BANISHED TO THE HOMELAND

DAVID C. BROTHERTON AND LUIS BARRIOS

BANISHED

TO THE HOMELAND

DOMINICAN DEPORTEES

AND THEIR STORIES OF EXILE

Columbia

University

Press /

New York

Columbia University Press
Publishers Since 1893
New York   Chichester, West Sussex
cup.columbia.edu
Copyright © 2011 Columbia University Press

Library of Congress Cataloging-in-Publication Data

Brotherton, David.
  Banished to the homeland : Dominican deportees and their stories of
exile / David C. Brotherton and Luis Barrios.
     p. cm.
  Includes bibliographical references and index.
  ISBN 978-0-231-14934-1 (cloth : alk. paper)—
  ISBN 978-0-231-14935-8 (pbk. : alk. paper)—
  ISBN 978-0-231-52032-4 (ebook)
   1. Dominican Republic–Emigration and immigration. 2.
Deportation–Dominican Republic. 3. Deportation–United States. I.
Barrios, Luis. II. Title.

  JV7395.B76 2011
  325–dc23

                                                  2011023883

Columbia University Press books are printed on permanent
and durable acid-free paper.
This book is printed on paper with recycled content.
Printed in the United States of America

c 10 9 8 7 6 5 4 3 2 1
p 10 9 8 7 6 5 4 3 2 1

CONTENTS

ACKNOWLEDGMENTS

AS USUAL, THERE are so many people to thank for their help over the years in making this book possible that we most certainly have overlooked some of you, albeit unintentionally. For this mistake we ask your forgiveness in advance. First and foremost, we must thank the many deportees and their family members who participated in this study, inviting us into their lives, however briefly. For some participants, of course, who acted as informants and cultural brokers, such as Manolo, José, and Luis, a considerable amount of time was spent with them, hanging out, listening to their stories, observing their progress, and sharing the ups and downs of Dominican deportee life. We hope the end result was worth it and that we did justice to your extraordinary generosity of both spirit and time. Further, we must mention the direct contributions of Yolanda Martín, Ralph Larkin, Antonio de Moya, Omar Bautista, Rene Vicioso, Gipsy Escobar, Maria Heyaca, Lino Castro, Kalil Vicioso, and William Cossolias, all of whom performed critical tasks at various times, including face-to-face interviews, transcriptions in both Spanish and English, in situ expert advice, editing suggestions, and contributing photographs.

We must thank once again the academic institutions that we have long called home, John Jay College of Criminal Justice and the Graduate Center of the City University of New York. In particular, we want to thank members of the sociology department, most notably Barry Spunt, Danny Kessler, Louis Kontos, Douglas Thompkins, and Maria Volpe, who read drafts of this book and at various times lent their resources to the overall project, and members of the Department of Latin American and Latina/o Studies, including José Morín, Jeannette Sucre, Jodie Roure, and Marcia Esparza. In addition, we want to send a note of appreciation to the immigration study group of Jock Young, Michael Flynn, Fabiola Salek, Cory Feldman, and Fenix Arias. We also want to acknowledge the support of Jeremy Travis, president of John Jay College, and former John Jay dean James Levin, who, along with former John Jay president Gerry Lynch and former John Jay provost Basil Wilson, supported an early conference on deportees at John Jay in 2004. In thanking our institutions, we need to mention the special place in our research occupied by the law faculty at the Universidad Autónoma of Santo Domingo, especially Franklin García Fermín and Enrique Chalas, who provided integral support to the first-ever conference on Caribbean deportees in 2003 in the Dominican Republic. These conferences were crucial for opening up the public discourse on deportees, providing the public space for scholars and activists to come together on such a growing yet occluded social and political problem, and helping create the networks that allowed us to extend our sample, which finally made the project possible. The erstwhile criminal justice reform organization, the Justice, Equality, Human dignity, and Tolerance (JEHT) Foundation, was a major underwriter of the John Jay event, but during the financial crisis it sadly fell victim to the multibillion dollar skullduggery of Bernie Madoff et al.

Finally, we must thank our executive editor Lauren Dockett, editorial assistant Avni Majithia-Sejpah, and production editor Roy Thomas, as well as the good staff of Columbia University Press, who once again opted to support and encourage our project through thick and thin, sticking with us over the numerous missed deadlines and ensuring a finished product that we hope will cause some reflection on one of the most tragic crises of our times.

Last but not least, we want to remember those deportees in our study who passed away during the making of this book. The last of them, Pedro, was executed by the police in January 2011 in Santiago. All of their deaths were untimely, unnecessary, and preventable; they were still in the prime of their lives, and it is only the soul-destroying conditions that characterize life as a deportee with double and triple stigmas that forced them to succumb. Thus, this book is both a tribute to and in memoriam of the following:

Frankie
George
Eddie
Alex
Freddie S.
Pedro
Omar
Freddie

PEDRO (*RIGHT*) WITH HIS BROTHER KALIL A FEW MONTHS BEFORE HE WAS KILLED BY POLICE IN THE DOMINICAN REPUBLIC.

BANISHED TO THE HOMELAND

INTRODUCTION

The production of "human waste," or more correctly wasted human (the
"excessive" and "redundant" that is, the population of those who either could
not or were not wished to be recognized or allowed to stay), is an inevitable
outcome of modernization, and an inseparable accompaniment to moder-
nity. It is an inescapable side effect of order-building (each order casts some
parts of the extant population as "out of place," "unfit," or "undesirable") and
of economic progress (that cannot proceed without degrading and devaluing
the previously effective modes of "making a living" and therefore cannot but
deprive their practitioners of their livelihood).

(BAUMAN 2004:5)

BAUMAN'S PRESCIENT ANALYSIS on the processes of social exclusion
that appear to be endemic to late modernity frames our study of the lives of
subjects who formerly resided in the United States, sometimes for considerable parts of their lives, either as "permanent legal residents" or as "undocumented residents," but who now find themselves forcibly dispatched to their
country of birth, the Dominican Republic, as "criminal deportees." Our study
traces the lives of these embodiments of "human waste" (in Bauman's terminology) and their bulimic journey (Young 1999, 2007) across the Caribbean
as they get pushed, pulled, and ultimately vomited out by a nation whose foreign policy has rarely veered from its early imperial path of Manifest Destiny
and whose economy is so dependent on the world's surplus labor pool. These
twin, mutually reinforcing characteristics of the United States are key to an
understanding of our subjects' fates, past, present, and future, and provide
the sociological and political economic contexts in which their lives unfold.

There have been more than thirty thousand Dominicans forcibly repatriated in a little more than ten years, a population little noticed by the general public until the recent protests of the undocumented and their supporters. We begin with a letter from one of them, Pedro.

12 January, 2005

Dearest Professor Brotherton

I sincerely hope this letter finds yourself, friends and family in the very best of health and spirits. As for myself, suffice it to say that I and others like me continue to struggle and try and make sense of it all.

Sir, I wrote you previously but after speaking to you over the phone I said to myself let me shorten this up because time is limited.

First off, I applaud your efforts, admire your work however little of it I was able to see, and thank you not only as one of the many affected by these unjust laws, but as one human being to another.

May the good Lord keep you strong and bless you always. Professor, people, that includes governments, always lament the atrocities when it's too late to do anything about it. I guess hindsight is always 20/20 but it is the observers, the conscientious objectors, the ones on the outside who must always point out these things while they are happening.

Because for any evil to win, the Good must simply let it happen, and evil is committed at the time by good people who happen to have good intentions but who simply forgot there's 2 sides to everything.

There undoubtedly exist those in power who simply and deliberately don't care because, as the saying goes "shit rolls down hill not up."

Sir, not all men leave prison the same. You cannot paint us all with the same brush. I do not believe that the founding fathers meant for all this to have taken place.

How many good men throughout history have come out of prison? Quite a few. But let me fill you in on what is going on down here.

The military and law enforcement are the true Dominican mafia. They are involved in everything. Narcotics, murder, rape, crime, etc. they routinely hire men like myself as gunmen or drug enforcers and then send a team of cops to kill us. Coming from me it may sound unbelievable but the facts speak for themselves and time proves and reveals the truth as well as the lie. The drug of choice is heroin for the deportees. No employment is available. Some have nowhere to sleep much less to eat, a lot are uneducated and the few who were educated in the U.S. can't find work here.

The cost of living is sky high here. In the Dominican Republic if you have no money, a car to get around in, and a house or an apartment you will go through many, many changes. Some make it through alright some or rather many don't.

The rise in crime is easily blamed on the deportees. I should say conveniently so. Professor, we the deportees are not a threat to the U.S. government. No-one can make me believe that.

A more real and serious threat are the Bush's and others like them. People in power who allow and sanction drug importation, prostitution, murder etc . . . Do you really believe that hicks from the Dominican Republic will topple the U.S. government? No sir they won't! Many will say, "Well, you're on a tropical island" and so on and so forth. That doesn't hold water either. Many like myself are raised there in New York all our lives, that's all we know. In prison I went to college for a 2 year Associates, a degree as a paralegal, preparing for my eventual release.

Did I get into a lot of fights in prison? Of course I did, but who didn't. It's prison for Christ's sake! Yet never was the good looked at, only the bad.

At the end I was told I would be deported to a country I basically knew nothing about. To a culture I do not understand and that's more than wrong.

I paid my debt to society and hoped and prayed to be with my family. To sit with them, laugh, cry, to walk down familiar streets, to ride a train, a bus and see the changes.

My personal plight is more of an emotional one, I guess. Does it make it any less important? No sir! I believe it only makes matters worse. My family in the U.S. is trying desperately to keep sending me money but what happens when they can't?

Who will feed a deportee for free? Or house us? Or anything?

Do you know the stigma that goes with being a deportee? The media has made us out to be animals who should be caged forever or killed for the good of society. In the D.R. law enforcement and their justice system has no problem doing either although they prefer the latter.

We can't even get a visa out of the country for up to a year or maybe more. That's because as soon as we arrive we are put in their prison until someone comes to claim you like luggage. Then you are fingerprinted, taken pictures of and you now have a criminal record in the D.R. without having committed a crime here.

We are on parole for six months and then given a document of good conduct but the record stays. You can't get a job without the good conduct paper by the way, because everybody asks to see it. You also need a cedula (stamp in English) or a government I.D. card which you can't get without the good conduct paper.

Then when all this is done and you go to get a Visa to Europe or anywhere, excluding the U.S. naturally, you can't get it because the government of the D.R. has you pegged as a criminal, and with today's global atmosphere of paranoia you undoubtedly get denied. So we are in essence boxed in, forced to live in poverty and like it.

We are left with no other recourse because if you get a job here it's a miracle. With a criminal record you'd be lucky if they let you pump gas at a gas station so what do many of us do? We head back home. Home is where the heart is and we are N.Y. bound, sink or swim, that's the overall opinion. Better to live in prison in New York than free in the D.R. We simply don't care about getting caught for re-entry, that's the sad truth.

No-one leaves here with the intent of getting caught. We wish only to be with our respective families, and most, not all, wish to simply work off the books in the U.S. It's that simple. I just came from prison. Crime is on the rise. The Prison population is overcrowded. Did deporting 25,000 Dominicans matter at all? Do you see my point?

Sir, so much more I can write on this but for the moment I believe I touched base with you on most of the important issues and details of what we are going through.

I thank you sincerely for your time. May God help you always and I remain one of the many in the struggle.

Very Truly Yours

Pedro V.

Pedro, the brother of a psychology graduate student at the City University of New York, was deported in September 2005 after spending thirty-three years in the United States, coming to Manhattan, New York, with his family at the age of four. Pedro never became a citizen; like many Dominicans, he gained legal residency and felt able to travel freely back and forth between the Caribbean and his new homeland without thinking about the legal implications of being a noncitizen. That is, until the 1996 Illegal Immigration Reform and Immigrant Responsibility Act (IIRAIRA), whose provisions created hundreds of thousands of quintessential examples of social rejection known as "criminal aliens," who eventually become "criminal deportees." The act passed in the same year in which Congress, with President Clinton's prompting, ended welfare as we know it, eventually becoming law after being revised three times in the same year—each time increasing the severity of its penalties and widening the net of its criminal categories. The result was a complete reshaping of the nation's immigration policy, signaling a reversal of the more enlightened immigration legislation of 1965, which ended the Eurocentric and racist practice of quotas.

As Pedro balefully asks, How did this happen? How did this happen to him and hundreds of thousands like him? What happened to the country he was raised in? Was it not supposed to be the beacon of democracy and due process? Was it not based on giving immigrants a chance to prove themselves? What did he do to deserve such vindictive treatment from the criminal justice system after he had served his time and paid for his crime, as the expression goes? What can he do to adapt to his lot, a lifetime in exile in a country from which he is culturally estranged, where he is blamed for every spike in the crime index, and where he is regularly used as the stuff of moral panic by the government and the media, thus diverting attention from the corruption of the state and from the deepening inequalities that lie at the root of the country's fraying social fabric?

Yet, while Pedro veers between the sanguine and the desperate, he has not yet succumbed. Despite relapses, he has not become dependent on heroin to counter his depression as have an increasing number of deportees in a country that previously saw little hard drug use. Nor has he entered the illicit economy to counter the punishing levels of unemployment and underemployment while supplementing the meager income sent by his working-class family in New York City, who do their best to keep Pedro out of absolute poverty. Instead, he lives in the hope that, some day, he will be back in New York where he was raised, back with his mother and his brother, as he had dreamed while serving his sentence in those other New York State warehouses of human storage: Attica, Sing Sing, Comstock, and the rest.

For Pedro, the once-irrepressible immigrant, the street kid who as a youth wandered into the "wrong crowd," the question remains: Who took away his dream? What system does this to its quasi-subjects? Is this another form of inappropriate social control that ran so powerfully through America's twentieth century that it threatens to unravel the country's democratic traditions in the new millennium? This book is in many ways a study of what happens to the immigrant's dream when it becomes a nightmare in which a young bilingual, bicultural boy or girl attending a New York public elementary school at the age of seven becomes a permanent exile at the age of thirty-two. What happened in between? Where did the immigrant as subject go wrong? Why did no one warn him or her of the lifelong consequences of their actions? What does it feel like to be thrice removed from the most important people in one's life, first through emigration, then through prison, and lastly through deportation? And finally, how does the immigrant-turned-deportee socially, economically, culturally, and psychologically survive in his or her newly enforced environment?

Questions such as these will be addressed in the ensuing pages as we analyze the data from our seven-year ethnographic study and apply a range of sociological theories in social control, immigration, transnationalism, and cultural criminology. It is our hope that shedding much-needed light on this population and the processes of inclusion and then exclusion will make a timely contribution to the escalating debates on immigration control and on the punitive sanctions that now take the place of a rational, humanistic, and progressive criminal justice and immigration policy. In so doing, we will have shown the humanity of these subjects who are mostly just numbers on the United States Immigration and Customs Enforcement's (ICE) annual report of "deportable aliens," or just another case number in Immigration Court as the judge for the umpteenth time dismisses the vain efforts of the noncitizen to forestall his or her deportation back to their respective homeland.

1.1 LUIS BARRIOS (*LEFT*) AND IMPRISONED DEPORTEE (*PHOTO:* DAVID BROTHERTON).

1.2 DAVID BROTHERTON (*LEFT*) AND JUAN, A DEPORTEE (*PHOTO:* WILLIAM COSSOLIAS).

CHAPTER ONE

THE STUDY

IN ITS OVERT and covert existential meanings and its descriptions of the microworlds of the deportee and the macrostructures of daily life, we can identify in Pedro's letter (see Introduction) the major conceptual themes of our analysis: the punitive turn in the criminal justice system that overdetermines immigration policy; the traumatic experience of social and cultural exclusion that the French sociologist Sayad (2004) calls the "suffering of the immigrant"; and the efforts of subjects to come to terms with their new roles and identities as deportees. These areas will be carefully developed throughout the remainder of the book. But first, how did this project come about? What are its aims? How does the literature guide our study and contribute to our analysis? How did we collect our data (primarily interviews and observations) from some of the most stigmatized members of our society? And finally, what does the rest of the book look like?

HOW IT ALL BEGAN

This project occurred quite accidentally. As is the case with much research, it happened through serendipity. In our previous work we focused on the political transformation of New York City street subcultures into what we called "street organizations" (Brotherton and Barrios 2004). During our research we found that a substantial part of the groups' memberships was composed of first- or second-generation Dominicans. In 1998, after delivering an address on youth deviance among the Dominican immigrant community in New York at a criminological conference in Santo Domingo, we were asked during the question-and-answer session to talk about the increasing phenomenon of Dominican youth with gang affiliations returning to their country after being deported from the United States. At the time, we had little to say on the matter; however, we agreed that this would be an important topic for future investigations, and we vowed to start following this process from cities such as New York, Boston, and Miami.

Four years later, in September 2002, we kept our promise, and the first author, David Brotherton, began a year-long sabbatical in Santo Domingo. By that time, we had completed some informational interviews with Dominican lawyers and community organizers in New York City and observed that, although the phenomenon of Dominican deportees was growing rapidly in the wake of the Illegal Immigration Reform and Immigrant Responsibility Act of 1996, there was little community organization or media coverage around this issue. In Santo Domingo, the opposite was the case. Articles in major daily newspapers such as *el Listin Diario, el Nacion,* and *el Caribe* were being published almost weekly. These articles focused on how new deportees were arriving at the capital's airport and often noted that serious felons, including murderers, rapists, armed robbers, and drug dealers, were among them. Some reports also highlighted the tragedy of deportations with reference to family separation and the difficulties of reintegration while warning of the demonization of deportees.

The second pathway into this subject was through the life experience of the second author, Luis Barrios. Barrios has long been connected to the Dominican community through marriage, political activism, and his predominantly Latino congregations (first in the South Bronx, then in Central Harlem, and now in Washington Heights) to whom he has been ministering for the past twenty years as an ordained priest in the Episcopal Diocese of New York and the United Church of Christ. Barrios's spiritual work drew him to the deportee issue by involving him in the struggles of family members to prevent fathers, mothers, husbands, sons, and daughters from being deported and in the plight of deportees who have illegally returned to live in the city's "shadows" (Chavez 1997).

Consequently, as researchers committed to the community and its concerns, we wanted to know more about this emerging subpopulation that was traveling in the opposite direction of the Third World to First World flows conventionally imagined in immigration studies. A host of questions came to mind: What were the characteristics, contexts, dynamics, social networks, and historical roots of this population? How does this population occupy and develop within a transnational space? Why was this process of emigration, immigration, and repatriation occurring now? Although the phenomenon of deportees was largely a product of state-sponsored sanctions (Zilberg 2006), how were local communities responding to these exiled populations? Do deportees succeed in creating new networks, subcultures, and organizations to fill the gaps in social support and solidarity? What happens to the self-identity of deportees as they adjust to their new life-worlds? And finally, how do we articulate the pathos of social rejection or the resourcefulness in the mentalities of resistance?

To answer such questions, we had to get as close as possible to the everyday life experiences of deportees, to observe them, engage them, listen to them, and learn from their memories of the past, the narratives of their present, and their strategies for dealing with the future. To do so, we chose the methods of critical ethnography, an approach used in our previous study on street gangs, in which we emphasized the following:

> Our orientation begins from the premise that all social and cultural phenomena emerge out of tensions between the agents and interests of those who seek to control everyday life and those who have little option but to resist this relationship of domination. This . . . approach . . . seeks to uncover the processes by which seemingly normative relationships are contingent upon structured inequalities and reproduced by rituals, rules and a range of symbolic systems. Our approach . . . is an holistic one, collecting and analyzing multiple types of data and maintaining an openness to modes of analysis that cut across disciplinary turfs.
>
> We have chosen a collaborative mode of inquiry. . . . By this we mean the establishment of a mutually respectful and trusting relationship with a community or a collective of individuals which: (i) will lead to empirical data that humanizes the subjects, (ii) can potentially contribute to social reform and social justice, and (iii) can create the conditions for a dialogical relationship between the investigator(s) and the respondents.
>
> (BROTHERTON AND BARRIOS 2004:4)

Toward the end of this chapter we will describe in more methodological detail what we managed to accomplish. Before doing so, let us briefly discuss the literature that illuminated our way.

THE LITERATURE

What does "the literature" have to say about the 30,000–50,000[1] Dominicans deported during the last twelve years (1996–2008), many of whom were legal residents, and the current rate of deportations, which is nearly three hundred per month? How does the literature deal with the sociological contexts in which these policies emerge? What about the racial, class (Johnson 2009), ethnocentric (Cashdan 2001), and gendered (Boris 1995) nature of such policies as upwards of 50,000 legal residents are forcibly repatriated from the United States to cities and villages throughout the Caribbean and Latin America every year? Unfortunately, the literature does not say a great deal, but the following is a brief summary of what we have found in both the social scientific and journalistic literature along with some of the theories that can best explain this extraordinary phenomenon.

THE DEPORTEE AS SUBSTANCE

The focus on the dynamics behind deportations and the lived experiences of deported populations from the United States has only recently been the subject of serious social scientific inquiry in the English-language literature. Hitherto, only six articles (Griffin 2002; Lonegan 2008; Morawetz 2000; Noguera 1999; Precil 1999; Zilberg 2002) and three books (Brotherton and Kretsedemas 2008; Coutin 2007; Kanstroom 2007)[2] have appeared that discuss the general and specific political, legal, economic, cultural, and criminological causes behind the expulsion of so many Caribbean, Mexican, and Central American legal and nonlegal residents from the United States during the 1990s.

Noguera (1999) argues that increases in the rates of deportation have coincided with changes in the population flows to the United States, particularly from the Caribbean, in the latter part of the century, as large numbers of working- and lower-class urban and rural immigrants were drawn to the United States by its demand for cheap labor. Such immigrants are vulnerable to labor market fluctuations, are easily exploited and victimized, and have little cultural capital to pass on to their children. The resulting combination of poverty, low social mobility, the lure of the informal economy, and the unprecedented expansion of the social control industry have effectively criminalized entire African American and Latino communities, an effect reflected in the race/ethnic distribution of both state and federal prison populations (particularly in states such as New York, California, and Texas). Thus, the increasing arrest rates among immigrants of color combined with drastic changes to immigration laws have inevitably given rise to mass detentions and expulsions, among which Dominicans rank prominently (see also Ojito 1998; Rohter 1997; Lonegan 2008).

Meanwhile, Precil (1999) placed the issue of Haitian deportees in the broader context of the increased expulsions of other Latino and Caribbean populations. Precil argues that this persecuted population has arisen largely in the wake of the U.S. Antiterrorism and Effective Death Penalty Act of 1996 and has functioned to relieve the overcrowding of U.S. prisons at the expense of increasing instability in the receiving countries. In the earlier work of Griffin (2002), the author uses the notion of "geonarcotics," a concept linking drugs, geography, power, and politics, to analyze the phenomenon of deportation. For Griffin, the problem is the combined result of changes occurring in other social and political domains such as (i) "get tough" antidrug efforts by federal and state governments, (ii) new legislative oversight on immigration, (iii) increased resource allocation to the U.S. Immigration and Naturalization Service, (iv) restrictions on discretionary relief from deportations for foreign nationals, (v) congressional initiatives on "administrative removal" procedures, and (vi) early release programs that grant parole to some inmates in exchange for immediate deportation. Another study by Zilberg (2002), based on field work in Los Angeles and San Salvador, focuses on the transnational processes behind the deportee gang member phenomenon and what the removal of this contemporary "folk devil" means for the construction of urban social spaces, state social controls, community identities, and the politics of simultaneity (see also Smith 2000). Meanwhile, Coutin (2007), focusing on populations from the same geographical area, asks what the consequences of legal categories such as "citizen," "alien," and "deportee" are for immigrant subjects whose "multiple realities" in a globalized world frequently render borders meaningless.

Other research worthy of note include studies of expelled Salvadoran, Belizean, and Mexican gang members and Haitian "delinquents." The first, completed by social scientists at the University of Central America, El Salvador (Santacruz Giralt and Cruz Alas 2001), looked at the levels of social cohesion and violence of gang members returning from California. The authors found that many deportees had been socialized into violence as children, spanning both El Salvador's civil war and the intergroup violence in the streets and barrios of Southern California. In a second study on the recent wave of Mexicans drawn to New York City, Smith (2005) discusses the lived realities of transnationalism, describing how returning Mexican gang members have affected the local youth culture by changing notions of public space and bringing new forms of subcultural violence to the community. These findings are echoed in a third study on the Garifuna ethnic community of Belize, many of whom migrated to Los Angeles and who now watch their children being transported back to their native country as urban gang members (Matthei and Smith 1998). Finally, DeCesare (1998) provides an in-depth journalistic report on the hyperalienation experienced by expelled Haitian youths who neither know the Haitain culture nor its language, Creole.

The substantive literature on Dominican deportees reveals many of the same themes as deportees in other countries. We have written on the everyday lives of deportees in Santo Domingo, citing the massive increase in deportees since the passing of the U.S. Illegal Immigration Reform and Immigrant Responsibility Act (IIRAIRA) of 1996, their health problems, levels of drug addiction, struggles with indigence, and efforts to organize (Brotherton 2008; Brotherton and Barrios 2009). Gerson (2004) similarly raised the growing issue of drug abuse among deportees—especially heroin (see also Martín 2010)—the interlocking U.S. systems of criminal justice and immigration, and the collateral effects on the families left behind. This latter theme is taken up by Brotherton (2008), who has described the trauma of appeals processes in the United States for Dominicans and their families and the vindictive, irrational nature of deportee policy in its present form.[3]

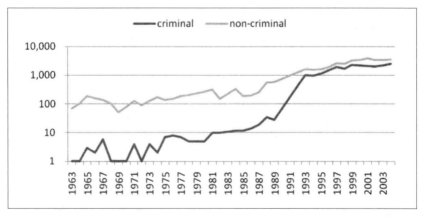

1.3 FOLLOWING THE ENACTMENT OF THE IIRAIRA IN 1996, THE NUMBER OF DOMINICANS DEPORTED FOR NONCRIMINAL OFFENSES INCREASED EXPONENTIALLY. ALTHOUGH THE OVERALL NUMBER OF DEPORTEES HAD INCREASED EARLIER, THE INCREASE IN THE DEPORTATION OF INDIVIDUALS WHO COMMITTED NONCRIMINAL OFFENSES OCCURRED DURING THE PERIOD THAT THE DOMINICAN GOVERNMENT BEGAN TO REGISTER AND MONITOR DEPORTEES FROM THE UNITED STATES. THE DOMINICAN GOVERNMENT CURRENTLY DOES NOT DISTINGUISH BETWEEN DEPORTEES REPATRIATED FOR COMMITTING CRIMINAL AND NONCRIMINAL OFFENSES (VENATOR-SANTIAGO, UNPUBLISHED MANUSCRIPT, 19).

In summary, the substantive, mostly empirical literature on deportees offer the following findings: (i) cultural estrangement and stigmatization are rampant among deportees; (ii) deportees experience high levels of direct (i.e., interpersonal) and indirect violence (i.e., the denial of basic material and social needs that allow human beings to become self-actualized [see Salmi 1993; Maslow 1954]) prior to their expulsion; (iii) the transnational social and (sub)cultural strategies and practices of some deportees that might find their origins in the United States include gang membership, drug use, involvement in criminal enterprises, and the establishment of self-help groups; (iv) U.S. immigration/deportation policy has become increasingly restrictive and draconian due to the passing of three acts: the Immigration Reform and Control Act of 1986, the Immigration Act of 1990, and the IIR-AIRA of 1996 (see graph in figure 1.3). Immigration and deportation policies have in turn been heavily influenced by the war on drugs (especially the Anti-Drug Abuse Act in 1988, which introduced the term "aggravated felony") and the war on terrorism (particularly through the Antiterrorism and Effective Death Penalty Act of 1996 and the Patriot Act of 2001); and (v) deportation policies wreak enormous collateral damage on both U.S. families and communities as well as on the communities of the receiving nations (Baum et al. 2010).[4]

1.4 AN ARTICLE FROM THE LEADING DOMINICAN NEWSPAPER *LISTIN DIARIO* (APRIL 9, 2002) READS, "SIXTEEN THOUSAND DEPORTEES, BUT THEY ARE NOT ALL THE SAME: THE INFORMATION THAT DOMINICAN AUTHORITIES RECEIVE WHEN THESE PERSONS ARRIVE DOES NOT SPECIFY THEIR LEVEL OF PARTICIPATION IN THE CRIMES."

Edición Digital, Santo Domingo República Dominicana

A   La República
> Zona de Contacto
> La Opinion
> Las Provincias
B   El Deporte
> Zona Deportiva
> Sacando Chispas
> Miniaturas del Béisbol
C   La Vida
> Espectaculos
D   El Dinero
> Las Mundiales
> W.S. Journal
E   Las Sociales

> Ediciones
> Obituarios
> Cartelera
> El Tiempo
> Horoscopo
> Contáctenos
Revistas

¿Necesita Usted?

**Dar a conocer
sus productos**

A   **LA REPUBLICA**

EEUU deporta 51 criollos que cumplieron condenas

■ DELITOS FEDERALES

Rafael Castro
AEROPUERTO LAS AMéRICAS-

Los deportados llegaron ayer en un avión de D9 escoltados por cinco agentes del FBI.

Llegaron deportados ayer otros 51 dominicanos que cumplieron condenas en diversas cárceles de Estados Unidos por narcotráfico, homicidios y otros delitos federales.

El avión que los trajo, un D-9, tuvo que trasladarse a Puerto Rico a reabastecerse de combustible debido a que en Las Américas no había disponible en el momento, pero poco después las autoridades dijeron que el suministro se había normalizado.

La aeronave, en la que fueron deportados los 51 criollos, arrendado por el Servicio de Inmigración y Naturalización norteamericano, matricula número N806- US, arribó a esta terminal, a las dos y 32 minutos de la tarde de ayer procedente de Estados Unidos.

Los deportados, consistentes en 49 hombres y sólo dos mujeres se encontraban guardando prisión en distintas cárceles norteamericanas cumpliendo condenas de 5 a 15 años por la comisión de narcotráfico, crímenes, asaltos, violaciones y falsificación de escrituras federales.

En el área de rampa del aeropuerto Las Américas, se estableció un amplio dispositivo de seguridad en el que participaron oficiales del Cuerpo Especializado de Seguridad Aeroportuaria, CESA, de la Dirección Nacional de Control de Drogas, DNCD, y de los organismos de seguridad del Estado para recibir a los expresidiarios.

Agentes federales

El grupo de repatriados llegó escoltado por cinco agentes del Buró Federal de Investigaciones (FBI) y de la Agencia Antidrogas Norteamericana, (DEA), quienes procedieron a entregar a los deportados a las autoridades de Migración de servicio en la terminal aeroportuaria. Con este grupo de cincuenta y uno se extendió a 102 el número de criollos deportados al país en el primer mes de este año, tras cumplir condenas en recintos carcelarios de Estados Unidos, acusados de diferentes delitos criminales.

1.5 ANOTHER ARTICLE FROM *LISTIN DIARIO* (ONLINE EDITION; JANUARY 4, 2003) READS: "51 DOMINICANS HAVING COMPLETED THEIR PRISON SENTENCES DEPORTED FROM THE UNITED STATES."

THE DEPORTEE AS THEORY

To theoretically frame these experiences and analyze their meanings in broader terms, we need to isolate the literature that provides the best signposts for our data. There is, of course, an enormous body of literature on immigration and migration studies (see inter alia Cordero-Guzman et al. 2001; Hirschman et al. 1999; Foner and Fredrickson 2004), and we have no intention of embarking on a long review of these areas that are best left to more seasoned scholars of the subject. However, the theories we are most interested in are those that pertain to social control and the immigrant because we are, after all, dealing primarily with the subject of social exclusion. To this end we have divided our review into four discursive domains: social control paradigms and the U.S. immigrant, assimilationism and its critics, segmented assimilation and transnationalism, and crime control and resistance.

These bodies of literature, when brought together, provide a "constitutive criminology," or a criminology that draws on multiple theoretical traditions to explain historically contingent criminal or deviant phenomena. The late modern emergence of the deportee as a sometimes free, sometimes incarcerated, yet always highly stigmatized subject that currently makes up 25 percent of all U.S. federal inmates is an instructive case in point.

SOCIAL CONTROL AND THE IMMIGRANT

The theory of social control was a peculiarly "American" social scientific project at the beginning of the twentieth century (Melossi 2004), based on beliefs about consensual democracy in the wake of authoritarian regimes in Europe and influenced by theories of Spencerist evolutionary development and Durkheim's notion of anomie. It is important to emphasize that the notion of social control was always intertwined with the notion of social change, especially given the rapid social, economic, and cultural transformation of the United States. Behind the notion of social control was the philosophically pragmatic premise that human beings are in their nature adaptive creatures and will find ways to coexist with their specific environments. As Melossi explains:

> The concept of social control . . . encapsulated within the Chicago School of Sociology and Pragmatism—the only genuinely "American" philosophical orientation. It was a concept of social control that was all-pervasive because it responded to the need of the new society to incorporate large masses of newcomers in its midst, on grounds of a factual cooperation rather than through the traditional authoritarian instruments of politics and the law.
>
> (MELOSSI 2004:35)

The paradigm of social control had very much to do with how American society would effectively deal with the immigrant phenomenon and has come to be defined as the capacity of a social organization to regulate itself; the opposite of this paradigm was and is "coercive control, that is, the social organization of a society which rests predominantly and essentially on force—the threat and use of force" (Janowitz 1978:84). This narrative about integrative socialization (the inculcation of norms and values that leads to a consensus) and social processes was widely promulgated by early social scientists, such as Park (1961), Burgess (1921), Wirth (1928), and Thomas and Znaniecki (1927), who shaped criminological and sociological approaches to immigration issues for decades to come. Park, in particular, described immigration and settlement as a process of ordered segmentation, as newcomers were expected to pass through several universal stages of competition, conflict, accommodation, and, finally, assimilation.

Perhaps the highest empirical expression of the Parkian paradigm was Wirth's (1928) *The Ghetto*, in which he described two waves of Jewish immigration, showing that despite the problems of social and cultural displacement, immigrants through their self-organization and willingness to adapt over generations found mobility in the flexible, expanding, and pluralistic metropolis. Thomas and Znaniecki found both similar and different processes in their study of Polish peasants; their two-volume work is an optimistic narrative about the processes of immigrant adaptability. Nonetheless, they clearly state that this process cannot be achieved without enormous costs to the community as it endures stages of disorganization due to cultural conflict and reorganization.

Thus, although social control was one side of the adaptational equation, social disorganization was the other, and through much of the last century this social contradiction has been continually invoked to describe the emergence of gangs, crime, and delinquency in largely immigrant and migrant neighborhoods (see Thrasher 1927; Shaw and Mackay 1942; Cloward and Ohlin 1960). Importantly, for the Chicago School, although the emphasis in social relations was on the voluntaristic, resilient nature of the immigrant subject in civil society, it was always imagined within a broader ecological context, albeit with sometimes unexpected outcomes for the social order.[5] Nonetheless, the notion that immigrants accused of criminal offenses would be removed en masse from society is not present in any of this early literature.

WHAT ABOUT ASSIMILATION?

The Chicago concept of social control and the immigrant was largely a humanistic and optimistic one and did not foresee the time when hundreds of thousands, if not millions, of subjects would be socially excluded across borders or incarcerated in internal gulags. Until the 1950s, most sociologists adhered to the view that there were few, if any, structural constraints or contradictions that could undermine their belief in the progressive American century. In fact, the immigrant was proof of America's openness, social mobility, possibility, and "pragmatism"; it was evidence of a natural process of global selection as well as the New World's seductiveness.

These narratives of America's voluntaristic openness and the effectiveness of the natural evolutionary processes of assimilation (see particularly Warner and Strole 1945) shifted markedly in the 1950s with the more unified and functionalist notion of social systems developed by Parsons at Harvard and then by Lazarsfeld and Merton at Columbia. In this era, social science veered strongly towards *homus economicus* in terms of its scientific methodology and away from the more open-ended, naturalistic inquiries of Chicago. Little was left to chance, as social policy took its cue from sociological systems-based paradigms involving schooling, the family, the university, law, the factory, and the criminal justice system. In this heyday of social engineering, the narrative of the U.S. immigrant, especially any authentic, resilient one, was sidelined by the pretensions of and presumptions about American social, economic, and technological progress.

Oscar Handlin's 1951 book *The Uprooted* was one of the last of these optimistic narratives on settlement, arguing that immigrants would assimilate into U.S. society without contradictions or countervailing tendencies. However, a decade later, a different reading of the immigrant's social and cultural voyage was offered by Oscar Lewis (1965) in his widely read *La Vida*. In Lewis's work, the socially committed anthropologist offered detailed observations of the everyday colonized life worlds of Puerto Ricans in New York City and in San Juan, Puerto Rico, elucidating the lack of mobility of this population and their self-destructive behaviors—behaviors that, as he reasoned, constituted a culture of poverty. Although his descriptions of everyday family life were meant to show the situated culture of a transmigrant community reacting to the marginalizing pressures of "free-enterprise, pre-welfare state stage capitalism" (quoted in Bourgois 2002), the theoretical weakness of his culturalist argument and the psychological reductionism used in his analysis have overshadowed critical contributions to the immigration debate contained in his work.[6] As Bourgois (2002) argued, we cannot deny the very real suffering experienced by urban, inner city residents, including immigrants, for fear of essentializing urban poverty. Lewis exposed the deep, intergenerational social injuries being inflicted on a vulnerable immigrant population that ran counter to much of the literature and still seems to be a difficult subject to embrace, both theoretically as well as empirically.

SEGMENTED ASSIMILATION AND THE COMING OF TRANSNATIONAL SOCIETY

The governing concept of assimilationism in both immigration and race relations studies was fundamentally shaken by the rebellion in the streets of the United States during the race and ethnic revolts of the 1960s. As a result, new academic departments, with very different visions of the immigration project, were established throughout the academy. Nonetheless, although segregation and institutional discrimination were definitely prominent features of urban immigrant life, there were still wide swaths of the American population that were passing from their immigrant to their ethnic stages of social integration, which meant that some kind of assimilation was taking place and needed to be better represented and theorized (see Alba and Nee 1999). Addressing this conundrum, Portes and Zhou (1993; see also Portes and Rumbaut 2001) developed the notion of "segmented assimilation," bringing together several models of the integration process in U.S. society with a strong emphasis on the intersection of social and economic capital; they saw the possibility that significant cohorts of second-generation immigrants might find themselves excluded on a more permanent basis and therefore downwardly mobile. In a classic summary of their position, the two researchers described the three models as follows:

> The first replicates the time honored portrayal of growing acculturation and parallel integration into the white middle-class; a second leads straight in the opposite direction to permanent poverty and assimilation into the underclass; still a third associates rapid economic development with deliberate preservation of the immigrant community's values and tight solidarity.

(PORTES AND ZHOU 1993:82)

Still, there were problems with the immigration model despite these theoretical advances. First, how do we understand an "underclass" assimilationism without taking into account neocolonial and global postindustrial processes (Gans 1992)? Second, what was the historical and cumulative role of the state in processes of social exclusion and its part in increasing punitive legislation against the immigrant (see Zolberg 2008; Ngai 2004)? Third, the "interstitial" zones of urban areas were still presented as "black boxes" with few empirical studies to explain the dialectical processes of both inclusion and exclusion that must always be part of the immigrant/outsider narrative (see Young 1999, 2007).

One way to address these critiques is through the theoretical contributions of researchers working in the field of transnationalism. In their efforts to describe and theorize the increasing percentage of humankind residing permanently within, between, and across cultures, states, and societies, researchers such as Basch et al. (1994), Guarnizo (1994), and Smith (2005) have described relationships and tensions that emerge between the global webs of macrostructures and the flows and movements of people driven to cross or circumvent borders, building counter-hegemonic or new sociocultural spaces as they do so. Out of this discourse has emerged a focus on the existence of multicultural or hybrid populations that have been described by Robert Smith as "embodied in identities and social structures that help form the life world of immigrants or their children . . . constructed in relations between people, institutions and places" (Smith 2005:7).

Of particular interest to us in this literature is the work of Michael Peter Smith (2000), who takes to task those who bring to our attention the changing forms of domination prompted by global capitalism but omit from consideration the actions and consciousnesses of the ordinary citizens and noncitizens that allow such structures to function. For Smith, an essential ingredient of transnationalism is its focus on the way global society is constituted not above our heads but through our everyday efforts to make sense of the world—to create meaning through processes of accommodation, assimilation, resistance, and contestation. As such, he lists five tenets of transnationalism that are particularly relevant to our study:

1. Global structures are made and they can be unmade—the logics of capital formation are not a given but must be worked out, implemented, and produced. Such logics, therefore, do not represent a totalizing force.
2. The urban community is the key site for investigating the processes of transnationalism. It is a transnational locale in a world of migrations, expulsions, flexible capital accumulation, and political simultaneity (e.g., the mimicking of criminal justice policies such as "zero tolerance across borders" that are most notable [see Zilberg 2004]).
3. The culture that is produced by the intersection of transnational structures and agencies must be documented to understand the precise nature of accommodations, assimilations, and resistances.
4. All action is historically situated but is not locked into a periodized framework of analysis such as "postmodernity" and other epochal narratives. To overemphasize the period detracts from the peculiarities of the contemporary and its transitional, contingent, and unfinished nature.
5. The global and the local must not be made into a binary opposition; rather, they are interconnected spaces, places, and processes that conceptually and empirically help us better understand the construction of space, identities, and "place-making."

Strangely, despite the wide-ranging discourses in immigration and transnational studies, rarely do such discussions venture into the territory of criminology (Martinez and Valenzuela 2006; Rumbaut 2006). This is unfortunate because so much of the early sociology of immigration laid the groundwork for studies of crime, whereas so many contemporary immigrant communities are the subject of increasing penetration by the state into all spheres of daily life.[7]

SOCIAL EXCLUSION, CRIME CONTROL, AND THE CONTRADICTIONS OF LATE MODERNITY

By casting for terrorists using every tool at its disposal—most notably immigration and criminal law enforcement—and then selectively detaining and deporting non-U.S. citizens for typically minor immigration or criminal law violations, immigration law socially controls immigrant communities through the deportation threat. Imposing this threat, or that of detention pending deportation with no consideration of individual merits, is a highly effective instrument of social control.

(MILLER 2005:27)

Miller, a judicial scholar, highlights the use of an array of criminal justice and immigration laws and their apparatuses to socially control immigrant communities. This observation accords with the work of Young (1999, 2007), who argues that state threats against immigrants are a particular form of othering in late modern capitalism, a process of circumscribing or thwarting social citizenship that he describes as bulimic rather than just exclusionary. In Young's words:

None of this is to suggest that considerable forces of exclusion do not occur but the process is not that of a society of simple exclusion which I originally posited. Rather it is one where both inclusion and exclusion occur concurrently—a bulimic society where massive cultural inclusion is accompanied by systematic structural exclusion. It is a society which has both strong centrifugal and centripetal currents: it absorbs and it rejects.

(YOUNG 2007:32)

Young is referring to the tendency of advanced capitalist societies, particularly Britain and the United States, to culturally include yet socially exclude large sections of the population, particularly those from the lower classes and so-called "minorities." This highly contradictory process is carried out through several intersecting dynamics: (i) the pushes and pulls of the political economy with its restructuring of work, redistribution of wealth, irrational reward system, and heightening of class divisions; (ii) the universalism of consumer culture and its promotion of need, individualism, and freedom; (iii) the technological revolution of information generation and dissemination; (iv) the evolution of the social control industry with its rapid expansion of gulags, laws, surveillance systems, and constraints on civil and democratic liberties; and (v) the porous and fluid nature of all physical, social, and cultural borders. Together, these processes make it difficult for individuals to formulate a coherent sense of self and lead to a ubiquitous condition that he calls "ontological insecurity."

In this process of bulimia, Young (along with legal and criminal justice scholars such as Welch [2002], Simon [2007], Kanstroom [2007], and Kurzman [2008], and sociologists such as Bauman [2004]) cite the radical shift of society during the 1980s toward what has been described as a "new penology" (Feeley and Simon 1992) and a "culture of control (Garland 2002) based on a set of beliefs about the pathological nature of criminals and other types of socially constructed human pollutants. In this brave new world of governance through crime and fear, there is a presumed need to take preemptive action and exact extreme punishments to ensure that risks to the good, the pure, and the healthy (Douglas 1966) never materialize. Kanstroom (2007) and Kurzman (2008) in particular show the impact on the deportee of three conjoining wars: the war on drugs, the war on terrorism, and the war on immigration. Welch (2001) adds that the moral panics used to mediate, rationalize, and frame these strategies reflect the needs of an industry of crime control (Christie 1993) in which the deportee has become a source of revenue and an object of financial desire on the part of multinational corporations specializing in security.

But what of resistance? Is it all such one-way traffic? Theoretically it is critical to locate agency in these chaotic and contradictory processes and not to relinquish social and political will to the obsessions with order (Bauman 2004). Therefore, we seek a language to consider the many acts of individual and collective defiance performed by immigrants who are not simply adaptive and acculturating creatures (see, in particular, the critical anthropological work of De Genova [2005] on Mexican immigrants in Chicago and the critical theological work of Barrios [2010, 2008, 2007a]).

What takes immigrants over the border in such numbers? Is it simply the lure of the American Dream? What lies behind the sacrifices of family and friends as tens of thousands of dollars are spent on trying to reunite spouses with their children despite the massive indebtedness incurred? Who have the will and intellect to defend themselves against a criminal justice system that has consistently denied subjects information and adequate legal representation and has kept them isolated from any form of social support (see Pedro's letter in the Introduction)? How is a culture or subculture formed among the stigmatized? And how is life lived, engaged, and enjoyed rather than endured? Such questions all speak to the other side of the deportee experience and to what Katz (1988) calls that transcendental emotional quality in acts of deviance or what Ferrell and Hamm (1998) and Lyng (2004) might see as the existential "edge" that subjects reach for, knowing that they will cross the border or emerge intact from their heroin high. To guide us toward the answers, aside from those cited above, we have found the vibrant field of cultural criminology with its pointed criticism of the atheoretical positivism that dominates academic crime talk particularly stimulating (see Ferrell et al. 2008; Hamm 2007), while we have consistently referred to the fertile resistance discourses developed by Gregory (2007), whose work in the Dominican Republic focuses precisely on the relationship between dependency, the informal economy, and social citizenship.

TOWARD A TRANSNATIONAL METHODOLOGY

According to the literature, much about the deportee population remains an enigma, and this is particularly true of the Dominican deportee. We know little of any profundity about either the criminal or noncriminal biographies of its members, its genesis, and its evolution as a heavily labeled population, or its sociocultural interface with current Dominican society.

Such research is, by its nature, transnational, which means that we needed to design a project that could access data reflecting the cultural fluidity of the subjects while also examining the more fixed locations from which they are currently speaking. Clearly, such research is not logistically easy to accomplish; consequently, we had to devise a project that had one central field site, the Dominican Republic capital Santo Domingo (where most Dominican deportees now reside), and a secondary field site, New York City (from which most of them are deported). Four different stages of data collection constituted our ethnographic approach, as we endeavored to accomplish one of the first transnational ethnographies of the deportee.

STAGE ONE: SETTING UP THE FIELD SITE

To gain access to such data, perspectives, and processes, especially in this somewhat occluded transnational space (Smith 2005; Glick-Schiller et al. 1998), required entering into the life worlds (Habermas 2001; Katz 2003) of subjects that are quintessentially "hidden" or "hard-to-reach" (Morgan 1996).

In September 2002, the first author, Brotherton, set up the Santo Domingo field site in the Dominican Republic and started to make contacts with other qualitative researchers who might have direct or tangential relations with this population. Through such contacts, Brotherton developed a relationship with José, a deportee from New York City who worked as a street hustler and tour guide (see chapter 9), and Manolo, another deportee who was and still is a tour guide. Both José and Manolo, thus, became our first key informants and were paid 100 pesos (approximately $3.50) for each successful interview (15 in all) in addition to 100 pesos paid to each interviewee.

STAGE TWO: EXPANDING THE INFORMANT BASE

In January 2003, in conjunction with members of the faculty at the Universidad Autónoma de Santo Domingo (UASD), we organized the first-ever conference on deportees in the Caribbean. The event attracted more than 300 participants, including 40 deportees, 5 of whom broke their silence and spoke out publicly about their experiences of being deported. These relationships led to a purposive sample of 35 deported men (25 interviews in Spanish and 10 in English), ranging in age from 21 to 52 years old, and 5 deported women. We used the format of face-to-face, life-history interviews to elicit narratives that were descriptive, self-reflective, and highly phenomenological (Behar 1993; Katz 2003) and that provided us with nuanced and detailed insights into the historical, social, economic, emotional, and cultural nature of the deportation experience.

These subjects resided in different working-class and poor barrios in Santo Domingo, including the Zona Colonial, Villa Duarte, Villa Mella, Capotillo, San Carlos, Cristo Rey, and 27 Febrero. The interviews were carried out in a range of settings, including respondents' houses, a key informant's house and office, park benches, cafes, UASD, and barrio churches. In addition to the deportees, Brotherton interviewed a range of social actors involved directly in the lives of returned deportees, including priests, academics, law enforcement personnel, U.S. embassy and Dominican government officials, and Dominican journalists.

As in our previous research with street subcultures, from the outset we pursued a methodology that has been termed "collaborative" (see Moore 1978; Brotherton and Barrios 2004), which ensures the active participation of subjects in the research act. This was accomplished through the two informants helping us develop our interview questionnaire, suggesting different strategies to engage and develop rapports with the subjects, and constantly informing us of the changing dynamics of barrio and street life.

1.6 FATHER ROGELIO CRUZ AT A POLITICAL RALLY (*PHOTO:* LUIS BARRIOS).

STAGE THREE: INCARCERATED DEPORTEES AND THE *YOLAS*[8] TO PUERTO RICO

Stage three consisted primarily of face-to-face interviews with deportee inmates in two Dominican prisons and a visit to Nagua, a small coastal town on the northern side of the country, from which many immigrants attempt to sail to Puerto Rico in boats known as *yolas*. In Nagua, we made contact with a well-known priest and advocate of the deportees, Father Rogelio Cruz, who acted as an intermediary and provided us with important information on the scale of the exodus. We completed fifteen interviews in this locale with non-urban participants (ten men and five women).

STAGE FOUR: INSIDE THE LEGAL PROCESS OF DEPORTATION

In this penultimate stage of the research process, Brotherton participated in the appeals of eight Dominican deportees as an "expert witness," observing the courtroom interactions in which subjects were making their last bids to remain in the United States (see Brotherton 2008). Most of these events took place in a federal court building in Manhattan, but some occurred in penitentiaries outside New York City. This research yielded both field observations and multiple informal interviews with immigration lawyers and deportees' family members.

These multiple sources of data form the bases of our analysis and have enabled us to document with empathy and cultural sensitivity the lives of subjects who once immigrated to a country where most of them assumed they would remain for the rest of their lives but from which they have now been permanently banned.

Finally, it should be mentioned that this story is told by two researchers who themselves are personally familiar with the journey of the immigrant. The first author, Brotherton, immigrated to the United States from Britain more than twenty years ago and spent a year as an undocumented alien in California before becoming "legal" and entering graduate school. The second author, Barrios, a native of Puerto Rico, was first brought to the Lower East Side of New York City as a five year old by his mother, who at the time was seeking refuge for herself and her eight children from the domestic violence of her husband.

STAGE FIVE: RETURNED DEPORTEES IN NEW YORK CITY

The fifth stage of the data collection was performed by Luis Barrios, who, through his "insider" contacts within the Dominican community, interviewed eighteen deportees who had returned illegally to the United States. Barrios's task was to elicit data that focused on the strategies of survival for such a vulnerable population, the mode of reentry, and the processes by which subjects developed the psychological and material resources to make this journey.

CONTENTS OF THE BOOK

Here we describe the outline and contents for the following eleven chapters of the book. The order of the book follows the life flow of deportees as they move from the Dominican Republic to the United States and then pass through prison and detention camps before being returned to their native country and, in some cases, making the return journey to their surrogate homeland. Although we have tried to keep this book sequential, based on the chronological narratives of the subjects, the reader may also choose to read chapters out of sequence because we have presented the data in such a way that each pathway stage can be read independently.

The next chapter takes us into the setting of the study. As explained earlier, the bulk of our interviews and research takes place in Santo Domingo, although numerous interviews were completed in prisons, in the city of Nagua, and in New York City. Thus, chapter 2 is devoted to a brief description of the history and conditions in the Dominican Republic followed by a summary and commentary on some of the main characteristics of our deportee sample.

Presenting the interview data for the first time, chapter 3 looks at the factors influencing the decision of subjects to leave their homeland, the contradictory feelings of loss and hope, and the mythical constructions of America imbedded in the daily lives of Dominicans placed in their historical context. This orientation toward the United States is discussed in its narrative and ritualized forms as both male and female subjects reveal the multiple scripts and practices that made their emigration seemingly inevitable. At the same time, we analyze the feelings of loss and ambivalence as well as the memories of family and community life left behind. We also describe the many means of "making it" to New York, Miami, or Boston, including nightmarish crossings to Puerto Rico, stowing away on ships from Santo Domingo, hiding in trucks along the Texas border to be later delivered like a package in the mail, and of coming as a child with skimpy clothing in the middle of winter.

In chapter 4 we focus on the lived experience of deportees, who are both first and 1.5-generation immigrants, as they struggle to adapt to a rapidly changing urban America during different epochs and time spans. We highlight the adequate and inadequate preparations made by subjects to make their transition successful and the realities of working-class, multiethnic barrio life in the First World. We pay particular attention to subjects' accounts of neighborhood conditions, their experience of schooling, their plans for the future, the highs and lows of transnational family life, and their constant search for viable, meaningful work in a world of racially segmented labor.

In chapter 5 we consider the criminological "drift" of subjects into risk-prone social environments and the multiple sociocultural and economic influences that constitute their deviant trajectories. We show the great variety of orientations toward crime among the subjects, the importance of agency in their life course, and the webs of social control experienced by the Dominican community in various ethnic enclaves of the United States. Finally, we discuss the role of street subculture in the lives of subjects during their adolescence and their need to "fit in," particularly among other lower class New Yorkers.

In chapter 6 the testimonies of deportees regarding their prison experiences are recounted, and this physically and psychologically arduous time is critically analyzed. Not a single interviewee made light of this period in their lives as they revealed multiple levels of privation, humiliation, and dehumanization endured in local, state, and federal prisons; in prison dormitories; in small, multiple-inmate jail cells; and in solitary confinement. We discuss how the subjects created strategies to withstand their years of incarceration, their decision to stay neutral or to join other prison gangs, their resolution to fight their case from the inside, their drive to organize other Dominicans, and their determination to pursue an education, however limited. We also highlight their feelings of social estrangement and culture shock that accompanied their confinement, the multiple levels of racism that are rampant in the prison system, and their constructive relationships with other inmates. In doing so, we also point out the ways that prison has changed during the recent era of mass imprisonment and the increasingly common roles played by immigration detention centers in the incarceration industry.

Chapter 7 begins the exiled part of the book. We discuss what it means and feels like to be deported from the subjects' perspective. We answer questions about how deportees are processed, legally represented, and finally expelled through a court system that virtually predetermines the outcome. The deportees' only chance for appeal is to prove that they will be tortured by agents of the receiving governments and that such practices are policy. For women, there is a second line of defense under the U.S. Violence Against Women Act of 1994, in which a deportee must prove that she faces certain violence and possibly death at the hands of a former husband, lover, etc. This too is almost impossible to prove in court; the numbers of imprisoned deportees winning their cases is minute. Using observational field notes from court hearings and personal testimonies of deportees and interviews with immigration lawyers and judges, we paint a vivid portrait of this critical turning point in the subjects' lives and their range of responses, which vary from high levels of resistance to phlegmatic resignation.

When deportees arrive back in the Dominican Republic, what do they face? How are they received by their motherland? What levels of culture conflict do they experience? In chapter 8 we analyze these questions, focusing on the processes of stigmatization that are fueled by their pejorative or ambivalent identities as felons, deportees, Dominican/New Yorkers, failures, etc. We show how the Dominican media, politicians, and police leaders have contributed to the moral panic surrounding deportees as they are blamed for soaring crime rates and increasing interpersonal violence. Meanwhile, we analyze the psychological and cultural trauma experienced by many deportees as they come to terms with a society that is more parochial and homogeneous than the one they are used to. In many ways, this cultural encounter is the other, darker side of their transnationalism as they contend with their new master status.

Our analysis in chapter 9 focuses on the efforts, strategies, and models of personal and collective development of deportees. As we trace the economic strategies of our sample in their quest for daily survival, we provide a picture of the economic opportunity structures that await them and their attempts to build social capital and use whatever cultural capital they possess. With little tradition of meritocracy, massive levels of corruption and patronage, and highly unstable domestic formal and informal markets (including illicit drugs and the sex trade), we highlight the importance of social capital for deportees' economic well-being. Finally, we discuss what happens to those deportees who cannot socially fit in or who cannot adapt to the economic climate and instead turn to drugs as a form of self-medication for depression or as a means to escape the endless rituals of degradation that daily life seems to bring.

Chapter 10 highlights the experiences and plight of those deportees who end up back in Dominican Republic prisons. Although the rate of deportee recidivism is low, there are significant numbers placed in preventive detention after indiscriminate sweeps through the neighborhood, during which deportees, many of whom are innocent, are singled out for crimes.

In chapter 11 we present the final segment of our data based on interviews with deportees who have returned illegally to New York City. Here we analyze the individual and collective strategies that subjects used to support themselves and their families and stay undetected. These are quintessential transnational subjects resisting their legal status, refusing to abide by the discriminatory rules of the colonizing nation that pulled them here and pushed them there.

Finally, chapter 12 is our summation of the entire work, bringing together the major findings and the range of contributions these make to the development of theory. We also make a number of policy suggestions that would ameliorate the conditions and plight of so many hapless victims of these inhumane laws.

2.1 MAP SHOWING THE DOMINICAN REPUBLIC IN THE CARIBBEAN (*PHOTO:* SHUTTERSTOCK).

CHAPTER TWO

SETTING AND SAMPLE

La creación de la consciencia moral es el fin último de la evolución social. Lo que persigue al ser humano es lo bueno. Lo bello, lo útil, lo justo y lo verdadero están dirigidos al establecimiento de una sociedad en que la consciencia social esté tan educada y evolucionada, que la bondad sea un principio naturalmente ejercido por todos y todas.

(BOSCH 2009)[1]

The U.S. has a strong interest in a democratic, stable, and economically healthy Dominican Republic.

(U.S. DEPARTMENT OF STATE WEBSITE 2009A)

THE QUOTE FROM the Dominican writer, historian, educator, and former president of the Dominican Republic, Juan Bosch, expresses the legitimate aspirations of the Dominican people that unfortunately have never been realized. The Dominican Republic's history and its contemporary situation present themselves in stark relief to these ambitious and thoroughly democratic principles. Bosch's experiment lasted all of seven months, from April to September 1963, when it was overthrown by a military coup backed by the United States.

The participants in this project were born into the Dominican Republic, a country whose history has been shaped in large part by outside powers. These individuals then emigrated from their home country, attracted by the promises of the United States, and eventually were forced to return to the Dominican Republic, a place where, in their eyes, little had changed for the better. In this chapter we provide a brief background of the nation where the bulk of our interviews and data were collected.

HISTORY

In 1492, having been "discovered" by Columbus, the island of Hispaniola became a colony of the Spanish Empire. In 1697, after the virtual extermination of the Taino[2] natives, Spain officially recognized French control over the western third of the island. On January 1, 1804, Haiti proclaimed its independence after the first successful overthrow of slavery in the world, led by Alejandro Pétion and Toussaint L'Ouverture. The eastern two thirds of the island[3] became an independent country in 1821 known as Santo Domingo (Holy Sunday). Some contend that this part of the island was then colonized for twenty-two years by Haiti before it gained independence in 1844 and was recognized as the Dominican Republic, led by Juan Pablo Duarte, prior to the abolition of slavery in the Spanish Caribbean (Wucker 2000).

In 1861, the Dominican Republic returned to Spanish rule; two years later, Dominicans launched *la Guerra de la Restauración* (the Restoration War) that resulted in renewed independence in 1865. Many Dominicans view the struggle to gain independence from Haiti rather than from Spain or from the United States as the most significant event in the nation's formation (Moya Pons, 1998, 2008; Bosch 1970, 2003).

In the wake of this final independence, several unstable governments followed. In 1916, the U.S. government, as part of its Monroe Doctrine (i.e., the U.S. foreign policy, announced in 1823, that Latin America would be solely under the sphere of influence of the United States), invaded the Dominican Republic for the first time, laying the groundwork for a series of pro-U.S. governments. Horacio Vásquez Lajara was the first leader installed by the United States, and he governed from 1924 to 1930; Lajara was succeeded by the first totalitarian dictatorship in the hemisphere, that of Rafael Leonidas Trujillo Molina—better known as "El Jefe"—who ruled from 1930 until he was assassinated on May 30, 1961). In December 1962, the country saw its first free elections, in which Juan Bosch was elected with more than 60 percent of the popular vote. After just a few months, however, a military coup led by the Dominican General Elías Wessin, with the support of the U.S. government, deposed the democratically elected regime. This coup was followed by a civil war in April 1965, during which workers, peasants, and certain military leaders sought to return rule to a government guided by the country's constitution, drafted in 1963 (Fiallo 2003).[4]

For a brief period, the "Constitucionalistas" (as the Boschists were called) successfully outmaneuvered the antiprogressive forces under the leadership of General Wessin and elected Colonel Francisco Alberto Caamaño as President

2.2 DOMINICAN PROTESTS AT THE U.S.-LED INVASION IN APRIL 1965 (*PHOTO:* ARCHIVO GENERAL DE LA NACION-DOMINICAN REPUBLIC).

of the Republic and legitimate heir to Juan Bosch, who was currently in exile in Puerto Rico and unable to return during the political standoff. The ascendancy of Caamaño and the collapse of the militarists were interpreted by the U.S. Ambassador as a threat to U.S. hegemony in the form of communist sympathizers and pro-Castro elements. United States President Lyndon Baines Johnson quickly announced to the world that "the U.S. cannot, should not, and is not going to permit the establishment of communist governments in the West." A second U.S. military invasion of the Dominican Republic was ordered on April 28, 1965, on the pretext of protecting American property and lives and preventing a Cuba-led takeover of the Dominican Republic. On September 21, 1966, the United States and an Interamerican Peace Force (the countries represented were Brazil, Honduras, Costa Rica, and Nicaragua) withdrew their forces from the Dominican Republic, installing Joaquin Balaguer, former right-hand man of Trujillo, as the head of the country's new government (Chomsky 2006; Galeano 1973; Grandin 2006).

This transfer of power to the counter-revolutionary Balaguer occurred after a national election was held in June 1966, during the U.S. occupation. Despite the presence of Juan Bosch on the presidential ticket, the Balaguer victory was a foregone conclusion because it was the only result that would be recognized by the United States. Balaguer continued to rule dictatorially from 1966 to 1978.[5] Thereafter, three political parties, the Partido Reformista Social Cristiano[6] (PRSC), the Partido Revolucionario Dominicano[7] (PRD), and the

TABLE 2.1 LIST OF PRESIDENTS AFTER THE JUAN BOSCH GOVERNMENT

President	Political party	First year
Joaquín Balaguer	PRSC	1966
Antonio Guzmán Fernández	PRD	1978
Jocobo Majluta Azar	PRD	1984
Salvador Jorge Blanco	PRD	1985
Joaquín Balaguer	PRSC	1986
Leonel Fernández Reyna	PLD	1996
Hipólito Mejía	PRD	2000
Leonel Fernández Reyna	PLD	2004

Note: PLD, Partido de la Liberación Dominicana; PRD, Partido Revolucionario Dominicano; PRSC, Partido Reformista Social Cristiano.

Partido de la Liberación Dominicana[8] (PLD), have alternated control of the presidential palace, always pursuing policies that have been subservient to the interests of the United States and its political leadership, whether Republican or Democrat (see table 2.1).

THE CONTEMPORARY SOCIOGEOGRAPHY OF THE DOMINICAN REPUBLIC

The Dominican Republic is a geographically diverse tropical country with forested mountains in its central, northern, and eastern cordilleras; great fertile valleys such as the Cibao; rich tropical sugar-producing regions such as the Samaná peninsula; and excellent natural ports such as Santo Domingo. The Dominican Republic has not suffered the same degree of deforestation as its neighbor Haiti, and the warm waters of the Atlantic Ocean and Caribbean Sea provide abundant species of fish along eight hundred miles of pristine white sandy beaches that lure tourists from around the world. In short, the Dominican Republic has all the natural resources to support a thriving society. However, most of its population of 9.4 million (see table 2.2) continue to struggle in this land of apparent promise where so little has been accomplished for the well-being of the majority of its citizens.

TABLE 2.2 POPULATION BY AGE IN 2007

Age	Percentage	Men	Women
0–14 years	32.1	1,532,813	1,477,033
15–64 years	62.2	2,971,620	2,851,207
65 years or older	5.7	247,738	285,407

The largest city in the country is Santo Domingo, with a little more than 2.2 million residents; other large cities include Santiago de los Caballeros, La Romana, and San Pedro de Macorís, with populations that range from 125,000 to 370,000. Many city residents have migrated from rural areas during the last twenty years and still have strong ties to the countryside. More than one million Dominicans live year-round or temporarily in New York City, often referred to as "Dominican Yorks," and a substantial number live in the state of New Jersey and in the cities of Boston and Miami.[9]

The racial composition of the Dominican Republic is a controversial issue because a person's African heritage has long been subordinate to his or her Caucasian, Latino/a, or Spanish "blood," due largely to the nation's longstanding enmity with Haiti. Thus, according to official reports, 73 percent of the population is of mixed race, i.e., a combination of descendants of Spaniards and other Europeans, West African slaves, and natives; 16 percent are classified as Caucasian; and 11 percent are black, including the Haitian minority, many of whom cannot claim Dominican citizenry as a result of the biased laws of the Dominican Republic (Central Intelligence Agency 2010).[10]

THE POLITICAL ECONOMY OF THE DOMINICAN REPUBLIC

By 1961 the debt with international banks was around $14.8 million. Today, we have a foreign debt of $10.2 billion, and with respect to five decades ago…even the agricultural goods are nowhere to be found in the market, or have a price so high that they cannot be acquired by the working and popular masses. The poverty level has increased. And over 40 percent of the national budget goes to interest payments and repayments of the foreign debt.

(SANTOS 2008)

2.3 A TYPICAL STREET SCENE IN ONE OF SANTO DOMINGO'S POOR BARRIOS (*PHOTO:* WILLIAM COSSOLIAS).

This recent commentary on the financial state of the country from a noted journalist correctly emphasizes the steadily declining fortunes of the political economy after years of mismanagement and policies that enriched the elite (Ramírez 2008; Solís 2008). Although incorrectly assuming that the Dominican Republic's economy was strong in the 1960s, i.e., after the time of Trujillo (it is estimated that Trujillo and his associates owned approximately 60 percent of the country's resources), Santos accurately states that the country held little foreign debt and that it was able to produce much of its own food and energy. Today, that situation has changed markedly, with much of the country's revenue going to service its foreign debts. Its greatest sources of income are tourism, exports from the free trade zones, and money sent home by Dominicans living in the United States and other large capitalist economies (some $3 billion annually versus $6.5 billion for all exports). In other words, the Dominican Republic's plunge into economic dependency has lasted for several decades (Hoy Digital 2009; González-Acosta 2008; Bolívar-Díaz 2009; Barrios 2004, 2007a).

This subservience to outside interests can be clearly seen in the country's signing of the Central American Free Trade Agreement in 2004 (along with Costa Rica, El Salvador, Guatemala, Honduras, and Nicaragua), which allows

U.S. businesses even more influence over the domestic market.[11] Another example of this issue can be seen in the Dominican Republic's domestic energy production and distribution.

Much of the country's electricity production has been privatized in recent years, like most of the nation's other resources, as the government has turned increasingly to neo-liberal economic doctrines as the framework for domestic policies. Until 1999, the Dominican Electric Company (Corporación Dominicana de Electricidad), which replaced a private company in 1955, produced and controlled most of the nation's electricity. In August 1999, under the privatization plans of the first government of Leonel Fernandez, three distribution companies were established: Edenorte, which covered the northern region; Edesur, which covered the southern region; and AES Distribuidora del Este, which covers half of Santo Domingo and the eastern region.—Although the government maintained 50 percent of the shares of these new companies, multinational energy companies from Spain and the United States among them Union Fenosa, AES, and Enron—owned the rest of the shares with extremely favorable terms, placing most of the investment risk on the shoulders of the government (e.g., state subsidies to the electricity sector exceeded $1 billion in 2008).

To date, the results of this privatization have been catastrophic in terms of efficient, affordable, and dependable energy production, with frequent power outages throughout much of the country. Some of the poorest regions in the country receive 10–12 hours of electricity per day, and sometimes none for days or even weeks at a time. As the U.S. State Department website (2009) ruefully notes, "The electricity sector is highly politicized; the prospect of further effective reforms in the sector is poor. Debts in the sector, including government debt, amount to close to U.S. $600 million. Some generating companies are undercapitalized and at times unable to purchase adequate fuel supplies."

This failure of the electricity industry only mirrors the unregulated, untaxed, dependent, and unplanned nature of the rest of the Dominican economy (Díaz 2009). Another example can be found in the sugar industry, which was denationalized in 1996 and virtually given away to the lowest bidder. In addition, much of the former lands of the Consejo Estatal de Azúcar (the state sugar company) was unaccountably bequeathed to a range of functionaries, military leaders, and friends of various governments, turning the Dominican Republic, once the most famous sugar-producing nation, into a sugar importer (cf. the sugar industry in Brazil, which takes advantage of the demand for sugar as energy).[12] Meanwhile, the natural resources of the Republic's pristine beaches, warm seas, and limitless sunshine have been auctioned off to almost entirely foreign tourist companies, which pay minimal taxes on their repatriated profits while offering low-pay, highly segmented employment to tens of thousands of desperate Dominicans hoping to don a corporate uniform (Gregory 2007).

Finally, players in the country's banking and financial services industries have been active in the Dominican Republic, speculating in the property market, laundering drug money, and lining its own coffers in much the same ways as their U.S. counterparts, such as Bernie Madoff, Richard Faud, Henry Paulson, and Lloyd Blankfein. A perfect example of such practices was the collapse of Banco Intercontinental, the country's third largest bank, in May 2003. In a celebrated case of grand larceny, bank president Ramón Baez was arrested for fraud, money laundering, tax evasion, and distributing about $75 million to government officials and other influential people for "favors." In the investigation that followed, Baez was found to be using two sets of books to siphon off $2.2 billion, a sum equal to nearly 67 percent of the Dominican Republic's annual national budget and 15 percent of its yearly gross domestic product. In 2002, the U.S. Drug Enforcement Agency listed the Dominican Republic as one of the top centers in the world for laundering drug money. A year later, the Colonel of the Presidential Guard, Pedro Julio (Pepe) Goico Guerrero, was arrested by the police and charged with smuggling more than 1000 kilograms of cocaine into the country from Haiti. As of this writing, Guerrero has had no trial, and the accused is expected to escape any punishment (International Monetary Fund 2009; *Diario Libre* 2007; Perelló 2010).

Of course progovernment economists undoubtedly will remind us of the success of the free trade zones, also established in the late 1990s, which produce more than 70 percent of the nation's export earnings, primarily in the form of garments and medical equipment.[13] Such economic initiatives, however, as critical observers of global development remind us (Tonelson 2002), engender a "race to the bottom" in the wages, conditions, and opportunities of workers as the international labor force competes against itself while multinational companies move their manufacturing plants in search of the lowest labor costs.[14]

WHAT HAPPENED TO THE CARIBBEAN MIRACLE?

It is hard to believe that when the Republic's gross national product grew at a rate of 7.7 percent per year (1996–2000), the nation was viewed as an exemplar of overcoming Third World underdevelopment by actively participating in the global markets. As one economist has noted, however, it was precisely when the Dominican Republic was becoming the model for a U.S.-inspired economic "take-off" that the country lost what was left of its independence and a "de facto dollarization of its banking system" took place (Sánchez-Fung 2008).

In effect, the miracle was nothing of the sort for most Dominicans. Poverty rates of around 40 percent were relatively constant, the opportunity structure for most of the country's population remained much the same, the class divide was as great as ever with 12 percent owning 57 percent of the nation's wealth (for 1995–2004),[15] infant mortality rates were still around 29 per 1,000 births,[16] official unemployment constantly hovered between 15 percent and 18 percent, and the per capita income never moved much above $8,200.[17] In addition, the country consistently failed to change its ranking as one of the poorest providers of social investment in Latin America, with 23 percent of the national budget being spent on education and health,[18] all of which has prompted the following conclusion in a recent report on the nation's state of human development:

> What is most startling about this situation is that the inequality of opportunities in the country has not been caused by a lack of funds, but by the poor choices made by those who have had the power to decide how resources are allocated. For all these reasons, human development is a matter of power.
>
> (HUMAN DEVELOPMENT OFFICE 2008)

It is not surprising, therefore, that 57 percent of Dominicans say that they want to emigrate and 50 percent think that positive change in the country, i.e., change that will improve the lot of the majority, is not possible (Human Development Office 2008:28). Clearly, when all else fails, when hope is no longer sufficient to help them make it through the day, when the "remesas" from their families in the United States or Europe fail to arrive or keep up with the cost of living[19] (Valdez 2009), then the last resort is to escape this dance with want and misery and aim for the promised land (as we shall discuss in chapters 3 and 11).

More than 40 percent of all the undocumented aliens interdicted by the Coast Guard since fiscal 2004 have tried to enter the United States through the Mona Pass. In recent years, as many as 7,000 to 10,000 migrants have traversed these waters annually, often in handmade, unseaworthy and overloaded boats called *yolas*. The numbers could be even greater—no one can be sure how many vessels and lives have been lost.

(BECKLEY 2008)

FROM INDIRECT TO DIRECT VIOLENCE

Thus far we have highlighted what Salmi (1993) calls the "indirect violence" experienced by most Dominicans. What are the chances that Dominicans, especially poor ones, will experience direct violence at some point in their everyday lives? Official homicide statistics indicate a troubling trend in that the murder rate has nearly doubled between the years 2000 and 2008, increasing from 14 homicides per 100,000 people to approximately 25 (see table 2.3). Various explanations have been offered to account for this trend, including the marked increase in deportees over this period. However, because the homicide trend has held constant and the numbers of deportees has been steadily increasing, it is unlikely that the deportees are a substantial part of this particular problem. Other changes in Dominican society are more likely to be the key factors. In research that extends over a decade, long-time students of violence in the Dominican Republic Brea de Cabral and Cabral Ramírez (2009a, 2009b) focused on four principal areas:

1. A socialization process (heavily influenced by commercialized popular culture) in which violence features as a major resolution of interpersonal conflict and hyper-machismo performance and imagery is widely sanctioned and encouraged.
2. A sharp increase in the possession of firearms as citizens seek to protect themselves in the face of an ineffectual, corrupt, and potentially vindictive criminal justice system.[20]
3. The constantly high levels of social inequality reflected in unrelenting rates of both absolute and relative poverty and low opportunity structures create great reservoirs of frustration for the country's poorer youth and lead to the inevitable rise of gangs, intergroup conflict, and higher crime rates.
4. A sharp increase in the local and international drugs trade has been observed as more drugs stay in the country. The combination of increased drug and alcohol use at the local level combined with more gangs fighting over local markets must be placed in the context of an unrelenting demand for drugs in the United States and the failure of the country's own campaign to eradicate the drug problem (Brotherton and Martín 2009; Nadelman 1998).[21]

Clearly, a rising a level of physical insecurity is accompanied by a constant feeling of economic anxiety that has been made worse by the present downturn in the world economy. In the poorer sections of urban Dominican society, the conditions of public and personal security are much worse, and it is not uncommon to hear residents of these neighborhoods explain how they

TABLE 2.3 HOMICIDE RATES IN THE DOMINICAN REPUBLIC, 1991–2008

Year	Homicide rate (per 100,000)	Homicides	Total population
1991	13.0	908	6,967,000
1992	11.3	807	7,129,000
1993	12.7	930	7,293,000
1994	13.5	1,005	7,425,000
1995	13.3	1,007	7,558,000
1996	13.4	1,032	7,694,000
1997	13.2	1,038	7,832,000
1998	14.1	1,121	7,973,000
1999	13.0	1,066	8,117,000
2000	14.6	1,210	8,263,000
2001	12.8	1,095	8,411,000
2002	14.9	1,279	8,563,000
2003	21.8	1,902	8,717,000
2004	25.2	2,239	8,873,000
2005	26.3	2,394	9,100,000
2006	23.6	2,144	9,195,000
2007	22.1	2,111	9,361,000
2008[a]	24.8	2,396	9,659,278

[a]Projections based on data from January to August 2008.

avoid going out after dark, especially on streets where street lamps are often absent or broken and where power cuts ensure that little is illuminated.

For women, the incidence of victimization is particularly worrying as rates of domestic violence have been steadily increasing, as seen in the following report:

Violence against women continued to be widespread. In July the Public Prosecutor of Santo Domingo Province called the level of domestic violence in the Dominican Republic "alarming". According to official statistics, between

January and August, 133 women were killed by their current or former partners. A report entitled Critical Path of Dominican Women Survivors of Gender Violence, issued in June jointly by several Dominican women's rights NGOs, found that the great majority of survivors of gender-based violence were revictimized by the justice system. It found that a high percentage of victims abandon the legal process and highlighted the lack of judicial personnel trained to deal with the issue.

(AMNESTY INTERNATIONAL REPORT 2009)

Finally, Dominicans are not just confronted by the individual and social pathologies of daily life in the form of muggers, robbers, and aggressive behavior from a range of civilian actors but also by threats from those who are supposed to help ensure safety and justice for the population. In a recent report by Amnesty International (2009), the authors concluded that "police violence is best understood as a social control mechanism used to maintain 'order,'" which has become necessary because "the government is not meeting the population's basic needs or responding to legitimate social demands." The authors continued:

> There were widespread concerns about the escalating level of violent crime and the government's inability to combat it effectively. According to figures from the General Prosecutor's Office, 298 people were killed by the police between January and August, an increase of 72 percent over the same period in 2007. There were concerns that a number of these fatal shootings may have been unlawful. In October the Dominican Interior and Police Minister described the levels of fatal police shootings as "alarming" and called for corrupt officers to be expelled from the force and for improved police training. With no independent body to investigate allegations of abuse by members of the security forces, impunity remained the norm.

In another reputable analysis from the United Nations Office of Drugs and Crime (2007), the authors reported:

> The national police itself reports an average of 36 shooting deaths per month by the members of its force. In 2005, 18 percent of all violent deaths/homicides were a result of police shootings. Though the ages of the victims are not known, anecdotal evidence suggests that a large number of these are youth: one study cited 23 unprovoked killings of street children by los cirujanos ("the surgeons," a police unit that conducts night sweeps) in three neighborhoods in Santo Domingo over an eight-month period.

In the most recent statement on the provision of human rights, the U.S. Department of State (2009:1) drew the following conclusions:

> Although the government's human rights record continued to improve, serious problems remained: unlawful killings; beatings and other abuse of suspects, detainees, and prisoners; poor to harsh prison conditions; arbitrary arrest and detention of suspects; a large number of functionally stateless persons; widespread corruption; harassment of certain human rights groups; violence and discrimination against women; child prostitution and other abuses of children; trafficking in persons; severe discrimination against Haitian migrants and their descendants; violence and discrimination against persons based on sexual orientation; ineffective enforcement of labor laws; and child labor.

There is great consternation both within and outside the country regarding the methods by which social order is being maintained, the effectiveness of the criminal justice system, and the degree to which Dominican society is practicing policies that make it more democratic. Perhaps under the new Obama administration, the buzz words of change and hope used to mobilize millions of previously excluded U.S. citizens will have an effect on its partners in the Caribbean. We shall have to wait and see. We can report, however, that in recent years the Dominican police, at the behest of the Fernandez government and with material support from the former Bush administrations, imported largely repressive policies by incorporating different versions of the infamous "zero tolerance" approach aimed at "hot spot" barrios. Under two policy initiatives known as the "Plan for Democratic Security" and "Barrio Seguro" (safe neighborhood), a four-point strategy was implemented to achieve the following aims: (i) the reform and professionalization of the national police; (ii) a more visible and positive role of the state through improving public services but also through a more pervasive police presence[22]; (iii) the strengthening of local community organizations; and (iv) a closer relationship between society and government. In a rare academic evaluation, Brea de Cabral and Cabral Ramírez (2009) note that, although these policies have had some positive effect on crime rates, they have several weaknesses, including the state's inability to respond in long-lasting ways to the multiple economic and social causes behind violence in marginalized communities, the impossible task of reforming the police without sufficient resources, and the limited capacity of barrio organizations to fulfill their preventive roles. In other words, both direct and indirect violence continue unabated while the country's citizens await those with the political will and vision to bring about the kinds of real change momentarily glimpsed more than four decades ago.

THE SAMPLE

Below is a list of demographic characteristics of our deportee samples. All of these are purposive samples produced by snowball methods of data collection (Biernacki and Waldorf 1981), which make it difficult to know how representative they are of the general deportee population. Where possible, we have compared our data to the only other analysis of a Dominican deportee data set we have encountered, that performed by Venator-Santiago (2005a, 2005b) from a database of 475 Dominican deportee records.

The vast majority of our sample were men (84 percent), which is lower than the percentage in Venator-Santiago's study (94 percent), but this seems to indicate that males are much more likely to be deported than females (which also reflects the disparity between male and female prisoners in the U.S. prison system). The average age of the subjects in our study was 33 years old, which is similar to the average age of subjects in Venator-Santiago's sample, in which 63 percent were between 29 and 41 years of age. This concurs with our observation that most deportees are in the prime of their working lives, with many potentially productive years ahead of them, whether in the Dominican Republic or back in the United States.

Among the subjects in our study, the average time served in a U.S. prison was just over four years; however, there were a number of subjects who had spent in excess of ten years behind bars on both violent and nonviolent convictions, primarily related to drugs. Our sample is again similar to that of Venator-Santiago, in which more than 73 percent of the subjects had served similar prison terms for drug-related offenses. This is not at all surprising

TABLE 2.4 DEMOGRAPHIC DATA: PLACE OF INTERVIEW, GENDER, AND AVERAGE AGE

Place of interview (N = 98)	Gender		Average age (years)	Gender ratio (%)	
	Men	Women		Men	Women
	57	8	36.5	84	16
Dominican Republic: Streets (n = 65)	15	—	24	100	—
Dominican Republic: Prison (n = 15)	14	4	32.5	78	22
New York City (n = 18)	86	12	33.17	84	16

because there was a sharp increase during the 1980s and 1990s of noncitizens and African American and Latino/a citizens going to prison as a result of the criminalizing effects of the Rockefeller drug laws in New York and tougher federal sentencing laws as part of the overall war on drugs (Brotherton and Martín 2009; Nadelman 1998; Wallace-Wells 2007). Regarding problems with drugs, again this is hardly surprising when one remembers that 80 percent of those incarcerated at New York City's largest prison, Riker's Island, report problems with drug use (see Wynn 2002).

The average time spent living in the United States was eleven years, which is not far removed from the time of residency for Venator-Santiago's reduced sample of 196 subjects, in which the majority had spent more than five years as U.S. residents. The level of recidivism was very low among our civilian sample, which aligns with statements made to a House Committee on Foreign Affairs regarding estimates as low as 2 percent (Northern Manhattan Coalition Report 2009).

In terms of education, nearly 60 percent of our subjects do not have a high school credential, which is quite believable, especially for those who have been involved in the criminal justice system. Again, the numbers at Riker's Island prison are revealing. Among its inmates, 80 percent failed to graduate from high school (Wynn 2002); in the New York correctional system as a whole, 50

TABLE 2.5 DEMOGRAPHIC DATA: TIME SERVED IN PRISONS AND RELATED DATA

Sample (N = 127)	Number of participants	Average time in U.S. prison (years)	Average time living in the U.S. (years)	Proportion of charges related to drugs (%)	Participants with drug problems at deportation[d]	Average time in a Dominican prison since returning (years)
Dominican Republic: Streets	65	4.2[a]	15	74	15	2.2
Dominican Republic: Prison	15	3.8[b]	13	66	3	4.2
New York City	18	5.0[c]	10	83	—	2

[a]The longest term was 22 years; the shortest term was 15 months.

[b]Most subjects were in preventive detention. Of those sentenced, the longest term was 15 years; the shortest term was 10 years.

[c]The longest term was 8 years; the shortest term was 6 months.

[d]Drugs include alcohol, heroin, and/or cocaine.

TABLE 2.6 DEMOGRAPHIC DATA: CRIMINAL OFFENSES IN UNITED STATES

Sample (N = 98)	Drug sale	Drug possession	Gun possession	Homicide	Other
Dominican Republic: Streets (n = 65)	23	25	9	4	4
Dominican Republic: Prison (n = 15)	6	4	1	1	3
New York City (n = 18)	12	3	2	—	1
Totals, n (%)	**41 (41.8)**	**32 (32.7)**	**12 (12.2)**	**5 (5.1)**	**8 (8.2)**

Note: We do not know how many of these cases are based on conspiracy charges or are a result of plea bargaining.

percent of inmates lack a high school diploma or its equivalent (Brotherton and Barrios 2004). In addition, 25 percent of Dominicans over twenty-five years of age in New York City during the 1990s lacked a high school diploma, and only 4 percent had attained a college education (Brotherton and Barrios 2004).

The employment figures in our sample are interesting. Although the civilian sample is what one might expect, with an unemployment rate of approximately 27 percent, i.e., more than the general unemployment rate in the country (estimated at approximately 20 percent),[23] the rates for the incarcerated sample (however small) may seem contradictory. However, as we shall see in chapter 9, this could reflect the undue attention paid to deportees who often find themselves in preventive detention only to have their charges later dropped by the time they come to court.

The legal status of deportees is again revealing and confirms to some extent what we already know from other reports and data. Lonegan (2008) estimates

TABLE 2.7 DEMOGRAPHIC DATA: EDUCATION LEVEL

Sample (N = 98)	Less than high school	High school	Some college
Dominican Republic: Streets (n = 65)	37	25	3
Dominican Republic: Prison (n = 15)	10	4	1
New York City (n = 18)	8	10	—
Totals, n (%)	**55 (56)**	**39 (39.8)**	**4 (3.8)**

TABLE 2.8 DEMOGRAPHIC DATA: EMPLOYMENT STATUS AT TIME OF INTERVIEW

Sample (N = 98)	Employed full-time, n (%)	Employed part-time, n (%)	Unemployed, n (%)
Dominican Republic: Streets, n = 65 (%)	27 (41.5)	20 (30.7)	18 (27.6)
Dominican Republic: Prison, n = 15 (%)	6 (40.0)	5 (33.0)	4 (27.0)
New York City, n = 18 (%)	18 (100)	—	—
Totals, n (%)	**51 (52.0)**	**25 (25.5)**	**22 (22.5)**

that about a third of all deportees are formerly legal residents; the Northern Manhattan Coalition for Immigrant Rights (2009:2) concluded that members of the Dominican communities "seldom can be deported on grounds of unlawful status (i.e., undocumented status) alone." Venator-Santiago (2005a, 2005b) found that 42 percent of 102 deportee cases in his sample were residing legally in the United States, and another 16 percent could not be "normalized." Our sample of civilians and imprisoned deportees is definitely skewed toward the legal resident, although we have collected a sample of 18 individuals who were undocumented residents. We speculate that, due to the long established familial roots of the Dominican community in New York City and along the eastern seaboard, most "criminal" deportees are legal residents, which might also denote, as Venator-Santiago concluded, that legal residents are more likely to become involved in crime-related opportunities in their communities.

Our data on marital status differs somewhat from those of Venator-Santiago's sample, in which most of the subjects with available data (N = 124) were single but 85 percent had family ties in the United States, including children. Venator-Santiago also noted that an unspecified number were in consensual relationships without being counted as marriage. In our sample, we saw that a substantial number of deportees (both documented and undocumented) have children who may reside in either country. This social fact is important for the assessment of the collateral damage that occurs when families are fragmented permanently because of deportation or when members of the household are put in preventive detention (as is the case with many in our Dominican prison sample), which usually means that the main source of income for the family has been removed.

TABLE 2.9 DEMOGRAPHIC DATA: LEGAL AND MARITAL STATUS, FAMILY MEMBERS

Sample (*N* = 98)	Legal status in the United States		Marital status			Average number of children	Number with family members in the United States
	Documented	Undocumented	Married	Divorced/ separated	Single		
Dominican Republic: Streets (*n* = 65)	45	20	32	20	13	2.5	58
Dominican Republic: Prison (*n* = 15)	15	—	15	—	—	3.0	15
New York City (*n* = 18)	—	18	18	—	—	2.5	18

TABLE 2.10 DEMOGRAPHIC DATA: AGE UPON EMIGRATION FROM THE
DOMINICAN REPUBLIC TO THE UNITED STATES

Sample (N = 98)	<5 years old	6–15 years old	>15 years old
Dominican Republic: Streets (n = 65)	40	15	10
Dominican Republic: Prison (n = 15)	10	3	2
New York City (n = 18)	11	7	—
Totals, n (%)	**61 (62.3)**	**25 (25.5)**	**12 (12.3)**

The age at which our sample first left the Dominican Republic shows that the majority emigrated to the United States as children and subsequently spent much of their socialization there. In other words, the majority of subjects in our sample are first-generation immigrants to the United States who primarily came during two prominent waves of immigration. The first wave came after the dictatorship of Trujillo ended and the civil war and military invasion that ensued (see earlier in this chapter and chapter 3), and the second wave was a massive exodus of Dominicans seeking economic opportunity in the United States in the 1980s.

3.1 AN EXAMPLE OF GRAFFITI THAT CONTRASTS THE NEED TO ESCAPE THE COUNTRY AND THE ASSERTION THAT THERE IS STILL LIFE IN THE BARRIO—SHOT IN GUACHUPITA, NOVEMBER 2000 (*PHOTO:* LUIS BARRIOS).

CHAPTER THREE

LEAVING FOR AMERICA

David Brotherton (D.B.): Tell me about where you were born.

Danny: I was born here in Santo Domingo on October 22, 1962, and on August 8, 1963, my father took me to New York. They took me as a little baby. I was only 10 months old and so I grew up there all my life. I came back here in 1966 for a couple of months and in 1981 and 1991 for a few weeks. Then I came back here deported in 1999. I was born here but I really don't remember anything from here. (July 2, 2006)

IN THIS CHAPTER we seek to answer questions that are in the forefront of the emigrant's experience but are often sidelined due to an overemphasis on the settlement processes in the immigration literature. We agree with Sayad's statement (2004) that it is impossible to have a sociology of immigration without a sociology of emigration. The gain of one country is a loss for another; for many in the United States, however, the introduction of new immigrant labor and their families is now construed as a "burden." When emigrants leave their homeland, they are, by definition, displaced, both socially and culturally, even though they may eventually become "acculturated" or even "assimilated." The process by which people leave and experience their leaving is an essential part of this all too common journey in the global marketplace, and this experience becomes a marker, if an often buried one, as subjects form and reconstitute their sense of self in the new society.

We divided our data into three themes drawn from the respondents' narratives as they hearken back to a much earlier period in their lives: (i) reasons for leaving; (ii) feelings of loss, and (iii) modes of entry. For most of our respondents, the decision to leave for the United States was a difficult, highly traumatic, and often contradictory one. Some were too young to remember much about the decision-making process beyond the fact that they had to join their parents or their grandparents in *Nueva York*. For most, however, the decision was linked to the struggle for economic survival and a quest for some sense of a future that they felt they deserved. In other words, the act of leaving was a way to negate the psychosocial condition of fatalism that is common in colonized societies. In such narratives, quite naturally, poverty was the primary condition from which they wanted to escape, but often the experience of poverty was infused with the experience of repressive state policies, especially for those who left during the eras of President Balaguer and subsequent authoritarian governments of Balagueristas. As briefly mentioned in chapter 2, overlaying (or perhaps overdetermining) these experiences are the sociohistorical colonial relations between the United States and the Dominican Republic. These relations between what used to be called the center and the periphery maintain the issues of marginalization and subordination and are encapsulated in the hegemonic notion of the "American Dream."[1]

In the second theme, we concentrate on the issue of "loss." Here we are confronted with notions of cultural memory, of narratives that depict a social state left behind that will be difficult if not impossible to return to. This loss is also about the end of a period of life during which greater community trust and social solidarity provided a modicum of personal security at the local level. In a society where few are provided with any economic guarantees, the certainty of mutual family obligations and close-knit social circles built on reciprocal relations is a welcome respite. Such relations, of course, become difficult to maintain across borders and are in stark contrast to the individualized culture that is so dominant in the United States.

Finally, the third theme deals with the experiences of subjects as they made their way in airplanes, on ships, in trucks, on foot, and in "yolas" (flimsy Dominican sea craft) to the shores of the United States. How were their trips organized? What kinds of social networks were necessary? What were the dangers of such trips? Would they be prepared for yet another such voyage (see chapter 11)? These are some of the questions we ask in this section as we excavate the complex terrain of leaving for America.

REASONS FOR LEAVING

D.B.: Can you tell me what you felt when you left your country?

JUAN: When I left it was with hope because people always said when you arrive over there your life will change. You are going to earn dollars.

People always leave if they want to go forward, always if they want to find happiness. But, when you go for the first time you are going to another place, you are leaving your old life, someone who you were and you feel it. You are born right here, the first son, 20 years old and I left, okay, looking to improve my family. That's it. (November 3, 2002)

In the literature describing the reasons for Dominican emigration, the primary cause is said to be economic (as expressed in Juan's response above), followed by "political pushes" (i.e., the population's reaction to repressive domestic regimes or to subsequent periods of liberalization) and changes in U.S. immigration laws that might allow more Dominican applicants, particularly for the purposes of family reunification (Bray 1984; Grasmuck and Pessar 1991; Guarnizo 1997). According to our respondents, the first two reasons were prominent in their narratives, and there was little mention of the third.

SEDUCED BY THE AMERICAN DREAM

Among our respondents, the theme of the American Dream was prominent, particularly for those who had emigrated to the United Status in their teens or later. Those who emigrated earlier spoke mostly of their parents or of other family members who were similarly attracted to the promise of a better life "over there." Such messages of American prosperity and superiority are omnipresent in the swirl of First- and Third-World themes and images that constitute the urban Dominican's daily semiotic fare. Blaring from the television screens in most colmados (neighborhood grocery stores) and in so many homes in the Dominican Republic is a constant diet of Hollywood-made productions in which the middle-class lifestyles of Los Angeles, New York City, and Miami are heavily represented. Similarly, Hollywood films are the staple diet of most Dominican cinemas, although the cost of entry is generally too expensive for working-class residents of the capital. The process of seduction continues in the U.S.-based popular music industry that is granted significant air time, although it is on television programs that American-themed music is primarily distributed. This trend is balanced somewhat by the Dominicans' healthy respect for indigenous musical traditions, and it is notable how much air play is given to meringue and bachata rather than to rock and roll or rap music. Nonetheless, perhaps one of the most important ways in which the American Dream is communicated is through social networks of family members and friends who are more inclined to talk of their "positive" American transition than of the difficulties of settlement and any notions of "failure."

Although the idea of American prosperity is certainly alluring, no one can predict how it might be attained. Some emigrants have achieved the American Dream legitimately as they studied, found jobs after leaving school, kept their nose clean in the neighborhood, and generally followed the examples of their hard-working parents. For others struggling in the lowest tiers of the segmented labor force, the only way to realize their goals was through the informal economy, a classic case of Mertonian innovation. The immigration literature describes various ways in which emigrants move toward the Dream after they have arrived in the United States, but less is heard from people who have seen the Dream slip farther away despite their efforts. One of our respondents, Celio, recounts being beseeched by his brother-in-law to join him in Puerto Rico after his brother-in-law had received an amnesty, a stroke of fortune that is equivalent to winning the lottery.

> D.B.: Why did you emigrate? Was it for the American Dream?
>
> CELIO: The idea came from my brother-in-law. He was in Puerto Rico and at that time had an amnesty which they gave in '86. He was always telling us," You've got to go, you've got to go." Until he damaged my mind and I went. But I don't regret it, in spite of losing everything. I'll repeat myself, I don't regret it because I learned a lot and I've got something that every man wants to have, a son. He's not with me, but I have him. God and I are witnesses that he is there. I don't regret it. I helped my family a lot when I was over there. It may have been drug money, but I helped them a lot. I was my family's economic support when I was in the United States, when I was in Puerto Rico. Therefore I say these days that I don't regret it, because I did bad things but also I did good things. (December 2, 2002)

Celio talks of his mind "being damaged" by the seduction of the Dream; it is an interesting choice of words and refers to the psychological pressure placed upon him by his family. Celio's words could also speak to the impact of American culture on the self-esteem of a people whose efforts at independence have been struck such cruel blows by the foreign policies of Washington, D.C. Perhaps both meanings are present, for one should always bear in mind that the immigrant/emigrant is living through multiple consciousnesses, constantly piecing together the narratives of his or her journey in a never-ending quest to construct something approaching a unified self (Ewick and Silbey 1995; Riessman 1993). The tragedy for Celio lies in his permanent separation from his son (though he still clings to the possibility of some day, somewhere, getting in contact with him), which is countered by his insistence that it was all worth it. The hopes behind the original journey—the ability to make good on his family obligations, the experience of fatherhood, however fleeting, and the taste of America, particularly of New York—still mean something.

Below, Manolo reminisces about his childhood, a time when he was living the American Dream as part of a working-class immigrant family in the early 1960s.

D.B.: Did you miss the DR [Dominican Republic]?

MANOLO: I didn't miss the DR for nothing, I was too young to know, I was basically too excited to be over there rather than over here. It was plenty over there, but 'specially the train. The train got me very excited. My mother used to take us down to Macy's. She used to get paid and my father used to get paid and they would say, "Let's get the kids," you know. 'Specially when the winter time was coming . . . the coats, the boots, the long johns to protect us. We used to go down in the train. My mother used to hold on to me tight and my father used to hold on to the little girls, and we'd go inside those big department stores at 34th street and on 14th street . . . all that stuff specially at Christmas. My God, Lord have Mercy . . . bags for the kids, trying on the new clothes with my mother who used to take up her hair special. And then with all this stuff she'd get us ready for school, to go out in the snow. And then the weekends, the ice skating, after we'd bought the skates, ice skates, hockey skates. Man, it was very exciting, man, wow! (April 2, 2003)

Leon was also struck by the material and social benefits of his new surroundings. In talking about the American Dream, he remembered the following, again as a young boy:

D.B.: How was it when you started to hang out?

LEON: I didn't hang out 'cause I was only a little kid, but I saw everything. I saw big rooms, a nice bed, more food, food in the refrigerator . . . because back then we had no refrigerators in the D.R. I see the refrigerator and its cold and the cabinet full of clothes, you know, it was nice. Then when they took me to school, you know, I felt good, like a different environment, I felt safer. (March 3, 2003)

Safety and educational possibilities are both important elements of the Dream for deportees, as evidenced by Alex who wistfully remembers his experience of public schooling and its promise of social ascent for the poor.

ALEX: God bless them (the United States [added by the authors]) because you know, they offer you a lot of things, they offer you school, they give you money while you're going to school, you know, they give you free college and things. I don't how they call it but you have a lot of opportunities over there. But when you're young you don't realize those things, especially when you don't have no family next to you that can give you the proper guidance. (March 5, 2003)

In contrast, Andres, below, asserts that the Dream was more about people keeping themselves to themselves, staying out of "your business." It should be noted that cultural conformity is held in high regard in Dominican society, with a strong emphasis on the collective conscience, quite different from the U.S. traditions of individualism and personal autonomy.

D.B.: What did you like about the United States?
ANDRES: Well, I liked a lot of things. The United States is nice, things are easier there. With a little money you can buy a lot. The food is cheaper, the clothes are cheap, many things that in all honesty in your own country are difficult.
D.B.: Did you notice any competition with other groups, like with people who wanted to be better than you or mess with you?
ANDRES: No, no, no, because over there people live within themselves. They live for themselves. They don't live, let's say, uh, mistreating you, criticizing the way you dress. No, no, no, over there every one is trying to better themselves and move forward. (January 9, 2003)

Nonetheless, the American Dream does not produce the same bounty for everyone. Some of the respondents recounted how betrayed they felt by the Dream. Their expectations unfulfilled, they admitted to having been deluded, to having given up everything for this mythical life. For some, the cost of missing the Dream was severe, especially the sense of dislocation and disruption that it caused to their previous lives. One might consider this to be "sour grapes," that the subjects may not have prospered in any case, especially given the limited opportunities that existed in the country generally. Nonetheless, Cecilio's comments are noteworthy.

What happened is that I went crazy with the idea of seeking the American Dream. And therefore I left the country. If I had stayed and not been carried off by the American Dream I would have gone on to study. I would have gone to college and I would be a professional by now. Instead, I was in Puerto Rico from '89 to '96, between Puerto Rico and New York, that's practically seven years. In those years I could have graduated here, but seeking the American Dream I lost it all, except my life which is most important! (March 3, 2003)

DEALING WITH POVERTY

The Dream, of course, is very much linked to the experiences of unrelenting poverty in the Dominican Republic, where so many are living in permanent hardship with scant social mobility (see chapter 2). For many respondents, poverty was a normal state of affairs, especially growing up in neighborhoods during the 1970s and 1980s, with little notion of relative deprivation. In the following, deportees talked about the various ways they experienced poverty during a more general discussion that focused on their reasons for leaving.

> D.B.: Can you tell me about the neighborhood where you were raised? Did you see or live through poverty in your childhood?
> AGUSTIN: Yes, lots of poverty, the first I remember was Jualee, then later in a place they called Lenguaazul, that nowadays is called Sánchez Jaumatinamella. Then I remember going to El Faro, that's up that way, then Cristo Rey and lastly here in Villa Duarte where I have been all this time. (May 3, 2003)

> D.B.: Could you tell me if you experienced poverty during your childhood?
> ANDRES: Well, my grandmother was very humble. She was a dressmaker and used to sew in a dressmaking workshop so we could eat and take care of the house. I used to do the house chores, help out our aunt for my grandmother. You know, we lived the normal life of people . . . the simple life. (January 4, 2003)

> GIPSY ESCOBAR (G.E.): Tell me a little about the neighborhood where you were raised?.
> EIXIDA: It was peaceful. I had many friends, boys and girls and it was beautiful.
> GE: Did you see much poverty?
> EIXIDA: Yes, there was, yes.
> G.E.: In what sense? Did people not have enough money to buy food?
> EIXIDA: No there wasn't, that's to say, you could only afford to buy one piece of clothing a year and then you had to worry about eating every day. My father was always worried, always worried about providing food for the household. There was nothing, no refrigerator, no water, no light, nothing. (May 2, 2003)

In the first quote, Agustin is naming a number of poor barrios of Santo Domingo, with Jualee among the most deprived areas in the nation. These areas are assiduously avoided in conversation, with any mention of their names provoking a raised eye brow, an unsubtle reminder that these zones of deprivation (as expressed in the third interview) are seen as pathological places where indices of interpersonal violence are as high as almost anywhere in the Americas.[2] Poverty, therefore, was identified as a very real structural constraint, a condition that determined the school one attended (if one attended school at all) and dictated the space available for housing and even the number of people with whom one shares a bed.

D.B.: Did you like to study in school?

SANTO: Yeah I liked studying but it wasn't that easy because I had to work and therefore I had to quit school. (May 8, 2003)

D.B.: Did you see a lot of poverty?

SANTO: Yeah, lots of poverty, yes.

D.B.: And how is the experience of poverty?

SANTO: There is still a lot of poverty, lots of poverty still remains.

D.B.: Poverty as in people don't have enough to eat?

SANTO: To eat you have to work. You have to go to the country and even in the country there isn't a lot of work right now, there's not much production.

D.B.: And at your home, was there enough room for the whole family or did you have to share a bedroom with other people?

SANTO: I shared a bedroom with the other siblings, because the house was very small.

D.B.: How many bedrooms did you have?

SANTO: 4 bedrooms.

D.B.: For 10 children and the parents.

SANTO: For everyone, yes. (laughs)

D.B.: So, did you have to spend a lot of time outside?

SANTO: Of course. (laughs) (April 3, 2003)

LUIS BARRIOS (L.B.): Tell me about your childhood.

NESTOR: About my childhood? There was little happiness because back then, I always had to sell things. My mother never bought me trousers, never bought me a pair of shoes. I had to sell things with my brother, selling bread, what they call "pan bolita" and "caramelitos" that are made from coconuts, and cleaning shoes. From that I earned my money which got me my trousers. Half my money would go to my mom so she could buy things for my sisters. (May 3, 2005)

3.2 A TYPICAL DWELLING IN THE POOREST NEIGHBORHOODS OF SANTO DOMINGO. APPROXIMATELY 70 PERCENT OF SANTO DOMINGANS LIVE BELOW THE POVERTY LINE. THE CONTRAST BETWEEN THE DAPPER, SELF-CONFIDENT "LEONEL" IN THE POSTER AND THE DISHEVELED HARDSHIP THAT PERVADES THE COUNTRY IS MORE THAN JUST AN IMAGE. (*PHOTO:* LUIS BARRIOS).

D.B.: So you saw a lot of poverty?

JOSÉ: Lots of poverty, I lived in here in a yard, where there were like 14, 15 dwellings, like bedrooms, 8 or 10 people lived in each bedroom. Sometimes 10 in a bed! (May 28, 2003)

In the Dominican Republic, a heavily patriarchal society, there is a tradition of men fathering children without taking responsibility for them, as Luis attests below.

LUIS: Well, it wasn't too difficult because my dad never gave me the support that I needed, do you understand me? My mom raised me, my mom was my dad and my mom. She gave me what I needed. May God have glory even on my dad, let's say, because the feelings I once had are gone. Before I could not forgive him because he put me through a lot of hard times. If my dad had supported me, I wouldn't have gone to prison in the United States. Why? Because I would've been devoted to working and I wouldn't have had such a materialistic mindset, do you understand me? But because he didn't give me any support I said: "OK, I'm leaving my

country and I'm going to make money any way I can." So I began to do things that weren't right, do you understand me?

But poverty has also changed, particularly in more recent times. Part of the change reflects the great increase of commodities flooding into the Dominican Republic and the new social strata that have emerged. As the formal economy has developed with more foreign investment, the informal economy has grown with a massive increase in drug trafficking. The country is now a major transit point for Colombian drug cartels, with a growing local trade primarily in cocaine and heroin; concomitantly, its banks ensure that it is one of the world's leaders in money-laundering (U.S. Drug Enforcement Administration 2002). According to the U.S. Federal Bureau of Investigation, the Dominican Republic is also a leading producer of false personal documents such as passports, identity cards, and social security cards.

> D.B.: And were drugs being dealt there?
> AGUSTIN: Now there are drugs everywhere, even your own children and your little brothers can get involved. You tell them to stay out of it, to not get involved with people not knowing what they are doing. If it turns out they carry drugs and they get arrested, you also get arrested. So as someone who knows I tell them not to hang out with those types of people.

> D.B.: Were there any drug sales when you were growing up?
> AGUSTIN: Down on that street, not on this one, in El Proyecto, they used to sell, they used to sell drugs down there. (November 28, 2002)
> DB: Tell me about your neighborhood.
> JAVIER: My neighborhood is one of the most well known in Santo Domingo because famous politicians like Leonel Fernandez have come from there. It's also where the most drugs are dealt, one of the most notorious neighborhoods for drugs, most recognized for robbery and gangs. (June 5, 2003)

Deportees also talked about their struggles to emerge from poverty with emigration as the last and not the first resort. Andres discusses this below, as he tries to explain the obstacles facing youth and adults who reside in poor and criminalized areas. The reader should be reminded that the Dominican Republic still practices "preventive detention" which means that suspects can be arrested and placed in prison while they await trial, which can take several months and even years (see chapter 10). The lack of due process in the system ensures that many youths and adults have criminal records that stay with them for life which severely affects their employability. As Andres attests, all the will in the world often does not trump the constraints of dependency, discrimination and the normative level of poverty wages paid to labor.

ANDRES: Some youths, if they have a record won't easily be given work. Why? Because they see them as antisocial. They see them as not able to work. Why? Because they fear this person might do something crazy. They fear losing their business, so they make it difficult for you. But there are many ways you can earn a living. It could be selling chimichurri on a corner, running a corner store, selling water in the streets, there are many ways to earn a living. It's not necessary for you to go over there (The United States [added by the authors]), but you resort to having to go over there because things are made a lot easier than here. There, at least with your small or large earnings, you manage and help your family, but working in your own country, you work a lot and earn little. (January 9, 2003)

Finally, it should be mentioned that some deportees understood poverty differently. They described it in culture conflict terms, as the result of the newcomers with different customs moving in and creating the conditions for social disorganization. Such new residents usually came from rural areas, and there was a hint of prejudice in the respondents' answers. However, the same respondent also saw strength in these poverty-riddled communities as residents came together to share and give each other much needed support.

D.B.: Tell me about the neighborhood where you were raised. Did you live through a lot of poverty in your childhood?

ALBERTO: The neighborhood where I was raised was a very humble neighborhood. Still the neighbors were calm and human. If you needed something the neighbors gave you it, but as time passed, you know neighborhoods bring in other people, let's say, with other customs. Then the new customs hurt those that live there. If you live here and a fucked up neighbor moves in, problems start and right then they start to produce problems. So the neighborhood was calm, but later people started changing it, people were coming from the south, from different places until they had completely occupied the neighborhood. I told them this is what can cause problems, you could even cause deaths with this, let's try to make it for our children, because we need each other. (January 9, 2003)

FOLLOWING THE SOCIAL NETWORKS

Although many Dominicans emigrate for the structural reasons we have described, there are many who emigrate on the basis of the more personal circumstances of the transnational networks they were born into (Levitt 2001). This is particularly true of deportees who were taken by their parents, grandparents, uncles, or aunts and had little choice in this particular life trajectory. Of course, the underlying causes for the move may well be poverty or political repression; for many women, it is the insidious effects of patriarchy as expressed in domestic violence or intrafamilial abuse. Whatever the structural roots of the move, many subjects remember their emigration—if they remember anything about it at all—on a personal level, as the result of someone else making a decision to join the family "over there," of being displaced with few questions asked. In our sample, more than half of the subjects left the country before they were 5 years old. Below, Danny, Luis, Alex, Ferna, and Jose provide typical accounts of this process; Ferna, however, was much older (18 years old), and the gender-related reasoning behind the move is obvious.

> D.B.: It must have been confusing with your mom just leaving for the United States with your sisters. . . .
>
> LUIS: Well, she had to go.
>
> D.B.: She had to? I'm just trying to think of what you felt back then as a little kid.
>
> LUIS: As a little kid, well, like every kid missed their mother, you know, it was a little tense, but then, since they explained to me that things were getting better and I could see in my surroundings that there was more food, more milk, more clothing, I felt better. You know, they kept telling me that I will be going soon, so that kept my spirits up. (April 2, 2003)

> ALEX: Yeah, he [the father] had three more kids, girls. And then he had his life going on and I needed to have my life going on too! And he asked me: do you wanna go to the United States over there? You wanna leave me? And I started crying, I said, "Papi, yeah, I wanna go to New York but nobody has come to bring me to go to New York." That year I went to New York, to my mother's house, but it was like a nightmare when I went to New York, even though I love New York, you know, I went to the wrong neighborhood. (March 5, 2003)

> D.B.: Yeah. So, tell me about the move to the United States, how did that occur?
>
> FERNA: Because my parents told me not to stay here, they wanted me to stay over there, marry an American and get a better life. (May 9, 2006)

DB: Do you remember your father saying to you, "Look, we're leaving for New York?"

JOSE: Oh yes, I remember that clearly. He came in 1966 to get me when I was 3 years old but my mother told him "You can't take him, he's too small. Come later when he's bigger." He had the ticket and everything, the passport, I had the suitcases made and then my mother said, "No." My father got mad and then came back four years later when I was 7 and then my mother said" Ok, you can take him, he's bigger now." (May 1, 2003)

In another example of the influence of these networks on decision making later in life, Leonid remembers being pressured by his grandmother to come to Miami because of its "opportunities" and his "facility" for schooling. Leonid's grandmother had been helping keep his family above the poverty level in Santo Domingo, as was the lot of so many in his neighborhood (in this case Villa Duarte); after years of this support, Leonid made the move to Miami in his late teenage years.

D.B.: Tell me about school.

LEONID: I went to San Juan Evangelista. I went to different schools, I had the facility to learn. My grandmother lived in Miami, Florida, and wanted us to have a good education even if you had to pay for it. So, we went to some private schools here in Santo Domingo.

DB: And how did you move to the U.S.?

LEONID: Well, I moved to the United States when I was 15 back in 1988. I was still in school of course and I went as a student, with a student visa to continue my studies. That's what I did. I went in August, August 5, 1988, and in September I was already enrolled in school in Miami, Florida. I remember that was Kinlock Park Junior High School. I started in 9th grade and I already passed because of my language.

D.B.: So, you went to Miami in the 9th grade. But, why did you go? Did your mother send you or what happened?

LEONID: Exactly, my grandmother sent for me because she was a U.S. citizen.

D.B.: What did she say?

LEONID: Better education, more opportunities and you'll get a better job. (April 10, 2003)

And then there is Luis, who, as an adult, traveled to Miami for a holiday and then followed his social network up the eastern seaboard to the Dominican community in Boston, joining a neighborhood friend who was "dealing drugs."

This was an unfortunate combination because it lands the subject in a Massachusetts prison for four years after barely setting foot in the United States for three weeks (see chapter 5).

> LUIS: I stayed there (New York City [added by the authors]) for about a week. By the end of the week I called my house and I talked with my mom and asked her where my brother was living so I could go there to spend my vacation. When I got there he told me that his apartment was very small and that he was waiting for a larger apartment so we could live together. So I said to him how can I wait . . . the entire time I was thinking he was going to help me out. Then my friend from Santo Domingo found out that I was in New York and called me up and said: "I'm coming to get you tomorrow." The next day he showed up with his wife, he lived in Boston. He told me: "Let's go to Boston because in Boston I am alone. I don't have anyone, up there, we can work together on things." I told him that I've been thinking, about selling drugs some day but not yet. He told me don't worry "I'll help you with whatever you need." We went by car and when we arrived in Boston on Washington Street in Lynn, he took me to an apartment in Hannover Street, then told me: "Look, we're going to live here." He had a Boricua friend, a Puerto Rican, who sold drugs with him. Then he told me:"Come see how things are done." I told him that what I want to do first is find my way, even if I have to go back to my country and then return to find out. So, we left, I made an appointment with a lawyer who was charging me $2,500 to work on my residency. I made an appointment for December 5th of '89. I was living there in his house for three days, then on the 4th day he said to me: "Let's go check out Lynn." We went for a walk, a Puerto Rican in a car showed up with a police officer in plain clothes and he told my friend, "Listen, this friend of mine is looking to buy drugs." My friend told him: "I don't sell drugs" because he didn't know the other guy, who was a cop. So he told him: "Listen, I've known him for a long time. Whatever happens I'm responsible." From then on he began the conversation with the police officer in English and I didn't know what they were talking about. Although I could figure out more or less what they were doing because I was watching their movements. (February 27, 2003)

Finally, there is the respondent who undertook the journey to the United States to "make it on his own." But to do so he needed the networks that were already in place: someone to talk to about the process, a contact to cross the borders, and a family member on the other side to welcome and settle him. In the following, the respondent describes his journey; although he insists it was all due to his individual determination, it is obviously a highly coordinated effort involving family, friends, and acquaintances:

S.: I went to the United States because of the situation here, life was too hard, so I scraped together some change working here and decided on the United States.

D.B.: Do you have connections over there in the United States from before?

SANTO.: No.

D.B.: But, what happened to the family, your father. . . ?

SANTO: Oh, I have one of my uncles that lives over there, he lives over there for 40 years.

D.B.: But was it because of this connection with your uncle that he said, "Look, come to the United States to. . . ."

SANTO: No, I decided to go on my own.

D.B.: And what happened? Did you go to the embassy to get a visa?

SANTO: No, it was at the Mexican embassy that I got a visa, I went to Mexico. I stayed one month in Mexico and from Mexico I crossed over to Texas and from there I moved across to New York.

D.B.: So were you legal or illegal?

SANTO: In the United States I was illegal, but in Mexico I was legal because I went with a visa from here.

D.B.: So you arrived in New York in '78 and what happened?

SANTO: I called my uncle and he came to pick me up where the person that brought me had left me—because it's a person that brings people back and forth, from Mexico to there. So I called my uncle and he came to get me. So then I went to live in his house and from there he presented me to various people and I was meeting friends, from there I met my wife and then we married like in 6 months. She got pregnant and after two years we had a child. And then from there to here she sent me to ask for my residency, after like four years they gave me residency. (May 2, 2003)

FROM THE INDIRECT VIOLENCE OF POVERTY TO THE DIRECT VIOLENCE OF REPRESSION

Many respondents in our sample had experienced various acts of state brutality and repression in their everyday lives. These objective and subjective experiences of moving from the indirect violence of poverty to the direct violence of state vindictiveness strongly influenced respondents' decisions to emigrate and comprise an important part of the process of exiting (Salmi 1993).

> D.B.: Tell me about your role during the Revolutionary period.
>
> ROGER: I was a young boy, 14 years old, and joined a squad of school students to resist the marine invasion of Santo Domingo in 1965. I was a sniper and I used to shoot the marines when I could and then disappear. I saw people die right in front of me, right there, with blood all around me. It was a very scary time for me but I was defending my country. We were being invaded, you have to understand that. After the resistance died down they were searching for all boys in the capital of my age. My father said that I had to get out of the country as soon as possible otherwise I would probably be killed. It was a crazy time back then and a lot of people were disappearing. They would see some young boys on the street in the evening and they would just come and disappear them. It was that kind of time. So I got out and I left for New York to join other members of my family. That's why I left here. (October 1, 2002)

> D.B.: Was there a lot of political violence during this time?
>
> JAIME.: During the time I grew up yes because Balaguer was around for 12 years, lots of murder, the Banda Colorada (a group of assassins formed by Balaguer to murder opponents [added by the authors]) were killing and if you weren't with them you were a communist. You know the system that we have, if you were not with the regime you were an opponent and you were in a mess. Here this is always a presidentialist and militaristic country. Here the military are the ones that rule. (December 3, 2002)

> JUAN: During the time of Balaguer? For 12 years that was a bad time.
>
> D.B.: What was bad about it?
>
> JUAN: When you were young you couldn't feel safe, because anybody could do anything to you. They would say you were a communist and you just meant nothing, nobody cared. If somebody in the government was saying that you were a "hot head" you could die that day and nobody could say nothing.
>
> D.B.: So, did you lose any friends?
>
> JUAN: Not really friends, but people that I knew.
>
> D.B.: They were killed?
>
> JUAN: Yeah, they got killed. (April 12, 2003)

D.B.: Do you remember any of the political violence back then?

LEON: Actually, they were talking about Trujillo and I felt a little bit scared because I used to see the people running away. They used to say, "Trujillo is coming, Trujillo is coming" and everybody used to jet into their houses and close the doors, you know. So I never really actively saw Trujillo, I used to hear about it because people would run from him and they were scared of the police, scared of the cops. Every time I used to see a cop I'd think: "Oh, wait a minute, he's gonna kill me, he's gonna kill somebody." Because that's what everybody thought, that's basically the only memories I have. (March 15, 2003)

D.B.: Did you see a lot of violence growing up?

JOSE: Yes, my uncle was head of the PDM, the PDM was the Popular Democratic Movement, communists.

D.B.: It was your uncle?

JOSE: Yes, and my uncle was tough, tough, tough. My uncle, the whole family, we are combatant aggressors, you know what a combatant is? (Cell phone rings, interview is interrupted.)

D.B.: So the violence, tell me what happened?

JOSE: Pow, pow, pow, pow, it was a deal like this, and like I said the police fired at him and he fought the police.

D.B.: Really?

JOSE: Yeah, and he jumped over the wall.

D.B.: Your uncle used to live with you guys?

JOSE: Yeah, but my uncle now is in the States. He got out of here, yeah. (December 8, 2002)

These interview excerpts refer to a period roughly between 1965 and 1985, during which time it is estimated that 5,000 Dominicans disappeared at the hands of police, military, and other units working on behalf of the state. It is important to remember that, unlike other countries such as Chile, Guatemala, and South Africa, the Dominican Republic has never had its Truth and Reconciliation Commission. The victims' families and friends still do not know what happened to their loved ones, and the nation has never fully confronted its past, which would be the hallmark of a potentially vigorous democracy.[3] As we shall discuss later, there are many remnants of this authoritarian past alive and well today. In this vein, Juan's words resonate strongly: "Here this is always a presidentialist and militaristic country. Here the military are the ones that rule."

FEELINGS OF LOSS

We have discussed some of the reasons for emigration from the Dominican Republic, providing the emigrants' own words where possible. Leaving one's homeland is a complicated cultural and psychosocial process that involves hope and a feeling of relief combined with a sense of loss and regret. Each emigrant's experience depends heavily on the precise circumstances of the departure, the age of the subject, and the welcome at the end of the journey; nonetheless, removing oneself from the close-knit, fairly homogenous cultural community of the Dominican Republic is emotionally difficult. In addition, the landscape for those moving to the United States under these conditions has changed radically in the United States in recent decades. As the welfare state has been shredded and the country has moved further toward free-market ideology and government through crime and fear, everyday life has become more fraught, less secure, and more risk-based (Bauman 2004; Beck 1992; Simon 2007; Young 2007). In this period of rapid societal change and cultural instability, deportees had to make sense of their pasts, looking back to a period that for some felt more collective, more reciprocal, and less ravaged by disunity, competitiveness, and socioeconomic instability. This may seem to be contradictory, given that the period being discussed was one of extreme political repression; nonetheless, for some, this period of authoritarian paternalism was one of greater social calm:

> ALEX: I used to live here in the Colonial neighborhood, decent people . . . before it was better than now, now you can't even talk to people. Before you used to meet people in the same neighborhood, we used to cook and invite them to come here, when they had no food. Now, these days, nobody do that no more. Before they used to leave the door open, now they don't do that. Things change. . . . (March 5, 2003)

> D.B.: Tell me about where you grew up.
> MIGUEL: Back in the days it was a lot different. Everybody got respect for other people, you know what I mean. It's like in older places, you know what I mean, it's a neighborhood, you know, black people, all together. . . . (January 25, 2003)

> MANUEL: I went to school here under the dictatorship, it was very disciplined. We had to have our shoes shined, our khaki pant pressed, our shirts pressed, they used to give us breakfast in the morning, it was very disciplined. The schools here they used to run like schools, not like now.

Before they was more strict, check your ears, check your nail, check everything, no fucking about. (January 26, 2003)

D.B.: How was it back then?

FREDDY: During that time it was good. Yeah, there was not so much evilness, There also was not as much corruption as there is now. That's to say we youths were calm, we always liked playing ball, passing the time. But not now, now the boys are growing up with knives, guns in their hands, and there is too much corruption. (February 4, 2003)

Freddy's use of the term "evilness" is instructive. It refers to changes in Dominican life that he finds incomprehensible. For him, the rise of intra-community violence is about doing antisocial acts for the sake of it, for the high (Ferrell 2001), and for the emotional not economic satisfaction it brings. Although he was raised on the streets of New York City after emigrating at nine years old and has spent more than a decade back in his homeland, he cannot abide this growing insecurity in his daily life. Many deportees lament the passing of a more communal era, and they are confused and demoralized about the present fragmentation of the local community and what this augurs. They are in an ideal position, however, to see the Third World meet the First World for they have often been socialized in both and they do not always like what they see.

For example, the deportees constantly remark on the youth around them, particularly on what they regard as a desperate search for identity in symbols of consumption and hedonism. Freddy's comment about young people's penchant for artifacts of violence must be viewed in the context of their struggle for daily survival, the mushrooming gang culture, and the new Hobbesian approach that complements the adoption of market solutions for the nation's underdevelopment. Many subjects often reflect upon how difficult it is to comprehend the transition from a culture of state violence under the previous authoritarian regimes to a culture of interpersonal violence. Part of the challenge lies in the disjuncture between the ideology of individualism and the long awaited meritocracy that should come with deregulated markets and westernized "efficiencies." The stark reality is that the Dominican labor market is highly segmented, with poorly paid Haitian workers doing most of the construction, road repairs, and agricultural labor, whereas the better jobs are often regulated through patronage and clientalism. As a result, the deeply unequal socioeconomic power relations are maintained, and the three or four families that control great swaths of the economy continue to reap massive profits.

Working-class and poor youth are caught within these contradictions, and they react and adapt accordingly, searching for respect in the street world (Bourgois 2002) and trying different modes of innovation (Merton 1938) to exploit their inherited opportunity structures (Cloward and Ohlin 1960). Nonetheless, their actions lead to a form of implosion, an insidious form of social reproduction that is only partially resisted (Brotherton 2007).

These new currencies of youth violence are unprecedented, aided and abetted by police and military forces that are themselves socialized and trained in techniques of violent repression. This contradiction cannot be resolved as long as the country remains in its dependent state, riddled by what Freddy sees as "too much corruption." Looking back to look forward is difficult for the deportee, caught between the tangled webs of transnational experience in the past and their more static and fixed locations in the present. Essentially, they are stuck in a particular form of arrested psychosocial development, and they respond by imagining, lamenting, and waxing nostalgic, reinventing both the Dominican Republic and New York City as they do so.

GETTING TO AMERICA

This section focuses on how subjects journeyed to their destination: the levels of planning involved, the roles played by family members and friends, the social networks, the formal and informal mechanisms used to cross borders legally and illegally, and the sheer determination required to carry all of this through to the end. Getting to New York, Miami, or Boston is not just a boat ride away for many deportees. Although most of our sample went to the United States as children, legally brought there by family members, a significant number arrived illegally. Many of them tried to emigrate during periods when the United States was increasing restrictions on Dominican entry (particularly after 1986), and it was no longer a time when, as one deportee put it, "All you had to do back then was go down to the embassy and ask for a visa. No questions asked. Seriously, it was like buying a bus ticket. Of course they (the United States [added by the authors]) wanted to buy the peace here after the Revolution, after the Marines came in. But that's how it was. It's hard to imagine that now. . . ." (November 9, 2002)

Carlos's experience is typical of that for many of the respondents. His economic situation was making life impossible, working for nothing, barely scraping by, and so he inquired about how he can make "the journey." Carlos traveled to the north of the island, around the town of Nagua, which is the favorite staging post for many emigrants to make it to Puerto Rico in privately owned boats. He knows someone who knows someone, and with a couple of thousand pesos, usually around $500 to $1,000, one can buy a place in a boat with a range of other hopefuls, men and women of all ages and from all over the Dominican Republic.[4]

> L.B.: What's the best strategy to leave from here for the United States?
> CARLOS: Well, I had to go on the journey because of what was happening. Why? Because work does not provide me enough, what I was earning, then I was presented with an opportunity to take a short trip in a raft. They asked me for some money, I scraped it together, and I gave it to a gentleman who helped me go to Puerto Rico and from there I got to the U.S. little by little. I knew a friend of mine over there. . . . We were from this same place, the same area and through him I earn a living and with time I managed to go to New York. (November 29, 2002)

Most of the social science literature on crossing the border relates to the divide between the United States and Mexico (e.g., see Chavez 1997). There are few accounts of crossing the border into the United States from the Caribbean and fewer that detail this journey from the Dominican Republic. The literature that does exist is primarily journalistic and is often prompted by a tragedy, such as the publicized case in which Dominican emigrants spent days on a boat trying to get to Puerto Rico and, according to media accounts, resorted to cannibalism (Vargas 2001). Most attempts to cross the border fortunately do not turn out so tragically for Dominicans; nonetheless, these are extremely physically trying and emotionally draining experiences that require a great deal of personal and collective resourcefulness as described by Celio:

> CELIO: There were 76 of us. We arrived Friday during the early morning hours which was actually Saturday. We spent Saturday waiting and making calls for them to pick us up.
> D.B.: How did you get there?
> CELIO: We entered through Rincones beach.
> D.B.: On board what?
> CELIO: A makeshift raft, made from large wood, about 30 feet.
> D.B.: How much did you have to pay at that time?
> CELIO: In those days I paid around 1,500 pesos. It was a sister of someone that lives here who helped me, her name is Lucía. She spoke with him and trusted him and he told me, "Get me 1,500 pesos." He almost did it for me for free because he usually charges more money. Then, nothing,

I waited a month and then they called us and took us to Miche and from there we left. This was in '89.

D.B.: Were you scared?

CELIO: No, I wasn't scared because I was 20 years old, when you are 20 years old you don't have experience.

D.B.: It was kind of like an adventure?

CELIO: Exactly, and I am the adventurous type, I like adventures a lot. I won't tell you that I wasn't scared in the beginning because you are in the sea and you look from side to side and you don't see anything, the only thing that you see is water and one spot what they call Desecheo, which is after the Mona Channel. The ship felt something like a blow in the bow, in front, and water was coming in. We had to remove water, then I was feeling a little scared, but then I thought, I said: "Ok, there's 76 of us, I'm not going to die alone, 75 more will die." And so, from that, from that, that helped me a lot. (March 3, 2003)

As Celio indicates, the boat ride can be extremely hazardous and drownings are not infrequent. There is usually little shelter from the elements; most of the boats do not have sufficient life jackets for the passengers, and they are often dangerously overloaded. We can only imagine what it must feel like to be sailing in the middle of this vast expanse of water, completely at the mercy of the crew and the weather. Who will be there on the other side? Will I get past the U.S. Coast Guard? Will my contacts still be there? How will I make it to New York City? All these questions are going through the head of the deportee, but Celio likes to remember it as an adventure; perhaps this is his defense mechanism, one that is used by many subjects who found it difficult to talk at length about this aspect of their past.

There were some deportees who never made it across the border at all, at least the first time. Caught by authorities on their arrival in Puerto Rico or at the Mexican border, they were returned to the Dominican Republic, sometimes spending time in an immigration jail or detention camp before being sent back to the Dominican Republic. Those who were denied initially often managed to gather the material and psychological resources to try once more, as Eddie reveals below:

D.B.: You tried to go how many times?

EDDIE: Several times, one time, I was going to go to but I turned back. I decided that I wasn't going to go no more.

D.B.: Where from?

EDDIE: Miche, from Miche to Puerto Rico in a big boat, wood with two motors, a big yola, like 80 people.

D.B.: That was your first time.

EDDIE: Yes, that was my first time. The second time I tried to go by the pier and I was gonna take a ship and the ship, it say on the top "Puerto Prince" but the guys with me they read it as "Puerto Rico", so everybody say Puerto Rico 'cos you could only see half the word. So I arrived at Puerto Prince. I remember that I thought it was strange here. I look at the people and I thought in Puerto Rico they don't have so much black people and the language. I thought, oh, maybe I'm in Jamaica.

D.B.: So what did you do?

EDDIE: I spent six days there and I got to the border and I waited on the border, I waited there for two days on the border and then I crossed back again at night. I left Haiti at 10 o'clock and at 7 o'clock in the morning I arrived back again in the Dominican Republic. We were walking a lot. I remember the guide, we rented a house, I gave him 150 Dominican pesos or 14 Haitian pesos.

D.B.: How did you get the money?

EDDIE: I found a Dominican woman who had a beauty parlor and she gave me the money to get back.

D.B.: And the third time?

EDDIE: I had good luck. I took a tourist ship from here to Puerto Rico. That was good. I got into Puerto Rico the next day and when everybody gets out, I had like 7 dollars, I got a car and he put me in old San Juan. I met a guy on a bus and they put me off at Barrio Obrero and I met some guys I know from here and I spent a year there working and then I left for New York. I got some Puerto Rican papers and I was able to find somewhere to live on 109th and Columbus Avenue in Manhattan, and go to school at Booker T Washington and then Washington Heights School and I used to work on 32nd street, behind the bus station. (January 14, 2003)

Eddie provided details of the long, hard process to finally make it to the United States during the mid-1980s, before Homeland Security operations were established, before the border controls were tightened, and before a 700-mile wall to thwart the "illegals" was proposed. In our sample, approximately 25 percent of the respondents had made multiple crossings to the United States as undocumented immigrants, including a small number who now live in New York City (see chapter 11). How do they move back and forth? Obviously they can make it through this arduous route either by yola or as a ship's stowaway to Puerto Rico, or over the Mexican and sometimes Canadian border via a coyote, but an easier way is to have false documentation. Eddie again describes how he solved the problem of having been caught and the inevitable recording of his illegal efforts.

D.B.: I don't understand how you got back again and then returned. I mean you did it several times.

EDDIE: Well, I realized that I had to get out of the United States because of my situation. You know, as I told you, I'd went after this guy who tried to kill me. He shot me three times and left me for dead. You know, I was laying there and I said to myself I can't let this guy get away with it. So I found him. I found him in New York and he paid the price. So now I thought well, I need to go back to my country. I need to get away from the city, from the U.S. and just get some peace. So what do I do? In this world there are lots of drug addicts and they die and no-one knows what's happened to them. These guys have documentation, they have i.d.s, passports, and all kinds of papers. So that's what I did, I took over somebody else's identity. I used their Dominican passport that had a visa in it and I came and went. (January 14, 2003)

CONCLUSION

We have shown the beginning phase of the journey to the United States as the subjects remembered it. It is a complicated process, socially, culturally, physically, emotionally, and economically. Although tens of thousands make this journey as a matter of course in their lives, as a seemingly inevitable choice if they are to escape from ever-present danger or have any sense of opportunity, we should not underestimate the toll this takes on individuals.

The experience varies greatly and is contingent on a range of factors. Subjects who left as children remember, for the most part, the good things about leaving. They remember rejoining their families, having basic necessities such as food, electricity, and hot water just being there, seeing consumer items such as refrigerators and televisions (with real channels) that had been so scarce in their barrio now part of everyday life. For older subjects, the memories of their experience are influenced by whether they were able to enter the country legally or illegally. In the case of the former, their memories of leaving are cultural in nature as they had to deal with contradictory feelings of displacement and excitement, Caribbean heat and East Coast snow, the slowness of island life and the daily velocity of a "New York second." For the "legals," we will see in due course that the major experiences of their transnational journey come with settlement. For the latter, those who entered the United States illegally, their memories of the journey are quite different. When an illegal subject reaches the other side, there is enormous relief and hope and they set about the task of settling, of doing what they have to do to survive and to ensure that money is regularly sent home to their families. This obligation was of primary importance to them and was one of the most positive memories of their stay in the United States. In other words, they had experienced, for at least a short period in their lives, the ability to contribute to their families' household income. This finding should not be underestimated because it bears out the truth in Maslow's conception of the hierarchy of human needs, a truth that has been difficult to achieve within the post-colonial, dependent relations that always frame the Dominicans' struggle for political and economic survival.

4.1 MANOLO (*TOP RIGHT*) AT THE AGE OF SIXTEEN WITH HIS MOTHER, BROTHER, AND SISTERS AT THE FAMILY APARTMENT IN MANHATTAN.

CHAPTER FOUR

SETTLEMENT

David Brotherton (D.B.): When you arrived in the States, how was that?
Juan: When I arrived that was very bad, I was trying to stay for a year to bring
   my wife and family. But I saw that New York wasn't good for them. I was trying to get my kids over, but I didn't think that it was good to live there . . . .
D.B.: What did you see?
Juan: I saw a lot of guys in the streets selling drugs and they used to do it
   freely. I thought that was a bad environment for my kids. (March 1, 2003)

D.B.: When you think about those early years in school, how do you remember them?
Manolo: Well, yes. I wished I just could go back again with the mentality I
   have now. Those years were the best years in my life, I mean compared to
   now, now is not good. Back then it was very good. We had programs, we
   did things together, we used to have tournaments, a baseball tournament,
   a swimming tournament, I mean, everything that is necessary for a young
   man to do during those years it was there for me. Um, I mean, incredible:
   Yankee Stadium, Shea Stadium, Madison Square Garden, the New York
   Knicks. I've seen everything: football, the Giants, everybody. Bob Hayes
   used to come, all of them. I got very familiar with the football, with the
   baseball, with the hockey, I mean, I really got into it. (April 2, 2003)

IN MANY WAYS, the contrast between the recollections of Manolo
and Juan was seen in the recollections of many of the subjects. Sometimes
deportees seemed to have had a rich, fruitful early life in New York, and for
others it was always a struggle, always a battle against poverty, the seduction

of the neighborhood, and the small refuge found in the major socializing institutions such as schools, the family, or the church. In fact, few subjects talked about the influence of the church, even though we asked questions about the role of organized religion in their lives. Nonetheless, for the majority of the subjects who had spent much of their early years in the United States (primarily in New York City), this period was a mixture of positive and negative experiences, the hopes of the immigrant tempered by the harsh reality of New York's opportunity structure, the fun and experimentation of youth, and the price that is sometimes paid with acculturation to neighborhood subcultural practices (Kasinitz et al. 2008[1]). However, what came across strongly during this settlement period, both for legal residents and the undocumented, was a lack of fatalism. They spoke of missed opportunities, yes, and they frequently made statements such as, "If only I knew then what I know now," but very few among them outright regretted their experience, even if it was cut short. It was their shot at "making it"; they appreciated the time they spent hanging out with characters on the block, their school days, their participation in the "crazy" years of New York, and their memories of family, of their parents, their siblings, their grandparents, and their children.

This mixture of urban, transnational agency, of making the best of life in the socioeconomic margins, reflects the multiple levels at which the abstract concept of "segmented assimilation," as described in chapter 1, is played out concretely. The class, ethnic, and gendered backgrounds of immigrants—their human, social, and cultural paradigms intersecting with the opportunity structures of the receiving society—are encountered here in their immediate locales but set in a much broader periodic and structured epoch. Thus, much depends on the period when an immigrant enters the country. Is this a period of industrialization where blue collar jobs are plentiful, as might have been the case in the period after World War II? Or is this the era of economic downturn and local and global restructuring such as was evident in New York and other former manufacturing bastions of the United States during the 1970s and 1980s? Similarly, is the immigrant entering an ethnic enclave where a vibrant, microeconomy is being developed, or is he entering a neighborhood of disinvestment, one in which scarce resources and stiff competition for every social and economic opportunity underpin ethnic and race relations? And most importantly for our respondents, is this a period of extreme punishment in criminal justice and immigration policy, an era when the "good" immigrant is imagined against the "bad" and the state declares a so-called "war" on the rapidly changing "Others"?

In this chapter we describe how respondents remembered and continue to live out (for deportees who have returned illegally) their settlement in the

United States, principally in New York City. We focus on the themes and areas of life that were most prominent in the interview data, including various descriptions of the neighborhood cultures in which they grew up, with references to their encounters with violence, the drugs trade, gangs and interyouth conflicts; family life; their housing situation; the experience of schooling; and their work careers. There are some inherent differences between legal residents and the undocumented emigrants, given that many of the latter came to the United States as adults, whereas many of the former were raised in the United States for a substantial part of their childhood. Consequently, most of the data for this chapter, which focuses on settlement, comes from the legal residents. Nonetheless, we include some data from our undocumented sample because they are trying to settle too, and it is not accurate to assume that they are here temporarily by design, working in the United States until they make enough money to return home. Although some emigrants do plan such a return to the Dominican Republic, they did not appear in our sample as evidenced by some of the incredible stories recounted by those trying to enter the United States, sometimes repeatedly. For these emigrants, staying is an ongoing struggle, but with hard work, innovation, and social networks they have managed to do just that.

THE NEIGHBORHOOD

D.B.: How was Williamsburg back then?

ALEX: Wild, real wild, we used to have black people and Puerto Ricans, you see, and when you mix blacks with Puerto Ricans you don't get nothing good (giggles), specially Puerto Ricans from the street and blacks from the street, and you're in the middle. If you told me, if you told me that I gone to Queens Boulevard, or Townsend Avenue where you have Italians, ahm, and Irish people like that, maybe I would have met an Italian girl that goes to college and I would have been motivated to follow her. Instead I stood in Brooklyn for a while, and I never really liked Brooklyn. I was there because my mother was there, my sisters were there and that was the first place I went to South Street. It was real wild. (February 3, 2003)

In Alex's description of his early years in Brooklyn, we hear about how "wild" it was. This is in the late 1970s, and these parts of Brooklyn were indeed "wild." The South Bronx was burning from fires set by landlords, Bed-Stuy had just rioted, the city was the first experiment in neo-liberal supply-side economics (Harvey 2007), and the national political economy was struggling to emerge from recession, the oil shock, and the massive debts incurred through the Vietnam intervention. These were not auspicious times to be trying to make your way as a young immigrant in the United States. The city was dirty, the infrastructure was in great need of improvement, the public housing (the largest in the nation) was in serious disrepair and highly segregated, and the public schools had gone through disastrous defunding during the fiscal crisis of the 1970s as well as massive battles to decentralize (Katznelson 1982), all of which had produced horrendous statistics on drop-out rates and underperforming students, particularly those of color. Alex remembers these days as "wild," and he was not the only one for a variety of reasons.

HOUSING

The memories of deportees paint New York City in a stereotypical light, the exemplar of the urban jungle as seen in Hollywood films such as "Escape from New York," made during the 1970s, and "Last Exit from Brooklyn," made a decade later. It was not, however, as challenging as the respondents' tales regarding housing arrangements in the Dominican Republic.

On the whole, the subjects came to live in apartments with multiple bedrooms (although they rarely had one to themselves), a working oven and a refrigerator; their parents could buy furniture, and they had a television. All of these things were not plentiful in their country of birth, and they were appreciative of this dramatic improvement in their material well-being. Soon after their arrival, families usually tried to find larger residences in the same neighborhood to raise the three or more children, as was typical of Dominican households. Nobody spoke of being evicted, having their heat cut off, or spending time in a homeless shelter, despite the stubbornly high rate of poverty among the Dominican community (Brotherton and Barrios 2004). The vast majority lived in lower-class neighborhoods where the density of housing tended to be the highest and where the provision of green spaces, high-achieving schools, and a wide selection of shops, especially good quality groceries, were often in short supply. They had also moved to a far colder climate, but because most of them had spent much of their lives in these conditions, they tended not to remark on it beyond their memories of first arriving from the Caribbean.

LUIS BARRIOS (L.B.): Where were you living in Washington Heights? How many bedrooms did you have?

R: First when we arrived I stayed in a hotel with my mom and my sister. Then we went to 109th between Broadway and Riverside Drive, a little room like this with one bed. I slept on the floor on a mattress.

L.B.: How long were you there?

R: One year and then we moved up to 167th to an apartment with two rooms. I slept with my sister and my mom in the other room.

L.B.: How long?

R: Until my mom could find something else. She found another apartment with three bedrooms. I had a bedroom, my sister had hers and my mom and dad had theirs. (May 29, 2005)

A few, however, definitely remembered some privations:

L.B.: Tell me about the physical conditions in your home when you arrived.

RAFAEL: As I remember it, someone had just died there and no one was living in it. I think that's how we got it. We stayed there for about two months. It was completely empty, it had nothing, no bed, no sheets, no proper kitchen, nothing. It had a bedroom but it wasn't what you would call adequate. (June 1, 2005)

RACE AND ETHNICITY

Almost all of the subjects lived or are living in working-class neighborhoods, most of which are predominantly Latino, such as Washington Heights, the largest ethnic enclave of Dominicans in the United States. Residing in these areas where so many share the same culture and language is quite comforting, and networks abound that provide the immigrant with a number of opportunities to get by economically and become acculturated over time. José describes his experience:

D.B.: Wasn't it difficult in the U.S. from the point of view that the culture was so different?

JOSÉ: No, because before I left I studied English here for a year through a grant that I won. I always liked to speak English and I was so keen to practice it. So, in other words, things went well for me. Not only that, in Manhattan where I arrived, it was full of Dominicans, in the grocery stores, everywhere, everything was in Spanish. (May 1, 2003)

Similarly, Tony, who came to the United States as an eleven year old, sometimes referred to as the "1.5 generation," and Danny (who was brought as a baby) felt comfortable in the Queens neighborhood, on the fringes of Washington Heights and Harlem:

TONY: In the neighborhood where I was living was a lot of Latinos, you know, Puerto Ricans, Cubans, Dominicans, Colombians. Queens, specially the neighborhood I used to live near Corona. There were many Spanish people there. But I never experienced the question you asked me about racism. (April 1, 2003)

DANNY: The neighborhood was a mixed neighborhood, I remember that there was still a lot of Spanish, Latinos, or Dominicans, Puerto Ricans, there was Black, there was American whites, it was mixed. (April 1, 2003)

However, this was not the case for everybody, and, like Alex, a number of subjects who lived in mixed-race/ethnic neighborhoods, all of them poor areas of the city such as the South Bronx, Spanish Harlem, South Brooklyn, and Williamsburg, remembered tension between the groups. Andres and Miguel were typical of those who recalled such times:

D.B.: Did you experience racism with other groups, for example, with black or white Americans?
ANDRES: Yes, you always get these kinds of problems with people who see you as something different. They see themselves as "medium rare," as we say, and they see us as "rare," or they might say, "we've never seen this type around here." They always try to provoke you, but if you're intelligent you avoid it, you talk to them or you just walk away from situations when problems arise. (March 4, 2003)

D.B.: How was it for you?
MIGUEL: Well, the first week I wanted to come back to this country, you know. I couldn't support that kind of life. You have to stay like in the apartment, you can't go out, people saying: "It's not good here, there's a lot of danger on the street." I didn't know anybody, people don't like you, and you're Spanish. There was a lot of Italians in the neighborhood so you're Spanish and you can't be yourself. (January 25, 2003)

Typically, however, they did stay and tried their best to adapt, sometimes joining in with the dominant practices of their peer group. In this environment, gangs were commonly encountered. Alex, Luis, and Pedro remember these early years during the 1970s, a period when there were more than 50,000 street gang members across all five boroughs of New York City (Brotherton and Barrios 2004).

ALEX: There were Black Cats and Dirty Ones, I was in the Dirty Ones. All the way up by Graham. So many gangs in one little place. But we didn't have no guns. It was fist fights, chains and sticks, it was fun. But now is not fun, now is different, now it's machine guns.

D.B.: Did you have a club house?

ALEX: Yeah, we used a basement, a big basement, all young kids. Everybody is young there. We used to drink a lot of beer, Colt 45. All young people drink that when they're young.

D.B.: You must have been about what, 14, 15?

ALEX: Yeah, but I was only one of the leaders. The other leader was Juan from the Black Cats. But when there was problems I was the leader. So, I told him, "John, we gotta talk about this. How come you're the leader and when there is problems I'll be the leader?" Then he told me, "Ok, we don't need another leader from now on." So, I said, "OK, bye." He went to jail one time and I was walking around with his woman so the rest of the gang said: "Yo, we wanna speak to you. We know that Juan is not here and she gotta be with you. We have no problem, you can stay with us." So Juan came out and he wanted to kill me. I said to him, "How are you gonna kill me?" That was my life in New York! (March 5, 2003)

D.B.: When you were 15 there was a lot of stuff going on in the streets. How did you get involved?

LUIS: Well, I started getting involved, actually when I started to get in the gangs.

D.B.: Which gangs did you join?

LUIS: There was a gang called The Satan's Disciples.

D.B.: What year is this?

LUIS: This is like '73, '74.

D.B.: Is this the same time as The Savage Nomads, Black Spades, Crazy Homicides. . . ?

LUIS: (laughs) You know them, oh yeah, Dominican Power, Black Spades, Playboys, all those people, I was in that area right there. (August 22, 2003)

PEDRO: It started out as Real Master Dancers, then it turned into a wannabe biker club. And then it was Mad Dogs.

D.B.: It started as what?

PEDRO: Like a break-dancing crew, then we just all turned wannabe bikers, for real. Because in order to be a motorcycle club, wear a patch that says MC, you had to have a certain amount of motorcycles. The only club that actually had bikes at that time was the Dirty Ones. Crazy Homicides started getting bikes. The Savage Nomads started getting bikes. The Killing Nomads started getting bikes. Who else?

D.B.: Savage Skulls?

PEDRO: The Savage Skulls started getting bikes.

D.B.: Black Spades?

PEDRO: Black Spades. But we were what you would call Street Commanders at that time. But we didn't have bikes. But we'd all wear the leather vests, the patches. You never turned your patches over. That's like a cardinal sin. You gotta wear your MC boots, the Lee bell-bottom jeans, stuff like that. The Garrison belt, the knife, your rebel hat, you know, but this is what bikers wore. This is the regalia that the Hell's Angels were wearing, and I guess they made it real popular. They had a club there on Church, what was it? 3rd street? Something like that, in Manhattan.

D.B.: The Angels did?

PEDRO: Yeah. And they sponsored a lot of our clubs. Once we started maturing, we'd go under them. But sponsoring is just a fancy name, we had to pay them dues. So I guess they made money out of us. They leaned toward the business side at a very early age.

D.B.: How old were you when you first started hanging out?

PEDRO: I remember the first big rumble that I seen was between the Brotherhoods and the Hell's Angels. They came all the way to Queens to get them. And then, they had the Pagans, too, at that time. And then, let me see, what other clubs? I could tell you so many clubs. They had the Hell Burners, they had the Assassinators. All the clubs were Brooklyn and Queens, you know. We were like, brother and sister boroughs. They had Cocaine City Crew, which later changed their name to Crash Crew. They had the Ball Busters, which people always says was predominantly Dominican, but it was actually South Americans that ran that crew, guys from Ecuador. (August 10, 2006)

All three talk of their involvement in different groups, reflecting the complex mosaic of street collectives that overlaid the urban grid. For Alex it was the Black Cats, for Luis it was the Satan's Disciples, and for Pedro it was the Street Commanders. Most of these gangs had similar structures, with Presidents, War Lords, Secretaries, and so forth, as described in our earlier work on the Latin Kings (Brotherton and Barrios 2004). It is interesting to note that all three individuals remained in gangs (although different ones) during their prison terms as adults, which is discussed in a later chapter. At the same time, for all the race-ethnic competition that was so much a part of their settlement experience, there is no indication that the gangs they joined were ethnically based, although two of the groups mentioned alongside their own, Dominican Power and the Black Spades (African-American), were known as ethnically and racially based organizations.

Why did they join? Alex and Pedro answered this question, at least partially. One reason given, which is played out in various discourses on delinquency, emphasizes that young men are drawn to gangs in search of fun things to do with their time. Living in inner-city neighborhoods with little and sometimes no parental supervision and trying to adapt to local conditions are all part of what Vigil (1988) calls the processes of "street socialization," which are typical trajectories for marginalized second-generation, lower-class, immigrant youth in urban settings. Another explanation states that such organizations are the norm (Sánchez-Jankowski 1991) and that not joining them would be more unusual, especially when one is seeking to "fit in." Finally, for followers of the Chicago school of sociology, it might be the lack of viable community institutions in the area, due to the rapidly changing populations, that leave youth without adequate, norm-sustaining adults to help them become integrated. Whatever the reasons for gang membership, which is always a mixture of subjective and objective factors, the presence of such groups was a common component of the subjects' social ecology. Two other themes that accented the processes of settlement were violence and drugs.

VIOLENCE

D.B.: Did you see much violence in the neighborhood growing up?

MANOLO: In those days it was the Vietnam War. They had the big posters because we lived right next to Columbia University. It was a lot of protests, the hippies, a lot of people coming from Vietnam. . . . And then they had the Black Panthers and the Young Lords, so it was a whole bunch of things going on politically in the United States. Then this guy Robert Kennedy gets killed and then Martin Luther King. That's the kind of violence I remember. (April 2, 2003)

Manolo described the general mood of the country during his youth. Violence was in the air, on the television dispatches sent from Vietnam, on the streets as minority groups struggled against the privileged structures of race, class, and gender, and among the country's more radical leaders who seemed to be picked off one by one. Manolo smiles when he thinks back to this time as if to say, much like Alex, "It was wild back then, man, totally crazy." In these crazy times, when the world seemed to be turning upside down, our respondents had to make sense of the every day, which often included violence but of a more interpersonal kind.

CHINO: Over there (in the United States [added by the authors]) I started hanging out with the wrong people. I bought a little car, I met a Puerto Rican girl, I started drinking a little bit, a little bit of heroin, I was doing a little bit of heroin here and there. And a friend of mine had a fight, it wasn't class time, it was about 3:00, 3:30, everybody was out playing baseball, and then this guy had a fight with the baseball player. I grab a bat and I just made a swing but I didn't hit him . . . then all the people was against me, they went against me. They made a party at night in the college and they was waiting for me. I tried to tell them, "Listen, I was trying to stop this man, I wasn't gonna hit him." But they kept fucking around and so I had to leave there and then I started hanging in the street, selling dope and using.

D.B.: In the Bronx or in Washington Heights?

CHINO: No, I was in Washington Heights. And then came vacation time, summer. I told my mother, "Listen, I wanna get out of here, I wanna go back to the Dominican Republic. The life here is horrible, I see people killing each other for a dollar. "I need a dollar to buy a bag," "oh man, you don't got a dollar? I'm gonna get it from you." I see people going out of their minds. (March 22, 2003)

D.B.: And your brother . . . did they go to the same school?

ADONIS: Yeah, my big brother went to the same school. Then my little brother had a little problem with some of the dudes and they had a little fight, so, my mom, she moved us to New Jersey 'cause of my little brother, 'cause of that little problem he had over there in school. So I moved with her, but my people were over there in the Bronx, that's when I used to come from New Jersey and back to New York.

D.B.: So, your mom is going to New Jersey to get your brother away from the problems. Was your brother hurt or did he hurt the other guy?

ADONIS: No, no. He was trying to hurt him. They were trying to shoot him. (May 3, 2003)

These violent encounters forced the subjects to move to another location to escape the environment and the increasingly perilous situation. They did not want that environment to rule their lives or dictate their futures. Respondents also chose to leave for an extended stay in the Dominican Republic to avoid being caught up in the everyday events of their neighborhoods. Of the legal residents in the sample, seven reported doing this as a way to "keep clean" and to "stay out of trouble." Danny and Leon, meanwhile, talked about how the violence could escalate and go beyond fists, baseball bats, and knives. Danny blames this on what he calls the emergence of "warrior gangs," whereas the second respondent associates the increase in gang violence with the turn toward drugs.

DANNY: Well, there was violence, but not like those places like Brooklyn or stuff like that. There was violence, but in those days there weren't so many warrior gangs, there was this fighting . . . one guy would fight with the other one, and he would get the champion from this block or his big brother, and they took it out and that would be it, but it was not warrior gangs, I was in a street gang, but it wasn't really gangs, just young kids who try to be like the others . . . and . . . yeah, we were young . . . we were just more like a club. (May 2, 2006)

D.B.: So, there were a lot of gangs.

L.: Lots of gangs, they really wasn't selling drugs, maybe some of the gang members were doing that because you used to see them real nice with money and cars, and you wonder, "How the hell did he get the money?" So, then I started to realize, then got involved with them, you know, and got even bigger than them.

D.B.: So, back then when you were first hanging with gangs it was more of a social thing.

L.: Yeah, it was a social thing. Fighting with the little gangs and stuff like that, with chains, there wasn't no guns, or none of that, only chains and little knives, you know, actually no real violence. We used to beat up guys, you know, not to kill them. (August 22, 2003)

DRUGS

In the respondents' comments above, we read of changes taking place among the gangs, with the second respondent implying that these changes had something to do with an increase in local entrepreneurial activity related to drugs. Their references to the increase in violence among gangs is supported by the rising homicide rates in inner city neighborhoods across the nation in the late 1980s and early 1990s, particularly in New York City. The rise in the death toll among inner-city youth, many of whom were involved in gang-type organizations, has been linked to the deadly mixture of new structures in the illegal drugs market, easier access to guns of higher quality than in the past, and mushrooming rates of relative deprivation (Blumstein 1995; Fagan 1990).

Many researchers (Bourgois 2002; Curtis and Wendel 2007; Sánchez-Jankowski 2003; Venkatesh 1997) have described the decentralization of the drug trade that accompanied the introduction of crack and created ideal conditions for the corporatization of certain gangs and the arrival of new ones. Entrepreneurial drug gangs (as opposed to social gangs or what Danny calls "club gangs") and pseudo-gangs (what have been called drug posses), focused on creating and defending markets and redrawing territorial and spatial boundaries in the poorest urban communities, now inserted themselves into the subcultural mix of such neighborhoods. During this period, roughly 1985–1991, the violence rate among inner-city men under 18 years of age escalated. One important factor is the increased frequency of market and territorial disputes as the drug trade became more open and business conflicts were settled with the use of extreme force. This change in the texture of the city left powerful and lasting memories in the respondents.

Nearly 80 percent of the formerly legal residents, who had lived in various cities, described illicit drugs being openly sold in their neighborhoods. For many this was a facet of everyday life that they remembered as children, and for others it was something they encountered as young adults. Marijuana, crack, powdered cocaine, and heroin were all mentioned as items being preferred extensively in the informal economy, and a number of them later became involved in this market either as buyers for personal use or as buyers and sellers as full-fledged participants in the drug market (see chapter 5). For many of the subjects, this relationship to the drug trade marked the beginning of the path that led to their deportation. Of course, this makes perfect sense if we remember that the intersection of the war on drugs with the war on immigrants (see Payan 2006; Haywood 2005; Welch 2003; and chapter 1) is an essential structural factor that produces this criminogenic outcome. Quotes from eight of our respondents describe this era and how it affected them in different ways.

In the first series of quotes, the respondents describe drug dealing in their local environment as something to be observed, as an indication of how the neighborhood was changing in different ways, with one respondent interestingly relating the increase of the drugs trade to the arrival of more Dominicans.

D.B.: How was the barrio in New York?

S.: Yes, a lot of drugs, a lot of violence and a lot of delinquency.

D.B.: Many gangs?

S.: No gangs.

D.B.: Just drugs.

S.: Selling drugs, yes.

D.B.: This was in the '80s?

S.: I'd say around '87.

D.B.: What kind of drugs?

S.: Cocaína. (February 19, 2003)

DANNY: In the early days, I remember when I was 7–8 years old it started to change. A lot of Dominicans came . . . then a lot of drugs started coming around the neighborhood. There were probably drugs before but I was too young to notice. Now it was like more flagrant, more in the open. . . . (May 2, 2006)

D.B.: How was the neighborhood back there? Were drugs being sold when you were growing up?

FREDDY: Back there, yeah, I saw something of everything: drugs, violence, everything but it wasn't like here. Over there the people who were doing it were the older guys. Over here it's the young ones. (November 2, 2002)

A second series of quotes shows respondents in much greater proximity to the drugs trade.

D.B.: Did you see many drugs in your neighborhood as a kid?

ALEX2: Drugs? (he laughs) Are you kiddin' me? My mother married this guy, a Cuban, and he would be like cookin' up crack in the kitchen when I got home from school. That's the sort of shit I grew up in. What was I supposed to do, just sit there and do my homework? They used to put me to work, I swear. I used to be there like putting stuff in little bags and I'm like a kid. My parents were some of the first to be selling this stuff on the streets in the Bronx. That was my environment, can you wonder I grew up to be like this, like in this situation? How was I supposed to avoid it? (November 15, 2002)

D.B.: Tell me about your drift to the streets.

J.: One day I wanted some sneakers but my father said he had no money for that, and then a friend come and say, "Jose to buy a pair of sneakers you have to do this and take this to there and I'll give you $100." $100 back then, that was a lot of money!

D.B.: $100?

J.: Yeah, $100 to take some drugs to another apartment. Of course, I said yes, no problem. So he gave it to me. I had my book bag for school and my scooter and I went and gave it to the guy. From then on this was decent money and from there I started getting into the streets getting easy money.

D.B.: How old were you?

J.: 13 or 14, I used to go to school during the day and then come home and do that, buy drugs. (December 3, 2002)

D.B.: Tell me about your neighborhood in Queens, how would you describe it?

TONY: It was a nice neighborhood, quiet, when I first got there it was quiet. Everybody got along with the neighbors, you know. But things started to change, people used to move out, new people coming in, and things started to change.

D.B.: For the worse.

TONY: For the worse, the street wasn't the same. Before you had safe streets, you know, you walk any time in the night and nothing happened, then there was a time that you couldn't stay out that late.

D.B.: What year is this?

TONY: I would say late '80s, early '90s.

D.B.: Because of the drug sales?

TONY: Right, a lot of drugs, a lot of stealing going on, people looking for money to buy drugs. (April 1, 2003)

D.B.: So, this was the early years, and what happened after that?

LEON: That was in the early years, in the '60s. After that I went to another school, but then they didn't accept me, I don't know for what reason. So they put me like in another school where they had more Blacks and more Hispanics, and I started getting more involved in the class. And then we moved back to 109th Street and Columbus between Manhattan Avenue and Central Park West, we moved there, now this area around there I saw a difference, because I used to see a lot of drug addicts. They used to have a lot of signs, I mean, commercials in the street about drugs. I always was afraid of that, afraid of drugs and I always used to see blood. I was always scared to see that blood. (April 23, 2003)

D.B.: Did you see people using?

JOSE2: Yeah, in the buildings in the hallways I used to see the junkies shooting up and I used to get scared sometimes. Sometimes it was 2 or 3 o'clock at night I used to see these guys shooting up in front of the building and the super used to go, "Go on, get out of here." (May 28, 2003)

In the case of Alex2, both his mother and stepfather were heavily involved in selling crack in its early years, and he links this exposure to his own entry into the criminal justice system (see chapter 5). Jose is in a similar situation with drug sales and the opportunity to partake coming through his peers and acquaintances. Tony, Leon, and Jose2 spoke of their revulsion at the continuous sight of junkies, the residues of their practices, and the increasing feelings of danger and vulnerability. These respondents remembered circumstances that were far from auspicious for young adults. Their descriptions of the problematic environment into which they were thrust demonstrate how heavily this environment influenced the pace and quality of their acculturation. The term "segmented assimilation" captures some of this encounter between the working-class settler and the receiving society that he or she enters, but all too often the concept is used schematically, usually with large secondary data sets, in an attempt to understand why some immigrants fit the assimilationist model so poorly.[2]

In these narratives of the drug environment we see the lived "context" of segmented assimilation, the everyday "aspect" of the inner city's social ecology, pregnant with different meanings. For some it is simply the background to life and can be observed, ignored, and kept at a safe distance; for others it is unavoidable, it must be dealt with, and it is quite seductive. Some adapted perhaps a little too well, and in retrospect they should have retained more of their ethnic traditions and resisted the lures of the American street. Others avoided the street and got "busted" anyway because their race, class, and gender met the profile of a discriminatory criminal justice system in the age of punishment.

Portes and Rumbaut (1994)[3] are correct in that it is not simply gumption, fortitude, and work skills that guarantee an immigrant's future; rather success is derived from how the different capitals that the newcomer brings, the social connections, the money in the bank, the educational background, etc., intersect with a range of opportunity structures, institutions, and the cultural milieux that are part of a reflexive socializing process. The following three sections of this chapter focus on three institutions, the family, schooling, and the working world, that along with the "neighborhood" are key elements of the settlement process and together give a strong indication of their future trajectory.

FAMILY LIFE

For our respondents, family life was a complex and often unstable institution in which parents worked hard to secure their children's future in low-income, blue-collar, and service industry occupations while living in Latino ethnic enclaves or mixed-race poor and working-class neighborhoods. None among the sample spoke of moving out of such neighborhoods with their families and into the suburbs or anything approaching middle-class living conditions. That kind of mobility was not experienced by these subjects. Perhaps their first- or 1.5-generational status explains this as the immigration route takes time to build momentum, but it is more likely a reflection of the race and class context of their entry into the U.S. mosaic (Hersch 2008). In this section, we discuss the major themes on the role and state of the family in respondents' lives during this settlement period.

Respondents from our sample who were raised as children in the United States had parents with working-class occupational backgrounds. Only one respondent in our sample, a woman who emigrated to the United States at sixteen years old, was raised in a middle-class household in the Dominican Republic. In our sample, most of the fathers were in blue-collar occupations; if the mothers worked outside the home, it was usually in service sector jobs. The typical story of parental occupations is reflected in the following two quotes from Manolo and Joel.

> D.B.: And what are they doing now?
>
> MANOLO: My mother now works, she's always worked. My mother knows how to sew and my father worked as a maintenance man in the building when we first got to the United States, and then a friend of my father got him a job in New Jersey where they make rubber cushions. My father worked there for at least 20 years. Now he's retired and he's getting his retirement benefits. (April 2, 2003)

> D.B.: And your father was always working?
>
> JOEL: Yeah, he worked for 31 years in Mount Sinai hospital, he was a porter. He died 2 years ago. (August 1, 2003)

For these families, the main reason for coming to the United States was to provide the family with basic work opportunities. For most legal residents, both parents tended to work, though in those families with three or four children it took the mother more years to get out of the house. There was little indication in any of the interviews that the parents saw much social mobility, and for the most part they appeared to be locked into patterns of segmented labor (Grasmuck and Pessar 1991).[4] No respondents spoke of their parents encouraging them to study or becoming particularly involved in their education.

> D.B.: Do you blame your mother?
>
> JOSE: In a way yes because she was supposed to try to help me more, to tell me what to do, I was on the street right there and I didn't have nobody. My father used to get up at 6 o'clock in the morning and from that time I didn't have nobody, I used to go school but nobody knew where I was going. I could have been doing anything and then my father used to come out at 4 o'clock. (May 1, 2003)

4.2 MANOLO AT THE AGE OF FOURTEEN
OR FIFTEEN WHILE LIVING IN MANHATTAN.

This is not to say that their siblings did not make more of the educational opportunities than the respondents did. However, it is difficult from the data to tell how much the limited cultural capital of the parents (only two of the street sample of 45 legal residents revealed that their parents had attended college) influenced the respondents.

D.B.: Did you go to college?

NIURKA (SISTER OF MANOLO): Yes, I got an AA and then went on to work as a legal secretary.

D.B.: Why didn't Manolo take an interest in college?

NIURKA: Manolo was always hanging out with a different crowd. He liked to go to discos and the guys he was with, they weren't college types . . . they were into the fast life and he got mixed up in that . . . Manolo preferred to have a good time than study. (May 5, 2005)

D.B.: So you went to college and your brother went to prison. There's quite a difference there.

KHALIL (BROTHER OF PEDRO): Yes, we were close but we had very different paths. He was older than me. He was very smart, he is very smart, but he also liked to fight and hang out. I guess he liked to cross the line and my parents didn't really know what to do. I'm not sure they knew what he was up to but it might be a case of they didn't really want to know. You get that with some immigrant parents. It's their way of dealing with certain things that don't fit with their traditions. (September 3, 2006)

FATHERS WHO PLAY AROUND AND SOME WHO ABUSE

Some fathers did not stick around for very long or moved in and out of their children's lives. Sometimes they went off with other women but still kept in touch with the children; other times they opted for other lifestyles and basically abandoned the children. Then there were those who seemed to return only to beat the children.

> MANOLO: My mother works at a hospital that takes womans who are getting abused by men, my mother gives advice. My mother never was abused but she went through some things with my father, 'cause my father liked other ladies, that's how I got other sisters and my mother divorced my father, and in the process everybody would feel a little bit depressed, but that's the way life is. And then my mother met another guy, a very nice man named Raul, and they got together. My mother sat us in the living room and told us about this man, very nice man and he stood with my mother for about 15 year. They got married and then he passed away of a heart attack. (April 2, 2003)

> DANNY: I was a good child with him but he would just come at me, like beat me, you know? And then say this is what you get for having dinner waiting, so I was often sad. I still love him and everything, but when I think back, you know? He was abusive, he abused my mother too. That was one of my earliest memories. He used to beat my mama . . . and my brother and I used to hide upstairs and stay scared in there . . . and the last time I remember, he wanted to beat me up, you know. I remember one time I was playing outside and I saw my father coming up with his hand bleeding, my mum couldn't take it anymore, she started stabbing him with a knife. Well she didn't want to stab him, but she probably was trying to get away from him to stop any death. I think that was the final battle 'cause she still had to divorce him. By the time they were divorced, I was about ten, and it was me and my brother. My sister was born on 7th street. She was born in '70, she was still a baby. . . . (May 2, 2006)

> ALEX: I don't know, my father used to love my mother a lot but he always was beating her like every day.
> D.B.: Why would he do that do you think?
> ALEX: I don't know.
> D.B.: Fucked up?

ALEX: He married my mother when he was too young, and then he used to beat me and beat my sisters. But I used to love him too because after he beat me he come and give me love. He used to love me, asked me to forgive him, and then he would start drinking and then started crying and kiss me. You know. He could get to you, you know. And then my mother never got that thing, grudges, you know what it means? Grudges are when you hold something against somebody. She never gave me love! (March 5, 2003)

Manolo and Danny reveal different aspects of their father's lives that were heard quite frequently in the interviews. Of the legal residents who were socialized primarily in the United States, only 50 percent lived with both parents during most of their youth. Of course, this is influenced by the economic precariousness that often leads to fragmentation because the father is forced to look elsewhere for employment. For many respondents, recounting this aspect of their life was seen as an ordeal and often emotionally upsetting.

RELATIONS WITH THE SIBLINGS

DANNY: As a kid I was close to my brother but then, then he got diagnosed with schizophrenia. He works for the government, well, at least he works at times. My sister is a pediatrician, she lives in California. She went to North Indiana University and graduated from there. She's now living over there, somewhere in California. She's really busy, she hardly calls me. My brother is schizophrenic, so he doesn't like talking much over the phone, you know? He's on medication, you know, we hook up a little bit sometimes, but he won't call me or I won't call him. . . . (May 2, 2006)

Most of the legal residents who grew up in the United States had siblings, and most of these still lived in the United States, although there were three respondents whose brothers were also deported although at different times. The majority of deportees described close relationships with their siblings in childhood and still had regular contact with them, even though they were deported. For example, Pedro explained that it was precisely his efforts to protect his brother from neighborhood toughs that put him on the path to fighting and eventually delinquency (see chapter 5). However, others saw themselves as the "black sheep" and found it difficult to understand why one child went in one direction and another ended up in prison. In many of the interviews, respondents spoke haltingly about their relationships with their siblings, perhaps because doing so brings back painful memories and emphasizes their complete isolation from their family in the present.

Danny was very much in this category. A bright, articulate man of forty-four years, he is also a heroin addict and a former felon with several terms in prison. It is difficult to know what Danny's early years were like with his siblings, although he starts by talking warmly about his brother, then pauses to reflect and then reveals something about his brother's mental state that keeps him even more removed. He also talks about his sister. He seems proud of her but infers she wants nothing to do with him, not in his present condition.

MY HUSBAND WAS A "MONSTER"

D.B.: Then you took care of the baby, you were like a single mother basically?

FERMIN: Yeah.

D.B.: And what were you working at before?

FERMIN: I was a go-go dancer.

D.B.: With your sister?

FERMIN: After three years my sister told me, "You can do it and you can make a lot of money." So, I became a go-go dancer.

D.B.: And then you got your baby and then you met this guy.

FERMIN: He was the bouncer at that go-go bar in Queens Boulevard. I met him at Nichol's on Queens Boulevard.

D.B.: Ok, ok. You started going out with him and he turned out to be very shady?

FERMIN: Aha. He was a monster.

D.B.: He was a monster?

FERMIN: Yeah, very much, for six years. He got me into drugs, you know, stuff like that, you know, and drugs drive you to do stupid things, you know. (August 4, 2006)

Fermin, above, was sixteen years old, much older than most children when she arrived in New York City. She originally came with her mother after her father died suddenly of a heart attack in his fifties. However, within a month of arriving, her mother also died, which left Fermin alone in California. As a result, she went to New York City to live with her sister in Queens. Fermin was one of the few cases of rapid downward mobility experienced by the deportees in the United States. She went from the status of a well-educated and affluent household, from a successful and happy childhood during which she recounted her years as a talented ballerina and then as a champion swimmer in the Dominican Republic (her mother had been a professional dancer and her father was a military general), to the life of a go-go dancer on Queens Boulevard with a baby in tow. During this chaotic "incorporation" into U.S. society, she met a man who promised to take care of her, only to habitually abuse her as he became increasingly strung out on crack. Eventually, after she was forced to take part in criminal activities, she went to prison for several years, separating her from the one element of stability in her life, her children (see chapter 5). For Fermin, domestic abuse was the norm; this was also the case for Elixir who, unlike Fermin, was undocumented:

GIPSY ESCOBAR (G.E.): You married him over there?

ELIXIR: Yes.

G.E.: How did you get to know him?

ELIXIR: We were neighbors and I became his girlfriend. It went from there, later he sent for me.

G.E.: He was older than you?

ELIXIR: Yes, four years older and I married him. He turned my life into a hell here.

G.E.: Why?

ELIXIR: He brought me here to Washington Heights on 159th, brought me where he was dealing with drugs, it was hell.

G.E.: He was involved with selling drugs?

ELIXIR: Yes, he was a drug dealer, sold drugs and mistreated me terribly. He locked me up, kept me locked up for six months.

G.E.: You couldn't leave?

ELIXIR: No, he wouldn't let me get out, no way, I couldn't do anything without him. He even tried to kill me once, tried to shoot me. At the time I didn't know what to do. I was illegal and was worried about telling the police. But I told them later, my lawyer told me to tell the police everything. And now he's away in prison. He's away away for five years on a hate crime. (May 3, 2006)

SCHOOL LIFE

D.B.: What was school like?

ALEX: Wild. They have big schools though, nice schools, where you get breakfast, good lunch and good teachers and everything.

Like most things American, schooling was a mixed bag for the respondents. In the literature, much has been written on Latino youth who are left behind in schools due to a lack of adequate English language skills, parental alienation from the school culture, peer pressure, race and gender socialization, a tracking school culture, and the general social and psychological problems that come with poverty (Suarez-Orozco and Suarez-Orozco 2001). All these factors colored the school experience of most respondents. At the same time, a number remembered this period favorably and waxed lyrically about the "good times" and the individual teachers who encouraged them and connected with them on different levels. However, the schools they attended were all low-tier institutions.[5]

SETTLING DOWN TO THE REGIME: SCHOOL WAS COOL!

CHINO: I went to Inwood 52, that's in Dyckman. I seen nobody drink milk like this. I saw a little container of milk and oh, my God, this is heaven (laughs). And then I started drinking milk, because I love milk. I say: this is free, this is good. I start getting big, eating, you know, nice, fun food, the hot dogs. Goddamn, this is heaven. It was nice and I used to play basketball, do exercise, and then they put me in a bilingual school, bilingual class, because I didn't know English and I was doing so-so. They put me with a tutor, like somebody who teaches English, two or three days. . . . I liked the school, because of the food, because it was nice. If it's cold you got the heat, if it's hot, you got the air conditioning, oh, it's fantastic. And then I went to my class and everybody was courting. I didn't know what was that, so I go to my class, and then when I was in high school that's when trouble begins a little bit. (June 3, 2003)

Chino belongs to the group of respondents who thought school was cool, at least in the early years. For him the provision of food, heat, cool air, free lunches, breakfasts, and school milk was most remarkable, a "heavenly" largesse that many respondents recollected. Coming from a country where want was the norm, especially in public educational institutions from the 1970s on, this experience of the differences between the First and Third Worlds made a lasting impression. But it did not last; by high school, the social side of school began to become more important than the academic side, a schooling process that James Coleman analyzed in his classic study "The Adolescent Society" (1961). It is also a time when youth increasingly start to resist the social order of schooling, question the meanings of its ideological content, and chafe at the stratification that appears to be rationalized by the tracking systems both within schools and across the larger society (Bourdieu 1977; Oakes 2005). Alex talked about the "social side" of his school experience, what he called his "happy days."

D.B.: Did you have good friends in school?
ALEX: Oh, yes, I had girlfriends and boyfriends. I say boyfriend because if you are a boy and you are my friend you are my boy friend. I got friends both females and males.

D.B.: So, when you look back to school now do you think you had good times would you say?

ALEX: Oh, yes, it was happy days, very happy days. Sometimes we used to skip classes to go to somebody's house, if your mother wasn't home, anybody, buy drinks, drink and smoke weed. But I never liked weed. (March 5, 2003)

Many of the respondents, when pressed on the academic aspects of schooling, came up with a range of positive experiences. It was striking how they spoke more substantively about their U.S. school experience than their Dominican experience, regardless of the years spent in each. For example, Alex and Raphael fondly recalled their favorite subject areas of history and math, respectively. These scholastic predilections, however, did not last during high school. The cross-cutting influences of their immigration status, the problems of identity that come with teenage psychosocial development, the seductive culture of the street, chaotic family dynamics, relative deprivation and poverty, and the mixed messages of educational ideologies all take their toll on the habitus, often leveling out the aspirations of new students. This in turn cancelled what Ogbu would argue is the essential difference between voluntary and involuntary immigrants (i.e., that Dominicans have not been conquered socially and culturally by an imperial power, unlike Mexicans and Puerto Ricans, and consequently Dominicans should do relatively better in school as they should show less resistance) (Ogbu 1978).

D.B.: What was school to you in the United States?

ALEX: Oh, it was beautiful. I liked it. My favorite subject was English and History. I used to like Human History, American History and Mexican History.

D.B.: Did you have good teachers?

ALEX: Yes. I never forget Mr. Silverman. He used to tell me, "You are a very smart kid." I used to go to him and ask him, "What does this mean?" "In what year was it discovered?"

D.B.: And this is in Manhattan or Brooklyn?

ALEX: That's in Brooklyn.

D.B.: So you got on pretty well at school, you say?

ALEX: Yeah. (March 5, 2003)

L.B.: When you were in school did you have good relations with your teachers?

RAPHAEL: Yes, of course, all the professors liked me, they said I could stay with them and help them during recess, help out with the other students. I always had good grades in school. I always excelled especially in math. I used to study at George Washington High School and at the Junior High School Institute. (July 9, 2003)

Mike Rose (1999) has written about what it feels like to be left behind, placed at the back of the class, in the wrong section, in the wrong year, and sometimes even in the wrong school. He explains what it feels like to be treated like there was something wrong or deficient with you because it happened to him in the Los Angeles School District and was a formative experience for his life's work as a specialist in reading at UCLA's acclaimed School of Education. Race and class play a big part in where you sit and how you get treated (Spradlin and Parsons 2008) but attitude to schooling also has a considerable effect (Ogbu 1978; Fordham 1996).

> D.B.: Who were the kids in the school? Were they Irish? Italian?
>
> L.: All of them but the majority was White. Of course I couldn't tell if they were Irish or that, but for me they all were White. I looked at my color and I looked at their color and I say I'm kind of different from them, you know, and they treated me different because they didn't want me to get close to them. Back then that's what their family was saying. I remember one teacher never let me sit in front, he said, "Go to the back." Always seated in the back never in the front, you know. There was only one Black teacher, he had like a little accent, I can't remember her name right now, but she used to explain to me, "Don't worry, I'm gonna help you, I'm just gonna teach you how to read 'cause you are the only Black guy in the school." Well, she didn't tell me I was the only Black guy, but she was like paying more attention because she was Black and she was helping me, you know. She paid more attention to me than to them because they had their own teachers. They didn't even look through my books, you know, drawing nothing, they didn't even look at what I'm doing, nothing, anything, nothing, they don't care if I was the last one going to class, they didn't ask me, none of that stuff. She was the only one. (January 10, 2003)

> D.B.: What do you remember about school?
>
> J.: I remember a lot of things. I remember about basketball, I remember about baseball, I was a good player. I used to play 2nd base for George Washington but from there I took to the street.
>
> D.B.: Did you like school?
>
> J.: Yeah, I liked the school,
>
> D.B.: Were you a good student?
>
> J.: Not really, I was a bad student.
>
> D.B.: Do you remember any good teachers?

J.: Yeah, I remember Mr. Gray, he was a big black guy. In a good way he used to try to teach me a lot of thing. He used to call me to the side, because at the time I didn't know too much English, and I used to try to show him in Spanish and he would teach me English like it was some kind of game. (January 15, 2003)

In L.'s comment above, he describes how his seat placing was tied to his race and this, in turn, was somehow tied to his language acquisition. Fortunately, there was one teacher who took an interest in him and committed to work with him, perhaps out of racial empathy. The efforts of a solitary teacher are rarely enough to make the difference in a child's complex sociocognitive development, and the institutional forces that are so heavily weighted toward social control rather than social empowerment often win out. J. also remembers his school days as pretty good times, mainly because of his involvement in sports. But he considered himself a "bad" student, someone who was not particularly accepting of the academic expectations of his institution. Was this because of his language problems, his limited English proficiency, and the expectation that overwhelming numbers of first-generation Latino students would fall through the cracks in large, underfunded, crisis-plagued, public schools?

THE STREET COMES TO THE SCHOOL

The environment of the neighborhood was hard to escape, and you simply had to adjust, get used to, and negotiate your way through the different forces that pulled you this way and that. You could join a gang but you did not have to. You could just hang out and skip your homework, but it was your choice, no one was forcing you one way or the other. There were so many dilemmas for the first-generation immigrant child, so many cultural questions to comprehend, especially when you are caught between cultures and so few adults can explain the appropriate codes, especially when you are trying your best to be an "American." In the face of this, the school still could be depended upon to be a small haven, a place where you might get some relief, more established social order. In the following interview excerpts, presaging what Devine (1996) has argued, the streets were starting to penetrate the school during the respondents' earlier years:

L.: I moved there and then to public school, Booker T. Washington, I went to Booker T. Washington. The people at that time, the teachers didn't care, so kids were doing whatever they wanted. There used to be a lot of drug businesses around there so I started to open my eyes, and see things, you know. I saw money and stuff like that. I always saw people that if you don't have no money you're nobody, you always have to have money.

D.B.: What are the drugs that are being sold in the late '60s and '70s?

L.: The drugs, I always used to see, I believe that it was heroin, you know. Yeah, a lot of people shooting up, kids, everybody, even teachers I used to see.

D.B.: Really?

L.: Yeah, and they didn't mind, you know, back then. "What are you doing?" "Nothing, it's a medicine that I'm using." So, I didn't pay it no mind, you know, because I was a young kid. The teacher told me it was just medicine, so, I don't care, you know, I thought he's probably sick or something. (March 7, 2003)

GRADUATING AND NOT GRADUATING

For some respondents it appeared that, no matter how hard they tried, something or someone would always conspire to pull them down and send them off course. Even their teachers, those they should have respected, sometimes worked against them. Danny, now a strung out heroin junky in Santo Domingo, tries to put his school days in perspective. Was it the family situation? The move to Miami? The neighborhood in Harlem? The accident? It is difficult to say what caused him to be, in today's parlance, "socially disconnected."

DANNY: School? I did well in school, until my . . . family got divorced. I had a lot of trouble and they started sending me to see a psychologist. . . . I was like in fourth grade, that year I had got in a lot of trouble in fourth, fifth grade, and then sixth grade I did much better, seventh grade I got my leg broken by a car, I was riding a bike, and the car broke my leg so . . . I started school late that year and got behind, and I started messing around, that's when my mum, who was fifty and she had a new man and that was kind of hard for me. I didn't do well in school. I started messing, playing hooky and stuff, and that's it. I went back again, and I was left back in seventh grade, then the next year they just get me out of school and sent me to ninth grade, so I can go on to Harlem High School, which is one of the worst high schools in New York, number 12, I think in the country. It's a high school right by me, and uh . . . I went to that school, but I never went to school, I basically played hooky all the time, you know. Then I moved to Miami when I was 16. I ruined my GPA. . . . (May 2, 2006)

AND A FEW WENT TO COLLEGE . . .

As if to buck the trend, three respondents attended the City University of New York. Chino tried his hand at different subjects at Lehman College close to where he lived in the Bronx. He liked the social sciences, and he was a thoughtful, playful analyst of daily life. He had lived for so long between social and cultural worlds, in a liminal state of flux, that he could make interpretations and provide insights that would impress his professors. Chino also liked hedonistic pursuits, and the pull of drugs and the social scene that went with it enticed him more than scholarly activities. For a while he was able to mix the two; he could "maintain" when he had to, but gradually he fell further behind and so did his self-esteem.[6]

D.B.: So you graduated?

CHINO: Yeah, I graduated from Kennedy, I got my ring and everything, beautiful, my mother was happy, they give me a certificate, an award because it was a great achievement, after all, throwing me out of here, out of there, then I improved and graduated. I improved because I was doing exercise and my mind was focused, everything was nice. And then they sent me to Lehman College. (March 23, 2003)

Tony is different. He lives in a small apartment that he shares with a tenant. He is virtually penniless, and there is hardly any furniture. He has a small bed and he prizes his radio. But Tony is dapper and keeps himself fit and trim even though he might only eat once a day. He used to be a good athlete and played basketball, baseball, and learned karate; he had many ladies on his arm. He also has a young daughter that he cannot find, and a picture of her as a child is stuck to a mirror on his wall. Tony had ambitions; he wanted to be an architect and does not know exactly what went wrong or when. Below, he remembers attending La Guardia College for about 18 months—it was the high point of his scholastic career.

TONY: In the beginning it was very hard because of the language. You know, the teachers used to speak in English to me, and it was very hard for me to understand. But I was taking Spanish classes as well and I really liked everything because to me it was something different, you know, I was learning a new language and everything.

D.B.: Did you graduate from high school?

TONY: I graduated from high school, yes, at Middle Town High School. And then after that I went to La Guardia College for about a year and half. I was taking a B.A., Business Administration. But then I dropped out, you know, when I was 17 or 18 years old I left school. I got a new job, I started working to make money and so I didn't really care too much about school after that. (April 1, 2003)

4.3 TONY IN HIS SANTO DOMINGO APARTMENT (*PHOTO:* WILLIAM COSSOLIAS).

Manolo spent a short time at the Borough of Manhattan Community College, even though he failed to graduate from high school. Back then, in the late 1960s, the system was more accessible.

> D.B.: So, you didn't get your GED.
>
> MANOLO: No, I didn't get my GED, but they accepted me in college and I went to Manhattan Community College. I took a test which I passed and they told me that I had a lot of potential. That got me through four semesters in Manhattan Community College. (April 2, 2003)

GETTING A JOB

Most of our respondents enjoyed their U.S. schooling, but it did not leave them well prepared for the labor market, especially coming from their place in the sociocultural pecking order. But work they did, and they were proud of it. They paid their taxes (most of them), they rented houses and apartments (only one respondent spoke of having bought a dwelling), and they did a moderate job of taking care of their children (see chapters 6 and 7). Both the men and the women tended to have children with different partners, and it was difficult to keep straight which children were with whom during the life histories (according to the demographics, more than 75 percent of the sample had children). Almost all of the respondents were in low-end occupations, like those held by David, Danny, Manolo, Javier, George, and Pedro (below). Only one member of the sample ascended to a profession that might be considered "middle class."[7]

DAVID: When I got there I got a job with the Supreme Oil Company in New Jersey. The first day they were checking me out. I was looking at one of the guys working at a machine and he had this chain down here and trying to seal a can. I was looking at him and was thinking that I could do that also. The next day I started to do the same thing as if I'd always known it. I am not slow to learn, I see a thing once and that's it. . . . (May 23, 2003)

D.B.: Were you working there?

DANNY: Yeah, I was working in McDonalds, I would get jobs in McDonalds, doing security and then you go to factories. . . .

D.B.: And this is what happened in New York?

DANNY: I went back to New York, right then, and I was doing messenger work. I was a bike messenger, and then I stopped because I got into crack. This is about 1986. . . . (May 2, 2006)

JAVIER: OK, on November 1966, I leave here on Pan Am flight 245, I remember that exactly. I get to New York and I worked for two weeks, across 92nd and Columbus Avenue, it was a Cuban guy who had a grocery store, one of my aunts talked to him to see if he needed somebody and he said yes. But he laid me off in a couple of weeks because he said I didn't have the experience. And it's true when you go from this country to any country of the world it's a different city, so people don't understand, but I was a kid, you know. I was 16 years old but I was more skinny than I am now, and I didn't have no experience at that time. And then after that I went to a factory for one year at 34 West 14th Street, a few steps away from 5th Avenue, yeah, I worked there for a year. (May 22, 2003)

MANOLO: When I came out (of prison [added by the authors]) I went down to Wall Street and got a job. That's how I learned about containers; I went inside the shipping industry. Yes, I went right into the shipping industry. I started as a personal messenger for Vitto Martina, I used to carry a lot of money on stocks, I went to buildings that people couldn't go into but they used to let me in because I had a special ID and commission. I even used to go in limousines. They used to send me in a limousine to the ships to bring in the manifests, everything that was going on the cargo. Man, you go straight up to the cargo. I used to bring them the yellow envelopes, with all the manifests, the letters, everything that is going out of the Unites States, export documentation. I used to bring it to the captain up there, "Oh, are you Manny?" I said, "Yes, sir." He used to say, "What do you wanna drink? Do you wanna drink something? I said, "No, man." He used to call the guys that worked on the ships, "Give them anything they want, give them Coca Cola and sandwiches." So, I stood down there for about close to four years near Wall Street. (April 2, 2003)

GEORGE: I got out of here (the Dominican Republic) at age 14, because I was wild at that age you know. I was not interested in going to school. Maybe I was a bum, I learned to do things my way. I met this guy, and then this other guy, and I got involved with Mormons who spoke English. It was with the Mormons that I learned English—it was no problem for me. Actually I learned Spanglish, because I'm an intelligent person. I'm not the average John Doe, so I learned, you know, but in school they don't really have Spanglish. But I went on with my life, with this senseless shit, worked, ate, drove cabs in New York. I also worked in factories at a very young age in Brockton, Massachusetts. (July 3, 2003)

PEDRO: Yeah, I started driving trucks at different lumber yards. I was always a hard worker. I used to help my father. I don't want to leave that out. Like when he needed help in the warehouse, I used to put five and six pallets, you ever seen pallets? Put them together for him. And I'm not talking about the little wood pallets I'm talking about the metallic ones that go in the belly of cargo frames. I used to drive high and low and put it on there. I actually knew how to do weights and balances, and knew how to load a frame. And if I would've stayed in the U.S., I could've gotten a lot of money for that. So the frame won't be bottom-heavy or top-heavy. And he taught me all that, how to fill out airweigh bills. He used to love taking me to work. It helped me stay away from the streets. Then I worked for another guy for two more truckings. . . . Then got laid off there. . . .

B: After how long?

P: Maybe close to a year. I always held onto jobs. . . . Then I got a job at American Roofing . . . that was a good job. I was driving a straight job for him. That's not an 18-wheeler, but it's a big truck. It's like a 20-footer. I was driving that all over the city, New Jersey. I never crashed. Always went to work, was always at work on time, would go home, see my wife and kid. I was doing good.

B: But you get laid off about '88, '89?

P: Yeah. (August 10, 2006)

CONCLUSION

Chapter 4 focused on the lived experiences of first- and 1.5-generation immigrants as they struggled to adapt to a rapidly changing urban America during different epochs and time spans. In these data we see both the processes of segmented assimilation and social bulimia at work.

Highlighting the respondents' adequate and inadequate preparations to make their transitions successful and the realities of working-class, multiethnic barrio life in the poorest zones of the First World, we paid particular attention to subjects' accounts of neighborhood conditions, their experiences in school and at work, and some of the highs and lows of transnational family life. Although all of the subjects who have spent significant time in the United States look back nostalgically at their former lives, the acculturation process was never a smooth one. They experienced a range of exclusionary pressures in the form of inadequate school systems, relatively low-status jobs, or the informal economy that is constantly luring them to attempt a shortcut to achieve the American Dream. We heard of the tremendous pressures from within the family as parents, siblings, and other real and fictive relatives provide invaluable support structures but at the same time have a habit of breaking under the strain of poverty and transnational instability. Through all this, the subjects struggled to keep their feet on the ground, but they never quite made it. Although most of them lament some of their past decisions, in general they feel they did the best they could with what was available to them. In the chapter 5 we discuss how our respondents fared in the next stage of their lives.

5.1 RENEE IN HIS 1970S HEYDAY IN WASHINGTON HEIGHTS.

CHAPTER FIVE

PATHWAYS TO CRIME

*By 1976 Jamaican DJ Dillinger's song "Cokane in My Brain"—an unlikely
smash hit in Kingston, New York, and London—announced that the white-
line pipelines out of the Andean "snowfields" through the remote Caribbean
cays into the First World's leisure centers were open. In a 1981 story featuring
a martini glass filled with cocaine, Time magazine toasted the "all-American
drug," the powder that made you "alert, witty, and with it."*

(CHANG 2005:207)

THE NEIGHBORHOODS WHERE many of the subjects were living are often
referred to as "at-risk" environments. These are the social and urban spaces
where the working-class immigrants are attempting to settle, reminiscent of
what the Chicago School would call "interstitial areas" in the early part of
the century. For example, the neighborhood of Washington Heights, where
a substantial number of the interviewees came from, had some of the highest rates of poverty and crime in the city throughout the 1970s, 1980s, and
1990s, the periods during which many of the subjects were growing up.
This is not to say that such structural and cultural conditions predetermine
that someone will lead a life of crime. Rather, the opportunities to commit
crime, the social networks that lead to crime, the subcultures that seduce one
into crime, and the set of definitions that make crime and other transgres-
sions normative, as in Cressey and Sutherland's (1978) notion of differential
association, make the criminal pathway difficult to avoid. This is a continuation of the discussion started in the earlier chapters with the theory of segmented assimilation that is now de rigeur in immigration studies and social
bulimia in criminology. We see now in much finer detail the role of agency,

the notion of resistance, and the cultural context of transgressive behavior (Young 2007; Katz 1988; Ferrell 1996).

In the respondents' narratives we get a sense of how slippery the slope is. Rarely does anyone refer to the guiding hand of a parent. No one mentions an intervention that happened in prison that might have steered them to a different path when they returned to civil society. Even though most were ambivalent about their school experiences, many still expressed early hopes about their education, enjoying the relative luxury of school meals, heat, air conditioning, books, and teachers who, for the most part, seemed to have their best interests at heart. Nonetheless, there are few accounts of strong teacher–student bonds that might have taken the place of absentee parents or of parents who are simply overwhelmed by the long hours of work or by the demands of large families. Nor does anyone talk about mentors in the community or the guiding influence of community institutions, such as the church. Such institutions existed in some form in these neighborhoods, but nowhere in the subjects' narratives do we hear of their importance or influence as the adolescents are increasingly surrounded by and attracted to the culture of the street and its diverse practices, performance codes, transcendental properties, and opportunity structures for licit and illicit incomes.

In this chapter we lay out the primary themes that emerged from the data as the respondents recounted their entry into the criminal justice system. It was not sudden; it did not happen overnight. It was not easily compartmentalized into neat life stages; rather, it took place as a layered if somewhat predictable sociocultural process over a number of years. For legal residents, it often started in their teens and was a slow progression, moving from experimenting with soft drugs such as marijuana, then taking on small-time, peripheral roles in the drugs trade, and then eventually becoming more independent players buying and selling a range of drugs including marijuana, powdered cocaine, crack cocaine, and heroin, sometimes accompanied by continued drug use. For others, the drug trade was accompanied by robberies and burglaries; these were the minority, however, and such practices depended on what their peers and older acquaintances were doing. In most cases, the subjects *drifted* into crime and often *drifted* out again, much as Matza (1964) had argued many years before. On the other hand, there were a few who took a more coordinated entrepreneurial path, building delinquent and criminal careers over several years, lured by lucrative drug profits and the attainment of a hedonistic lifestyle that now symbolized the American Dream, which was impossible to achieve in the legal job market available to them. Then there were those who became involved in the illicit economy for what they claimed were altruistic reasons, doing it for their parents, usually their mothers, helping lift them out of poverty by making the financial contributions their fathers could not or were unwilling to make.

We describe some of these routes into the criminal justice system, noting that the dividing line between the legal and illegal world should not be accepted as given. Rather, it is constructed and continuously reconstructed depending on the configuration of social relations in society (particularly the class relations), the ideological trends of the day, and the broadening of state powers that have the most powerful effect on those communities with the least resources (see in particular Hall et al. 1978; Venkatesh 2006; Wacquant 2002; Black 2005).

PATHWAYS TO CRIME

As we saw in chapter 4, the neighborhoods where most of the subjects resided and, in some cases still reside, provided multiple levels of risk as well as opportunities to engage in practices tied to the illicit economy. In these communities the dividing lines between the licit and illicit economies are not always clear. Bodegas often sold drugs or were used by drug entrepreneurs as "fronts" to wash their money and to distribute the illicit product. People were able to engage in full-time, mainstream jobs and then get involved on the side in a little dealing to supplement their income. In many low-income communities, there is often a vibrant trade in stolen goods as families struggle to survive utilizing their "from below" social capital and social networks just a few blocks from the middle- and upper-middle-class inhabitants of the Upper West and Upper East Sides of Manhattan.[1]

THE DRUGS ENVIRONMENT AND THE HOOD

Among respondents who lived in the United States during the height of the crack epidemic, accounts such as Chino's below, where he explains his movement between the two worlds: the mainstream and the streets, were not uncommon.

DAVID BROTHERTON (D.B.): Did you go back to Washington Heights?
CHINO: Yeah.
D.B.: Same neighborhood?
CHINO: Same neighborhood. And then, you know what was waiting for me over there? The boom of the crack, everybody was going nuts, what the fucking thing is this! Everybody going up and down the building, roaching here, roaching there. I said, "What's this man?" And then I said,

"Everybody's making money!" Bam, bam, bam, like that. And then I went to take a course, like I told you, as a bank teller. I wanna get a job, bam, bam, and then I went to the streets. I use both of them, the streets and the bank. (April 6, 2003)

Chino talks about returning to Manhattan after a brief respite in Santo Domingo, where his mother had sent him to calm him down after leaving school. Until then, he had no criminal record, but he did have his circle of associates with whom he had formed strong bonds at school. In contrast, Adonis did not involve himself in both of these separate worlds. For him it was the drugs world, his family and friends, and little else, and he moved very quickly up the ranks. This was a world that gave him opportunities to move ahead and try something new, and it provided for some basics. He got involved "right when [he] came out of school"; it was almost natural, like entering an apprenticeship at the shipyard or factory, only such legitimate opportunities did not exist for him. Instead his friend told it like it was: "You're not working, you ain't doin' nothing, let's start." His response was, predictably, "Of course." It made so much sense at the time that he failed to question it. This is an important point about most of the subjects' accounts; the sequence of events and the flows of their life course all seem so natural, so normative. Until, of course, they get busted, but even this has a ring of inevitability about it.

> D.B.: How did you get involved with selling drugs in the first place?
> ADONIS: I got mixed up with this friend, right, when I came out of school, I got mixed up with him. He took me to his, to his block where he used to hang out. He's a Puerto Rican dude, so we used to hang out together. I didn't know he used to sell drugs, you know, but then, he told me, "Yo, you're not working, you ain't doing nothing, let's start working me and you." So, we started selling marijuana, and then from there I jumped to the heroin, right, to the dope, you know, I was selling dope by myself. And now I'm making money by myself and he's selling his marijuana by himself. I was getting that dope by myself. They left me alone in there, you know. It was only me there, that's when the cops came, the undercover. That's when I realized that I didn't know how to move. I didn't know how to sell drugs, I didn't know nothing. So, I got caught! (April 11, 2003)

The normative structure of crime is also present in the testimonies of Tony1 and Tony2. "I never moved from there," Tony1 said. "I went right back over there to the same. . . ," said Tony2 as they recount the significance of place when crossing society's moral borders. In effect, they returned to the same environment where they were originally arrested; when they were caught again, they both received longer sentences (two to four years and three to six years, respectively). In another part of the interview, Tony1 remembered that he did try once and moved to Florida, but without the social support he found it too difficult and came back to New York after several months. However, as a felon and as an immigrant who spoke English falteringly and with an accent, the job options were minimal. Despite his demoralizing circumstances, Tony1 tried his hand at architecture at a local public college in the Bronx (see chapter 4), but Tony2 did not get that far.

D.B.: You did the 3 years.

TONY1: I did the 3 years. They didn't give me no chance. No work release, no breaks, you know. So I got out in 1989, went to Florida to stay away from the things I was doing and stood in Miami for 2 years, 1989 to '91. Came back to New York in '91 and went back to selling drugs.

D.B.: In Queens again?

TONY1: In Queens again, in the same place, I never moved from there. Ahm, I stood there, I don't know how long, but it was a long time, may be 20 years in the same neighborhood. Not in the same house, but in the same neighborhood. Then I got busted again in '92 and they gave me 2 to 4. (April 1, 2003)

TONY2: A sale, yes. It wasn't much, it was a $20 sale.

D.B.: Cocaine or crack?

TONY2: Cocaine.

D.B.: What happened?

TONY2: They sent me in for 4 months.

D.B.: 4 months?

TONY2: Like I said, it wasn't much, it was only $20, I got sent in 4 months.

D.B.: Rikers?

TONY2: Rikers Island. I stood there like 80 days, something like that. Then, I was free again. I didn't stay away from the street or my friends or the drugs. I went right back over there to the same that I was doing before jail. So, basically I didn't learn anything, 'cause 4 months wasn't much.

D.B.: When did you get busted the second time?

TONY2: It was like a couple of years after that, like '87.

D.B.: Sales again?

TONY2: Yes, drugs again, but it was a little bit more, and they gave me 3 years, my second time.

D.B.: To an undercover?

TONY2: Yes, an undercover, again. But this time around it was little worse, they gave me 3 to 6.

D.B.: Where did they send you?

TONY2: To Ogdensburg, and from Ogdensburg I went to Eastern. . . . (August 8, 2003)

SELLING DOPE TO DO DOPE

Another way to drift into the drug trade was through using the product. Both Manny and Danny recount the paths they traveled over time, characterized by their involvement in the use of hard drugs—crack cocaine for Danny and powdered cocaine and heroin for Manny. Both were also working in the legitimate economy, but they gradually became immersed in the life-world of the user, which requires significant levels of ready cash. This they attained through hustling and selling. Eventually they both served time in prison, which for Danny, in particular, came as a shock. At the end of the interview, he remembered entering the dormitory on Rikers Island. The darkness that Danny remembers is perhaps a metaphor for the future that lay ahead.

> DANNY: I was doing messenger work, I was a messenger, then I stopped because I got into crack. This is about 1986. . . .
>
> D.B.: When the crack really started hitting?
>
> DANNY: Yeah, right.
>
> D.B.: And you were living in Washington Heights?
>
> DANNY: At that time my mother had moved to Queens, Middle Village. I would just go there to sleep, come and stay three or four days. Then I would go off take some more coke and sleep again. So I did that and rented a little apartment . . . on 107th street.
>
> D.B.: How did you survive?
>
> DANNY: I was selling drugs. . . .
>
> D.B.: Selling crack as well?
>
> DANNY: Yeah, crack cocaine.
>
> D.B.: And then you got busted?
>
> DANNY: And then I got busted, exactly, in 1987 I got busted with about two ounces of cocaine, I got to do some time. I did a year in Rikers Island.
>
> D.B.: It was your first time?
>
> DANNY: Yeah, first time selling. It was like a first experience . . . when I went there I remember it hit me right away, it was so dark, I thought I was going through the back yard, and actually it was the dormitories . . . it was so dark in there, when you walk . . . and then I was there for nine months. (May 2, 2006)

Manny's experience was a little different. He came back to Manhattan after trying to make it in Puerto Rico with a girlfriend, but after several years the relationship fell apart. Manny was caught two-timing his partner, and she kicked him out. It was a sad day for Manny, and his life started to crumble.[2] Manny told his story like it was a conversation on the street, articulating the web of dynamic social and economic relationships that made up his life at this stage. Eventually he ran afoul of the law again, and this time he had immigration problems. He was the only one in his family who had not become a U.S. citizen.

MANNY: I had a situation with Myriam in Puerto Rico, I took a plane and left to my mother. When I got to the house, with my bag I sat down and started thinking: "Damn, I need some money." So, I went on the street and I see my friends, "Hey man, how are you?" I said, "I came back from Puerto Rico." "Yeah, you was down for a while." I said, "Yeah, about 4 years." "We thought you got busted and you was in jail." I said, "No, I was in Puerto Rico. I wanna go Downtown and see if I can find a job." "Hey Manny, if you wanna make some money it's over here, you know, we'll hook you up and you pay me whenever you want." So, I took an ounce of cocaine or 28 grams and I started selling, you know, and then I started sniffing again, coming home late and as time went by I see myself getting too out of control, so I went to Santo Domingo and that's what got me here.

D.B.: So, you were selling mainly coke?

MANNY: I was selling cocaine and I was consuming cocaine. I used to get it back in Harlem and that's what got me back over here.

D.B.: You started getting heavy into heroin as well?

MANNY: Yes, I started to do heroin again. I met a girl in the Lower East Side, that's the thing when you meet people. In the Lower East Side I had friends, I met a nice girl but the girl was into heroin too. She didn't look like she do because she didn't do it every day, like myself, I didn't do it every day, but once you start you keep doing it, like you do it today or you might not do it on Sunday, but you do it on Monday. So, that's what happened to me and it came to the point where I said, well, I'm gonna go to Santo Domingo. (May 10, 2006)

THE PEER GROUP

Peer groups are obviously crucial for explaining how subjects cross the borders of the law and end up in circumstances far beyond their control. Criminology is full of theories and studies that show the different influences of peer groups on behavior, from the differential association explanations of Cressey and Sutherland (1978) to the modeling of Bandura (1977), the lower-class cultures depicted by Miller and the neutralizing techniques of Matza. Subjects repeatedly told stories that revolved around the activities and influences of their peers, showing how these relationships helped foster a type of behavior, a set of expectations, a culture in which certain norms and practices were established and facilitated. It is worth noting that a number of deportees in this study knew each other in Manhattan when they were younger, and there are even two subjects in the sample who are brothers, both of whom were deported from Miami.

RUNNING WITH MY HOMIES

Manny described how he drifted into "activities," which was his way of saying "drug-dealing," through his desire to have fun. At the time he was a "virgin," meaning he was somewhat naïve and not particularly aware of the consequences of his actions. This state of mind is powerful, particularly among the working-class youth where the future appears a long way off and the tendency is often to live for the day and to be in the moment (Cohen 1955). Manny was clearly influenced by those whom he called the "seniors," other men in the neighborhood who hang around the streets signifying through their dress and their attitudes that money is not so difficult to come by. For Manny this is impressive and seductive. His family is not well-to-do, with his father working most of his life as a hospital porter and his mother doing her best to take care of eight children, so "plata" in Manny's house never went too far. Manny had to make the leap beyond the "kids' stuff," which he did through opportunities provided by his neighborhood social circle.

D.B.: Up until 16 would you say you were, you know, a regular guy, going to school, playing sports?

MANNY: Yes, I was a virgin.

D.B.: And then something happened.

MANNY: At the age of 16 when I first started looking at seniors, guys with a whole bunch of money in their hands. We're all surrounded. You wanted to go to the movies, you wanted to do this, you wanted to do that, so, we used to listen to these other guys, you know. "I just made 300 pesos." "I just made this," "I'm gonna buy that." So, that gave us a push to go out and make money, and do the activities that we want. Go down to 42nd Street, go down to the movies, we used to make money to go to the zoo, play around with the monkeys, and deal with the peanuts (laughs) and all of that. So we was basically into the activities, having fun, not realizing the consequences. (May 10, 2006)

Freddy, a childhood friend of Manny, has a somewhat different story, although his move into delinquency was enabled by a friend whose age he did not divulge. Freddy was taught how to burglarize, his friend's specialty, and in his eyes this led him straight to prison and eventually to deportation. His narrative of this critical period in his life is short and is encapsulated in a few sentences. In the interview, Freddy did not elaborate, despite attempts to pursue the issue of his "apprenticeship." Freddy decided there was not much to talk about any more—what's done is done. He discussed the logical sequence of events, as if they naturally flowed from one to the other. Freddy made no mention of a lawyer or of his experiences in prison; he simply passed seamlessly through a system over which he seemed to have no control, until he ended up back in his homeland.

D.B.: Well, tell me, how were your relationships with the police, what happened?

FREDDY: With the police? Nothing, I had problems, because I got a friend who got me into the good stuff, to make it big.

D.B.: How old were you?

FREDDY: I was like 18 years old. Then that friend of mine taught me what burglary was like, then we went out one day and did one of those things, broke into a house, and I was caught, then they put me in prison. After that I got out, how do you say it? In violation, then they put me, how is it called? That I have to stay at home as a prisoner for some time, but then I violated that too. It's because of the violation of probation that I was sent here. (February 11, 2003)

HOW DO I GET AWAY FROM IT?

One hears frequently during adult-led interventions, usually held in schools or in community centers and designed to prevent or stop delinquency, drug use, or gang membership, that youth must make choices in life. They (youth) do not have to go the negative route and they should think more seriously about the consequences of their actions, who they hang out with, the meaning of education, their chances in life without an educational credential, the dangers of having too much fun, of taking risks and so forth. Such scripts are common in youth empowerment programs when teachers, social workers, or youth workers do their best to have students consider alternatives to what they might think of as an inevitable path to delinquency, failure, frustration, and unhappiness. Relations between the straight world and the deviant one, however, are never that simple, never that black and white. Both worlds are extremely interconnected and contradictory, and the reasons for a youth's involvement in different forms of transgression, which may or may not be criminalized, are less straightforward than they appear.

Leonel recounted his days as a young adult when smoking marijuana was a common activity in his neighborhood. He went to a school outside of his neighborhood, however, a school where such behavior was not tolerated. His movement between these different worlds made it difficult for him to decide to which he belonged. Should a young person in such a situation choose to hang with the more hip, risqué, deviant crowd because they are "cooler," because they offer the immediate opportunity to make money, because in his 'hood it was expected of him? It is hard to say, but the phrase he used to explain his situation is telling: "I didn't have no way out." For Leonel, the immediate need for money versus the opportunity to continue his education was an easy choice. He did not actively seek this opportunity; rather, it came to him in that it was embedded in his local ecology. Is this other form of lower-class social capital, the process that supposedly cements lower-class subjects into systems of social reproduction and self-condemnation? Who are the "they" in Leonel's account of his trajectory toward crime? Can we say that Leonel's choice was particularly rational?

> LEONEL: I was about 18 or 17 then.
>
> D.B.: Why was it so bad?
>
> LEONEL: Because now my eyes started to open more, and I used to see my friends smoking marijuana, selling here, selling there, and always getting money. So it's like society was the one that put you that way, you know, they were the ones that carry you because . . . I used to go to a different type of school. Then they say, "No, you can't go to that school, you have to go to this school." So, actually they were the ones who was guiding you to get involved in criminal activity, you know.
>
> D.B.: So, a lot of your friends and a lot of people you knew then were selling dope.
>
> LEONEL: The majority were selling.
>
> D.B.: Where were they selling it?
>
> LEONEL: Around the school, the houses, the apartment buildings, everywhere, it was crazy. So, actually I got involved in that stuff because I didn't have no way out, I couldn't make no money and I couldn't get no jobs. (May 18, 2003)

Lifestyle Dilemmas

We have seen different versions of the drift into the life worlds of low-level crime. These are not the well organized worlds of the mafia or even mid-level drug dealers, rather they are the loose, peripheral edges of the local informal economy that include drug-dealing, small-time burglary, and other relatively minor felonies. These crimes are committed by youths as they search for economic niches, social spheres to belong to, creating and adding some meaning and edge to their early adult street lives. This is also the 1970s and 1980s, when the streets of New York City were alive with the culture of art, dance, music, drugs, sex—many versions of collective pleasure are everywhere. It was an era of numerous street gangs throughout Manhattan, the Bronx, and Brooklyn. Tribes of hip-hop aficionados moved from their stomping grounds in the South Bronx behind such leading practitioners as Afrikan Bambaattaa, Kool Herc, and the Rock Steady Crew (Chang 2005) to downtown trend-setting clubs like the Roxy and the Peppermint Lounge. As Jock Young opined in the early 1970s, in certain eras the straights are the deviants and it is crucial to put so-called normative, mainstream behavior in context, especially when writing from a social and temporal distance (Young 1971).

HOW CAN YOU STAY IN THE STRAIGHT WORLD?

Both Chino and Leon are cases in point. Chino knew the "normal" life, the 9-to-5 life, but it was the streets and its freedom, its flexibility, its offerings that were clearly more seductive, and once in that world the self, or what he calls his "image" under the influence of illegal substances, began to change. Chino's pathway into deviance is a story often told by the substance user; people who want to get high and are open to the deviant pleasures in life (Firestone 1959) enter those worlds just below the surface of the urban grid of normalcy and straightdom. Chino said that the straights do not have time for all that pleasure, for all that "hanging out," i.e., an escape from the regimes of time managed by employers, bureaucrats, and social institutions. A straight who does "hang out" runs into difficulties when he tries to get back to the mainstream, back to the workaday world in a bank; he finds himself shunned, perhaps stigmatized by his persistent deviance, and so the world of drugs and self-indulgence pulls at him again and again until he develops "a problem." It was during this latter phase of his street deviance, when he slips into a daily heroin habit, that Chino finally served time in prison, which led to his physical removal from that environment.

D.B.: Throughout your life, the way you're talking, the street has always been sort of a problem and also a big attraction?

CHINO: It's like . . . when you have free time you go to a corner, you meet people, but the thing is the people, like the people from the street they're different from people that work 9 to 5, because people from the street they are all hanging out, "Let's go to a party," "Let's go get high," "Let's go play pool," you know, and people that are 9 to 5 they don't have no time to do this. And, you know, I like normal life, I like work, I like to study. Then I start getting into problems. I don't know if my image turned into one of the street guys. Maybe, because when you're using drugs you change your attitude. Like I never made the effort to get a job but when I made an effort I'd say I never got the chance . . . I mean, I used to go out trying to get a job, filling in applications, but nothing worked. . . . Still, I did work in one bank and then another bank for over two years. (March 23, 2003)

Leon's story was similar, but it wasn't drugs alone that seduced him but the entire lifestyle, especially the material things, the props, regalia, adornments, and signifiers of the fast life—the spoils of "getting over." This is what consumer capitalism is all about. The possessions become part of your identity, and you cannot do without them because without them you have no identity and suddenly you are no one again. This is all perhaps part of a stage in the new political economy, what Courtwright calls "limbic capitalism" (2005:121): "By that I mean the reorientation of capitalist enterprise from basic services and durable goods to the more profitable business of providing transient but habitual pleasures, whether drugs or porno or gambling or even sweet and fatty foods." Leon put it this way:

D.B.: At that time did you ever think about how to get out of this shit?

LEON: Well, you say that, but it is not easy to get out when you're involved in it, 'cause you get addicted to money. You get addicted to living the fast way, it's very hard to just ignore it, 'cause you're young and you still got that energy. You don't think, you just throw away money. I didn't care. I'd go to the discotheque and spend 10,000 dollars in one night! I didn't care because I knew I was gonna get double, or triple the amount the next 2 or 3 days. Sometimes I thought about getting out of it but then I started to get a habit, you know, using drugs, and now I got the habit of the environment. It wasn't easy for me to run away from this situation 'cause I wouldn't feel right. I used to always have my jewelries, my cars, and then if I backed up I wasn't going to have all that. Who was I going to be now? (June 8, 2003)

I GOT INTO IT IN THE MILITARY—BESIDES, BACK THEN THE LAWS WERE DIFFERENT

Did all the deviants learn their deviance in the subterranean worlds of the street? Not at all. Many found their way into illicit drug scenes and other worlds of illicit pleasure seeking through institutions that are supposed to be the bedrocks of societal conformity. Tomas described how he got turned onto drugs in the military. First he was a user, hanging out and smoking marijuana with his fellow GIs; then he moved on to harder stuff, snorting cocaine when it was all the rage and finally setting up shop within the armed services before leaving with an honorable discharge. This was the early 1980s when, as Tomas says, the laws were different: "A police officer was stopping me in '84 with a few grams of cocaine and he does nothing to you."

D.B.: As soon as you came out or while you were coming out of the military?

TOMAS: I was actually in the army when I started.

D.B.: A lot of people were using. . . .

TOMAS: Yeah, there was a few of my friends doing it. . . . I knew how to get the connections because I knew people in New York. Back then police wasn't doing anything about that, with cocaine, you know. I remember a documentary three years ago about police in Miami, Dade County. There is a guy talking back in '82 saying, "Cocaine is sort of a harsh drug, I'm addicted." This is what he is saying, that's the official thing. The Surgeon General of the United States used to say that was the official thing, but it wasn't a big thing in New York. A police officer was stopping me in '84, '85 with a few grams of cocaine and (laughs) he does nothing to you, as long as it wasn't being sold. He says, you know, "I'll let you keep it," but if he feels really bad, he might ask you to dump it and step on it, you know, up to an ounce, two ounces was ok, you know. So, it wasn't a big thing, it was in the open, everybody knew people were dealing drugs in the open, it was also sold mostly in Hispanic neighborhoods, you know, but everybody was coming there to buy, whites, everyone, and from all over the country. . . . (April 27, 2003)

SEGMENTED LABOR AND THE WRONG PLACE AT THE WRONG TIME

Some respondents had little direct involvement in deviant behavior, whether it be criminal or legal, except by virtue of the fact that they were undocumented immigrants. One such deportee was Elixida, who was caught in a drug bust at her place of employment in the Manhattan fashion district. Unbeknownst to Elixida, her employer was using his dress shop as a front for laundering drug money as well as for the discrete sale and distribution of cocaine and heroin. While the shop was under surveillance, Elixida was asked by her employer to answer a phone call because the caller only spoke Spanish. She was told to order 5 boxes of dresses and 10 boxes of blouses, which were codes for an order of cocaine from a distributor working in Colombia. When the police finally raided the establishment, Elixida was arrested as an accessory to a conspiracy to buy and sell drugs. She was held in Rikers Island for more than two years, during which time she gave birth to a son who stayed with her for six months before being taken away and placed in the care of a neighbor. On her re-entry into the "free world," the federal prosecutor dropped all charges and commended her on her cooperation in what became a successful prosecution of an illicit drug enterprise that involved both Russian and Colombian organized crime figures. However, on completion of her sentence Elixida was handed over to the immigration authorities who filed for her deportation. After four and a half years in the country, brought to the United States by her Dominican husband who virtually enslaved her, six months as an undocumented shop worker, and twenty eight months in prison, Elixida was deported by an apologetic immigration judge who said that "the law is the law." On hearing the judge's decision through an interpreter, Elixida wept and her body shook with grief and resignation. It took three sentencing proceedings because the judge could not decide if Elixida would really face persecution by her wife-beating husband, who would also be deported after serving three years in an upstate prison, or if the cartels in the Dominican Republic would kill her for her role in the prosecution's case. Before she disappeared into the parallel world of the undocumented, she gave this account of her ordeal:

GIPSY ESCOBAR (G.E.): What were you doing?

ELIXIDA: I was working at a store where they were selling drugs. I tried to leave, I was feeling like pressured, like I couldn't leave.

G.E.: Like a hidden threat?

ELIXIDA: Yes.

G.E.: What would you like to do, I mean, what would be your favorite job?

ELIXIDA: I like to work and I work in whatever I find.

G.E.: But don't you have like an ideal, like some people think of being an actress. Don't you have an ideal like that?

ELIXIDA: I liked it before, when I was younger, I wanted to be a model.

G.E.: Now you were going to talk about your experience with the arrest.

ELIXIDA: I was working at a store and those people got me in trouble, I was taken to the Rock (Rikers Island [added by the authors]), and was imprisoned for two years and a half.

G.E.: And what were the charges?

ELIXIDA: Conspiracy with drugs.

G.E.: What happened?

ELIXIDA: They came looking for me at home, I had been absent from work at the store for five days, and they looked for me at home. They told me that I had to be investigated. I said "Ok, it's all right."

G.E.: How did the police treat you?

ELIXIDA: It was good, or maybe it wasn't good or bad because they give me a name that wasn't mine.

G.E.: How was the case resolved?

ELIXIDA: They realized that I wasn't so guilty, I did one little thing, but, that didn't make me guilty.

G.E.: But did they realize that they were accusing you of being a person that wasn't you?

ELIXIDA: They realized that I was being accused of something that I didn't do, yes. (May 7, 2006)

WHAT OF RATIONAL CHOICE? THE EGOCENTRIC ECONOMIC DECISION

In recent years, a great deal of criminology has been influenced by rational choice theory, what Young (2007) calls "market positivism."[3] In our interviews with the subjects who were involved with small- or medium-sized criminal gangs or drug crews, we heard different versions of the rational choice narrative. Their statements were ambiguous, however, as some virtually stumbled onto a criminal pathway with little clear intention, whereas others knew full well the direction their choices were taking them. In the first excerpt below, Adonis confirmed what a number of studies have found (Levitt and Venkatesh 2000), namely that the drug trade often does not pay the foot soldiers very well, and it is positively dangerous to their health. In the second excerpt, Miguel embarked on a more racial interpretation, reminding us to view the kinds of life chances from a different perspective.

D.B.: Were you making money out of it?

ADONIS: Just a little bit. I was buying the stuff that I wanted to buy. I was buying my clothes, I was clubbing, I was going to hang out with my people, things like that. But I never made enough money to brag and say, "Yo, I'm selling drugs." But I got my money, nothing more than that. (January 19, 2003)

D.B.: Tell me what happened. You started working, 2 years and 8 months, and then what happened?

MIGUEL: Things, you know, the situation is hard at work, I met another girl, and we decided to get another son, so I have to get more money. Sometimes you don't have the fortification, you see the easy way, you know what I mean? 'Cause you're not from there, you know, you don't know the system. American people, they got another chance but like the Black people or Spanish people don't got that. You know what I mean? (January 25, 2003)

WHAT OF THE FAMILY CONTEXT?

And what of the family and its influences on all the 1.5-generation youth who are trying to make sense of the pell-mell pace of life in New York City? Some families were unified and strong, providing the children with a modicum of stability. For them, it was a mixture of the surrounding culture, the failed institutions, the climate of the times, and the changes in law that pushed them gradually out the door that would never open again. For others, there was a feeling that their parents did little to help them and that part of their trajectory toward crime was related to the way they were mistreated or undersocialized by the adults who should have been nurturing them. George and Alex both came from families where the father abandoned them.

D.B.: How old were you when you first started to get into this?

GEORGE: I was introduced to it at an early age but I stayed on the edges. . . .

D.B.: In the market?

GEORGE: In New York, not only in New York, I would say in the States. You don't put your nose where you don't belong. You mind your business. You can be a killer and yet you're my next door neighbor, I don't care about that. That's the way it is. So, I wake up on my 25th birthday, that's when I started to put my hands on it and of course it's in the mid '70s to late '70s. Thereafter, I got involved in crime. First using it (drugs [added by the authors]) then putting my hands in it, a little cutting and wrapping, and eventually I got into dealing in Brooklyn, which is big money, I made money.

D.B.: Is this in New York and New Jersey?

GEORGE: New York, New Jersey, and Boston.

D.B.: So, between the '70s you were living off of the earnings of that in New York and New Jersey?

GEORGE: Always, making good money and living off of that.

D.B.: So, you didn't work and had drugs stocked in some places?

GEORGE: I wasn't really that bad, but that kind of life is wrong. But I did that.

D.B.: So, that was from '75 through '85 or. . . ?

GEORGE: '77, '78 really, somewhere around then, to '84. '84 I got busted with 2 ounces and got 30. . . . See, that hurts, you know why that hurts, I was not expecting it, you are so used to seeing so much drugs, and you travel with so much around, and then you get busted with a little, you know, a little thing, they send you to jail for 30 years. That's your whole life. (July 3, 2003)

Alex told a different story. He thought back to his childhood and the drinking and domestic violence that was habitual in his household. At a "certain age" he left the house, and he turned to street gangs for succor, excitement, and meaning. He became a "real drug dealer," and during a raid by rivals he shot through a wall and killed his attackers; as he put it, "it was either them or me." Alex was sentenced to 15 years and was sent upstate, where he drifted from prison to prison and became an enforcer for the Latin Kings in Attica.[4]

D.B.: Tell me about your parents. Where did they work when you were growing up?

ALEX: The last time, ok, how can I put this . . . my father drinks a lot, right, and smokes a lot of cigarettes and he liked to beat up my mother. There always used to be a fight and then before the fight was over he used to pick on me, pick on one of my sisters, liked to beat the shit out of us and things like that. My mother went to the USA when I was about 4, then she prepared my papers and sends me to New York, to school and after a certain age I continued to high school. Then when I was 18 I left my house. You know how youngsters in New York are when they get to a certain age they think they are already a man or that they're already a woman, you know, and then I started meeting kids that used to be in gangs. You know, gangs like Spanish Kings. So I became a Spanish King when I was about 19. Then I started getting into problems, selling drugs, marijuana. So after marijuana I went to sell dope, and then I get arrested in Brooklyn for dope and they put me on probation. Then after I started doing things I went back to my mother's house.

D.B.: In Manhattan?

ALEX: That happened in Brooklyn where I used to live. Then she moved to Manhattan, I went to live with her for 2 or 3 years but we didn't get along, because I grew up with my father. So, then I became a real drug dealer. (March 5, 2003)

JUST WANNA HELP OUT MY MOM

Finally, there is the notion of the good son, the dutiful child who is committing crime only to keep his mom happy and away from the degradations of poverty. This might be seen as a way to adapt to the socioeconomic structure, a move in keeping with the immigrant version of the Mertonian innovator whose motives are more altruistic than egoistic. It is also a way for boys or young men to compensate for fathers who have abandoned the family, turning their backs on their own flesh and blood. The psychic pain of such abandonment was never far below the surface for our respondents, and their self-rationalizations of "I did it for them" helped them withstand the years of privation and isolation in prison.

D.B.: What was your plan?

ARIEL: At first, when I started, my plan was to help out my mom, you know, 'cause I didn't want her to live in New Jersey and if she was gonna live in New Jersey I wanted to buy a house for her. But my father did that already, he already bought a house for my mom. That was my plan in my head, to help out my mom and my father, because he's been working for like 23 years, since I was born, you know. So I wanted to help them both out, but I took the wrong way, you know. (April 23, 2003)

LUIS 1: Well, it wasn't too difficult because my dad never gave me the support that I needed, do you understand me? My mom raised me, she was my dad and my mom. She gave me what I needed. May God have glory even on my dad because the feelings I once had for him are gone, not even the dead would forgive him because my dad put me through a lot of hard times. If my dad had supported me, I wouldn't have gone to prison in the United States. Why? Because I would've been so devoted to working and I wouldn't have had such a materialistic mindset, do you understand me? But because he didn't give me any support I said, "OK, I'm leaving my country and I'm going to make money any way I can." So I began to do things that weren't right, do you understand me? (April 2, 2003)

Sometimes the respondents were desperate for their mothers and families not to know the true source of their income—a classic case of immigrant liminality, moving in the shadows of the shadows.

CELIO: I was thinking inside . . . about my family because as I told you, my family was an important part in this because they were hoping that I could, how should I say this, help them get on. Now, they didn't know was what I was doing in Puerto Rico, they didn't know that I was dealing drugs. I told them that I was working in a company. In reality I did work at a company but I left that. I was working for two years in that company. My family thought that I was working but what I was selling were drugs. I was going to bed at 1 A.M. or 2 A.M. every night and putting my life in danger. I did a lot of things that maybe I'm paying for now because God sometimes makes you pay. I say that maybe I'm paying for it because, well, it was either my life or theirs. . . . I didn't trust anybody . . . everyone was my enemy. They coveted what I had or what I was doing. As I sometimes say, "I am not a 1,000 pesos bill to be liked by everyone." (March 3, 2003)

FOR THE ABUSED, SOMETIMES THERE IS NO CHOICE

As seen in Elixida's story, the female pathway into crime and deviance was different from that of the men. Fermin explained the events that led to her arrest. We do not see a solitary figure making decisions and exhibiting the kinds of agency typical of many of the male subjects in the rest of the study. Rather, her actions are inseparable from her status as a victimized wife of a crack addict, someone who brutally kept her in check and forced her to act on his behalf. Her actions, however, were founded in a history of resistance. As mentioned in the chapter on settlement, Fermin was dealt a number of cruel blows as a young adult, losing her mother and father, finding herself alone and vulnerable in a strange country, with only her sister, who lived on the other side of the country, for support. After struggling to sustain herself economically in the "seedy" economy of bars and nightclubs while raising several children, she ended up on the losing end of a violent, macho culture. In this sense her victimization is not atypical, neither in the United States nor in her native Dominican Republic, where violence against women is still extraordinarily prevalent (see chapter 2).

FERMIN: My husband got wasted with that (crack [added by the authors]), I really hated it, he was crazy, and then he would abuse me so much. Abused me even more, and all the money you make, forget about it, if I didn't give it to him, he would catch me (she stops and pauses). You don't know what I went through.

D.B.: Did you ever go to the police?

FERMIN: Yeah, yeah, he got locked up many times but I went back and I, like. . . .

D.B.: In '96 you both got busted, how does that happen?

FERMIN: Ok, we were driving, he's just driving and I was by the window and he told me, "Call that person and when I tell you to snatch his chain, you snatch his chain." I was like, "I don't wanna do that." And he said, "If you don't do that I'm gonna break your teeth" (the interviewee clenches her fist, raising it to her face). So, I got scared, he's 6 foot 4, he's a big man, you know, and I say, "Ok." So, then he said, "Go," and then I went like this (the interviewee leans across with her arm out as if she's reaching through a car window) . . . and then, and then we got caught. The man went to the police and, I don't know, they found us, they saw us driving through and then they got us. They took us to the Hudson County Jail, that's where we did time. He got 10 flat and I got a 5 flat. (May 17, 2006)

OF ETHICS AND SOCIALIZATION: SNITCHES AND CORRUPT OFFICIALS

To get an idea of the world in which ethics and norms are regularly mangled on the streets, where good and evil, straight and deviant regularly interact and switch sides, we can listen carefully to Luis and Pedro. By the mid-1980s, Luis had done well with four drug spots throughout Northern Manhattan and was earning a good living, all cash and tax free. Like many drug dealers, he lived in a conspicuous fashion, turning his cash into possessions like cars, gold chains, expensive clothing, and "good times" with an assortment of women and associates. This was, after all, the middle of the crack cocaine era and there was money to be made as the mafia gave up control of much of New York's drug markets (Curtis 2003; Sánchez-Jankowski 1991). The notion, however, that law enforcement was in the business of serious crime prevention is a fallacy. As Luis3 testified, the spoils were shared between the rule-enforcers and the rule-breakers, and the rooted, systematic corruption of public morality, especially in the poorest areas of the city, was on display for all to see. Under such circumstances, how could one get out of the game? In fact, it is difficult to tell who is in or is out of the game.

D.B.: So, they had something on the guy and he snitched on you.

LUIS3: I don't even know the guy. I didn't even have drugs on me, nothing. I was in a store, you know, I think the guy was doing business . . . because I know the guy that works in the grocery store, I was related to him. . . .

D.B.: Is this in Manhattan?

LUIS3: Yeah, this is in Manhattan, 147th Street and Amsterdam Avenue. So, I'm talking to the guy that owns the store, I know him for a long time, since we were kids. Probably the informer came there and saw me talking to the guy and said, "Well, he's probably one of the guys that's selling drugs." So, when the cops came, they said, "You're one of them," you know, "You're being charged with possession of and distributing crack cocaine," stuff like that. I thought I was gonna get out of it, but the informer he got more power, you know, and started pointing fingers that I was involved in this and that, and I couldn't fight it, they told me, "You're gonna take it to trial?" I said, "Well, let's go and take it to trial." I had no problem.

D.B.: And so, did you have a number of drug spots?

LUIS3: Actually, yeah.

D.B.: How many did you have?

LUIS3: 4.

D.B.: And how many guys did you have working for you?

LUIS3: About 30.

D.B.: Did you manage to put any money away, save anything?

LUIS3: They took a lot of money from me, the cops. When they first arrested me, they took $250,000 and jewelry and they kept the drugs, they kept everything. They did a stick up and said go away. About 6 months later or a year later they came back again and took another $270,000, cars, jewelry, everything but never put me in jail. It was like they were robbing me. (June 10, 2003)

D.B.: You have this feeling that you can't be the breadwinner and then you come across these guys?

PEDRO: Yeah, they are like friends of mine.

D.B: And they're in the drug business?

PEDRO: They're collectors. They collect on what people owe. You see, the drug game is so dirty. People can be the best of friends, but once you start making more money than me, then I get a bunch of guys and say, "Stick 'em up" and you know, then you can't trace it back to me at all. "Oh, man, that's so terrible what happened to you?" And it was me all along! This is the type of flippin' that's in that lifestyle. There's no loyalties . . . I mean, in the US now, they call 1-800-TIPS. The guy's dealing out of the corner store. But the guy that's giving the tip is a major drug dealer too! He just wants the competition out! He can't deal with the guy personally, so he's going to set the cops on him. It's a filthy game.

D.B.: So you meet these guys, you get re-acquainted?

PEDRO: Well, I just bumped into them and they said, "Pete, man, come with us." And I always had a name in the neighborhood, you know, as a fighter. So they said, we need guys like this—more muscle. So, they said," Come with us." And me, like an idiot, and that's a nice word I'm using, I went along. And lo-and-behold, here I am. (August 10, 2006)

CONCLUSION

If one reads the bulk of the immigration literature, the first- and 1.5-generation immigrants in our sample are not at all typical of those making their new lives in the United States. According to most analyses of immigration and crime, the pathways to prison usually occur in the second generation (Martínez and Valenzuela 2006). The narratives in this chapter, however, help us see how quickly the Americanization process is working in another direction and how the need to "fit in," adapt, make it closer to the American Dream, help out the family, be a man, and survive intolerable relationships are key to the criminal trajectories of many of the subjects. These trajectories are characterized by the liminal contexts of the immigrant, who is caught between nations, borders, formal and informal markets, laws, subcultural norms, and street identities.

This process of deviance is made that much more certain with each new anti-immigrant legislative act, each new strategy in the crusade against drugs, each new raid on immigrant neighborhoods looking for the "illegals," and each new process of interagency intelligence sharing that is now conveniently organized under the ever-expanding auspices of Homeland Security.

6.1 A TYPICAL SCENE IN RIKERS ISLAND, NEW YORK CITY (© MICHAEL S. YAMASHITA/CORBIS).

CHAPTER SIX

PRISON

Rikers Island es un infierno.

THE STORIES TOLD by the respondents about their experiences in the U.S. correctional system are nightmarish. It is hard to believe that such stories could be produced by a civilized society. Of course, there is a great deal about the United States—the sanctioning of torture by the U.S. Justice Department, the establishment of Abu Ghraib by the U.S. military, the use of the death penalty in federal and state courts, the structured racism at the root of the human-made disaster after Hurricane Katrina—that makes us ponder how a society that presents itself as a modern democracy cannot guarantee basic human rights to so many of the people living within its borders. It is in this context that we understand the frightful experiences of so many of our research participants. Some of them, of course, were guilty of various crimes and would be the first to repeat the inmate's mantra: "If you do the crime, you do the time" (see also Sykes 1958). Others were innocent of the crimes of which they were accused, caught in the wrong place at the wrong time, often betrayed by associates who used their naïveté for their own opportunist ends; they were ignorant of the language and had no access to a competent lawyer. Regardless of guilt or innocence, we see a system bent on punishment, staffed by employees who have often been trained to treat their charges as the "enemy" due to the perverse power play between inmates and guards that marks modern prisons, especially in an era when rehabilitation is considered passé (Garland 1997; Parenti 2008; Christie 2000).

LEGAL REPRESENTATION

DAVID BROTHERTON (D.B.): Do you think that you had good legal representation?

RAOUL: No, no, he works for migration directly. I mean, he's a lawyer that gets money knowing that they're not going to solve any problems, but he takes my money anyway. There are even two friends of mine who gave him money, around $10,000 or $20,000. And the same lawyer went to call migration for them to be deported![1] (July 22, 2003)

Like Raoul, few of the subjects reported being well represented or at least satisfied with their representation in both criminal and immigration court proceedings. Many spoke of unscrupulous lawyers (both legal and nonlegal residents) who took their money, sometimes more than ten thousand dollars, and did little in return. This was especially true of subjects who had spent less time in the United States and did not have the kinds of community contacts who might have helped them navigate the intricacies of both the criminal justice and immigration systems.

Others spoke of being represented by court-appointed lawyers who did their best with what little resources they had at their disposal; these lawyers were usually overburdened with other cases, which is the norm for many public defense lawyers in recent years because of substantial cutbacks to agencies like the Legal Aid Society.[2]

D.B.: What did your lawyer do when he found out you had no previous record?

JUAN: Nothing. I got a Spanish lawyer. I think she was trying to do a good job, but she got no experience. She was there 9 months after she had graduated. She was very inexperienced.

D.B.: So they put you in jail? You had no option of bail?

JUAN: Yeah, but I couldn't make it.

D.B.: So they kept you in jail, how long did the trial last?

JUAN: They took 9 months.

D.B.: After you were in jail?

JUAN: The whole thing took 9 months to finish with the case.

D.B.: You must have felt like this was some kind of nightmare.

JUAN: Of course, that was it. I didn't know if I could take it 'cause it was so much. That's when I started to know God, that's what made me make it. . . . I thought that I could make it through an appeal since I was innocent. I said how can they put somebody for 15 years in jail and know that

I didn't touch it (the drugs in the car placed there by his friend [added by the authors])? I know that I didn't do anything.

D.B.: Did you have a chance to give a testimony?

JUAN: My lawyer at the beginning said that it was a better idea not to talk during the trial, and then she changed her mind but I didn't trust her. . . . I talked to a couple of lawyers in the jailhouse and they say that they didn't recommend for the defense to speak during the trial. I was very confused and I never got a good explanation. Then she said that if I weren't Spanish it would be better. She said that a lot of white guys on the jury are prejudiced against drugs and Spanish people. Then I say, ok, we try to make a better case in the appeal. That's what she did. She said that that was a good case, but we lost it. We took it to the Supreme Judicial Court of the State and they decided that I must stay in jail.

D.B.: How long did all that take?

JUAN: That took about 2 years, well into the spring.

D.B.: And then when you finally lost everything, what were your thoughts?

JUAN: I never give up, even when I was doing nothing in the case I still thought there would be a moment that I was going to make it. I used to tell myself, until the last day I spend in here I'm gonna take this case back to court, because I knew I didn't do it! I was trying that for 5 years and then finally after 10 years I got the right to go to a new trial, I get some new evidence and the trial judge finally said here it is.

D.B.: After 10 years.

JUAN: Yeah, after 10 years. We finished it after 12 years because you know that's the process. After 10 years I finally found a guy who helped me to get things together and do it the right way. In the end I had maybe five different judges, then that last one thought that I needed to go to court. And I won. I got out with 3 years to go! I spent twelve years in there for nothing. Twelve years when I didn't see my children, my wife, just my mother and my eldest daughter.

D.B.: Explain.

JUAN: My mother moved to the United States to be near the prison with my eldest daughter. So I saw them but when I got arrested my wife in the Dominican Republic was pregnant. The last daughter was born after I had been in prison for 4 months.

D.B.: Did you see your daughter at all in prison?

JUAN: No, I met her, the last one, I met her when I came out after 12 years.

D.B.: Unbelievable.

JUAN: And the third one also, she was only 2 years old when I went to prison, and I met her after 12 years too. (March 1, 2003)

THE SHOCK OF THE SENTENCE

For all that the subjects knew about the criminal justice system, through friends or family members, many of them were unprepared for the extraordinary sentences handed down to them, especially for nonviolent drug offenses. Mandatory sentences for drug offenses increased significantly during the late 1980s when both state and federal legislatures across the nation got "tough on crime," particularly drug crimes and other crimes committed by poor and minority residents (Elsner 2006; Reiman 2006; Cole 2000; Mauer 1999).[3] Respondents revealed how the length of sentences affected them. For Rafael, the threat of such a sentence communicated to him by his lawyer forced him to plead guilty, even though he argues that he was innocent, and this plea led to his deportation. For Guido, the sentence is not a threat but a reality. Guido spent seven years in a state prison before challenging his trial and winning an early release.

> D.B.: Then, you had a sentence. . . .
> RAFAEL: Well, I didn't want to declare myself guilty because I thought I could win the case, I had all the evidence. But then the lawyer scared me, she said to me, "No, they can give you 40 years." What do I know? 40 years!
> D.B.: 40 years?
> RAFAEL: 40 years of prison! Well, then I had a friend in prison who opened my mind and said to me, "When she comes, you tell her very clearly that they cannot give you 50 years. In the first place you are a first-time offender, never have been arrested." (January 11, 2003)

> GUIDO: When I went for sentencing, my documents went to another judge, and my lawyer told me, "Go in front of this man and do whatever you have to 'cause I guarantee you that if you go in front of this other judge you're fucked." This guy gave me 50 years, and I think it was 2 years for the firearms charge. I was scared. Never been in trouble in my life, this is my first time ever in trouble as a juvenile or as an adult, and it led to this. He gave me 52 years! Before I was thinking I would be out in 2 years, you know. (May 22, 2003)

PRISON EXPERIENCES

How does one survive in prison? It is not easy, as Sykes classically explained:

> Deprived of their liberty, stripped of worldly possessions, denied access to heterosexual relationships, divested of autonomy, and compelled to associate with

other deviants, the inmates find that imprisonment still means punishment however much imprisonment may have been softened in this modern era by an accent on humanitarianism and reform. I have suggested that it is these punishing aspects of modern imprisonment, these deprivations or frustrations, which play a crucial part in shaping the inmate social system. It is these deprivations, particularly as they involve a threat or an attack at a deep psychological level, that the inmates must meet and counter. And the inmate population's modes of reactions can be found ranged, I have suggested, between two poles. On the one hand, the prisoner can engage in a highly individualistic war of all against all in which he seeks to mitigate his own plight at the expense of his fellow prisoners; on the other hand, the prisoner can attempt to form a close alliance with his fellow captives and to present a unified front against the custodians.

(SYKES 1958:131)

And this was in the days when the rules in prison were much clearer, when there was "respect" between the older and younger generations and the inmate population was not as racially divided (Hunt et al. 1993; Parenti 2008). As many observers have commented, prison has changed significantly over the years as vast numbers of primarily poor and working-class men and women, particularly of color, have been incarcerated for longer periods and in greater numbers. These quantitative and qualitative changes have led to different processes of formal and informal social control as seen in the relationship between inmates and correctional officers.

The development of the prison-industrial complex (Critical Resistance)[4] within the security state has become what some openly call the "American Gulag" where the old codes of prison no longer apply (Dow 2004; Parenti 2009; Young 1999). As Hunt et al. (1993) found, today's imprisoned youth do not enter prison respecting the older inmates as they might have done in the past; in addition, daily prison life is more volatile, punitive, and predatory, and the risk of various illnesses is much higher. Therefore, disciplinary cells such as segregated housing units and "the hole" (solitary confinement cells) are increasingly used by prison administrations as they face an inmate population with high rates of HIV and AIDS as well as mental illness (more than ten percent of the prison population has some form of mental disorder). Widespread overcrowding, diminishing opportunities for education, highly conservative parole boards, and the endless web of punitive sanctions applied to ex-inmates in civil society[5] add to this toxic mix, making it easy to understand why rates of recidivism remain high and the prison population continues to grow exponentially despite drops in crime (Travis et al. 2001). As a result, frustration, paranoia, and resentment are the norm for inmates rather than the exception.

One result of the declining conditions of prison life is that many inmate populations today are organized around prison gang cultures, an experience recounted by both male and female participants (although rarely reported in the male-centered literature; cf. Owen 1998). We have interpreted the prison experience through several themes: (1) the prison-industrial complex, (2) surviving alone, (3) relationships with correctional officers, (4) gang life, and (5) life as a female inmate.

THE PRISON-INDUSTRIAL COMPLEX

Many of the participants who had spent time in prison commented on the extraordinary growth of the incarceration system and the myriad ways the system both used and worked against the individual. An interlocking culture of vindictiveness exists as judges dispatch inmates to needlessly punitive environments, with no relation to the severity of the crime. Is this the consequence of the "culture of control" (Garland 2002) as judges have become increasingly ideological and prosecutorial (Cross 2007), caught up in the popular crusade or moral panic of the day. This ideological turn is particularly noticeable among parole boards, with subjects recounting how difficult it was to get a sympathetic hearing from these carceral bureaucrats.

> GUIDO: First they sent me to a medium security receiving unit, I spent like about 8 months there then they sent me to a maximum security.
>
> D.B.: What for?
>
> GUIDO: (laughs) You tell me why! I was in the maximum security prison for a little over a year. Most guys there had violent crimes. I'm a non-violent offender with no criminal history. I have a level of education, yet I'm sent to a maximum security prison. Why would they send me there? I would say to run my time up. I would say they're putting me in an environment so hostile, that I could only do one thing. . . . After I went to prison the Republicans came to power in Virginia and they abolished parole and put more and more conservatives on parole boards. . . . The reason for the denial, I'll never forget this, "Your involvement with drugs so disregards the welfare of others." What the fuck excuse is that? (laughs) Talk to me about what I've done. Talk to me about the time I've been in prison. Talk to me about all the programs I've participated in, the people I help to learn how to read and write, the other students I helped to translate their letters, all the people I helped write grievances for. Talk to me about the good things, the positive things that I've done. Isn't that what rehabilitation is about? Don't talk to me about the shit

I did before I came to prison. Talk to me about your fucking crime bill, and your American shit with Newt Gingrich's revolution. Talk to me about your Anti-Terrorism and Effective Death Penalty Act. No! (May 22, 2003)

What does it feel like to be the raw material of this complex? How does it feel to be the source of profit for a system that no longer seems to have a purpose beyond punishment and social exclusion? How do inmates view the supposed reasons for this extraordinary peace time expansion of a system that before the 1970s was such a minor item (though always important) on a state's fiscal balance sheet? When we take into account the chilling economic and social fact that more is being spent on prisons than on higher education in California, Illinois, New York, and so many other states, what legitimacy remains in the eyes of the inmate?[6]

D.B.: Is that a medium security or. . . ?

GUIDO: That was a medium security, they sent me to a dorm, a room full of people, a big dorm, about 300 and something men up and down, packed, like a warehouse, a human warehouse. Basically, it was a concentration camp. (June 23, 2003)

Leon conceived another meaning for his presence in these remote locations. It's about business, the American way, a culture that promotes making a buck out of everyone and everything, even the most disposable of social classes. Leon's analysis is prescient (though it was before the recent financial meltdown) and accords with the work of other critical criminologists, such as Welch (2002, 2003), who argued that the business aspect of imprisonment is particularly important in the case of deportees because, according to the sordid logic of the profit-based system, the value of an incarcerated noncitizen about to be deported is worth more than the value of other run-of-the-mill U.S. inmates.

D.B.: What do you make of, I mean, of the huge explosion of prison population?

LEON: Before inmates used to be something that was like a burden for the government, a weight for the government, right now, inmate populations are not a weight, it's a business now. Like in upstate New York or in Denver, Colorado, any states you want, you know that the prisons are in little areas where there are poor people, now what they do is they go to the community and ask them whether they gonna put a jail over there, so the community agrees. Now the people in the community are gonna get jobs, they're gonna get everything. Everything that's been consumed it's gonna come out of that community, so the community grows, so they get taxes and everything, so it's becoming a business. A really strong business.

D.B.: It's pretty sick.

LEON: Very, very, now what they do is just lock up people, it's a modern slavery, that's what it is, and they don't have no exceptions. They have Black, White, everybody, they don't care. If you're smart you have to be very careful, they gonna lock you up, because they need people that are intelligent right now to run the computers, to run their business, you know, because people that run the jail are the inmates. They're the ones that run the administration, you know, it's not the police, they don't do nothing, they're just there—it's a big business (May 23, 2003)

SURVIVING ALONE

Once the convicted are in the system, how do they get by? How do they negotiate day-to-day life? How do they navigate their way through the various prison subcultures, the logic of the bizarre rules of the "total institution," the psychological pressures of the correctional stuff, or the various personalities among the inmates? How do you resist, incorporate, and accommodate the regimes of dehumanization and deindividualization on which the institution is based? Most of us will never know. It is difficult to even think of living in such confines, of going without our "freedom" for any significant length of time. When we do, even in a short-lived experiment such as that carried out at Stanford University more than two decades ago (Zimbardo 2008), the results are frightening.

This question of social and psychological survival for the majority of inmates is a recurring one except for the most institutionalized prisoners. Our respondents discussed how they "made it" without having to assimilate into the inmate subcultures.

D.B.: How long were you in jail before you started [getting involved in self-help programs]?

LEONEL: About 5 years.

D.B.: Did you get involved in any groups in jail? Prison gangs?

LEONEL: No gangs, no, I used to get involved with people that used to come from the street to teach the inmates how to manage violence.

D.B.: Oh, aggression programs.

LEONEL: Yeah, it was a program like that . . . AVV something like that, right, so from there I started learning and reading books. . . . . I came to them and told them that that's what I really wanna do, so they say, "You really wanna do that?" So they gave me books, they gave me materials where I saw how I could relate to those people, how I can work with them. . . . I'm there for these people to continue the rehab, you know, so I was doing that constantly. I didn't have no problem with that, I used to make basketball tournaments, racquetball, weights, all that stuff. I used to manage all that stuff, so they said, "How can you manage all that?" Well, they listen to me, you know. (July 25, 2003)

Alternative visions to violence (AVV) programs are anger management programs present throughout the correctional system. For many inmates, it is one of the few opportunities to have regular contact with teachers and social workers from the outside; it is something to occupy inmates' minds as well as a chance to reflect on their life course. For Leonel, his involvement in this program allowed him to socialize with other inmates and organize them outside of the gang structures. Leonid, below, had a similar strategy. He became involved in multiple programs to help other inmates adjust to prison life and overcome challenges such as dealing with addiction, getting divorced (a frequent occurrence), and losing close family members. In this way, Leonid created a new role for himself and alternative personal identity other than that of the prisoner.

LEONID: I didn't do college, I just did counseling, you know, people trying to commit suicide, rehab. I used to help people that had problems with drugs. I used to help a lot of people that used to have problems with their wives. I took them, just to help their kids, just to help young kids when they first come to jail, I had like a group meeting authorized by the federal government. They gave me an office, so I was like the head of that, and they see that what I was doing was positive because the majority of the kids that came, you know, came in real fast, so I used to slow them down, told them how to live in jail, how they're supposed to carry themselves, you know. This is not the street, there is no mother and there is no father here.

D.B.: So you became kind of a role model for them.

LEONID: Right.

D.B.: Did you enjoy that?

LEONID: Well, it helped me because I knew how to read people's mentality, what they're all about, you know, because I was doing it for so long.

Sometimes I used to make mistakes judging people, so that helped me get better. Now every time I look at a person I know how to judge them because I was doing that so long with criminals and people who are assassins, people who have violated kids, robbers, real drug dealers, drug addicts. I mean I got involved with all these people so I just learned how not to manipulate them, but to control them, put them on the straight track. I enjoyed that because guys used to come to me when they were going home and they used to thank me. Their families used to write me letters and told me how their kids are doing. They used to tell me that I was this certain person that helped them, you know. I felt real good about that. (April 10, 2003)

Some of our respondents managed to use their time in prison to resume their education, gleaning what they could from the small collection of books in the prison library and finding ways to take courses at local colleges. Pedro did both, becoming an avid interpreter of the law and earning a reputation as an inmate scholar and a "jail-house lawyer," i.e., an inmate who can provide legal advice to other inmates (Abu-Jamal 2009). In his account, Pedro described how he was helped by other inmate scholars, in this case by the infamous Jack Abbot.

PEDRO: I went to college in prison. I went to Skidmore University. I took political science and liberal arts. The first semester, I got an Associate. Then I got into anthropology or something like that. My friend got me into that. We studied the Yanomamo in South America. It was a beautiful experience for me. I thought, "Wow," I never knew books were this interesting. Then I got into all types of stuff. I ran into Jack Henry Abbot in solitary confinement. He's the author of "In the Belly of the Beast." Man, I never met in my life such an intelligent human being. I swear to God. I mean he was a little radical in his influence, but this guy was mind-blowing.

D.B.: How would you talk to him, through the walls?

PEDRO: He was my neighbor! Then we met up again in Wendel, he was my neighbor again. He said "Hey Petey boy!" and I said "Oh, snap?" it's you. He's Chinese and American Indian. But he's Jewish, you know, of the Jewish faith. He used to tell me about Norman Mailer, the guy that helped him get out. I said, "Damn, Jack, why'd you stab the guy?" And he said, "Pete, I didn't want to, I was on an automatic pilot. You just don't know what it is because you haven't been released from prison. But when you've known prison all your life you can't let anybody disrespect you.

And when you're let out to the street you wanna react right away with a knife or something, but you don't know where you're at. You gotta say, "Wait a minute, I'm acting like an animal. I'm in civilized society." But people don't know what 15 or 20 years in prison will do to you. I don't care who you are, it works on you. I was on automatic pilot and I stabbed the guy." I said, "Wow!" So he was fighting for his release. They beat him up real bad, the cops in Attica. He didn't want to go back there. (August 10, 2006)

And then there were some whose physical and psychological intensity signaled to everyone that this was not a guy to be messed with. These subjects managed to do "their time" in their own way. Marcos was such an inmate.

D.B.: Did you have to join a group when you were inside?

MARCOS: No, not really. Like if you're a man nobody fucks with you.

D.B.: Oh, I see, so you defended yourself.

MARCOS: It's like do you wanna die one day? Think of it like that. I don't make no trouble with nobody but if somebody is fucking with me I have to do whatever I have to do. You know, the jail here is worse, but over there you know a lot people. I prefer jail over there than being in this country right now. You don't know what you're talking about. It's crazy here. (July 25, 2003)

RELATIONSHIPS WITH THE CORRECTIONAL OFFICERS

There were few interviewees who had anything positive to say about the correctional officers with whom they had spent so many years. As far as the respondents were concerned, racism was rife in the prison system, and the guards were partly to blame for this dynamic. Below, Miguel describes the normality of the violence between correctional officers and the inmates, and he includes female officers in perpetuating the culture of abuse and sadism, perhaps as we saw in the infamous photos of Abu Ghraib (Mestrovic 2005). Miguel discussed how correctional officers are sometimes drawn from the same families across generations. In other accounts, we heard of more organized racial violence.

D.B.: How long were you there for?

MIGUEL: Almost 2 years. Then I fought my case. I was like 3 years in immigration fighting.

D.B.: So, you did 2 years upstate. How was the first prison time?

MIGUEL: Bad. Specially, in that jail, you see a lot of shit in that jail. The police is smacking people, you know, putting pressure on, you can't talk, you never see your family. I know you don't hear about it, about, they call it "icening," that's in Lakeview, Lakeview facility.

D.B.: Lakeview?

MIGUEL: Yeah, that's the shock program, that's a killer people over there.

D.B.: Really?

MIGUEL: These people are doing a lot of shit. But, like I said, nobody says anything, you know, like its Hispanic people, they're nothing. You can't say shit. I see the police smacking people for nothing.

D.B.: Did they smack you?

MIGUEL: Yeah! I couldn't say nothing, 'cause they say, you know. . . .

D.B.: Is this the correction officers or the cops?

MIGUEL: Correction officers and female officers too!

D.B.: Female and male.

MIGUEL: It's like a big family, everyone working like in the same county. May be some people don't speak English and they think it's showing disrespect. They get on the job at 9 o'clock and by 10 o'clock you have to go medical because it's whap, whap. It was crazy.

D.B.: And were there many Latinos there?

MIGUEL: Yeah! Like in the courtroom, you see five American people on the jury or whatever, all like "blanquitos" and you say to yourself, "But all you see in the system is Black and Hispanic people." (January 25, 2003)

D.B.: And how was the prison where you were?

MAURICIO: (scoffs) Another . . . you know Ku Klux Klan people? Something like that.

D.B.: KKK were working there?

MAURICIO: Yeah, with the fucking tattoos here (he shows his forearm), with the blacks on the trees. Plus when you work in there the whole day they give you $1 dollar a day!

D.B.: One dollar a day?

MAURICIO: One dollar a day! And if you don't work you get locked up, they don't let you out.

D.B.: And did they beat the inmates there too?

MAURICIO: Yeah! A lot of people, you know what I mean, people say in there they don't give a fuck what happens to you. . . . This motherfucker takes the people out and uses the club, you see him, smacking, putting you in the SHU (segregated housing units [added by the authors]). When the family go there he say you're not even there, you know. You try to make a phone call to your family and the motherfucker got the phone system blocked so he got all control. Like, I can't even send you my number. If I get locked up, put in the hole, I can't send you my number.

PEDRO: The mindset with those guys was different. These guys are like, I don't know. They like out of a movie, like a clan, maybe. I see some of the guards with tattoos of black babies hanging off trees! I said, "What the hell?" And they are all big, like 6'3" and they'll break you up. You know, they broke my ribs. Ask a medical doctor how difficult it is to break the ribs. There's a twig on certain plants that if you try to snap it the fibers like stay together. That's more or less how they explained that the ribs are. Mine actually separated. And if you put your hand in you can feel it, it fused back together like that. That was because they beat me. (June 10, 2003)

There was only one account that referred to the professionalism of the correctional officers.[7] Juan, who was incarcerated in Massachusetts, found that the guards changed over time as the system grew larger and larger and the laws governing inmates became more punitive.

D.B.: What were the guards like?
JUAN: In the beginning they was very professional, but they deteriorated, they got tougher, and tougher, and tougher, more security, more troubles, more disrespecting. When I left the things were getting ugly.
D.B.: Really?
JUAN: Yeah. So I just tried not to pay attention and blocked it from my mind when they provoked you.
D.B.: What would they do?
JUAN: Try to disrespect you, make you feel that you mean nothing and that they got power over you, over your life, over your thinking, over everything, and that they can abuse you and you can't do and say nothing. That's when many people get mad and do crazy things.
D.B.: They were mainly white guards?
JUAN: Yeah. Mostly.
D.B.: No Latinos?
JUAN: No, not many but sometimes they are even worse.
D.B.: Sometimes they're worse.
JUAN: But I don't blame no race, I think that it's the system. I got some guard friends and they say, "You just a step under me. They press on me, they push me and I gotta push you. That's the way it is. We don't feel comfortable about it but we gotta do it. (March 1, 2003)

GANG LIFE

One of the most common experiences recounted by the participants was related to prison gang life. Respondents joined a wide range of Latino and non-Latino gangs for various reasons such as social support, cultural affirmation, or self-defense. As stated earlier, the ubiquity of the prison gang culture is a fairly recent phenomenon that reflects the growth of the system in recent years and the racialization of inmate life at all levels of the institution. Some of the gangs joined by the subjects also have a street presence, such as the Latin Kings and the Ñetas, while others were purely prison phenomena such as the Rat Hunters and the Trinitarios.[8] The respondents were candid about their involvement in these groups, which reflected the normative place of these subcultures in the current system.

The Prison-Only Gangs: The Rat Hunters and the Trinitarios

The Rat Hunters

Pedro joined the Rat Hunters, a gang that was not well known outside of the prison system. This was a group unlike other prison gangs in that it was set up primarily to ferret out prison snitches. In Pedro's account we can see a number of his reasons for joining this particular gang. One reason has to do with a desire to maintain his affiliation with former acquaintances from the street—thus moving within and between subcultures, which is part of a successful transition from civil to incarcerated society. Another reason is normative in that Pedro is long used to the norms, values, and expectations of the gang culture. Third, the group has a specific purpose, which is to secure a certain order and root out those working with "the enemy," i.e., the administration; in this, the group appeals to Pedro's sense of righteousness and of a "higher calling" while giving him status and a feeling of empowerment, both with inmates and the administration.

> PEDRO: The Rat House was started in the Brooklyn House in 1979 by a Puerto Rican fellow by the name of Angelo Torres, they called him T-45, another guy called Toro, also Puerto Rican, and then a deceased brother, his name is Dino. Now, why did I get involved? A lotta the FMD's (Pedro's former street gang in the Bronx) who are no longer around got absorbed into the Rat House. A lotta the ex-bikers got absorbed into the Rat House. So it was a natural sequence or chain of events. We all got back together, but under a different name. A lotta guys from the

Bronx, Brooklyn, Queens . . . we used to, you know, sniff out confidential informants, and get rid of them. Some of the fellas went to extortion and they caused a lot of war. Because whether he's right or wrong, the war's already started, they shed his blood, so we had no choice but to get involved. But . . . we used to make the peace between the Dominicans and the Blacks. A couple of times we couldn't, 'cause brothers shed already, and that's just like the unforgivable sin. Before it got to that stage, if I happened to be in that prison I'd say "No." You know, you're not going to let good people go against each other. If you have real beef with him, then listen, you two guys fight it out. You wanna go hand-to-hand, or you wanna go knife-to-knife, but you two guys, as two individuals. Don't drag two of us into this, or the two countries for nothing. Believe it or not prison administrations started seeing that I had a lot of influence and it helped me somewhat because they would think twice about putting me in the box and administrative segregation. They'd say, "This guy's an asshole but he keeps the peace." So it helped, and then again it didn't help. 'Cause they're afraid of people with power like that and especially a thinker. (August 10, 2006)

The Trinitarios

A second group that also featured among interviewees were the Trinitarios. This group was formed in the late 1980s and was open only to Dominican inmates to provide a sense of cultural affinity and solidarity, taking its name from the three founders of the Dominican Republic: Juán Pablo Duarte, Francisco Del Rosario Sánchez, and Ramón Matías Mella, who had formed a secret society in 1884 with the same name to fight for Dominican independence. The group has a tough reputation within prison but is not seen as a predatory organization out to expand its power and influence. Rather, it is a disciplined, self-defense group that does not shy away from conflicts with other inmate organizations when the need arises. This is how Tony and J. explained their reasons for joining:

D.B.: How was Rikers? Was it a time of a lot of violence?
TONY: Yes, yes. There were problems, just to talk on the phone. But since I'm trained I'm not problematic. I have practiced every sport, I'm trained in all the 'hoods and I can fight. Then there are those Blacks who smoke crack and in winter what happens is they rob your car to get into prison, to be away from the cold. That's when they start lifting weights and they get like Tyson and they're crackheads! Then, when you have to talk on

the phone they give you about 6 minutes or a slot time after 5:00 pm. But you know if you talk with your family one day or you have to call someone after 5:00 when they arrive from work you have to slam too for them to respect you. Then one starts getting into the system, learning how it is. In the state system I organized myself with the Trinitarios, the families, the Dominicans of color. We were like among the first to have its own estatuto, not to rob, not to fuck faggots, but to take care of ourselves. That was while I was there, we had that respect, a lot of discipline. Immediately I was deported I didn't want to know about that. I don't talk about it to anyone. (April 1, 2003)

Julio talked about the threat of being victimized and the difference between the culture in New York City's jail, Rikers, and the upstate prisons, which can be close to the Canadian border.

> D.B.: You spent 1 year in Rikers; were there a lot of gang conflicts?
> JULIO: Yes, but I learned the state of that. While I was there at Rikers I was calm. I was working at the laundry room. I wouldn't get in trouble but when I went upstate, there it's different.
> D.B.: How is it?
> JULIO: When you arrive at first upstate to make time, you've never been there before, there are a lot of guys with felonies, a lot of veterans who believe that they're gonna take you up. That's what motivated us to organize, to be the Trinitarios. This is what we're gonna be to protect us as Dominicans because we have to be together or they're gonna exploit us. That's what motivated me to get into this with no intentions to go beyond that. In this moment you have to be there because you are alone, you can't call, "CO," because then you're snitch. If you're stabbed and you call the cops, then you're a snitch, and that's worse because wherever you're transferred to, when they see you, they open you up. . . . (February 18, 2003)

Thus, there are good reasons for the existence of the group, and, as Julio says, prisoners have nowhere to go with complaints. He recounts how the group started, amid a system of inmate semiotics, often linked to themes of nationalism.

> D.B.: What was the group's history?
> JULIO: There was already the Latin Kings and the Ñetas and there was nothing else. Some Dominicans arrived, transferred, and got together and

became a family. Then in Wyoming we started to talk, those of us that were there, who were older. We saw the groups of Boricua who would take your sneakers, steal your cigarettes. "Listen, let's get together here to take care of each other." So we go to church and look for black and green necklaces, break it down and put it together, small green balls and small black balls. The black one is for unity and the green is the symbol for bananas. So the Kings wear amarillos, the Ñetas would say hi with the fingers like this, and we go like this: God, patria, and liberty. (February 18, 2003)

As stated earlier, the group largely stays within the walls of the prison and does not have the ambition to take it to a subcultural level in civilian society. Tony was adamant that what he did in prison stayed in prison and that the context for his actions should not be confused with the person he is now. Tony felt threatened just by talking about that possibility.

TONY: There are still some who go on with that. Now there are a lot of groups, like the Bloods, or the 42, those are focused on gang activity. I have experienced this in prison but I have no relation of any kind with these since my deportation. I mean I've been in contact but I don't want it. I keep the pictures because it was me who was there, that's my green group, but I don't talk to anybody about that because I don't want anybody to know that I participated in that in case they think that I'm doing that here. And if I don't want problems you don't want to be associated with someone from the family who still does a robbery. No, no, the devil is not taking me away. (April 1, 2003)

The Prison and Street Gangs: The Ñetas and the Latin Kings

The Ñetas

Only two subjects spoke of having been members of the Ñetas, a prison organization in Puerto Rico that has a presence both on the streets and in prisons on the mainland United States. Celio's use of prison language is striking. His reference to the group as "brothers of pain" denotes a highly politicized sense of raison d'etre and empathy between members that refers to itself as the Association of the Imprisoned.[9] As Celio put it, he learned about equality through this group. His reference to himself as a "consultant in the discipline" and as "scheming" (i.e., joining the gang) shows how prison subcultures appropriate the language of civil society to express roles and actions in this parallel world of "nations."

> CELIO: If I had to beat someone who had it coming, who made a mistake then you gotta beat. Among ourselves we can't fight, because we're brothers of pain but if I fought and that guy earned 10 slams then I would give them with pleasure, because it's like a discipline that one has to follow, and I was a consultant in the discipline. After I was transferred to the White Bear at Aguadilla, I didn't scheme, like they say over there. What I did was eating and keeping quiet over there. But after I arrived at Bayamón I did scheme and I was a consultant again. I completed my prison sentence and that's when the feds came looking for me. But it was a nice experience, in spite of all the work that it means. I mean it's nice in the sense that you have to learn a lot and you're not afraid that someone might hurt you because the prisoners take care of each other. We're brothers of pain. Even if you're a killer, even if you've killed 15, even if you're a thief, everyone is equal. (March 3, 2003)

The Latin Kings

Of all the groups, the Latin Kings were the most popular. Eight of the subjects had been members of this group that, although originally started in Chicago, has a presence throughout the United States, especially on the East Coast.[10] Both Andres and C. discussed their reasons for joining and concurred that social support was crucial, especially for individuals who felt vulnerable.

> D.B.: Did you get involved in any prisoners organizations while in prison?
> ANDRES: Well, I had to be with the Latin Kings because I felt hopeless, I felt lonely. There were always fights, revolts, and since they were Latinos, I joined their gang, because, because at least I received from them the support that I needed in order to survive. Prison is something difficult for a human being. Being in a country where you don't have a family, where you only know a few people that had left before you to the United States. (March 4, 2004)
> D.B.: Could you tell me about that organization, the Latin Kings? Why did you find yourself obligated to join?
> CARLOS: Well, I benefited as follows. I received their support in case I had, let's say, any controversy with another person. They would at least come out for me, to defend me, this way at least I avoided having to confront a group of people alone. Then I looked for their support to be able to

have like a family inside prison. I felt I had the support of someone who could represent me when I had any type of difficulty, any problem. (June 7, 2003)

Alex's experience is somewhat different. For him it was a case of joining a subculture that he was previously used to. He felt privileged in that he had personally come into contact with the founder of the New York State Latin Kings, the infamous King Blood. Alex explained the day-to-day structure of the organization and the culture of violence within which it operated.[11]

ALEX: When I got to Collins I used to be a good friend of Humble, do you know who Humble is?

D.B.: Yeah, William Humble.

ALEX: He was the best there. And then I like disputing, I like that, I like invading and shit. So, we became really good friends because every time there was problem I was there and he checked me out. One day he said: "Yo, come here. Why are you always there every time there is beating around," I said, "I like that shit." "Do you wanna be a Latin King?" I said, "What?" I didn't know what was a Latin King. "Yeah, but we don't wear colors nothing like that." So fine and then that's when we started 1986. Then from there I went to Franklin and became crowned. I wasn't crowned by King Blood, he didn't bless me, it was another King who was there.

D.B.: In Franklin or in Collins?

ALEX: In Collins, because he was locked up, you know. Then, I don't know something happened and I didn't like it. I didn't like one part of it, that we gotta jump everybody against one, I didn't like that. I said, "Man, why we gotta do that? Only one man and we fucking forty jump on him. No I don't like this shit, I'm gonna get out of this shit. I'm not gonna say, "I'm a King" no more. After that there was a problem with a King, right, big problem. A Moreno (African-American [added by the authors]) beat the shit out of him, so they went and beat the shit out of the Moreno, so now the First Crown wanted to see me: "I want you to be a Latin King. We appreciate what you've done, blah, blah, blah." I said, "No, no, I don't want part of it." He said, "No because I'm gonna get transferred out of here I need somebody like you. Please, you've already shed blood for this Nation, and you're not a Latin King, you know, please." I said, "Ok, when you leave I'll be the First Crown." Then, some of them was jealous. "He just got here, how can he become a First Crown if he just came here," and he said "Ok, he just got here and he already shed his blood and you haven't done shit for the Nation." And that's how I became the First Crown.

D.B.: This was in Franklin?

ALEX: Franklin, yeah. Then I had it nice, I had those niggers running. I said, "If you got a problem nobody is gonna jump on no fucking body, ok, you gonna fight only one on one. We gotta prove and show the Nation men that we got hearts, show me you're fucking Kings, the one who doesn't take it I'm gonna beat the shit out of him." I used to get beat too, you know. Then I went to Altona and I became Third Crown, because sometimes you be First Crown, sometimes you be Third, I was always the Third or the First. Because the First is the one who give the orders and the Third, he is the chief of commanding. The one who gets the work done. Then they sent two brothers to beat me up and they were surprised when that didn't do shit to me. Forget about it. Then, before I left, there was a problem with the Kings and the Ñetas and I got in, because if you're a King you're always gonna be a King, you can never be nothing but a King and over there in jail they keep it real, it is very dangerous. You gotta respect it even if you're not in a gang. If you're the First Crown, right, and I'm a manito, for me to speak to you I gotta go to the Fifth Crown first, 'cause the Fifth Crown is an advisor, like your attorney, the one that gives you counsel. If you're First Crown you give the orders to the Third Crown: "Yo, you're going to war" then the Third Crown speaks to all. The Fourth don't do nothing but keep the money. (March 5, 2003)

As seductive as prison gang life can be, the paranoia, sadism, and internal feuding got to be too much even for Alex. The tipping point occurred when he became a victim of the gang's internal order system:

ALEX: But we kill each other! That's one thing I used to say to Willie, "They wanna kill each other." I remember I did some stuff to a brother up in Clinton, they wanted to hit me, stab me. I said, "What kind of brothers are we, we're not fucking brothers. You know, if you respected me you would call me outside, "You're in a violation, don't touch the crown for 6 months." When you're really a Latin King, they hurt you by taking your crown. Don't give your brothers a salute or nothing. Not sending your freaking brothers to beat you up. They even got Latin Kings that became Bloods for the treatment that Kings was giving them! (March 5, 2003)

And the Women Have Gangs, Too . . .

Most accounts of female inmates do not include much data on gangs. Rather, the general assumption is that women form "families" in the prison, with inmates playing the roles of mothers and children (Owen 1998), and not warrior gangs that struggle for control of the political economy or for power within the contested matrix of race and ethnic relations. Both Fermin and Elixida, however, found a different set of circumstances.

GIPSY ESCOBAR (G.E.): Tell me about your experience in prison?

ELIXIDA: Rikers Island is hell.

G.E.: Tell me why.

ELIXIDA: Oh, my God, there are lots of gangs, a lot of women kill there, everything happens in there. A hell.

G.E.: What type of gangs are there?

ELIXIDA: All of them: Latin Kings and Queens, the Bloods, lots, lots, and there is a great deal of racism inside, too much. The other women, the dark ones want to hit you, want to humiliate you, don't want you to eat. A lot of racism, even inside the officials.

G.E.: And you never belonged to any of those gangs?

ELIXIDA: No.

G.E.: And did you feel pressure on their part?

ELIXIDA: Yes, lots, lots. I was pregnant, one time I went to the table to eat the food, which was the worst thing in this world and she pushed me, a Black one, another inmate pushed me and I was gonna fall, pregnant. Lots of racism. The worst thing I've ever experienced.

G.E.: Tell me a little of what it was that those gangs that you mention did, the women of the Latin Kings. . . ?

ELIXIDA: They were the groups who fought.

G.E.: Against others. . . ?

ELIXIDA: To cut their face.

G.E.: Didn't they have like meetings for Latinas or . . .

ELIXIDA: The ones that have gangs are the Puerto Ricans and Blacks.

G.E.: And it was mostly to fight.

ELIXIDA: Yes, to jump on people who they didn't like.

G.E.: And you never had any problems with them?

ELIXIDA: No, because Blacks liked me, some Blacks did, others wouldn't let me do anything. (June 8, 2006)

D.B.: Did you make any friends in prison?

FERMIN: I made a friend, I used to help her out. She's a Puerto Rican friend from the Hudson County Jail; we went together to Clinton. I don't even remember her name, she was from the Ñetas. . . .

D.B.: Asociacion Ñeta?

FERMIN: Yeah. She had problems when she went to prison with the colors and the stuff, I never went into none of that. That's why I had so much problems because I didn't wanna be . . . .

D.B.: You didn't want join in.

FERMIN: No, my friend did, but not me, for what? They wanted me to be a Latin Queen, I said, "I'm no Latin Queen (laughs)." I never belong to that. I wanted a normal life. I didn't want a life from the ghetto, you know, forget it. I was scared. (May 7, 2006)

THE FEMALE PRISON EXPERIENCE

All the female subjects had harrowing tales to tell about their prison experience. Gang tensions, racial rivalry, humiliation by guards, and enormous levels of pain and suffering at being separated from their families. In much of the literature on female inmates, a familiar refrain is that the worst part about prison is the ending of the inmate's family role. Both Elixida and Fermin talked about this in their accounts, but first they talked about surviving, about creating a persona that prevented them from being taken advantage of by the other inmates. For outsiders, this view of some female inmates as predators might seem surprisingly masculine.

G.E.: How were your relationships with other female inmates?

ELIXIDA: More or less ok, because I wasn't afraid of them, I didn't let them humiliate me, I pretended to be strong so that they wouldn't do whatever they wanted to me.

G.E.: Did you make any friends?

ELIXIDA: Yes, I made lots of friends, lots of friendships. Lots of good women, quiet, who were in prison. There were a lot of innocent inmates.

G.E.: Based on what you saw what was the composition of the inmates?

ELIXIDA: Blacks, Dominicans, Colombians, Puerto Ricans.

G.E.: Lots of Dominicans?

ELIXIDA: Si.

G.E.: Lots of Colombians?

ELIXIDA: Yes, lots. More than other nationalities. Puerto Ricans weren't too many, lots of Jamaicans. Yes, all the countries. And more Blacks, because there are more Blacks than any other in prison. (June 8 2006)

FERMIN: Oh, my God, I was scared when I first got there. I thought it was like in the movies, and I never had done nothing wrong in my life. That was the first time and I went right to the big house. I thought they were gonna rape me. All of that. I had all the big shit on me plenty of times.

D.B.: They did?

FERMIN: Yeah, 'cause they said I was a White girl, you know, and blacks don't like Whites. And I was like, "No, I'm Spanish, I'm Dominican." And then they didn't bother me anymore, you know. I went to "lock up" once because I broke some girl's face with a tray. She had me up to here, you know, every time she takes my food and I didn't eat, so, you know, the usual stuff. After a while I know how to act in jail, like they say, I talk like they talk. (The interviewee stands up and makes a menacing face holding her fists out like she's going to attack someone.) "I got my love for you baby" and this and that. I learned how to talk the street talk. I did not know that before, you know what I'm saying. I adjusted to the system. I had no choice. You have to fight or you get your ass kicked every day.

D.B.: How long did it take you to adapt to the prison life?

FERMIN: Like 5 months. (June 7, 2006)

Fermin spent almost 5 years in prison, and Elixida served just over 2 years. The most humiliating part of Elixida's experience, however, was giving birth to her child while incarcerated. Bringing an innocent baby into the world under such criminalizing and oppressive circumstances is a tragic irony.

G.E.: Let's talk about the prison.

ELIXIDA: We used to sleep like 50 inmates in a room. Everything happened in there, everything, women having sex with one another in the bathroom, one sees a lot of ugly things.

G.E.: And then they put you in a cell for pregnant women.

ELIXIDA: Later they put me in a building for pregnant women only. It was a little better.

G.E.: And tell me how it was when you had your baby.

ELIXIDA: They took me to Elmhurst Hospital. There I had my son, foot-cuffed, tied all the time. Only when I was pushing the baby did they let me free, but then at once they handcuffed me and I had two policemen with me, one in front and one behind, looking at me, with the pain and everything, always.

G.E.: As if you were going to run away?

ELIXIDA: They sent me back with the baby to prison. I filled out an application because I didn't want them to take away my son, I wanted them to let me have my son. There I lasted one year. After the child was one year old, the same day he was one, they sent him home, because he couldn't be with me any longer. That's what hurt me the most in my life.

G.E.: That separation.

ELIXIDA: That separation, because I had him the whole day and night, every hour and then they take him away from you. Nothing hurt me as much as that in my life!

G.E.: How much longer did you last in prison after they took your son away from you?

ELIXIDA: About one more year.

G.E.: And you sent the child to your friend Catalina?

ELIXIDA: To Catalina.

G.E.: Did they bring you the child for visits?

ELIXIDA: Sometimes but I didn't want it anymore because it hurt them. They came crying, they just wanted to stay with me there. (June 8, 2006)

Strange things happen in prison, and relationships can develop across the inmate–officer divide. Perhaps this happens in women's prisons because there are so many more men working in such institutions than females in the male institutions. Nonetheless, for Fermin it was both a surprising and a pleasant experience to receive support from this unlikely source, providing her with some respite from the unforgiving attention of the criminal justice system. Eventually, however, it amounted to little and she was deported anyway. For the second time in her life, she was wrenched away from her children.

FERMIN: All of a sudden I got a big money order, two packages and stuff. I didn't know who was sending me that. Then they send me a number, so, I call him. He told me, "Take my address, you can come to my house and get an address for when you come out on parole." And I was like, "How do you know I'm gonna go out on parole if they're gonna deport me?" And he said, "No, they're not going to." And it turned out that the guy was Sergeant X from Hudson County Jail. He was this guy that fell in love with me the first time I got locked up, and he helped me out a whole lot.

D.B.: Really?

FERMIN: He helped me out with everything: clothing, money, every week. It was incredible. He even rented me an apartment. But I didn't love him, you know. But he helped me a whole lot. A sergeant from the Hudson County Jail fell in love with me (laughs).

D.B.: Interesting.

FERMIN: Yeah. I used to call him all the time. He was older like in his 60s.

D.B.: So, you get taken by surprise when you're informed that you're gonna be deported.

FERMIN: They told me, "You're going home, baby." And I said, "What are you saying? Why don't you just shoot me? I don't wanna go back over there." Ha, ha, he was laughing, he was laughing. And I told him, "Why, why, why?" And they explained because of that dime. But it's a dime (this is related to a charge that the subject maintains was the deciding factor in her deportation case [added by the authors]). I thought they would give me a chance so I can go to court.

D.B.: So, you were with your children again at this time.

FERMIN: Yeah, I had my kids. But they don't care, they don't care.

D.B.: So, that must have been awful.

FERMIN: Yeah, my kids went to see me when immigration caught me, they took me to Hudson County Jail, 'cause I was living in New Jersey Park. They took me back to Hudson County Jail and the guy from immigration, the guy from the jail came and picked me up and sent me to another jail, an immigration jail far away, near Trenton. I don't remember the name of the jail. They said my kids were running after the van. Priscilla was running after the van, "Mommy, mommy," but I didn't wanna see it. It was awful. . . . (the interviewee is weeping). (June 7, 2006)

CONCLUSION

In this chapter, we explored the different prison experiences shared by our respondents. Most of the experiences were negative, although some respondents stated that they made the best of their situation and gained skills and knowledge that would be difficult to replicate elsewhere. Nonetheless, the time in prison was generally traumatic and life changing. The respondents adapted as best they could to their situations, using their own specific forms of social and cultural capital to endure the years of captivity for their crimes. The circumstances of the crimes were wide-ranging, from transporting drugs (sometimes unbeknownst to the subject), to being a player in the drugs economy, to being the unsuspecting accessory in a money laundering and drugs trafficking enterprise, to homicide; however, they were nearly all played out in a lower-class environment. Most of the crimes related to one of the largest and most profitable aspects of contemporary capitalism, the illegal drug trade.

Whatever the background to the crimes, all the subjects served their time; they paid for their crime in the most punitive criminal justice system in the Western world. Furthermore, they served their time during a period when most of the rehabilitative supports from a previous era had been removed; even where such supports were present, they were not allowed to avail themselves of such opportunities because they were noncitizens. The most insidious aspects and characteristics of the human condition—racism, violence, alienation, vindictiveness, humiliation, exploitation, predation—all appeared in the respondents' recollections. None of the respondents entered therapy once they were released from prison to help them cope with the profound psychological trauma and sensory deprivation they had experienced. They kept these stories inside themselves until, per chance, they encountered an empathetic social scientist interested in such narratives or—perhaps much more likely—they are re-institutionalized in a mental health facility. If they are fortunate, they find a relationship within which they can unburden themselves. In the classic prison study by Sykes (1958:64), he stated that, although it might be assumed that the normalcy of torture and death for the incarcerated has been replaced by a Western rational system of deprivation of liberty and material goods, "we must explore the way in which the deprivations and frustrations pose profound threats to the inmate's personality or sense of personal wealth."

7.1 ROGER, A DEPORTEE WHO WAS ACTUALLY A U.S. CITIZEN. SEVEN YEARS AFTER BEING DE-PORTED, HE EVENTUALLY PROVED TO U.S. IMMIGRATION THAT HE WAS ILLEGALLY REPATRIATED (*PHOTO:* WILLIAM COSSOLIAS).

CHAPTER SEVEN

DEPORTED

I lost my residency for $15 after I worked for over ten years there! Taking money out of my check, they didn't care about any of that. No, instead I'm deported to this country like a dog, without clothes or anything. Woken up at 4 AM, "You're going to your fucking country now!" Fuck that, man. They're going to pay for that sooner or later. They're going to pay because they're doing too much injustice . . . tied up behind by the feet, by the hands, they don't even give you food in the airplane. A small sandwich like this (puts his fingers together) and a small glass of soda and I'm tied to that airplane. To go to the restroom you have to be tied up, too. It's an abuse. You're a prisoner inside an airplane. What are you going to do, jump from up there?

(MR. S., DEPORTEE, APRIL 5, 2003)

DANNY: They deport more Dominicans than from other countries. Every week there are 50, 40, 30, every week, and this government doesn't care about it. Every week it's people and more people, more deportees. Next week about 70 will come for little things not worth it, for half a gram, deporting somebody, for half a gram! (Feburary 22, 2003)

AS DESCRIBED AT the end of chapter 6, the act of deportation is harrowing and deeply traumatic, not only for deportees but for their loved ones as well. In the criminological literature, this is sometimes referred to as "collateral damage" (Mauer and Chesney-Lind 2002; Petersilia 2003; Uggen and Manza 2002; and Travis 2002). This phrase is mostly used to explain the broader, unseen, and often unconsidered ramifications of sending the hundreds of thousands of men and women to prison in the United States as a matter of course. Little has been written about the social consequences of deportation, even though tens of thousands of U.S. residents who have significant social and cultural ties to the United States have been deported after they have completed their prison sentence for their crimes.

What does it feel like to be deported? How are the legal processes experienced? Who plays a role in this tragic saga? In this chapter we focus on the experience of being deported, the anguish of the deportee, the absurdity and inhumanity of the court room drama, the vindictiveness of the state, and the logics of immigrant social control policies.

In the rest of this book, we will critically analyze the act of exile, which is the "natural" result of the three wars on the globalized "other": the war on drugs, the war on terrorism, and the war on the immigrant. In this analysis, we must remember the "bulimic" character of this process (Young 1999), i.e., the United States, in all its mythical splendor, culturally sucking in immigrants, socializing them in the factory system of schooling, feeding them the promise of social mobility, and then expelling them through a celebrated yet cruel performance of so-called due process. The actors and actresses play out similar roles on different stages of the criminal justice system across the United States every day of the week. Sometimes the immigrant subjects are not even given a court in which they can perform their role; for the sake of costs, some are granted only a video conference, during which they are told of their inevitable deportation by a judge hundreds of miles away.

We begin this chapter with a long, reflective field note taken during a deportation hearing for a Dominican-born man who had been living and working legally in Manhattan for twenty-seven years.[1] He and his family lived "just off Bleeker," that fabled thoroughfare of the West Village where tens of thousands of immigrants have staked their claim to be "Americans." This exposé of the courts and the legal process of deportation is followed by an analysis of five themes prominent in subjects' experiential accounts: (1) resignation to one's fate, (2) incompetent or fraudulent legal representation, (3) experience of the immigration detention camps, (4) legal resistance, and (5) the flight back.

Field Notes (February 13, 2006): We arrive at Eastern Correction facility in Ulster County, New York State, a fortress-like maximum security prison built for human disposables around the 1920s. The building is impressive in its colossal, symbolic might, peering over the Catskills like some hungry ogre. Nearby is the Ulster correctional facility, which houses the immigration court. I enter its doors through a reception area and undergo the usual inspections by its security personnel. As we walk back and forth through the security scanner while our bags, coats, and shoes pass slowly through an x-ray machine, the guard in charge emphatically announces: "No keys, pens, cell phones, or pills, just some papers needed for the court for those who are testifying."

Meanwhile, lounging on two rows of padded black plastic chairs, seven guards are hanging around relaxed, friendly, and chatting while observing the events, perhaps this is the end of their shift or they are awaiting the beginning of it. The guard in charge returns to the business at hand.

"You're here for the Delgado trial?" directing his question at me.

"Yes, and this is my assistant," I responded, motioning to my colleague who is standing at my side.

"They only said one of you was coming. We only have a permission slip for one person. We've already had twenty-one of them come in. That's the most we've ever had here for a court appearance. Usually it's three or four but twenty-one! That's almost more than our entire staff here sometimes," he adds with a wry smile. "Isn't that true guys," he says, addressing his fellow workers. "Sometimes we only have seven people here on duty and there's this family with twenty-one of them!"

"Well, I guess they're all here to support him," I retorted.

The guard glances up, raising his eyebrows, "I suppose so. I suppose that's one way of looking at it. So you're the expert witness, are you? You do a lot of this? I mean, you know a lot about this deportation thing?"

"Yes, I do a lot of it," I reply. "I spent a year in the Dominican Republic seeing how deportees are living. It's very difficult for them, very difficult. There are no jobs, the cops blame them for everything. They don't have a chance."

The guard looks at me straight on, shakes his head and says, "Crazy isn't it? I mean, they've already done their bids and then they get this at the end of it. I guess they'll have to come right back over here again, won't they. You know, they'll have to get in any way they can and just hope they don't get caught cuz you know it's another three years in the federal pen if they do."

"Yes," I said, somewhat taken aback at the guard's sympathy and candor, "That's what some of them do but then there's a lot that stay over there and try to make it."

Finally, he finds the permission letters, hands us each a visitors' badge, and escorts us to an office positioned next to two security gates. There our hands get stamped with a special ink that can only be read by a special machine.

"There'll be another guard here in a minute to escort you," says our man-in-charge, "Here she comes now."

Standing on the other side of the double gate is a tall, well-built Hispanic female who nods at us, then signals to someone in the security office. Suddenly, the gate on her side is electronically opened and she enters into a sort of no man's land. The gate behind her abruptly closes, immediately followed by the gate in front of her opening. After several minutes of this security ritual she is standing next to us.

"You got everything?" she inquires.

I nod affirmatively, a little bemused at the question.

"Let's go then," she continues and gestures to a guard to open the gate again. Our escort is affable and jovial and we quickly strike up a conversation as we traverse the grounds.

"How long have you worked here?" I ask.

"Ten years," she answers, "Came from Bedford Hills."

"Yes, I know it. It's the prison for female inmates," I reply, "Did you like it?"

Her pace slows slightly as she turns her head toward me, as if for emphasis.

"The women? Oooh! They're crazy," she answers, elongating the word 'crazy.' "Compared to the men, pure crazy."

"And here? How are the inmates here?" I respond.

"Here, they're fine, no problem."

We reach the immigration court via a path that passes between several inmate dormitories. For a prison (or a distribution center for recently adjudicated inmates mainly coming up from Rikers Island, which this is), the accommodation looks relatively cheery and clean. The surroundings are bucolic with snow-capped hills providing the backdrop and the sound of a rushing stream breaking the silence. Of course, I can't help thinking how ironic it all is, the inmates so unfree while this beautiful wintry nature appears as free as a bird.

At the entrance to the immigration court building another guard greets us, inspects our visitors' badges, and checks our names against a list. He then escorts us to a room where those asked to testify must congregate and wait to be called. While waiting, I talk to Mr. Delgado's father, mother, niece, and fourteen-year-old son. The father and mother are clearly agitated, talking almost manically about the need for their son to come home and to put an end to this tragedy. They talk as if they are trying to wake up from a nightmare.

"He should never have pleaded guilty," he says in a heavily accented Dominican Spanish, "the lawyers said if he pleaded guilty he would only do three years. He never said anything about being deported. He said he might have to do fifteen years if he didn't plead guilty. My son didn't do anything. He's a good boy. He's always lived with his mother and father. How can they do this to us? All he wanted to do was play baseball. When he couldn't play anymore he started to drink. He started to get depressed. But why does it end up with this. Oh God, Oh Maria, we are good religious people, we go to church. He was raised a good boy. Why this?"

The father continues in the same desperate vein, speaking rapidly. He is not willing to accept what is happening or what might be about to take place. The mother is the same. She starts to pray and calls upon God to help reunite her with her son.

"I am an old woman, I have terrible blood pressure, I cannot take the stress. My heart, my heart can't take it. I love my son. I don't want to see him taken away. He's my baby, my son, I can't stand it, I can't."

The niece then starts to explain to me about the background to the case. She recounts how her uncle got into a physical altercation with someone in a bakery when he was drunk and how the owner of the bakery called the police two days later when her uncle returned to buy something.

"There was no evidence, nothing," the niece intoned. "They couldn't produce anything that he stole, nothing. There was no weapon. It was just this guy's word and my uncle was drunk. My uncle is a good man. He wouldn't hurt anyone. They forced him to do this, to say that he was guilty. You know how they do. We are a vulnerable people. We are Latino immigrants, when the lawyers tell these things to us we believe them. When they say that you'll do fifteen years you believe them. To us they are the law. We are always afraid, always. That's why he's in this mess. It's crazy. What kind of justice is this?"

Suddenly a guard appears, "A Dr. Brotherton? Is there a Dr. Brotherton here?"

"Yes, that's me," I said, and I bid my farewell to the family.

Inside the court room, seated along the back and the front side walls, are the rest of Mr. Delgado's family members, including his five sisters, his seven-year-old son, his nieces, nephews, and brothers-in-law. It's an example of the central importance of family in Dominican life, especially when this micro-community is under such pressure.

The judge beckons, "Dr. Brotherton, please stand here and raise your right hand."

"Do you swear to tell the truth and nothing but the truth, so help you God?"

"I do sir," I said.

"Please take a seat," said the judge.

The lawyer for Mr. Delgado looks at me, smiles and begins his cross-examination. He first asks me to describe who I am and what I do. He then asks a series of questions that revolve around whether or not deportees are likely to be tortured by the Dominican government or whether the police will torture them with the complicity of the government. I did my best to paint a picture that fitted this scenario but I couldn't honestly say that torture is something deportees should expect. Rather, I said that in the present climate where deportees are being scapegoated, then it follows that the police who are often authoritarian and out-of-control will abuse them. It also follows that many will land back in prison, after being put in preventive custody. Given the nature of the

Dominican prison system, its appalling lack of resources, and the normalization of brutality that goes on inside, it is likely that such deportees will suffer physical and psychological harm. The judge then countered that this was not the same as torture. Physical abuse and beatings by the police do not meet the criteria, he said. What was torture? It was the government-sanctioned use of extreme pain to extract information from a subject. It was the pulling out of people's finger nails, the attachment of electrodes to people's testicles, and the extraction of teeth without anesthetic. That was torture.

"As I have said, time and time again, Mr. Crichter (Mr. Delgado's lawyer), you fail to make the case that deportees will be tortured at the behest of the Dominican government. Rather, you assert repeatedly that, in general, harm will come to these deportees. I have no doubt that the country we are sending them to is a bad place. I have no doubt that the deportees do not wish to go there and that life will be difficult for them. I have no doubt that for some of them it will lead to serious harm. But that, according to the law of the United States, is not the same as torture. If I were to allow such evidence, if I were to agree with you that that is torture, this appeal will simply be turned down at the next level, which is the Board of Appeals in Washington. They have done this to me already. I had a gentleman here who was going to be sent back to Barbados with full-blown AIDS. The man desperately needed his daily cocktails. His lawyer argued that if he were sent back there would be no chance that he would continue to be treated and therefore be kept alive. I agreed with him and I ruled that in such a case we would be sending this man to his death. The Board of Appeals disagreed with me and sent him to what I am almost certain was his death. That, Mr. Crichter, is the law of this land."

The judge's words unintentionally exposed and explained the depth of cruelty and injustice that characterize these policies. Here was one of the firmest believers in American law condemning its lack of morality and rationality simply by recounting the evolution of a case that he had just tried. I'm not sure how this was received by all who sat there, but for me it was absolutely clear that poor Mr. Delgado will assuredly be spending much of the next twenty years in a country he hardly knows.

"If you wish to stay here and watch the rest of the proceedings, Dr. Brotherton, then please do so," said the judge.

"Thank you, your honor. I would very much like to observe the rest of the hearing," I answered and took my seat in the middle of the court room.

"Who is your next expert witness, Mr. Crichter?" boomed the judge.

"I want to call Hector Delgado, the father of my client, judge," said the lawyer.

The seventy-five-year old father entered the room escorted by a guard. He stood in the witness box next to the judge, who asked him if he spoke English.

"No, señor," he answered, whereupon the translator, a dark-skinned, middle-aged Latina seated in front of me to my right, began to translate word for word, exclamation for exclamation, the statements of the next two experts in this hearing.

The lawyer for the defense began to ask Mr. Delgado about how many times he had returned to the Dominican Republic during the last ten years. Mr. Delgado answered that he used to go regularly while his parents were alive. His father lived to be 95 and his mother 104, he proudly stated. But when they died in the late 1990s he would go less, and then when his son got locked up in 2003 he hardly went at all. The lawyer then asked him about what he thought his son would be facing in the Dominican Republic. Mr. Delgado answered, "Nothing but crime and delinquency . . . nothing but hardship, problems, injustice."

"Do you think your son will be tortured when he goes back?" asked the lawyer.

The father stood there and wondered for a while. He tried to grasp the real meaning of the question that in the eyes of the court, by saying yes this was the only way he could get his son to stay in this country. Finally, he said,

"Yes. He will face torture."

"How do you know, Mr. Delgado?" asked the lawyer.

"Because that is the kind of place my country is. It is a place where the police kill people for nothing, absolutely nothing. They don't care about anybody, especially the deportees."

"Have you seen the police kill anybody?" asked the lawyer.

"Yes, I have," answered the father.

"Can you tell us about it?" asked the lawyer.

"In the neighborhood where I used to live in Santiago I saw a jeep full of police come up and pull out their rifles and go boom, boom to some guy. He fell dead. I couldn't believe it. I said to a neighbor, 'What are they doing?' 'The police have just shot a guy,' the neighbor said. I didn't want to stay there. I moved away immediately."

The father then makes a gesture with his hands as if he's pushing away the words he had just uttered, as if brushing away a memory.

"So you actually saw the police kill someone?" said the judge.

"Yes, I did. I saw them kill this man and then bundle him into the back of a jeep and drive off. That's what the police do in my country. That's why I am so afraid to let my son, my only son go back there. I want him to stay here, judge. Oh God, Oh Maria, I want him to stay here with his family. Please, please, give him clemency. We are all known in our neighborhood. We have been here for thirty years. America has been good to us. We love America. We had nothing when we came here. My son drinks and gets depressed. The police, the police, they find him and bring him home. They say, "Mr. Delgado, look after your son. We found him drunk again. He's got to take care of himself."

At this point Mr. Delgado starts to visibly shake. The people around the room are now howling in tears. The sisters, the brothers-in-law, the seven year-old son, and the defendant, nobody is immune from the rising tension that has been created by the questions and by the desperation in the father's creaking voice. The guard picks up a box of tissues and starts to hand them out. First one, then another, then literally dozens of tissues are being issued to the audience who cannot control their grief and sorrow. The judge then turns to the defense lawyer.

"Mr. Crichter, was all this necessary? Did you have to put this father through this? I am a man probably the same age or even older than Mr. Delgado and I have a son like Roberto. I feel for this man but he is unable to answer your questions in the way you would like. He has not been able to state factually that his son will face torture by the government when he returns and that is the crux of this case. So why do you put your witness through this? Why are you putting this family through this? Your job is to present a case to me, Mr. Crichter. You cannot help it if you don't have a case and I am afraid you don't have a case. We have been here now for four hours. Normally, this hearing would last one hour. But with all the family members here who have traveled so far from New York to see their brother, their uncle, their son and to support him, I have decided that this trial has to play itself out. There is no other way. But, I must tell you that I find it disagreeable and unnecessary to put people through such emotional turmoil and pain like this."

"I'm sorry, judge," says the lawyer, "I am just trying to show the court the probability of what faces my client. I have to work with what I have. I am just doing my job to the best of my ability."

"Do you have any questions counsel?" the judge asks the lawyer representing the government.

"No, judge," comes the reply.

"Mr. Delgado, please take a seat," instructs the judge in a pleasant but firm manner.

The father walks somewhat bewilderedly back to the center of the room and sits down a couple of seats to my left. I look at him and smile but he fails to respond. His face expresses a mixture of disbelief, frustration, and anxiety. How can this be happening to him at this stage in his life? He has gone through countless hardships to raise his six children. He left the country of his birth in 1972, seven years after the Revolution, in the middle of the bloody Balaguer dictatorship, with his entire family. He never had another child in the United States. He has managed so far to keep all his family together. Everyone was doing so well with the exception recently of his son. His daughters got married, they had beautiful children, lots of them. He still lives in the same house as when he moved here in that fateful year . . . and now this. How could he prepare himself for this moment when the very country that he has believed in all these years, that gave him an opportunity to be somebody, to live decently, to experience joy and happiness, how can this country do this to him, to his son? It doesn't make sense. It just doesn't make sense.

"Who do you want to call now?" the judge asks of Mr. Delgado's lawyer.

"I want to call the mother of Roberto Delgado," the lawyer replies.

"Are we going to see the same thing, Mr. Crichter? Are you going to put her through this, too? Does she know what torture is? Have you schooled her? Have you?" asks the judge.

"Yes, I think so," says the lawyer diffidently.

The mother is brought into the court room by the guard. She looks very tense, as if she is just holding it all together. On entering the witness box she goes through the ritual with the bible and sits down. The defense lawyer begins the questions.

"Do you follow what is going on in the Dominican Republic, Mrs. Delgado?"

"Yes, I try to," she says.

"How do you do this?" asks the lawyer.

"Through listening to the news, through friends," Mrs. Delgado replies.

"What do you think faces your son if he is deported to the Dominican Republic?" asks the lawyer.

"Delinquency, nothing but delinquency. Nothing good can come of this. I know he will face terrible things, I know this. My country will harm him, I know this."

"Do you think your son will be tortured if he is returned?" asks the lawyer.

The mother just sits after the question is translated. She looks apoplectically at the audience. God knows what's going through her mind, the question is too pointed, too harrowing to be answered.

"Do you understand the questions?" asks the judge.

Again, the mother just looks at the audience and pats her chest. She then begins to talk, as if channeling something from another universe.

"Yes, I believe something terrible will happen to him. I believe the police will hurt him. I can't bear to think about it. I don't want to talk about it. I don't want to think about this evil. Can I say something? May I say something?" the mother asks the judge.

"Yes, you may," replies the judge as he looks down at his feet as if to communicate "here we go again."

The mother then gets to her feet and raises her hands in the air as if praying in a Pentecostal church.

"Oh God, Oh Jesus, Oh Maria, I pray to you, release my son from this trial. Oh Judge, please forgive my son. Please have the power, the pity to allow my son to go free. Allow him to come back to his mother and father, that's all we ask. He's a good boy. He doesn't mean ill to anyone. What use is this to take him away from us and his children. Please, please I beg you. . . ."

The mother continues for several more minutes, beseeching the judge to release her son. The family members are again sobbing uncontrollably, men and women alike are howling in grief. Even one of the guards, a bulky African-American man, is beginning to break down and I see tears start to run slowly down his cheeks. The mother suddenly stops, turns away from the judge and, looking glassy-eyed, collapses into the chair and closes her eyes. There is now pandemonium in the court room and the judge orders one of the guards to call a nurse. After about three minutes, the mother comes around, having fainted, and is holding her chest and breathing heavily. One of her daughters runs over and holds her head, stroking her hair gently and whispering softly that "everything's alright," which is about the furthest thing from the truth right now.

At this point a nurse comes into the room with another guard, and between them they get the mother to her feet and take her outside and place her in a chair. They are joined outside by someone who looks like a doctor with a stethoscope round his neck. The mother does not return to the room, and we find out later that she has been taken to the hospital where she is diagnosed with having suffered a mild heart attack. The judge, looking exhausted and exasperated, turns to the defense lawyer.

"Now what, Mr. Crichter? Now who are we going to have? Please don't let's go through this again. It is not helping your case. It is not helping Mr. Delgado." But his questions are misdirected. It is not the family that doesn't have a case, or the lawyer, but in a humane society it is the U.S. government that is on the wrong side of the ethical, rational divide, and everyone in the court room knows it. I would wager that even the guards would agree that this inflexible policy leading to mass social exclusion and family fragmentation, targeting mainly black and Latino communities, is senseless. There are no winners, only losers, and it is costing the U.S. tax payer hundreds of millions of wasted resources.

"I would like to call Jessina X. . . , the niece of Robert Delgado," answers the lawyer, somewhat chastened by the flood of undermining comments from the judge and, of course, by the inability of most of his witnesses to speak to the almost impossible subject of torture.

The niece enters the door led by a guard and confidently strides to the witness box. I had spoken to her earlier, and she had told me that she had recently graduated from John Jay College of Criminal Justice. I asked her about the case and, though she was better informed than I was about the history, she had very little knowledge of the Dominican Republic except through the occasional holiday. Neither did she know too much about the finer details of the 1996 immigration act or the subsequent anti-terrorist acts, all of which were playing a role in the expulsion of her uncle. After swearing the oath and taking a seat, the questions begin once more.

"Do you understand what is facing your uncle, Roberto Delgado?" asks the defense lawyer.

"Yes, I do. I have read about cases like his on the internet and I have tried to do some research around the subject."

"So you know that the only way we can halt your uncle's deportation is through proving the probability of torture when he arrives there?"

"Yes," says the niece, "I understand that this is his only chance."

"So, what do you understand by torture?"

"Well, for me, it is the application of extreme forms of pain and punishment to someone in an attempt to get information and just to terrorize someone. This punishment can be physical, it can come from beatings but also from the denial of food to someone. It can also be psychological and emotional," the niece makes an impressive statement and surprises me at how cool, calm, and collected she can be under the circumstances.

"Thank you," says the lawyer. "So, do you think that this form of torture will be facing your uncle when he goes back to his homeland? If so, why do you think this will happen?" asks the lawyer, who is now beginning to regain some of his composure.

"Well, let me see," says the niece. "I can't say for certain that this will happen to him, but I do know how Dominican society feels towards deportees, and I do know how violent and brutal the police are. I can tell you that Dominicans think of deportees as less than human. They are nothing to them and are blamed for everything that goes wrong in the country. And if they are thinking this, then you can imagine what the police are thinking. The police simply treat them like dirt. They beat them, kill them, torture them, they do whatever they like to them."

"How do you know this?" asks the defense lawyer.

"Because when I've been back there for holidays, when I've been staying in the capital, I hear what people say about them, and I have had dealings with the police just driving around," answers the niece.

"Now hold on here," says the judge. "None of this means anything. This has nothing at all to do with the conditions of torture that need to apply in this case. For a start, your definition of torture is all wrong. As I've said before, it is about pulling finger nails, taking out teeth, attaching electrodes to testicles . . . that's torture. Not all this talk about being denied food and psychological punishment, that's not what we're talking about under this law. And as for giving testimony on the probability of torture, you've proceeded to talk about how bad the police are and how nasty the people can be toward deportees, but that's irrelevant, absolutely irrelevant. You have to be specific, factual. Mr. Crichter, once again I must ask you, have you prepared your witness?"

"Yes, judge, as much as I could. I am just trying to show that. . . ."

"I know what you are trying to show, Mr. Crichter, and I am trying to keep this trial focused and it is proving impossible." The judge then turns back to Ms. X. . . .

"Ms. X. . . , do you understand what I am saying?"

"Yes, judge. I understand what you are saying, but do you understand what I am saying? I think I understand what torture is and maybe it doesn't satisfy the needs of this court and maybe I have it all wrong, but I don't think so. It is this court that has it all wrong. If you want to know what torture is, this is torture. What you are doing to my uncle is torture. Look at it here! Look at what the laws are doing! It is tearing up our family. It is tearing my uncle away from his children, his mother, his father, and his loved ones. What justice is there in this? I have done my research. I have studied criminal justice and I don't see any here today. There is torture, yes, and it is here. This is torture, but there is no justice."

"Thank you, Ms. X. . . ," says the judge. "I understand your feelings, you may step down. Who do we have next, Mr. Crichter?"

"I would like to call the son of Roberto Delgado, Roberto Junior."

The new expert witness enters somewhat hesitatingly with his head bowed, led by a guard. He is a handsome boy with long, thick black hair. He stares at his father who looks back at him with great intensity and tears in his eyes. The judge is kindly toward him and gently asks him to take a seat after being sworn in. The judge turns to the lawyers and says, "Mr. Crichter, I am allowing this witness, but only for very few specific and direct questions. Do you understand? I want no repeats of what has gone on before."

"Yes, judge," says the lawyer, "I understand."

"Mr. Delgado, do you understand what might happen to your father?"

"Yes," says the boy, "he's going to be deported."

"And do you understand what is meant by torture?"

The boy looks at the lawyer and slowly looks down at his feet. After a while, he shakes his head. The judge says, "You have to say something, Roberto. You cannot just nod for the court." The boy returns the judge's look.

"No," says the boy, "I don't understand."

The lawyer now looks down at his feet and shakes his head. It is interesting how bodily gestures are starting to mimic one another.

"Ok," says the lawyer, "Ok, that's enough. You may step down Roberto. Please step down."

The boy looks up and turns to the judge. The judge says gently, "It's ok, just take a seat."

The boy goes to the middle of the room and sits behind his father. He cups his head in his hands and begins to sob, silently, his shoulders and upper body motioning up and down rhythmically, but there is no sound. As I look around, I see his little brother staring at him with tears running down his cheeks and his eyes swollen and red. It is heartbreaking for me, as I think of my own children and how they would be reacting if I were to be taken from them. The process is simply insane.

"Now, we have had all the witnesses, is that right Mr. Crichter?" says the judge.

"Yes, that's correct, judge," the lawyer answers.

"I have allowed this court all the time it takes to come to some kind of judgment. Up till now I see nothing that alters the opinion of the court that Mr. Delgado will be deported. He will be returned to his homeland after completing his sentence which, I believe, has five months more to run. Now, Mr. Delgado, before I fill out the forms confirming your deportation, do you have anything more to say?"

"Yes, judge, I do."

Mr. Delgado stands up and looks around the room. Tears are in his eyes, and his face, too, is swollen from the strain and the crying.

"I want to tell you and my family that I am no thief. I've never taken anything from anyone in my life, not even a pair of nail clippers. What happened to me was wrong. It was a miscarriage of justice. I agreed to a plea for something I didn't do. I thought I was gonna get a short sentence and then be released. I thought if I didn't do that I was gonna get fifteen years, that's what they threatened me with. No one told me I was gonna get this. Ok, I have a temper and I can get violent. It happens when I drink and I'd been drinking when all this happened. I don't remember much about it except the guy gets the better of me and I go home. That's about it. But I didn't steal nothing from nobody. All I wanted to be was a baseball player, that's all. I got a scholarship to some university but it didn't work out. I didn't get picked up and so I got depressed. I get very depressed and I start to drink. I know I need treatment for this but I don't need jail and I don't need to be torn away from everything I love. This is my life here. I've been here since I was a kid. This is all I know. Here's my family right here. I don't have no family where you wanna send me. What am I gonna do there? Where am I gonna live? How am I gonna see my children again? Where's the justice in all of this?"

"Why, Mr. Delgado, didn't you become a citizen like your sisters? Why?" asks the judge.

"Because I can't read or write, judge. I knew if I took the test I wouldn't be able to write down all those names of the states. I wouldn't be able to write down the answers to all those questions that they were gonna ask me, that's why. I got a scholarship to a college when I was a kid, somewhere in Oklahoma, to play baseball but they never taught me to read or write. It's as simple as that."

The words that come out of Mr. Delgado's mouth are astounding. It's as if this whole theater is an exercise in different levels of humiliation. I was thinking how much courage it took for him to make this statement. The bitter truth of his situation reveals itself in his suffering that happened long ago, not just in the last few years. The marginality of his race and class, the cynical, mass packaging of the American Dream, the shattered hopes of the parental immigrant generation, the children left fatherless, resentful and traumatized, these are all the truths embedded in his final plea. Only this time there was no bargaining. The decision was non-negotiable. Mr. Delgado didn't even bother to ask for an appeal. At this moment he was a broken man. The unassailable logic of the immigration laws won the day. They had gotten their man. He was ejected with seemingly due process in the American way through the court system. Of course, objectively, the odds were massively against him from the beginning, but the appearance was maintained—as the judge often remarked, "This trial will play itself out." As we exit the prison, I turned to the translator who had performed so magnificently throughout, never wavering in her concentration for a second.

"Do you do a lot of these hearings?" I ask her.

"Yes, all the time. I've been doing them for years," she answers.

"It was quite a day, wasn't it?" I follow up, rather inanely. "I bet these kinds of scenes are quite unusual aren't they? I mean, the intensity of it."

She looked at me a bit puzzled and then, in a quiet, matter-of-fact manner, she retorts, "No." She said, "They are quite common. I work under these conditions very frequently. It is a very emotional job. I try to keep calm and professional, to be of maximum service."

On the drive back to New York City, my colleague excitedly and vividly recounts how he experienced the day's extraordinary events. After a while he begins to focus on a single, seemingly undeniable conclusion: "What kills me about this country is its self-representation. How it continually tells the world that it's the freest, the most democratic place on earth and yet its practice is totally the reverse. What's the difference between what this country is doing and what the Soviet Union was doing? Tell me, what's the difference?"

EXPERIENCING THE LEGAL PROCESS OF DEPORTATION

There is a great deal we can learn from Roberto's experience of the deportation process as he struggled to understand the irrationality and vindictiveness of society's rules. For Roberto and his family, however, it is impossible to accept the finality of this action. It runs counter to their understanding of being "American" and of everything that this identity constitutes, i.e., legal legitimacy, justice, democracy, and opportunity. Roberto's parents came from a country that, in their experience, possesses none of these qualities—this was an important reason for their original departure. To have the country of their dreams turn against them so many years later is unimaginable. To have this country so willfully and painfully fragment their family, an institution which is still the foundation of most Dominican sociocultural life, creates an existential crisis from which both parents will never psychologically recover—it may indeed hasten their deaths.

Roberto and his family are not the only victims in this scenario; it is clear that everyone connected with this act is somehow tarnished and diminished, their humanity harmed, undermined, and questioned. Even the judge, on the one hand a stickler for the Weberian execution of bureaucratic procedure and on the other a man protesting the pain that the family must endure, is caught in an impossible situation as he tries to make the court process accountable and transparent, doing his best to be an "American" who believes in the existence of "due process" and the neutrality of the law. The contradictions are there for all to see, a massive disjuncture between the most basic principles of human rights that one should not inflict harsh and undue punishment on others and the practices of the immigration legal codes. As we consider these data we need to remember that, as the Chicago school sociologists saw it, the more society turns to coercive mechanisms for social control, the greater the failure of the project. In this experience of expulsion, as remembered by the subjects, it is hard to discern who or what benefits from the current policies.

RESIGNATION TO ONE'S FATE—OR "WHAT YOU GONNA DO?"

The subjects had a clear understanding of the odds stacked against them in battling the system to win some kind of justice for themselves and their families. Many had spent years in prison, felt the discriminating opportunity structures of employment, discovered that school was often little more than a tracking device for skilled and unskilled labor, and lived in neighborhoods that always seemed to have fewer amenities and facilities than the well-to-do areas they passed through on the subway trains and public buses. When it came to the criminal justice system, they learned early that "their" knowledge of the receiving country's culture is not what counts; in fact, it could condemn them to many years behind bars. They also learned that it is difficult to fight back (though not impossible) and that fatalism—another name for "knowing your place"—is a common condition of barrio and ghetto life. What else can explain why so many signed without protest the agreement to be deported during their prison stay? Was it simply the codified language of the dominant culture that assured this act of compliance, or was it another example of the power differential that shaped their everyday interactions with authority? The prisoners are expected to comply and they do; it is only some time after the fact that they more fully understand what they have done (Venator-Santiago (2005a) found that only 13 percent of his sample fought their cases).

ANDREAS: The DA (district attorney [added by the authors]) told my lawyers how I was gonna cut up for three years (accept a plea bargain with sentence [added by the authors]). He was like, "Are you sure you gonna cut up for three years? I was like, "Yeah, I'm gonna take that, I ain't got no other choice, all I gotta do is my time. If they're gonna deport me, they're gonna deport me, at least I'm gonna be in my country." But then on July 3rd I was in the Island (Rikers [added by the authors]) and a couple of DAs from Immigration wanted to see me. I was like, "Alright, first I need to speak with my mother and father," because they didn't know about anything. So I was calling my father and he was saying that he was gonna do his best to get me out and not let them deport me. But then he got mad at me. . . .

DAVID BROTHERTON (D.B.): Your dad got mad?

ANDREAS: He was like, "Don't sign that." I was like, "Yeah, I need to sign this, if I don't sign I'm gonna stay over here like for two more years trying to fight this case and they still gonna deport me, so am I gonna lose two more years of my life? No." So I signed out quick. (May 27, 2003)

JUAN: I cut a big deal, you know what I mean, and I only spent eight months.

D.B.: You were supposed to do seven years but you only spent eight months?

JUAN: Yeah, because I signed.

D.B.: Did you know what you were signing?

Juan: Yeah, I just wanted to get out. (March 1, 2003)

GUIDO: When I went to court to see the judge, they didn't even take the handcuffs off, they didn't take nothing, I'm telling them: your honor, can you please take these off? He said, "We can't do that." But I said, "Look, you have about 300 cops around here, where am I gonna go, with guns and everything." They said, "No." I couldn't even write, I couldn't sign a paper, nothing, you know, so I was telling them, I said, "Your honor, but who's gonna take care of my kids?" They said, "Don't worry, the government will take care of your kids. . . ." I said, "But it's not the same. You're not gonna be there like a father." He said, "You was in jail for such and such amount of time, so what are you telling me now? Who was there when you was in jail doing whatever?" I said, "But your honor, I already paid for what I did, now you're gonna send me back to the Dominican Republic, why would you that?" He said, "I can't help you, you're gonna have to go." At first I told him that I didn't wanna come to this country, so they said, "Which country do you wanna go to?" I told them, "I wanna go back to England." (laughs) He said, "You really want to go back to England? The process is about six months." I said, "I gotta stay six more months in jail?" He said, "Yep, and we gotta send a letter over there to see if they accept you. Do you have any family over there?" I said, "No, but I don't wanna go to the Dominican Republic, I wanna go to England." So they said, "Ok, now you're gonna have to wait six months and then we have to write to the Prime Minister to see if they're gonna accept you, and they are probably not gonna accept you (laughs)." So I said, "Ok, I wanna go back to my country." They wasn't gonna send me, right? I'm asking you. (May 26, 2003)

INADEQUATE OR FRAUDULENT REPRESENTATION

As noted in earlier chapters, a large part of being poor and living in the cultural margins is reflected in the access one has to legal resources, especially when confronting the state in a legal matter. Immigrant communities are particularly vulnerable as a result of language differences, and many members of this population rely on neighborhood law offices to protect their interests and help them negotiate the various interlocking systems of criminal justice, welfare, immigration, education, and so forth. Sometimes, immigrants who find themselves in "trouble" with the law are afforded legal representation at the public's expense, such as Legal Aid in New York City. In such circumstances, there is a reasonable chance they will get decent counsel from skilled and committed professionals. Professionals in the public system are often overextended, however, due to increasing case loads and a lack of adequate public financing, and we consistently heard complaints about the quality of representation and sometimes no representation (ten of the original sixty-five respondents claimed to have been defrauded by their lawyers). Of the total sample, only three respondents spoke positively of their representation, which is extraordinary given the gravity of the legal predicament facing each of them.

D.B.: You spent three years?

MIGUEL: In immigration.

D.B.: Where?

MIGUEL: In Buffalo.

D.B.: Upstate New York?

MIGUEL: Yeah.

D.B.: Why did it take three years to fight your case?

MIGUEL: Almost more than the time they gave me.

D.B.: Why did it take so long?

MIGUEL: Because, I got a private lawyer, my wife helped me out. He was putting appeals in. He said, "You got a good chance for staying in New York." So I got in one year, and I was deciding I wanted to leave but my wife and family said, "You waited one year, you can wait more." But working in there, taking all that time, seeing no chances, I couldn't do no more.

D.B.: Must have cost a lot of money!

MIGUEL: Yeah, I paid like almost $5,000 dollars. But he was a fucking thief lawyer, he kept saying, "You'll get out, you'll get out." But you never get out. (January 25, 2003)

LUIS2: Well, the lawyer that I had, I sued him because when I was incarcerated he told me, "Get me $2,500 because I'm getting you out." The mother of my friend, the one I was in prison with, got me the $2,500. Then he lied to me because he kept all the money and didn't help me at all. Then he continued working for the court and took my money. I sued him, I still have the papers. The court answered saying that the lawyer had been suspended for a year due to malpractice. I couldn't continue with the suit because of my English and lack of experience. Some of the terms I've forgotten. I wasted a lot of time writing from here to see if I could take the case forward. Then I stopped the whole thing because I didn't have, how do you it say it, the means! (April 2, 2003)

Consequently, it was not surprising to hear subjects talk about being "tricked" into signing their deportation papers because they did not fully understand the immediate and long-term consequences of their action. Their main complaints were that they (1) were rarely given sufficient time to think about their choices, (2) had few people with the appropriate knowledge with whom they could consult, (3) had insufficient time to consult with family members, and

(4) possessed insufficient education and knowledge of the English language to fully comprehend their legal standing or their rights. In Roberto's case, it is clear that he had a lawyer who was willing to fight for him and a family who was going to support him, but this was an exception to the rule. In the majority of cases, the subjects were alone in trying to come to terms with something that was almost impossible for them to grasp, either conceptually or emotionally. Therefore, many subjects felt resentful at their treatment, in contrast to those above, who had come to accept the hopelessness of their new reality.

D.B.: Did you have any idea about the process?

SANTO: No, no.

D.B.: You had no idea from before.

SANTO: Let me explain to you. They took me to the immigration jail; I lasted six months there, fighting the case. Then, the last time the judge goes, "Look, even if you fight the case, we're going to deport you. It's useless for you to fight 'cos you're leaving for your damned country." The judge told me just like that. He told me not to fight the case and that I was leaving for my damned country. Then, I started to think and said to myself, "It's ok I'm going to leave." Then he told me, "Sign here." I didn't know what I was signing because he didn't even give me the papers for to read. I signed without knowing that it was about the deportation! After he said, "That's your deportation. Do you understand me?"

D.B.: During this time you didn't have any legal notification from a lawyer who was sitting by your side. . . .

SANTO: A court lawyer, but it's theirs, from immigration! The lawyer told me, "Regardless, you're going to your country, don't start fighting the case here." And the judge said, "Regardless you're going to your damned country, don't try fighting your case." In three days, they called me and deported me.

D.B.: Three days! Did you call your family?

SANTO: I called my family, but it was too far—they didn't have time to come and see me. I didn't know what, when, or who were going to deport me. Then around 4 am the security police came to wake me up, "You're leaving for your country." At 4 am! I came like this here without anything. If he had given me the papers I would have looked for someone to study the case, and I wouldn't have signed without knowing what it was. That was just a trap to get me. (May 3, 2003)

TONY2: I didn't know I was going to be deported because the previous time they even gave me work release. That was my second time back when they were deporting others, but they didn't deport me. They even gave me a break and sent me back to the street. It wasn't until my third court hearing that I got deported. But I didn't expect this because by this time I was married, had a kid over there, a little boy, so I thought they was gonna give me a break. But they didn't care—I'm just another Dominican who sold drugs. (April 1, 2003)

THE EXPERIENCE OF THE IMMIGRATION DETENTION CAMPS

Investigative journalist Mark Dow (2005) has written extensively on conditions in the ever-proliferating detention camps of the Department of Immigration and Customs Enforcement (ICE).[2] Dow spent time at one of the biggest of these camps in Florida as an English teacher, and he described these camps as follows:

> The Krome Detention Center of the U.S. Immigration and Naturalization Service is a sprawling complex at the edge of the Everglades. . . . The despair and frustration of the prisoners at Krome were unmistakable. . . . As I drove back to Miami Beach my mind's eye retained the image of large groups of mostly dark-skinned prisoners sitting around a yard or in a cement-block building in their bright orange uniforms—what my student referred to in his poem as his "uniform of contempt." Before the hopelessness that pervaded Krome had dissipated I would be back on the familiar freeways, passing the usual strip malls and subdivisions; in an hour I would be on the beach. I had realized that Krome was invisible.

(DOW 2005:1)

Practically all of the subjects had spent some time in camps such as these, often in states much further away from their families than where they were previously incarcerated. None of these subjects spoke positively about these facilities; rather, they recalled overcrowded conditions, a lack of recreational opportunities, rampant abuse by prison guards, a general atmosphere of despair among the detainees, and the gradual if not immediate recognition that their experience of the justice system would not improve during this last stage of their detention. Juan sums it up:

D.B.: You were waiting there to see the immigration judge.

JUAN: No, I was already deported by the judge. But we just had to wait to get a ticket.

D.B.: And how was that? Was jail any different to the prison?

JUAN: That was worse!

D.B.: Much worse?

JUAN: Yeah, they used to have riots over there all the time and they do things just to bother inmates.

D.B.: What sort of things?

JUAN: Lots of different things. The food was very bad, they got a lot of rules, they were abusive to most of the people that go there from prison or from the feds. No good treatment. No, they're accustomed to work with guys from the street. They think that people from prison have to be treated in the same way. But most of the people that go to immigration prison just want to leave and get out. We've just tired of being in custody. (March 10, 2003)

LEGAL RESISTANCE

There were, however, ten subjects who decided to fight their case, taking the system at its word and making use of the appeals process. Four did so with the aid of a lawyer, and six tried their best without professional representation. To take on such a responsibility requires a great deal of self-confidence and courage. It also requires a level of education that most of the study participants lacked. In addition, there were three participants who fought to have their sentences reduced in prison, arguing that they had been inadequately represented. These three were successful towards the end of their sentence; these successes might have been helped along by judges responding to the increased pressures to reduce both prison costs and overcrowding.

Guido discussed how he acquired his knowledge and motivation to fight. Although he did not succeed, he at least won some respect for his endeavors, and in his eyes he had somehow resisted the status quo and forced the system to take him a little more seriously.

GUIDO: I not once heard anything concerning long-term legal residents, not one thing. When I got parole, a couple of Spanish guys from El Salvador used to tease me, telling me, "You going back, shit, they're gonna send you back so fast." I said "Look, you believe I'm a fucking idiot? I've been here nineteen years." And they said, "I know a guy like that, wait and see, they got so many laws waiting for you." And when the guys from immigration picked me up, a Dominican guy and a Puerto Rican guy, the Dominican guy tried to play with me. He wanna be Puerto Rican, I guess, 'cause he had this resentment toward his own people. He was very rude and disrespectful. I asked him whether or not they were gonna send me back. He said, "Yeah, we're gonna send your ass back, you can forget about it, it doesn't matter if you've been here 50 years, you're going back!" In the

7.2 DEPORTEES ARRIVING AT A SANTO DOMINGO AIRPORT ON FLIGHTS FROM THE UNITED STATES THAT ARRIVE TWICE EACH MONTH (PHOTO TAKEN FROM THE INTERNET, PHOTOGRAPHER UNKNOWN).

bus I met this gentleman—I'll never forget his name. He was locked up in Greensville Penitentiary, Peter Bernard, from a small island in the Caribbean, St. Lucia. This guy did twelve years, just got out on armed robbery after he had done another bid prior for like six years. This individual was one of the smartest individuals I ever met in my life, especially when it came to law. He was a jailhouse lawyer. He showed me how to study the law books, helped me to stay interested in fighting my case. I learned how to read the law, look up files, and I started to write to the American Immigration Law Foundation. From the time I was transferred to Immigration and Naturalization Service custody, I used that whole time to study, learning everything about 212(c), retroactivities, the decision regarding retroactivity in the Supreme Court. . . . I had no choice at the time; my mother was dying of cancer and I had hired a lawyer for my board hearing, but I noticed the guy's level of competence and motivation were very low, so I said, "Shit, no one is gonna help me but me, so I gotta learn this myself, and show these people I'm able." So I studied those laws, I learned those laws to the point that I had the judge and the prosecutor looking through the books to understand my interpretation and to understand my arguments. . . . I appealed early but I lost after like I won. I left there showing you might have deported me and ruined me but still the judge said to me, "I've never seen no one coming in front of me defending themselves as you have. They didn't expect that." (May 22, 2003)

THE FLIGHT BACK

Finally, there is the flight back to the Dominican Republic. Their long wait in the prison cells of the United States is over, and the deportees are escorted by federal marshals on a commercial flight bound for Santo Domingo, to be delivered to officials of the Dominican Department of Deportation on the other side. The journey was full of contradictions. On the one hand, many of the subjects felt relieved that it was all over; they had emerged from prison intact and were now ready to start life anew. Others experienced pure dread as they returned to a place that they were no longer familiar with, where they had little to no family or social support and no economic prospects, and were often nursing quite serious medical and mental health problems. It is possibility and hope juxtaposed with anxiety and despair. Luis1 and Luis2 provided two examples of the fortunate ones. Luis1 still had his large, extended family waiting for him; Luis2 had very little family, but what he did have was crucial for his resettlement.

LUIS1: All my family helped me tremendously when I returned. They accepted me, gave me a roof, helped me out with money even though they have very little, and just helped me become part of the community again. (April 6, 2003)

LUIS2: So they said, "Ok, you may go back." They put me in another jail, and from there they put me on a plane. While we were in the bus we were handcuffed for about nine hours, uncomfortable like this.

D.B.: Totally unnecessary?

LUIS2: Totally unnecessary. From 4 AM to about 11 AM or 1 PM.

D.B.: So you came off the plane handcuffed.

LUIS2: I was still handcuffed in the plane.

D.B.: When did they take the handcuffs off?

LUIS2: About ten minutes to land before they took them off. Then they took me over to the police plaza. Boy, it was hectic there, but they actually let me go the same day.

D.B.: After only a few hours.

LUIS2: Yeah, they took me to my house. They said, "Give me an address." So they drove me over, and then from there over to here now.

D.B.: Who was here to help you when you came?

LUIS2: My cousin, if I wouldn't have found that cousin, they wasn't gonna let me go. Actually, I didn't have no family over here. I have nobody over here. I'm just living off what my family sends me. I live in my cousin's house, but he's not here—he lives in the United States. I stay in his house and I don't pay no rent, but if it wasn't for them I'd be sleeping maybe right here, you know (points to the park bench). I don't think my family is gonna leave me, I think that's how it's gonna be, you know. (May 7, 2003)

CONCLUSION

The data in this chapter reveal much about the invasive properties of the security state today as well as the lived culture and practices of repressive immigration policies. Although these "data" shed a humanistic light on the processes of immigrant incorporation and removal, which are often obscured by legal discourse, they also raise some important issues about the state of contemporary immigration theory and its departure from one of sociology's founding concepts: social control.

We have examined the multiple levels of experience of this final part of the social exclusion process of the deportees by following them through the immigrant court proceedings and their efforts to defend themselves through whatever devices are left to them. We have also documented their extremely conflicted experience on the return flight to their "enforced" homeland. Now they will have to adapt. For some, it is another process of acculturation; for others, it is a period of social and cultural rejection. Miguelito's expression of a common deportee sentiment provides an appropriate end to this chapter.

D.B.: Is there anything else you want to add?

MIGUELITO: I think at least if you're gonna deport someone, make it for a fucking capital crime. You deserve to get another chance 'cause they're selling you a lot of dreams over there. "Do your work," "Go and join this program," "You wanna be a new man? Put all your effort into your new life." This is what they tell you again and again, and yet you do all this and you still end up getting separated from your family. You're fucked! People have to think about all of this and why they give us no real reason for kicking us out for the rest of our lives. You're a resident of that country, that means you live there, forever! I understand if you killed somebody, or if you've done a bad crime, you know what I mean. Under the law they can even kill you. That's OK, I suppose, I understand that. But selling a few drugs! Or maybe even using drugs or whatever! Or for getting a traffic ticket! You get deported for this bullshit! (January 25, 2003)

8.1 SIGN OUTSIDE THE DOOR TO THE DEPARTMENT OF DEPORTEES (PSYCHOLOGY DEPARTMENT) AT THE NATIONAL POLICE HEADQUARTERS IN SANTO DOMINGO (*PHOTO:* LUIS BARRIOS).

CHAPTER EIGHT

BACK IN THE HOMELAND: PART ONE

THE SOCIAL-PSYCHOLOGICAL CRISIS
OF THE DEPORTEE

*David Brotherton (D.B.): How is the reaction of people here when they know
that you're a deportee?*

*Javier: Bad, and that's why I would like institutions here to take into con-
sideration that not everyone who engaged in illegal activities over there
continues to do so here. I mean, one did something there, but that doesn't
mean that he'll want to do it again here. Because it's not the same circumstances, or the moment, or the experience that one has, do you understand?
But still the deportee is marginalized here. We're all categorized the same,
as if we all robbed, assaulted, killed, or raped, and that's not true. . . . Look
at my case, I've been here for ten years. How much longer do I need to wait
to show that I'm not involved in anything? Twenty, thirty years? When I
starve myself to death? I'm being starved here, but I just pretend, so I don't
think about it. But I'm in a bad situation and I need help.*

(MARCH 1, 2003)

HOW DO DEPORTEES fare when they return? How do the different levels
of Dominican society react to the deportees? Do deportees adapt easily, using
their survival skills and extant social networks to resume their lives? Do they
feel shut out, feared and estranged by and from a society that many of them
are not familiar with? The quote above makes it clear how the majority of
the subjects, particularly those who had been socialized in the United States,
encountered their new homeland and felt "branded" in a dubious ritual that,
as Goffman (1960) reminds us, has been a constant feature of social interac-
tional processes at least since the ancient Greeks.

In this chapter we focus on the difficulties that deportees face as they struggle to come to terms with their social, cultural, and physical displacement from the United States, now understanding that any legal return is impossible. We deal more explicitly with the crisis of subjectivity in the deportation experience as the subjects contend with their marginalization and categorization as the transnationalized Other.

In our total sample, we found very few, perhaps 5 percent, who were "thriving" upon their return. Of course, this must be placed in the context of a country in which few of the population could be said to be particularly well off, with around 15 percent living a comfortable middle-class existence and a miniscule 5 percent living in sumptuous splendor, owning much of the country's economic and financial wealth (see chapter 2). However, despite the extreme difficulties that deportees encounter, there were surprisingly few who returned to a life of crime (see chapter 10). This finding is similar to that of Bernard Headley (2008) in Jamaica, whose analysis of the recidivism of deportees based on police archives found that the rate of deportees transgressing the law was less than the average Jamaican.[1]

To survey the social psychological terrain of the deportee-homeland encounter, we discuss several themes that were prominent throughout the interview data and our ethnographic observations. These data illustrate what many of our respondents felt was a deep social and psychological crisis from which it appeared difficult to emerge. We begin with a description of the official processing of deportees as they are accepted and recognized by agents of the Department of Deportation and the national police. Then we examine four essential issues that reflect the precariousness of the deportee's status in Dominican society. First is the notion of place—or displacement—as the deportees come to terms with the permanency of their new sociocultural and political location. In this analysis, we discuss three themes: (1) the issue of identity, (2) the deportees' view of culture conflict, and (3) the phenomenon of a double consciousness. Second, we investigate further the critically important experience of stigmatization and social bulimia. Third, we explore the different ways subjects viewed the "spoiling" of their identity and their consequent levels of exclusion from mainstream Dominican society. Finally, we discuss what might be considered the partial truths behind the stereotype of the deportee.

GETTING PROCESSED

GUIDO: I came here in '97, I was brought here, went through immigration, the airport, they sent me to the customs area. I spent the night there.

I didn't sleep, just sat there waiting to get the hell out. I asked them, "Why are you locking me up, I've already been locked up. Why do I gotta go through this?" I stayed up all night waiting. In the morning they asked me questions and released me. They didn't have my file at hand, so I was able to more or less pull everything down. I just told them that they caught me with a couple of ounces. I didn't talk about my firearm charges, 'cause I know I'd go to El Palacio (the National Palace of the Police in Santo Domingo [added by the authors]). I didn't really get into details. I kept it to the minimum. They took pictures and fingerprints, then released me to my uncle and grandmother's custody and we left. (May 22, 2003)

The procedures for deportees entering the Dominican Republic as described in Guido's account above are now out of date. Until around 2000, when the numbers being forcibly repatriated were not yet in the tens of thousands, deportees were handed over to deportee officials who were not known for their thoroughness. Typically, as Guido described, the officials would have little information on who was being returned and what the offenses had been that merited their deportation. Extraordinary as it may seem, neither the United States nor the Dominican government felt that this sharing of information was useful. Deportees were typically held for a night in a downtown Santo Domingo police facility or at the airport. A minimal case file would be opened on the deportee, listing basic information such as name, occupation, address in the Dominican Republic, and the date and time of arrival. Answers to questions about offenses committed would also be recorded. This is how one female deportee experienced her homecoming:

ESTRELLA2: We were received by a few Dominican military men, who physically beat us and took whatever money we had. Later, they put us in a bus and we ended going to the Police Department, where they opened a criminal file on each one of us and they took our photos and fingerprints. They kept us for two weeks imprisoned before allowing us to go, under the condition that we return to report ourselves to them every week. (January 22, 2003)

The current process is more systematic. All deportees, after going through customs, are met upon arrival by members of the National Police and representatives of the Department of Deportation. Deportees are transported by bus to the National Police headquarters for questioning (this usually occurs four or five times every month). A list of offenses committed by the deportees and the number of years served are provided to the receiving officials by the U.S. marshals who escorted the deportees on the plane.[2]

The deportees are questioned by officials and then kept overnight at a special holding facility. The next day, the deportees meet with a psychologist from the Department of Deportation, and they are told that they must return to this department each month for six months to report on their economic and social progress. In recent years, a representative from a non-profit organization (see chapter 10) set up to help deportees is often on hand to answer questions.

The final stage in the process of creating an official identity for the purposes of state social control and entry into the labor market is to obtain a *cédula* (an identity card) that citizens have to carry at all times, and a *nota de buena conducta* (good conduct note) that is required by employers in the formal economy (particularly hotels, offices, banks, and government) to show that a citizen does not have a criminal record and is in good standing with the criminal justice system.

THE EXPERIENCE OF SOCIAL DISPLACEMENT AND STIGMATIZATION

To understand the experience of resettlement for deportees, we examine two key themes: social displacement/exclusion and stigmatization. By social displacement we are referring to the way expulsion is felt as deportees are essentially removed for a third time from a settled environment. The first displacement is emigration to the United States; for most deportees who were legal residents of the United States this occurs when they are children (Torres-Saillant & Hernández, 1998:36). The second displacement is their imprisonment in the United States, when they are removed from civil society and their immediate families. The third displacement occurs when they are forcibly repatriated to the Dominican Republic.

In the first section of our analysis, we discuss four analytical categories prominent in the subjects' narratives: betrayal, confusion, and trauma; identity; marginal man; and double consciousness. Together these highlight the complex feelings of alienation and estrangement as deportees reflected on this most profound crisis of self in their life course (Gregory 2007; Barrios and Brotherton 2004; Brotherton and Barrios 2009; Brennan 2004; Brotherton, 2003a, 2003b, 2003c).

In the second part of this analysis, we focus on the concepts of stigma and social bulimia as developed by Goffman (1960) and Young (1999), respectively.

Here we concentrate on the social types used to label deportees as society at large constructs what Goffman calls an "ideology" to explain deportee inferiority and the threat they pose to social order. These analyses present the other side of the globalizing process, highlighting the subjugation of those who are systematically marginalized, humiliated, and made invisible by laws of legal and social citizenship and by notions of criminal justice (Glick-Schiller et al. 1998).

BETRAYAL, CONFUSION, AND TRAUMA

It is hard to express the feelings of loss and the pain of separation when our respondents realized they were being deported from the land where their spouses, children, and sometimes mothers, fathers, brothers, and sisters live, and where the vast majority of their friendship circles remain. The deportees saw themselves stripped of what they thought were their "inalienable rights," leaving them confused as they tried to come to terms with their new statelessness and the permanence of the removal process. It was a traumatic experience, a "massive" dislocation of their social life (Alexander et al. 2004) over which they had little control (Carlson and Dalenber 2000).

Although most deportees had been visited by an agent of the immigration service during their prison stay in the United States and thus knew in advance that this removal would eventually come to pass, it was difficult to accept that it would actually happen. Most, like Guido, Estrella2, Jaramillo, and Chasmin, were long-time "legal residents," not temporary visitors.

D.B.: So, now you get deported, did you see your family?

GUIDO: No. My family drove to the hearing in Arlington, and from there I was taken back and a few weeks later I was deported. I didn't see my family or nothing. I was just packed on a plane and sent to the Dominican Republic. (May 22, 2003)

LUIS BARRIOS (L.B.): Talk to me about your deportation process.

ESTRELLA2: I finished my three-year sentence at Sing Sing Correctional Facility and I was so happy because I was telling myself, OK, after this negative experience I need to get myself together. I thought my family was waiting for me outside the prison when I got out, but to my surprise, it was the immigration agents who arrested me and took me to the New Jersey Immigration Detention Center. In less than two weeks they sent me back to the Dominican Republic. These people kidnapped me. (January 22, 2003)

L.B.: How was your deportation process?

JARAMILLO: I had never felt a fear like I felt when they deported me. I was only out of prison three minutes before immigration was arresting me, taking me from the jail at Fishkill Correctional Facility. In all these years, I have never understood how it was that they sent me from New York to Laredo Detention Facility in Texas. I was isolated, and my wife did not believe me when I told her that immigration had arrested me and had me in Texas. She was crying on the phone and shouting, and then my children were asking me what time I was coming home. These were seven painful days, and every day I was looking for a way to escape and return to my family. My God, with all the frustration I felt so helpless. (January 28, 2003)

CHISMIN: Can you imagine? I left my country at the age of two with great pride because I came as a visitor and immigrant to the United States, and I returned to my country at the age of 28 dumped, despised, and according to these people a criminal. I felt like I had been kidnapped and left in Santo Domingo as waste. Even my photo came out in the newspapers where they said I was a drug dealer. My dad had to turn the sky upside down to get me a place to live where I wouldn't get hurt. Arriving in my country under these conditions and having been forced to leave my family took away all my desire to go on living. I have to confess that at that time the world seemed over for me. I was alone, desperate, and ashamed, and when they called me a deportee it just took away all my will to live. (August 22, 2009)

Virtually all the deportees recounted similar events, i.e., after the hearing where they were told they would be deported, they were transferred back to the prison and then usually to an Immigration and Naturalization Service detention center (see chapter 7). As described in various accounts (see Bernstein 2007; Dow 2004), these facilities provide a minimum of human rights to detainees and add to their state of trauma. Subjects often talked of "being lost" when they arrived in the Dominican Republic, of not knowing who or what would await them.

D.B.: When you got back here? What did you feel?

GUIDO: Totally dislocated, totally lost, totally confused, in a sense like a bad nightmare. I felt as if I'd paid my debt to society and I used my time in prison to reconstruct my life. I had completed programs which I planned to use, and already had a certain agenda for when I got out. Then a big hurdle was put in front of me. No matter how high I jumped, I couldn't jump that hurdle. So I felt discouraged, betrayed 'cause I felt something unjust was done to me, something unconstitutional. I felt like no one was on my side. (May 22, 2003)

As Guido recalled, deportees planned for some eventual future, but it had little to do with the reality they would face. They created narratives for themselves about what they would do upon "getting out," and many had taken courses in prison to this end despite the drastic cutbacks in prison rehabilitation services. When the time finally came, however, they made desperate attempts to reach family members so that some provisions could be made for their arrival. This was often an uncertain endeavor because many deportees have few relatives remaining in the Dominican Republic, and they had no way to know whether any relatives would be willing to lend their support to these negatively labeled subjects. Alex described being rejected in this way by his mother:

ALEX: We don't get along, her husband and I don't get along either.
D.B.: So, you don't see her?
ALEX: I don't to go to the house, I don't ask them for nothing, because when I got deported she told somebody, like years ago, she told somebody, "If he gets deported I ain't gonna get him and he better forget about me and I ain't his mother, because my name is never gonna be. . . ." Like, you know, like she's a sophisticated woman. At that time she was with the government here and she don't want the government to know that she had a deported son. When I found out about that I called my mother and I told her, "I ain't nobody, forget about me." (March 5, 2003)

Feeling abandoned, depressed, and estranged in their homeland, the totality of their social and cultural displacement often makes deportees suicidal. Not sure of who or what to trust, often racked with guilt and unable to think clearly about their prospects or about strategies to cope with their condition, deportees often experience the social-psychological version of what some theorists refer to as space–time compression (Giddens 1991). For deportees, however, it is a form of space that feels outside of time, or is in effect time dramatically slowed down, just like prison time. This is the other side of the postmodern self, the one not characterized by global flexibility and agency but rather by global immobility and dependency heightened by transnational social controls and the politics of simultaneity (Zilberg 2002, 2004). When asking "Americanized" deportees about the future, few will answer with any certainty or any semblance of hope and purpose. Responses are usually along

In the drawing:
My body is in The REPUBLICA DOMINICANA buT My MIND HAERT AND Soul is iN THE 'SA with my family.

A D.P. Life

8.2 "D.P. LIFE," A DRAWING BY A DEPORTEE WHILE IN PRISON IN THE DOMINICAN REPUBLIC (SEE CHAPTER 10) (*PHOTO:* LUIS BARRIOS).

the lines of "We take it day by day," or "We're hanging in there, it's all we can do." Both Javier and El Pelú vividly describe how this state brought them to the edge of self-destruction:

JAVIER: What did I do? I sold prescription drugs, I think it was morphine, to an undercover. For that I got seven years and deported to a country I hadn't been to in twenty years. All my family's over there, all of them: my mom, my dad, my brothers, my sisters, my children. My mom always said something bad would happen to me if I kept messing up, but this? I tell you, when I first arrived I wanted to kill myself. I was gonna take an overdose of something. I don't know why I didn't. (November 3, 2002)

EL PELÚ: This shit (being deported to Santo Domingo [added by the authors]) infuriated me in a way that I thought was going to drive me crazy. I have four sons who I could see every two weeks while I was in Wyoming Correctional Facility. Eighteen months later, I could not see or touch neither my children nor my wife because we were afraid that, having traveled to the D.R., they would have problems on their return to the United States. This was agony, like living in hell every day. Every night I spent there, alone trying to sleep, I was constantly thinking that the world had ended for me, that I had lost everything, my wife, my children, and my life. And on top of all that, I can't find a fucking job in Santo Domingo! I asked myself a hundred times, why the fuck am I living? A hundred times I had the intention of killing myself but did not have the courage to do it. I was walking like a robot, and everything I was doing was mechanical. I was not feeling that desire to live as earlier in my life. I was dead in life. (December 9, 2003)

IDENTITY

In anthropological work by Cohen (1978), identity is intrinsically connected to a subjective notion of ethnicity based on a population's experience of inclusion and exclusion. It is linked to their identification with place and their relationship to politics or, more specifically, to symmetries of power. This construct of identity was particularly true of deportees who emigrated as children and who were socialized from an early age in the norms, rituals, and ideologies of the United States. Although a few respondents left for the United States in their twenties, retaining their Dominican identity and extensive "homeland" social networks, others considered themselves "Americans" or "New Yorkers"; they attended U.S. schools, grew up in U.S. barrios, worked in U.S. factories, and spent time in the U.S. criminal justice system.

This is not to say that these deportees had maintained absolutely no contact with their former country; all of the respondents were transnational in some way, caught between two cultures and two societies. For example, some of the 1.5-generation immigrants[3] had spent a substantial amount of time traveling back and forth during their teens as their parents sent them away for summer vacations or to get them "straightened out" (a desperate strategy to counter the dangers and seductions of the inner-city street). Others, however, rarely returned, and although they might hear Spanish in the home, their first language—the one in which they dreamed and imagined—was English, while their Spanish had become Spanglish.

How did this new, enforced location affect their sense of self? This question is key to understanding the deportees' success in (re)integrating themselves into Dominican society. For many, it was difficult to see themselves as anything other than "American," regardless of the time they had lived in the Dominican Republic or of their mastery of Spanish. In a way, their selves were still in the United States; their cultural reference points, their most important memories, and the narratives they repeated to themselves were still embedded in New York, in their apartments on Amsterdam Avenue, in their elementary schools in the Bronx, or with their street gang affiliates in South Brooklyn. Rodrigo illustrates this in his drawing *A Deportee Life: My Body Is in the República Dominicana, but My Mind, Heart and Soul Is in the U.S. with My Family.*

Consequently, what they were experiencing was unreal; it was an endless dream (or nightmare) from which they awoke every day, where they did their best to eke out a subsistence living, where they never reached economic or social transcendence. For them, life was lived liminally, between and betwixt, in a series of stark contrasts between the abundance of the First World and the scarcity of the Third, between variable seasons of New York and the relentless heat of Santo Domingo, between the efficiency and relative openness of an advanced capitalist "democracy" and the inefficiency and opaqueness of a dependent quasi-democratic state. These constant comparisons in which many deportees engage reinforce their Americanness and have some similarities as well as differences compared with the findings of Guarnizo (1994), who argued that returning Dominicans tend to exaggerate their U.S. identity in much the same way as they exaggerated their Dominicanness in the United States.

> LUIS2: I just don't like this country, because I didn't grow up in this country, it's totally not for me; it's a different environment. I like to feel a different kind of way, with different types of people. I'm not saying these people are not civilized, but they're not at the level like in the environment where you lived. (June 10, 2003)

There are some deportees who quite consciously emphasize their "difference" from local inhabitants, brandishing their emigré acquisitions, be they property, objects of style, or language. The deportees in our study, in general, were not among this group of "sojourners." On the contrary, they tended to keep their identities under wraps, more private than public, more restrained and constrained than celebrated. Constantly aware of being Othered, they were likely to save such identity discussions for their backstage conversations with other deportees, which only occurred under conditions in which they felt socially and culturally safe. In a visit to a Dominican prison (June 8, 2007), a deportee approached us and, in reference to his treatment by the mostly Dominican inmates, laconically stated, "They're tough on Americans in here."

Marginal Man

> MANOLO: They are not civilized, they are not developed, although they think they are. They put a tie on and they think they have shit. Come on, your mentality is not good. You don't know how to treat people the way you're supposed to, you know. What's the use of having a tie if you don't know

how to treat the people? All you're thinking about is evil things to do. You know, rob them, 'cause that's what they do. . . . You can't even go to the police. The police! They're a bunch of fucking killers, they're evil; that's the first thing you gotta distrust, they're no fucking good, none of them, none of them is any fucking good. (May 10, 2006)

Both Manolo and Luis2 (previous section) express their alienation using the terms "civilized" and "uncivilized" to draw distinctions between the two societies. Such sentiments, which are common among long-time residents of the United States, sound suspiciously like a Huntingtonesque perspective of comparative world development. The social pathologies that they witness and experience on a daily basis have overwhelmed their tolerance levels, exhausted their frameworks of understanding, and left them susceptible to common sense notions of cultural deficiency as a marker of Third World behavior and as an explanation of underdevelopment. Now looking from the bottom up at a society that they have usually been able to view from afar, they are caught classically in the "marginal man" syndrome: The marginal man . . . is one whom fate has condemned to live in two societies and in two, not merely different but antagonistic cultures. . . . His mind is the crucible in which two different and refractory cultures may be said to melt and, either wholly or in part, fuse (Park 1961:11).

It is not surprising that the police are singled out as one of the main destroyers of any legitimacy behind the way rules or laws are practiced in the homeland. According to Gregory (2007), the police are often corrupt, undereducated, poorly paid, ill-trained, and generally willing to do the bidding of those with power, frequently victimizing those most in need of protection and "public safety." Manolo's use of the term "evil" is significant because it speaks to those vindictive qualities felt by deportees and reflects the cultural criminological aspect of oppression, the fervor behind the jack boot, the high attained from beating civilians, and the self-righteousness in the act of rejection (Young 2007; Ferrell, Hayward, and Young 2008). For Manolo, struggling in middle age to resolve his in-between cultural status, he had to learn to accept the limitations placed on his agency and any semblance of equality before the law. He had to become "acculturated" to a country that is often viewed by deportees as spiraling into a social, moral, and economic abyss; in doing so, the remembrances of his youthful visits are brought into stark relief:

MANOLO: It's not a system here. They don't help out others that are in need. There's too many poor people here, too many evil people like you see all over the world, but over here in an island like this, it's not supposed to happen. Plus, nobody likes deportees here. On this island, everything is, like, restrictions. Everybody is, like, not with each other. It's not a unity island. It's like a bunch of gangs, you know, nothing's united. This is the difference to when I used to come here on vacation. Back then, it was still, like, virgin, virgin. (May 10, 2006)

Manolo waxed nostalgic about the country he used to know, one from which he could return home after a month or two, and he compared it to the one in which he lives every day, year after year, suspended in time. He uses negative terms to describe the society in which he has to find a place, and he overlooks the other side of Dominican life, the warmth and magnanimity of its people, the vibrancy of its culture, especially in music and dance, and the long history of struggle from below against imperialism and colonialism that has been contained by U.S. hegemony through military invasions and economic dependency (Betances [1995] and Perkins [2004]). The injustices and privations that Manolo witnesses and reads about mediate much of Dominican life, just as Caldeira (2000) described the relationship between fear, inequality, and the social construct of crime in the Brazilian context.

What Manolo and other subjects experience is not specifically Dominican, but rather it is a generalized consequence of neo-liberalism (Gregory 2007). As an isolated individual, as a marginal man, Manolo can do little more than pour scorn on these conditions and on its supposed agents without engaging their "root causes." This resentment for his new country is fueled by the anger and frustration he feels for his own impotence (Fanon 1963).

DOUBLE CONSCIOUSNESS

Luis recalls his feelings of sociocultural dislocation, bewilderment, and estrangement. During interviews, respondents frequently began to weep as they relived their frustration, abandonment, regret for their deviant choices, and the loss of family, income, and future prospects. In many ways, deportees must live out a double consciousness that goes beyond the transnational norm. With many considering themselves part Dominican and part American, deportees' lives are more affected by their relationship to the past than to the present, which psychologically is difficult for them to reconcile. This is similar to the notion of double consciousness elaborated by Du Bois:

A peculiar sensation, this double-consciousness, the sense of always looking at one's self through the eyes of others, of measuring one's soul by the tape of a world that looks on in amused contempt and pity. One ever feels his twoness, an American, a Negro; two warring souls, two thoughts, two unreconciled strivings; two warring ideals in one dark body, whose dogged strength alone keeps it from being torn asunder. . . .

(1999:2)

As with African Americans, the double-consciousness takes three forms: first, deportees have to contend with their stereotypes while knowing who their true selves are; second, deportees are subjected to multiple levels of discrimination that undermine their sense of legal and social citizenship, reinforcing the social fact that they are both Dominican and not Dominican; third, their Dominican and American selves exist in constant tension and cannot be adequately reunited. This trauma, which poses as culture conflict, directly relates to and reflects their interlocking sense of self and social displacement. It is experienced as a form of devaluation and ultimately as dehumanization:

> ADONIS: We're human. Everybody makes a mistake. You're not killing nobody or nothing. You're separated from your wife, your kids, for life. They throws you in a place you don't know for fifteen, twenty years, how can you survive? These people don't think about that. It's hard here. You try to do the right thing. You don't do no crime and you are not going to the drug system, you don't go to the stolen system, yet he's making you out like you're a criminal. (April 11, 2003)

Adonis, clear in his own mind that he is not "going to" the illegal informal economy (Gregory 2007), is reminded of how he feels deposited and situated against his will in a place where he is out of place. He wonders how long the punishment will continue. What is its purpose? This double consciousness is a continuation of their U.S. experience, especially for the more "black" deportees who now face the racially policed hierarchies and boundaries of the Dominican Republic (Torres-Saillant 2000).

MORAL AND PHYSICAL STIGMA

Deportees return to the Dominican Republic with their identity spoiled on numerous levels and face being diminished and shunned because of both their moral and physical stigma, as Goffman (1960) stated over fifty years ago:

> By definition, of course, we believe the person with a stigma is not quite human. On this assumption we exercise varieties of discrimination, through

which we effectively, if often unthinkingly, reduce his life chances. We construct a stigma-theory, an ideology to explain his inferiority and account for the danger he represents, sometimes rationalizing an animosity based on other differences, such as those of social class.

(1960:5)

In the works of Douglas (1966), Sibley (1995) and Young (1999, 2007), we see how social exclusion is carried out against a range of Others from traditional to late modern societies as lines of demarcation are constructed, augmented, and transgressed. Young (2007) argues that social bulimia is perhaps a more apt term in the case of deportees because they experience both inclusion and exclusion. Nonetheless, the experience of stigma is probably the most difficult social and psychological issue confronting them, regardless of the degree to which they considered themselves integrated into Dominican society. The symbolic forms that this Otherness takes are manifold; we will concentrate on four of them: the felon, the dangerous Other, the Dominicanyork, and "the failure."

THE FELON

A good deal of research has been carried out in the United States (Schwartz and Skolnick 1962; Pager 2003; Western et al. 2002) on the stigmatizing effects of prison and its relationship to stratification. Pager (2003) pointed to the importance of "negative credentialing," which are the negative sanctions applied to ex-inmates through the exclusionary powers of the state. For example, they are precluded from certain types of jobs in health care and public sector occupations; they are prohibited from a range of social spaces including public housing; and find their basic political rights, such as voting, denied. Thus, this form of state-sanctioned stigma has a direct influence on one's life opportunities; the same is true in the Dominican Republic, where the influence of the state is assured through the deportee-stamped good conduct note. Given the paucity of jobs in the formal sector, the deportee has basically become an "untouchable." Fortunately, with corruption so rampant, it is sometimes possible to have this obstacle taken care of and have the stigma partially removed:

> LUIS: It costs about fifty dollars to have someone change the letter, to get that stamp off it. But, of course, you have to know the people on the inside. You have to know that one person who has the access. But it's possible. Here, if you have the money, everything's possible. (August 22, 2003)

8.3 TYPICAL NEWSPAPER REPORT FROM *HOY* IN SANTO DOMINGO (MAY 21, 2002). THE HEADLINE READS, "16,000 DOMINICANS DEPORTED IN NINE YEARS, THE MAJORITY OF THEM FOR VIOLATIONS OF LAWS ON THE CONSUMPTION AND SELLING OF DRUGS AND CONTROLLED SUBSTANCES" (*PHOTO:* DEPARTAMENTO EDITORIAL-PERIODICO HOY).

THE DANGEROUS OTHER

As Guarnizo (1994) points out, native Dominicans can often spot a deportee from afar, as their dress, their walk, and their language give them away. This physical otherness of the Americanized deportee combines with the corporate media campaigns, public statements by senior police officials, and actions by the legislature to create a form of moral panic that rationalizes and reflects the deeper ideological shift in Dominican society toward a neo-conservative ideology (Mayer 2001). At the level of law and order, this ideology reflects the drive toward more social control and the importation of U.S. policing strategies, one of which is the famed zero tolerance policy, which was rationalized by conservative East Coast criminologists. Jaramillo suggested how the print media aid and abet this process:

JAMARILLO: After one week, they deported me to Santo Domingo. There they treated me like a dog and I had to bear insults and humiliation by the police. I was not alone. I think there were about twenty of us, all guys. . . . A newspaper took a photo of our arrival, and guess what? The next day I was in the newspaper as a criminal. One more criminal that was coming to the Dominican Republic! (March 1, 2003)

This move toward more control of the streets is a central plinth of recent governments (particularly the Leonel Fernández administration) and appears to be taking precedence over funding to public schools and universities, the public health service, public works, affordable housing, and the infamous state of energy production and distribution. Tens of millions of dollars are procured from the World Bank and USAID to focus on the "incorrigibles" and neighborhood "hot spots" (for a critique of such policies in the United States, see Harcourt 2001 and Karmen 2001 inter alia). The aesthetic of dependency in this law-and-order policy is demonstrated by the new badges of the federal police, which are almost identical to their New York Police Department counterparts, and by the new Harley Davidson motorcycles now proudly owned by the transport police. Both the symbols and substance of these imported strategies play well with those who persist with the authoritarian policing culture.

These traditions of arbitrary police powers make deportees natural targets for police sweeps and investigations, largely with little justification. Between the denunciations of faceless neighbors, the demonization by the media, and the eagerness of the police and private security[4] to look for suspects among the deportee population, many deportees are loath to be seen in public spaces and thus restrict their movements. As the Director of the Department for Deportees admits:

> When they (the deportees [added by the authors]) finished their period of observation, they don't need to come to this office anymore. However, we always keep the file open because whenever there is a crime in an area where we have deportees, we begin interrogating them. This is already a matter of police procedure. (April 2, 2003)

Such victimization is an outcome of "geographies of exclusion" (Sibley 1995) and echoes what Douglas (1966) argued is society's penchant for purification or the distancing of certain sectors of society from what are considered human filth. In the treatment of the deportee, we witness the linking of tropes and metaphors such as "dangerousness" and "threatening" with their presence, which quite naturally increases their real and imagined sense of being "outcast."

D.B.: You don't like to hang around here 'cause the cops are coming down.
ADONIS: Yeah.
D.B.: Why is that a problem?
ADONIS: Police over here is not like over there. If they see you over here in the street or on the corner, maybe you're smoking a cigarette or drinking

MINISTERIO PÚBLICO | **Procuraduría General de la República**
Secretaría General
Centro de Atención al Ciudadano

Ref.:090010503565

CERTIFICACIÓN

Por este medio, certificamos que al momento de emitir el presente Documento, en el Sistema de Investigación Criminal de la Procuraduría General de la República no existe registrada ninguna información de casos judiciales abiertos en contra de ▓▓▓▓▓▓▓▓▓▓▓▓▓▓▓▓▓
antes o después a su
DEPORTACION de fecha **28 de enero del 1999,** por lo que se expide esta **Certificación** de **NO ANTECEDENTES JUDICIALES EN LA REPUBLICA DOMINICANA.**

Expedida, firmada y sellada a solicitud de **MARINO DE JESUS LEBRON RODRIGUEZ,** en la ciudad de **Santo Domingo, Distrito Nacional,** capital de la República Dominicana, a los Doce (12) día(s) del mes de febrero del año 2009. Su vigencia prescribe a los Noventa' (90) días a partir de su emisión.

LICDA. SENIA MIGUELINA CUEVAS SUERO
Encda. de la Sección de Certificaciones Generales

8.4 IN RESPONSE TO AN EMPLOYER'S REQUEST REGARDING A PROSPECTIVE EMPLOYEE'S CRIMINAL RECORD, THE COUNTRY'S ATTORNEY GENERAL ANSWERS BY STATING THAT THERE ARE NO OPEN CASES INVOLVING THE SUBJECT EITHER BEFORE OR AFTER HE WAS DEPORTED.

a beer, they're gonna stop you and be like, "Let me get your cédula." Even if you got your cédula and even if you got your papers, they're gonna take you to the prison, regardless. If you don't give them $50 bucks they're gonna lock you up for one day, make you sleep over there in the prison. That's why I don't like to be hanging out too much. (April 11, 2003)

Adonis discusses what is normal for deportees when they "hang out" in neighborhoods that are under more scrutiny with the new policy of "barrio seguro" (safe neighborhood; see chapter 2). Although fewer suspects today are kept in prison under preventive detention laws, the tendencies to arrest first and ask questions later, to threaten citizens unless they offer a bribe, to hold people overnight in the airless cells of the *destacamiento* (local precincts) for almost any reason, have not changed (see chapter 10).

It does not stop there, however. As neighborhood residents live increasingly under a climate of crime and fear and the country "adjusts" its public investment to suit the dictates of outsiders, the internal tensions compound. The threat of the deportee as a human pollutant grows inexorably, especially as their numbers increase. More than a decade ago, Guarnizo (1994) identified another layer of control that could easily describe the status of the deportee today:[5]

> A blatant wave of social discrimination against migrants has erupted, erecting barriers and exacerbating urban spatial segregation. Today, urban spatial segregation is drawn along class lines—a typical feature of Latin American urbanization—but also according to migration status.
>
> (GUARNIZO 1994:81)

THE DOMINICANYORK

> In stark contrast to their socio-cultural reaffirmation while overseas, migrants in the Dominican Republic are perceived as Americanized Dominicans whose behavior is seen by non-immigrants as an affront to authentic Dominican culture. Migrants' style of living, their tastes, and their manners, especially those of youngsters and the most prosperous (particularly excruciating in the case of those seen as drug traffickers), are judged as tasteless and revolting especially by the upper classes.
>
> (GUARNIZO 1994:80)

Guarnizo's analysis is still relevant, perhaps even more so today. Despite the fact that he was mainly talking to upper-middle class residents, it is clear that the Americanized Dominicans, the so-called "Dominicanyorks," are both morally and physically rejected. As both Santo and Manolo explained:

SANTO: If you go for a job over here, they ask you your age. Then they say, "Do you speak English?" I used to live in the Bronx. So then they're gonna ask you, "Are you deported?"

D.B.: Has that happened to you?

SANTO: Yeah, as soon as they ask you if you speak English, even if you speak English a little bit, they're gonna ask you, "You was living over there, but you got deported, what you did over there? Were you selling drugs? Did you get locked up for weapons?" You know, violence, that's all they ask you. (April 8, 2003)

D.B.: The Americanized deportees, do you see them like stay together, help each other?

MANOLO: Yes, they help each other, they stay together and they're more reasonable people. They think positive. They regret coming back here and they wanna leave. They get rejected here by the society.

D.B.: As soon as people know that they're deportees, they get rejected?

MANOLO: Yeah, they get rejected. People look at them as very evil. They don't wanna know about them. They get very, very depressed because of the way they're rejected.

D.B.: How do I know you are a deportee?

MANOLO: Well, news gets around, and plus when people see the difference in your physical, the differences in the conversations that you have with that person, most likely, they will ask you if you had been to the United States, "Are you deported here? And you tell them, "Yes, I was deported here." Right away, that's it. They don't wanna conversate with you no more. You must be a criminal. You gotta watch out over here because they're watching the deportees. Everything comes negative upon you, nothing comes positive. . . . (May 10, 2006)

Language, therefore, is one marker that sets the deportee apart, an attribute that obviously works in contradictory ways. On the one hand, having English is a great skill in the tourism-driven market place; on the other hand, it is a way to signal the deviance of the newcomer. Thus, what chance does the deportee have of avoiding this rampant practice of stigmatization? How does he or she escape the shaming process, after being charged with bringing "negativity" to the Dominican diaspora, of allowing "Americans" to think that Dominicans are nothing but drug sellers and violent gangsters? How are Americanized deportees to overcome deeply held suspicions about the nature of their character, which is thought to have been irreparably damaged, not by Dominican society but by their encounter with the land of opportunity, now conveniently read as that crime-ridden, materialistic, amoral corruptor of Dominican purity?

In response, the Dominicanyorks are brought together by their rejection, by their shared sense of stigma, but what resources do they have to share? How do they lend each other moral solidarity when their very association leads to more demonization and a downward cycle of rejection, dejection, retreat, and depression that are common stages of the exclusionary process? Manolo correctly linked the epidemic of depression found among deportees with the experience of rejection, yet there are no government services in this area, no counseling offered, no action taken by the authorities to lessen the suffering that clearly result. The master status is secure, therefore, and the deportee is a Dominicanyork with the finger being pointed from many directions, much like the "snitch culture" cultivated in highly policed societies.

Miguelito was desperate for work in 2003. In five years, he had only had a couple of temporary jobs. He had recently achieved a breakthrough and found a job just outside of Santo Domingo. Then a string of burglaries occurred in his community, and he was visited by the police.

> MIGUELITO: How they find out about my background, I've no idea. Someone, a neighbor, another worker always says something about my past. And as soon as my boss gets this kind of information, I'm fired. (January 25, 2003)

THE FAILURE

Added to the complexity of this exclusionary process is the blame that deportees receive for returning to their homeland, not only as an embarrassment to Dominican society, but as a "failure."

> D.B.: How do people treat you?
> JAVIER: They don't believe it can happen to a person. They think I must be stupid because I went there, spent twenty-five years of my life there, and didn't come home rich. (November 3, 2002)

Similar statements were repeated during our interviews or in informal conversations, but it was usually said after much reflection on the part of the respondent. Such treatment by the receiving society is extremely painful, even more than being rejected as a deportee. In being cast as a "failure" rather than just as a "felon," the deportees feel as if their struggles to survive, to fit in, and to endure the years in prison have been of no consequence. Discussion of their treatment by the non-migrant population is filled with resentment at the lack of understanding and appreciation for the deportee's past travails.

> LEON: It's the ones who don't leave who call us failures! The ones that didn't have the guts, the vision, the dream to get away. They blame us for wanting something better than this, for wanting a future . . . for not being able to stand this shit any more. It's like they're afraid or something. I don't know how to explain it. We're sort of blamed for trying, and it's like we've let them down because we've shown them that that place over there is not what it's cracked up to be. You know what I mean? The streets are not lined with gold, and that's a big letdown to them. (May 22, 2003)

Leon alludes to the complexity of this position. There are many "let downs" contained within this social construct of the deportee. It is true that those who typically tend to leave developing countries "voluntarily" for the more prosperous North (in the Americas) or the West and North (in much of Europe) might be seen as the entrepreneurial ones, those who have more drive and who are less able to tolerate the lack of opportunity in their homeland. For the non-migrant, this supposed division between the two worlds is assured, and when a Dominican is forcibly returned, he or she becomes living proof that there is a hollow truth to this belief, thus shattering the illusion and provoking an angry response. Instead of looking more closely at the relations of dependency, the victim is blamed. At the same time, the deportee produces another type of "let down" in the form of the shame that the subject has brought upon his ethnic community through being imprisoned and then being (un)ceremoniously ejected.

CONCLUSION

In this chapter we focused primarily on the felt conditions of deportees and how they have experienced rejection upon returning to their homeland. We have described primarily through the eyes of the deportees themselves the different ways social displacement is experienced, managed, and constituted. We have focused on the experience of stigma (both moral and physical) and social bulimia, which are powerfully evident in the processes of social marking (due to U.S. cultural inclusion) and socioeconomic exclusion. Regardless of how long the returning natives have lived in the United States, the stain of a criminal past on their identities are permanent. The majority of the sample felt that, despite their "freedom" in civil society, they were again "doing time" in a world to which tourists travel as an "escape"—the irony is that these tourists owe their experience of a "getaway" to the many deportees who work in this industry (Kempadoo 1999).

Finally, we also note that the deportation process not only produces psychological agony, but also spiritual desolation (see Barrios 2007a; Barrios 2000, 2004). Although notably absent from the literature, this area needs to be taken into consideration because so many deportees are repatriated to countries where the Catholic Church has a prominent place in the dominant culture.

9.1 LUIS AT HIS CHESS CLUB IN THE PEDESTRIAN STREET EL CONDE, ZONA COLONIAL, SANTO DOMINGO (*PHOTO:* LUIS BARRIOS).

CHAPTER NINE

BACK IN THE HOMELAND: PART TWO

ECONOMIC, SOCIAL, AND CULTURAL SURVIVAL

I've never seen the people deported to this country do bad things. Their major object is to go away from this country because they know they're not gonna live good in this country, you know. 'Cause the majority of the people really want to work but they also wanna make money. Over here if you work like in construction they're not gonna give you any good money. What is one or two hundred pesos when you have to pay ten, fifteen, twenty thousand pesos for rent and food? It's really not enough, so what they do is they hire people like the Haitians to do that type of work. They don't give no job to the deported.

(MR. M., DEPORTEE, JULY 25, 2003)

DEPORTEES MUST SURVIVE an ongoing social and economic crisis that befalls most Dominicans. For deportees accustomed to working- or middle-class life in the United States, its vagaries notwithstanding, the depth and spread of the nation's poverty is a shocking everyday reality for which many are unprepared. Economic marginality is everywhere. From the hundreds of youth and adults begging for spare change on sidewalks, to the legions of school-age children searching for shoes to shine from morning until night, to the hordes of individuals who swarm around cars at traffic lights selling cell phone adaptors, bottles of water, oranges, mangoes, peanuts, and sometimes puppies—these sights of the economically disposable are without parallel in the United States.

U.S. Navy Veteran deportee: I sleep anywhere, anywhere I can lay my head. It's rough out here; this is not like New York. In New York at least . . . in the morning you got a soup kitchen, here you don't get nothing. You survive on whatever. This is not my way to live. I don't know how long I will last like this (August 22, 2003)

No, the deportee in the Dominican Republic is in a completely different economic and cultural space. The array of legal and illegal jobs in the low-wage economy do not exist. State-sponsored training to prepare workers for changes in technology to avail them of new labor market possibilities is almost unheard of. Unions that provide access to decent paying jobs with health benefits are nearly impossible to find. All such norms are virtually absent in their new home, which seems to be based on a massive informal economy policed selectively by the state, a patronage system of job distribution that changes with every new party that comes to power, and the low-wage occupations in the formal economy, so many of which are tied to transnational capital (see chapter 2).

Gregory (2007) described this dual economy, split between the two interdependent sectors of formal transnational capitalism and informal localism. Gregory argued that workers in these terrains occupy spaces that on the one hand reflect the individual's and the nation's relationship to global dependency; on the other hand, they provide for different levels of human agency.[1] We saw numerous examples of deportees living out this contradiction between adapting to the parlous level of life chances and a refusal to acquiesce to these structured limitations. In addition to the usual ways of boosting income through the sale of labor and the exchange of both licit and illicit commodities, some deportees have the advantage of another income in the form of the "remesa" (money sent from the United States; see later in this chapter), an indication of the globalization of labor and of the Dominican Republic's peripheral economic status (Grasmuck and Pessar 1991).

WORK

Of course, work is crucial for the integration process. It provides sustenance, structure, self-esteem opportunities, and the basis for future planning.[2] In an analysis of the formal job market for 2005, according to official statistics, the Dominican labor force is structured as shown in Table 1 in Appendix A. The table gives a general indication of the distribution of jobs; however, there are a number of ambiguities that raise a host of questions. For example, it is clear that an enormous section of the working population, roughly half of the total, do not appear in the formal economy, i.e., that part of the economy receiving regular salaries and wages from an official employer. Are these people who are "without an occupational sector" among the self-employed, or, more likely, is this another way of referring to those in the informal economy? Furthermore, one must note the contradiction between the indicated age range of the working population begins at ten years of age and Dominican law, which clearly states that child labor under the age of sixteen years is illegal (Garcia 2009).

Despite these challenges and questions, we note several important facets of the Dominican economy relative to deportees. First, although tourism is said to be the country's number one employer (Ribando 2005), the data for tourism are much lower than those for manufacturing and commerce, which indicates that a substantial proportion of those working in the tourist industry may be involved in the informal rather than the formal economy. Second, the highest number of jobs in the formal economy appears to be in the commerce sector, which presumably includes all those occupations involved in trade and retail services. For many employers in this sector, formal records of good conduct are required, which places such jobs outside of the opportunity structure for deportees. Third, the actual population who are said to be receiving an hourly salary is only 1.4 million, which is less than half of those in the so-called working-age population, another indication of the limited formal opportunities for returning immigrants in a total population of almost nine million people.

In the analyses below we shed light on the work experiences of the deportees as they negotiate the occupational possibilities in a highly dependent society and seek ways to survive by a variety of means. We also discuss the importance of their support networks, highlighting the roles played by the family, friendships, and efforts to self-organize.

THE FORMAL SECTOR

THE TOURIST INDUSTRY

Although tourism was a target of investment by the Trujillo dictatorship during the 1970s, it was not until the Balaguer governments of the 1980s that that this sector of the economy was aggressively developed with the support of U.S. aid agencies and the World Bank. The number of tourists coming to the Dominican Republic increased dramatically from approximately 90,000 in 1970 to 3.7 million in 2004, 32% of whom came from the United States and 44% from Europe, with the British, Spanish, and Dutch most prominent among the sun-seekers (Pope 2007). Gregory (2007:28) noted that this form of economic development, which is largely based on "luxury tourism" (citing the work of Crick 1989), reproduces the "dualistic structure, the plantation system, of the colonial economy." This dualism is expressed in many ways, from the swelling coffers of the foreign and domestic business classes, who amass high rates of profits from the dozens of inclusive resorts while paying little or no taxes to the Dominican government, to the well-paid, largely expatriate management teams that run these establishments while the most menial and lowest paying jobs are reserved for the locals. It is in the race-, class-, and gender-bound system of labor stratification and colonial political economy that the deportee seeks to make his or her way in the world.

THE GUIDES

Ten of our subjects were working full-time in the tourist industry, some of them in formal positions with certifications as tourist guides, having gone through two months of training organized by the association of tourist guides in Santo Domingo. Such courses, which are paid for by the individual, consist of history lessons about Santo Domingo's rich colonial past and its development through the Trujillo years to the present, as well as explanations behind the different tourist sites in a city that has a number of firsts in the Americas (e.g., Columbus's first port-of-call, the first university in the hemisphere, the first cathedral, and the longest-serving dictator!). These positions offered a modicum of stability because tour guides would be offered work when a ship arrived in the harbor or a tourist bus descended on the colonial zone, with the official tourist union involved in finding bilingual guides. However, because the tourist trade was extremely unpredictable, not least due to the competition of inclusive resorts and the tendency of such resorts to keep tourists ensconced within their Westernized spaces, the extraordinary richness of Santo Domingo's past and present are largely missed by foreign visitors who come to this part of Hispaniola.

Another factor that inhibits tourism is the inability of the local and national governments to rid the River Osama of the massive amounts of garbage dumped daily into this natural open sewer by residents of the impoverished barrios along the water's edge. Such refuse, including discarded appliances, chokes the propulsion systems of incoming cruise liners, making their docking perilous. The stench and floating islands of detritus appalls the unsuspecting First World tourists.[3] Eddie[4], a deportee and long-time tour guide in the colonial center, aired his frustration:

> EDDIE: What's the damn secret? Invest in the people! Give us back our country so we can do useful things, so we can hand something down to our children. I wanna know, what's the damn secret? (May 22, 2003)

9.2 JAVIER IS A "GOFER" IN THE TOURIST INDUSTRY (*PHOTO:* WILLIAM COSSOLIAS).

For Manolo, however, the class, race, and gendered nature of the tourist industry's development is not always uppermost in his mind; he often ends up blaming the locals for not being sufficiently customer-friendly as the culture of capitalism has taught populations in other parts of the globe.

> MANOLO: I got motivated quickly and got into the organization as a tourist guide. A friend of mine said to me, "Manny, you know what your area is? You could be a nice tourist guide because you know how to deal with people." Over here they treat the tourists bad. They gotta get into taking care of the customer. Don't talk about your shit all the time . . . it's a whole different world. They don't know, they don't have that instinct. (June 2, 2003)

Despite Manolo's ability to take care of his customers—despite his biculturalism, his bilingualism and his social and economic networks that provide his customers with "good prices" on jewelry, clothes, cigars, and other local offerings—he is completely dependent on the few ships that arrive at the city's harbor for the $20 a day that he charges.

MANOLO: I ain't had a ship for three weeks . . . I don't know what's going on. There's nothing here. I come down every day hoping to hear about something, anything, and there's nothing. I try to keep myself busy, you know that. I don't want to drift off, fall over the edge like some of them who give up. I keep myself strong, always looking for an opportunity, but they not there anymore. You know I try. (August 5, 2005)

Manolo tries, and so did Roger, who also worked as a guide and who in 2005 won his right to return to the United States after proving that he indeed had U.S. citizenship and should not have been deported in the first place! Eddie also works hard, surveying the Conde and waiting for tourists to file down a chintzy shopping street in the colonial quarter, hoping to attract them with his broken American English:

EDDIE: You know how hard it is out here? I have to hustle, all day, every day, but I can get you whatever you want. I can show you all around here. (April 14, 2003)

THE GOFERS

Javier fills a role in the tourist economy below that of the guides, like a messenger or a "gofer," surviving off the tips from the "guys" above him and doing little errands for English-speaking tourists whenever he can get close enough to pitch his services. Javier is always living on the economic edge; he was deported seven years ago (at the time of the interview), leaving behind three children and an American-born wife on the west side of Manhattan. In his nervous Spanglish diction he explained how he experiences his occupational structures:

JAVIER: You go from day to day. Some days you can make five hundred pesos ($20), other days you make nothing. Mostly you make very little, just enough to buy a meal and maybe a beer. I do little jobs for tourist guides. I'd like to get a better job, but you need a "nota de buena conducta" (good conduct letter). If you're a deportee, it's stamped all over it, so as soon as the employer sees that it's all over. (November 3, 2002)

THE ATTENDANTS

Tony3 sits on his upside down tin can for twelve hours or more each day, parking the cars of the customers at the Café Americain then looking after them for twenty or thirty pesos while they eat meals that cost more than Tony's weekly income:

> TONY: Right now, this is my job; it's not, it's not really a real job, you know. I depend on tips. I don't have a paycheck. You know, the restaurant gives me a few dollars every week, a few pesos, but that's not enough. I just get by, with the emphasis on "just." (May 2, 2003).

These are the "tourist" workers, seen and unseen among the deportees. They are united by their common striving for a dollar here and there to provide them with a bowl of rice and beans for lunch—and when they are lucky, a piece of chicken or a thin piece of steak. On the occasional good day, or when a U.S. family connection manages to send them a few dollars, they might get a shot of rum or a bottle of Presidente beer to wash it down. But that's on a good day. . . .[5]

ZONA FRANCA WORKERS

Six of our respondents had jobs or had held jobs within the Zona Franca (see chapter 2). The great benefit for the employers in the Zona Franca is that they pay no business taxes, and there are few unions that are permitted to organize the work force in these areas; therefore, the exploitation rate is very high. Tomas, who worked in a call center in Santo Domingo, is one such worker:

> TOMAS: There are hundreds of deportees in these call centers. Both here in Santo Domingo and they have some more near Puerto Plata. I think we're almost all deportees in the one where I am because we speak fluent English. It's not as if the customers know about our history, is it? It's one of the few jobs we can get here. It's like there's actually a demand for us! I don't much like the work. It's monotonous, every day, one call after the other and you don't get paid much either. It's enough to survive on but you won't get rich on it. Someone's making money out of this, but it sure ain't us. (April 27, 2003)

Most of the call centers are legitimate, offering a range of services in the United States: giving driving directions, providing translations into English or Spanish, helping customers with insurance problems. There are some, however, that are set up as bogus enterprises, preying on the insecurities of gullible North Americans who are looking for some kind of comfort in the soothing words of fortune tellers.

MANOLO: Did I tell you about the call center scams going on here? This was a few years ago; it was hilarious; but a bit sad at the same time. There was this Dominican guy, he'd lived in the States and he had this idea to take advantage of Americans, you know the way they always call those people to hear some good news in their lives. You know, the crystal ball gazers. Well, that's what we did. It was crazy. These poor saps would call up from all over the U.S., especially the Mid-West, and we'd just tell them the biggest load of shit you've ever heard. You know, we'd tell them anything, anything that would make them feel better. We would have games in there, like who could get away with the biggest horse shit. Jesus, we used to laugh sometimes at what we'd say. We couldn't believe we were saying it, you know what I mean. We just used to get carried away, like we were acting or something. Still, I got a pay check every week for a couple of months. I used to get out of there on Friday afternoon and go straight down to Western Union and cash that check . . . that was something. (May 10, 2006)

EDUCATORS

Two of the respondents, Alex 2 and George, managed to find work as teachers in small English-language schools in downtown Santo Domingo. These were legitimate jobs, and they were paid a set amount per hour for giving English lessons at beginning and intermediate levels to Dominican students who were mainly in their twenties. George dedicated about thirty hours of work per week to this job. For George, who liked languages and was proud of his mastery of English, Spanish, and Italian, this occupation was a social, psychological and economic life line. It gave him back some dignity, allowed him to feel useful and wanted in a highly stratified Dominican society, and provided him with a small regular income from which he and his wife could eke out an existence.

GEORGE: Yeah. I've been doing a lot of teaching. I'm doing that, 90 percent of the time, the other 10 percent I have been taking care of my girl, my house, 'cause it's mine. No . . . I wanted to tell you something, at my school, nobody knows about why I was here or what I did. But I have respected the rules, and I'm a strong guide for learning, very intelligent, very thoughtful, and very honest. But I got that course by myself and I teach it right, I teach it consciously, all the English language classes that I teach. And I gotta say that most of them like it, you know . . . they have seen that I have the means to bring them out, to make them as good as possible. (March 2, 2003)

In 2003, when this interview was conducted, George was struggling to control his chronic diabetes. His wife, about fifteen years younger than George, came and sat with us during the latter part of the interview. It was obvious that their relationship was close, typical of the Dominican household; she took care of the domestic chores, and George brought in the income. During the interview, however, George revealed how vulnerable he was to the vicissitudes of the Dominican political economy and how, quite recently, his life had entered a particularly risky stage as the government bought into the neoliberal ideal of removing subsidies from all commodities, even those that are protected from the profit-based motives of the market in most advanced capitalist societies.

Field notes (March 2, 2003):
George tells me his story as he rocks back and forth in a cane mecedora. . . . George inherited his living space from his mother, who died earlier this year at the age of seventy-one. She was visiting one of his sisters in New York City when she passed away after suffering for years as a chronic diabetic, a disease which has been passed onto George. George's mother died in Manhattan, and her son was unable to visit her or even attend the funeral because of his deportee status. Tears well up in George's eyes as he tells the story:

I hardly ever go out any more. I bet you know the barrio where I grew up better than I do. Basically I teach my English classes and spend my time with my honey, thank God I have her. I make five thousand pesos a month (about $200), as long as I have ten students in the class. My rent is fourteen hundred pesos, I pay my phone bill, and I have enough to eat. My insulin is the most difficult thing to buy. It costs me two hundred pesos for each bottle and I need at least one a week. Insulin used to be cheaper, then the government cut out all the price supports for medicine. I think a lot of people die from diabetes because they can't afford the medicine. No one seems to talk about it, but it's true.

George, in fact, died about two years after this interview. When we visited Santo Domingo in the spring of 2005, Manolo advised us that George had had a stroke and was in the infamous Padre Bellini hospital.[6] George never left the hospital after the brain scan on the day after his stroke showed that it could not be treated, particularly with the family's lack of resources. Two weeks after the stroke, still in the hospital, George passed away.

Alex2, the second of the teachers, was a similarly tragic figure. He was the leader of the Dominican street organization, the Ñetas, and remarkably we had interviewed him five years earlier during another research project in the South Bronx. Alex2 had been deported in 2001 after serving three years in the New York state prison system. He had lived in the Bronx almost his entire life (twenty-four of his twenty-six years) and spoke with a strong New York City accent.[7]

> ALEX2: Yeah, I teach English over there (he points to an old building across from the Parque Independencia). I do ok. I have about ten students, and I come in a few hours every day. I get by. It's not enough, but it's all I can find right now. I have this ability, I know English fluently, I went to American schools, I'm not stupid and they wanna learn, so that's it.
>
> DAVID BROTHERTON (D.B.): Would you like to work more hours? I mean, would you like to be full-time?
>
> ALEX2: Of course I would. But, you know, I'm also a bit up and down myself. I'm trying to get myself settled, settle down. I have a girlfriend and we live together . . . she helps me out a lot, but I'm still a deportee. I don't belong here, so it's difficult. (December 3, 2002)

THE FARMER

Guido, the farmer, was deported more than a decade ago.[8] He was the only farmer in our sample who was working full-time. It was an extremely hard life—dealing with the vagaries of the market and the competition from much bigger agricultural concerns. For someone raised in a First World city, it was a tremendous culture change to struggle to make a living in the rural Dominican Republic. Guido liked the solitude, however; he liked being away from what he called the "craziness" of Santo Domingo where "things could happen to you." He also worried about his wife and two children, whom he wanted to protect and whom he thought would stand a better chance of making it "in the sticks." Guido recounted the pathway into his new occupation and his family travails:

> D.B.: Can you explain to me how you got into this line of work, farming?
>
> GUIDO: When I was small I used to always be around chickens, like here in this country. My most beautiful memories as a kid were here in the countryside. So when I got deported thirteen years ago, I had to decide what I was gonna do. I didn't wanna go to school and study 'cos I knew they weren't gonna pay you anything, not here. Don't forget I had two American kids and an American wife who came with me, so I had to bring in some money. So I thought it was better to start a business and start to earn my own dollars. I've always been that way, a bit entrepreneurial. I was the first to kill my own chickens around here and sell them to the supermarkets, and then I started to do the same with guinea hens. I was doing

ok, considering. You know how things are here. You never know if you're gonna have electricity, the workers come and go, and it's difficult to find people to rely on, but you get by, and my wife stood by me and my kids went to school here. It was tough for them. They were raised in Alabama and Virginia, and now they're here in the middle of nowhere.

D.B.: Is your family still with you?

GUIDO: No, I sent them all back a couple of years ago. I didn't want them to feel that they were paying for my mistakes. My wife still comes out once a year, and I see my kids sometimes during the holidays, they're both in college now. I'm not lying to you when I say it's difficult. I miss my family and I miss my kids. I'm just here alone most of the time, doing what I gotta do. That's just how it is. Nothing changes here except the date. Nothing gets better, I just have to do what I gotta do. But I've survived with no help from nobody except my family. (May 22, 2003)

THE PUBLIC SECTOR

Only one of the subjects had managed to penetrate the government payrolls on returning to his country. Using his political connections to the party in power, Luis2 managed to obtain a government job, a prized position in Dominican society, three years after being deported.

LUIS2: I'm working with the local PLD (Partido de la Liberación Dominicana, the party of President Leonel Fernández), I'm working on registering people in my neighborhood to vote.

D.B.: Why are you doing that? Do you like this party?

LUIS2: It's not about liking the party, they are all the same, but I have to get a job, man. The only way you get a government job here is to help the party in power, so when this guy gets in he has to pay me back for all the votes that I got for him, and I get him a lot of votes around here.

D.B.: So this has nothing to do with the qualifications for the job?

LUIS2: No, of course not, this is how our system works; the other party does the same thing. It will take a while, but it will happen a few months after he gets in.

D.B.: And what happens if he loses the next election.

LUIS2: I get fired and they give the job to someone else they need to repay a favor. (February 27, 2003)

This, more or less, is how the system works in the government sector. It is rare to find workers in government positions who arrived at their position

9.3 OUTSIDE LUIS2'S OFFICE WITH JUAN, ANTHER DEPORTEE (*PHOTO:* WILLIAM COSSOLIAS).

through any meritocratic route. For the vast majority, employment is obtained through patronage, a system of party paternalism that guarantees a deeply inefficient government culture, an indifferent work ethic, and a system that lacks transparency and accountability from the top to the bottom. Nevertheless, Luis2 was one of the lucky ones in our sample, and, with his law degree from the Autonomous University of Santo Domingo, he eventually gained a job in the city's real estate bureaucracy, where he negotiated land deals with potential developers.[9] He did this in the mornings, and in the afternoons he retired to his one-room law office in one of the city's poor barrios, where he represented an assortment of clients who found themselves in trouble with the local police or—much worse—in one of the country's notorious prisons. In such cases, Luis2 would be hired by families who paid him a few hundred pesos, sometimes just to have the charges explained to them in non-legalistic Spanish. Before Luis2 got his government job, he talked about his legal practice as we sat in his tiny office, with its noisy generator driving the air conditioning unit (it was just another day in the barrio of Villa Duarte without electricity).

D.B.: What sort of legal services do you provide?

LUIS2: I help my people with whatever they need. Someone gets picked up for being drunk, someone gets busted for drugs—there's a lot of drugs around here—someone faces eviction, another person has a fight with his wife, someone just wants to use the copier!

D.B.: Do you make any money doing this?

LUIS2: No, not really. I can't survive on what I make here, even though I'm the only lawyer around. The people are poor, there's no money here.

DB: How do you survive?

LUIS2: My wife works in a hair dresser's; she does ok, enough for us to get by. (April 2, 2003)

THE INFORMAL SECTOR

STREET SELLERS

We sat on a bench in the zona colonial near where Luis (pictured on the first page of this chapter) was selling a few Haitian and Dominican paintings at the side of the Conde. He was working as a street salesman for another small-time entrepreneur, making a few pesos to help pay his rent and give his life some structure. But trade is very slow for sellers of paintings that typically vary between the beach scenes or lush tropical gardens of Dominican artists to the colorful hubbub of urban life or village society that make up the work of Haitian artists. These paintings sell for as little as $5 or $10, and there is little unique about these popular pieces of art that are found all over Santo Domingo. Luis muses about life in New York and his "plans" for exile in the Dominican Republic. In a follow-up interview in 2006, Luis was in much the same position—still sitting on the Conde, still trying to sell these paintings, still talking of his "plans." However, in addition to his work as a street vendor, he had set up a popular chess club next to his selling spot, with several tables and about ten locals whiling away their free hours in pursuit of a checkmate over their opponents. Luis was hoping that this initiative might somehow lead to a "real" club, maybe the "government or someone could see their way to investing in us," he whimsically suggested.

D.B.: They (deportees [added by the authors]) can't find work?

LUIS: They gotta make money on their own, start up small businesses for any kind of selling. Look, when I first got here I sold paintings, paintings of bodegas, marinas, you know, what is called flamboyantes, um, colonial. You gotta get into something that you can make money off. If you know a trade like tailoring or something else, you might be able to survive here, working for yourself, but it's really difficult to work for someone else. First, they don't want you, and second, they work different here and they treat their workers terrible. I mean the pay's a joke and you've got no rights, nothing. People here would rather see a deportee dead than help you out, give you something useful to do. Maybe it's because they're afraid of them I don't know. So this is what I do to get by, to stop myself from going crazy. And the guys here hang around, playing their chess games, and it all helps a little bit. What can I say? What else can I do? Really, what else can I do? (August 22, 2003)

THE SEX TRADE

We have discussed the experience of the small number of deportees who were involved in the formal economy, whereas the majority of our deportees found themselves outside of these economic structures. Most deportees find themselves working below their capabilities, with their different forms of human capital going wasted. Two sectors of the informal economy that are always looking for workers are the sex and drugs trades. Several subjects working in the "tourist" industry were involved in both; José, one of our first respondents, was the most explicitly involved of the study participants.

During the first year of the project, José spent nine months in what might be loosely termed "the informal economy." It was difficult to know exactly what he did except that, based on observations of his street interactions and the constant ringing of his cell phone, he was involved as a broker (called "maipiolo/a" in Dominican Spanish), introducing European and American male tourists to freelance female sex workers, negotiating prices, times, and places, taking his own commission (Brennan 2004).

> Of the men, José used to say, "They want beautiful Dominican pussy, something they can't get back home. They want to spend time with them, like two or three days, you know, while they're on holiday. They want someone who can take care of them, looks good on their arm, gives them excitement. They can't get this in Rome, or Chicago, or some bum fuck place in the Mid-West. Sometimes they even fall in love and sometimes the girl falls in love. But for the girls it's different, they just want to get out of here. Many of them have children at home in the barrio, sometime they even bring their children with them when they are with the men. These are my people, do you think we like to live like this? (Field notes, May 6, 2004)

In an informal interview with one of José's clients, John, a fifty-five year-old filmmaker from Los Angeles, confided to me (D.B.) about his experience with a beautiful, lithe, twenty-eight-year-old Dominican sex worker with whom he had just spent a week in Samaná, a favored resort in the northeast of the country.

JOHN: Claudia, man, she's beautiful, I mean she's perfectly built, svelt-like, dresses the part and fucks when I need her to but there's no conversation. I drive along with her for miles and she doesn't say a fucking thing. It's like she's there till the money runs out. Man, I don't know about these Dominican whores, I thought they were supposed to be the best in the world, would do anything for you. But if they don't talk they are just fucking machines and how can a guy get off on that?

José's modus operandi was to hang out on the main thoroughfare in the Zona Colonial, el Conde, approaching English-, Spanish-, or French-speaking male tourists and engaging them in conversation about the not-so-secret pleasures of Santo Domingo. Local female sex workers would check in with him during the afternoons to see who was around and to learn whether José had done his work among the many young and middle-aged tourist "johns" on the lookout for a little Dominican adventure. A colleague and fellow social scientist who had employed José in previous studies gave us this insider's perspective on José's past:

José's nickname as a boy was "Chico Lindo" (Pretty Boy), a name that he was very fond of, and probably revealed to very few men or women. He was raised by one of his grandmothers as an attempt to rear an "exceptional" altar-boy child from a marginal community. This is somewhat akin to the so called "berdache tradition" (half man/half woman, or "two-spirited person"). This may have included the belief that he was the child of a luá (voodu/santería god or deity) and was born with a special (divine) "light" or aura. I remember he told me that his grandmother used to tell him that he would go from one problem to another because of his "bad head" (mala cabeza, not being very wise). Since he was handsome and lively, he developed the traits of a "charmer" and few people (women or men) could resist his seductive and non-aggressive jest. Our friendship was good because I always treated him as a friend and he treated me as a confidant, never as a potential client. I guess he was not used to this, but it worked as a sound basis of mutual respect. We talked frequently and I learned important things about his sexual culture. He got married (consensually) with a "hard-headed" (motherly) Dominican woman of his social class who controlled and stabilized him (she may have beaten him a couple of times, or at least she was quite demanding and jealous). He made the arrangements for her to get married with a Spaniard who took her to his country. During his teenage years and early youth he may be considered a "Sanky-Panky," that is, as a hustler, mostly to relatively well-off foreign gay men, although he maintained a relationship with a "rich" Canadian man for some years. He confided in me once about all the violence he had to endure to remain in the trade of sex tourism. Many of these mostly male client/lovers maintained communication by phone or fax with him, and they used to send money whenever he, his family, or some close phantom had any new real or imaginary need. He boasted to me about the thousands of dollars he made some of these "victims" spend. He traveled to the States, probably with the help of some lover, but was soon involved in cocaine consumption and sales. I think he spent some five years in a U.S. prison and survived by belonging to a gang. He was finally deported and spent some two to three years in quite bad shape and physical health, without money. I do not know how long he has suffered from diabetes, but it was something he started mentioning after his deportation. Jose's "functions" or roles were manifold. I would use the term "multifaceted" or "versatile" to describe them. He was as he needed to be in every moment, "opportune" rather than opportunistic. He was an abused husband, a foreign male gigolo (sanky), a pimp to younger female sex workers (chulo), a male hustler (bugarrón) to gay men, probably a gay lover with some men, and a procurer (maipiolo) for both male and female sex tourists who were not personally interested in him. (August 3, 2005)

Marcelo was also involved, primarily as a maipiolo and as a small time provider of cocaine (see later section). Others used women in another way to survive, through providing women to whom they were not particularly attracted with their bodies, their companionship, and their sexual prowess. Tony3 was one such chulo (although his definition of "chulo" is somewhat different than that explained above. Tony3's definition is closer to the role of a "gigalo"):

> TONY3: She wants me but she's fat, fat, like a blood sausage (prieta in Spanish [added by the authors]), "fat girl." Now this is how it is here, I teach you. She's over there (he points out the window to a house about fifty meters away), checking out if I'm here or not, I know that because her window is open. But I can't go over to her house because she has girls and they don't like me, although she has a son who really likes me. So, she wants me but I can't go over there to eat because of the rest of her family. Sometimes she sends her son over to get me but I don't go because of my pride, I mean, she wants me but I can't eat her, what's that? You understand? Anyway, it's another form of surviving here but I'm doing it the good way, right? (laughs) I'm doing it by being a "chulo"—I let the women take care of me when I want them to. Of course I want proper work, I would love to work, but there's nothing and I'm not going to rob. No, I'd never resort to that. (July 18, 2003)

Only one member of our small female sample, Ferna, was engaged in the sex trade industry. Ferna was not prepared to be interviewed about this aspect of her life, although from other sources it is possible to partially describe how she was surviving. Ferna had come from an abusive series of relationships in the United States and had spent several years in prison there. Part of her earlier working life was spent as a go-go dancer in night clubs in Queens. On finding herself penniless in Santo Domingo in 2003, she struck up a relationship with Tony, who earned his living parking clients' cars outside restaurants. Ferna was a tall, blond, shapely, bilingual Dominican in her late thirties who desperately missed her three children in the United States and faced considerable obstacles finding work in the formal economy. After six months without work, Ferna concluded that sex work was the best paid and most available work to her. She entered this massive industry as a freelancer and earned around $50 per client in the Colonial District and at the large casino hotels along the Malecón Boulevard, which faces the Caribbean.

THE DRUGS TRADE—SELLERS AND USERS

Few members of our sample were involved in the drugs trade, even though it was ubiquitous in the Dominican captial. Celio gives several reasons why:

> I sold drugs for a week and I said, "No, that's not for me." I let that business go. If I'm invited, I say, "No, no, I don't do that." Why can't I sell what I sold in Puerto Rico? Here it's worse, because if I pass here what I passed in Puerto Rico and I get caught, my family has no way to help me. How am I going to pay for a lawyer to get out of this? They would give me ten years, and you know that prisons here are like time bombs. Here an incarcerated person is easily a dead body. At any moment there could be a riot, and either the cops kill the inmates, or the inmates kill each other. I don't want to be confined there, I don't want to get into trouble. I want to be at peace. (March 3, 2003)

Of the few in our sample who participated in this part of the informal economy, some had been involved in the sex trade and also had relationships with drug dealers, particularly in the cocaine market, which gave them an additional product for their clients. In such cases, the provision of drugs was more of a sideline and not their principal occupation, although they were able to earn a significant mark-up on the price of a gram of cocaine (from $5 to $10). For example, José supplied his customers with drugs, mainly pot and cocaine, to enhance their experience with the sex workers. His drug contacts were usually European or Americans (between thirty and fifty years old) who visited throughout the day at the Café de Flores or at night at a brothel called the House of Models.

On drives with José through different barrios, he spoke of entering a "98 percent or 95 percent zone," which he said referred to the level of purity of the cocaine being sold in these neighborhoods. On one occasion, José met a seaman from the Dominican–Puerto Rican ferry that sailed twice weekly to Rincon on the Puerto Rican coast. This contact was said by José to be part of a drug supply network that was transporting kilos of cocaine. One week later, the newspapers were full of a story about a "bust" in which five of the crew had been arrested. José commented on the report:

> JOSÉ: I get the drugs when the tourists need them. If they don't ask me for them, I don't get them. I don't push drugs, it's just something I have access to; I've lived on the streets most of my life, so I know many of the players. You know there's tons of drugs coming in here and you know who's behind it. The militares, the policía, they're all involved in it, so you got to be very careful. They will take you out in a second, they are the worst gangsters. They are the real gangsters. We're just trying to survive, but they run the business. (April 18, 2003)

Others from our sample made up a small group of heavy drug-users, especially those who were addicted to heroin (Martín 2010). As a visiting New York journalist reported:

> The worst-off spend their days in a drug-induced fog minutes from this capital city's mammoth Palacio Nacional, with its palm-tree promenades and roseate marble walls.
>
> More comfortable speaking English than Spanish, they are members of a growing subculture: deported criminals who served time Stateside and are now wasting away in this Caribbean nation of eight million.
>
> "We try to stick together because we can relate to each other. We're Americanized. It's a different mentality," Hayden Lafontaine, thirty-seven, a convicted cocaine dealer raised in Brooklyn, said, "We're strangers in our own country."
>
> Lafontaine lives in San Carlo, a slum that another criminal deportee described as like the "South Bronx when it was burning down in the 1970s." Mornings he shoots up on heroin, or, if he doesn't have drugs, shoplifts or calls family members in America, begging them to send money. Then, pain dulled, he sits in his urine-stenched apartment waiting out the afternoon rains and discussing with other deportees anything from the presidential debates to the latest Yankees game."

(GERSON 2004)

We found that heroin in many respects was a perfect drug for some deportees' psychosocial condition and marginalized economic situation. It numbs their feelings, it helps them escape momentarily from their insoluble dilemmas, it blocks out the memories of their families and loved ones in the United States, and it often reactivates an addiction that they thought they had overcome. The deportee heroin user slides into addiction by a combination of the drug's seductive, euphoric properties and profound feelings of social rejection, economic helplessness, and cultural alienation. The deportee heroin user then builds his or her own circle of rejected associates who have a common bond: the drug and being deported. Some addicts are involved in injection use, others prefer to sniff the powder, which provides them with an illusory feeling of control over their addiction, i.e., sniffing is not as bad as injecting into the vein, it's not as invasive and, therefore, you are not as dependent.

MIGUEL2: We say, who's gonna get the "bolsa" (the bag). Each bag costs 150 pesos or about US $5. Some guys split a bag, depends what you need, how desperate you are, and how much money you have. The heroin comes in three colors, white, brown, and beige.

D.B.: Has it been cut?

MIGUEL2: Yeah, it's always been cut with something. It comes from Colombia, sometimes Pakistan, depends where the boats are coming from. One dealer has weak heroin, another strong . . . word gets around who's got what. A lot of heroin users call it "medicina"—"voy a conseguir la medicina" (I'm going to get my medicine) or "Curarme" (cure me), they say.

D.B.: So a lot of users treat it as medicine?

MIGUEL2: Yeah, kinda. Like Chino would say, "M., I'm sick, help me out." I'd say, "Ok, I'll do one and one." That's a line for each nose, and he'd go get the syringe and the works and shoot up the rest. You know, we call the works what you use to shoot up with. (August 9, 2006)

Addicts maintain the habit through various means. Often they live off remesas sent from family members in the United States, and some are fortunate enough to keep their work lives going (but these are few). Danny, for example, was able to maintain his work and drug lives simultaneously, but shooting up eventually took its toll.

DANNY: My mother came here in October, she helped me out a lot, brought me a lot of clothing and stuff. I wasn't doing too bad, I was doing well. I was working as a receptionist in the Napolitano Hotel, and I was selling

9.4 OMAR, A DEPORTEE ADDICT AND THE BROTHER OF CESAR (SEE FIGURE 9.5), OUTSIDE HIS FAMILY'S SHOOTING GALLERY. OMAR DIED FROM RESPIRATORY FAILURE IN FEBRUARY 2010 (*PHOTO: LUIS BARRIOS*).

communications also, and then I just started cracking up with drugs. Heroin . . . .

D.B.: When did that start?

DANNY: That started in 2001, yeah, 2001. I started shooting up. I never shot up before, all my life, I just snorted and smoked crack . . . and now I'm all fucked up. (May 3, 2006)

Others can only feed their habit by engaging in different forms of criminality, usually selling illegal drugs, working in the sex trade, shoplifting from stores (toothpaste and cans of tuna were favorite items for resale, just enough for a bag of heroin), or stealing from their families. Paulina explained how impossible it was for her to remain with her supportive family and how difficult it was to live apart from her adolescent son:

D.B.: How are your relations with your family?

PAULINA: Always they want to see me, but what happens is that I am not at home because of the problems with my addiction. I am going to be totally honest with you, they give me things to sell because when I get sick from the heroin I feel terrible. I'm in a lot of pain, my head hurts, then I get diarrhea, I just get completely sick. As a result, if I was around

9.5 CESAR *(LEFT)* AND RAMON OUTSIDE THE SHOOTING GALLERY IN SANTO DOMINGO *(PHOTO: LUIS BARRIOS)*

I would hurt my family in all kinds of ways, do you understand? So that's why I try to keep myself away from the family's house so as not to hurt my son, hurt all those who care about me. Do you understand? But whenever I'm feeling well again, when I don't need the drugs anymore, I go back to my house and they treat me well. Thank God. (May 3, 2006)

These are very psychologically depressed and socially alienated circles because the heroin drugs culture in Santo Domingo is not large (although it is growing; see Martín 2010), unlike New York. These individuals are well known to community residents, who regard them with disdain. They desperately need treatment and some form of outreach; otherwise, death awaits them. The only agency willing to deal with them is a private institution run by the Catholic Church called "Hogar Crea," which is located about an hour outside Santo Domingo and requires the "patient" to pay one thousand pesos to enter its doors—no exceptions.

In our sample, five of the addicts had spent time at the Hogar Crea facility, including Danny, who at one time had been a leading member of this community "in recovery." For all their expressed desire to leave their addiction behind, it was extremely difficult for these individuals to maintain sobriety when faced with so many social, economic, and cultural impediments to full social integration.

D.B.: So, you've been fucked up for five years now.

DANNY: Yeah, five years. I did six months in jail. Then I was in the program. I was the director of the program at Hogar Crea, and when I got out of jail I went straight into it and was there for two years, clean. I was doing great, and then I fucked up. I came out again and fucked up again. . . . (May 4, 2006)

A third exception was P., who, after two years of unsuccessfully trying to find work in the formal economy, eventually slipped back into a heroin habit he had picked up in New York City more than a decade before. P. described his induction back into the business and also his move out of it.

PEDRO: Since I saw you last I've been going through a roller coaster, you won't believe my life here. Well, I got back into my old habits. It was something I was trying desperately to avoid, but I couldn't do it anymore. I was too depressed and just down. So I started using again, and before I know I'm using every day and I'm really down, down in the gutter, literally. I just lived to shoot up, I couldn't help myself, and then I knew I had to get myself together otherwise I was gonna die. I'd already seen a few of the guys o.d. and it was just a matter of time for me. Anyway, I started to get out of it but I was still using . . . I was kind of in and out of it at the same time. Then someone knew a little bit about my past and asked me if I wanted to get involved again. I didn't want to but I was desperate, I didn't know what to do, but before you know it I'm in the mix again. I'm working for these military types, you know they run the trade here, I'm not kidding, and they're ruthless. I mean it, they'll just put your lights out no questions asked. Anyway, they took out my buddy, another deportee. They just got rid of him, just like that. So, I had to do what I had to do. You know what I mean, and that's when I got out of it. I got out of it completely, got myself a girl, got married, had a kid. I know, you can't believe it, can you? (June 2, 2008)

DREAMS OF SELF-EMPLOYMENT

Although many deportees talked of wanting to start up their own businesses, few had managed to do so. What were they realistically going to do? Where would they get the loans necessary to start a small business? The banks in the Dominican Republic, unless you are well connected, do not lend money easily, and the interest rates are generally usurious. A number of deportees had dreams like that of Luis3, who dreamed of owning a bodega in a local neighborhood.

D.B.: What are your plans?

LUIS3: My plans are that, if God helps me, you know, try to get a little bit of money, I'm trying to save up some money so I could get a business, a grocery store—yeah, that's my major objective, because right now I'm too old to be going back to New York and doing what I was doing back then. I'm not gonna get used to working for somebody else like in a factory, and I'm not a professional, I'm not a scientist, I'm not no lawyer, none of that. If I get a little bit of money, fifty, sixty, or a hundred thousand pesos for a store, I'd be my own boss and have people work and make my money, so that's my major objective. (May 23, 2003)

Like many others, Celia, who had relatively recently been deported, dreamed of using her cooking skills to set up a small dining establishment like many other that dot the barrios. Celia was probably correct to place her fate in the hands of God rather than looking to any local infrastructure to help her idea become a reality.

LUIS BARRIOS (L.B.): What do you think you'll be doing in five years?

CELIA: If God helps me, I'll have a chain of "comedores" (small eating establishments).

L.B.: You like to cook?

CELIA: Yes, I like cooking. Having a restaurant in Limon de Juna to get by on, if God permits it. (May 26, 2003)

REMESAS

LEONA: See, a person like me, I wanna live out of this country, you know, because I don't want my family to keep sending me money, you know, I'm tired of that stuff, I wanna have my own job. (April 1, 2003)

Money sent back to deportees from their families in the United States has become one of the largest revenue streams for many Third World countries; remesas are currently the third most important revenue source for the Dominican Republic (see chapter 2). The subject of remesas has become a favorite topic of transnational studies showing the deep economic interdependency of developed and developing nations and the reliance of the former on the cheap, quiescent labor of the latter. The latter exports their generations of surplus labor, helping prop up their strangled economies while reducing the potential for social discontent from excessive rates of mass unemployment.

Although the respondents frequently spoke with dismay, like L. above, about their dependency on support from family members in the United

States, they were extremely grateful when the money came through, usually to one of the Western Union offices in Santo Domingo. The family members abroad would pool their resources, with brothers, sisters, and parents putting in $20 or $30 each month so that the deportees could receive enough money to pay their rent. Sometimes the amount was more than the rent, depending on the financial well-being and disposition of the family, particularly of the parents (usually the mother); sometimes it was less, and sometimes it arrived once every two or three months instead of monthly. Most of the deportees came from poor or working-class families, which meant that this financial support was difficult to sustain.

For most deportees, the remesa was the difference between living on the street and keeping their bare apartments or single-room occupancies. If the deportee had managed to start a new relationship and a new family, the remesa would pay for the children's education, hospital bills, or the sudden upsurge in the cost of living, which is a frequent occurrence because the government abandoned many of its price support policies.

OTHER SOCIAL SUPPORTS

Social capital is crucial in the Dominican Republic. Returning migrants who have been away for substantial periods of time are challenged to build or rebuild social networks that lead to meaningful employment or bearable living situations. Some throw themselves into different levels of the Dominican transnationalist society, using their past relationships with the United States to build transcultural networks on the island. This is the case with deportees who have spent the better part of their lives in the United States. Others who immigrated to the United States later in life try to revive their past networks, reuniting with their family members and doing their utmost to develop new partnerships, new families, and new webs of meaning. Others who cannot do this, or are simply unwilling to become acculturated to Dominican life and the limited opportunity structures that are impossible to overcome, did their utmost to reenter the United States (see chapter 11) by a variety of means and routes. They are convinced that the culture conflicts are insurmountable. Victor was taken to the United States when he was four months old and never returned until he was deported in 1998.

D.B.: What happened at the end of your sentence?

VICTOR: I went to a detention center in Buffalo like a county jail. They have a floor rented to the INS. I did three days there and got deported back here; it was a commercial flight.

D.B.: You went back over the border?

VICTOR: Yeah, I couldn't adapt here. It was the first time I'd ever been here and I didn't speak Spanish that good.

D.B.: What did you do during those sixteen months?

VICTOR: I got together with a girl, she got pregnant. It's like I related to her as a woman but not to her culture, her background. I went from an industrialized country to . . .

D.B.: The Third World.

VICTOR: . . . a Third World country and it wasn't the same. (May 3, 2007)

THE FAMILY

Dominican society is heavily based on relations of organic solidarity (Grasmuck and Pessar 1991; Levitt 2001), interwoven, blood-related, and extended kinship networks that are cemented by ritual gatherings, mutual obligations, and reciprocal relations. Much of this is in the tradition of matrilineal Latino family structures in which the woman and mothers are simultaneously placed on a moral pedestal (the Marianismo syndrome) while being relegated to a subordinate economic and political position vis à vis men in the family. Most deportees, however, come from highly fragmented families; they are forced to attach themselves to whatever family relations exist in their new (in most cases) homeland. Despite obstacles to a relatively settled family life, a number of deportees were able to re-establish familial roots that aided the resettlement process. Of the sixty-five subjects, fifteen were currently living with family members and another ten had lived with family relations in the past (before overstaying their welcome). Nine other deportees had started new families with Dominican partners, all leading to Dominican-born children (mostly in addition to their children left behind in the United States). Seven deportees were living in apartments owned by their parents who lived in the United States. For most deportees, the family in its various forms had proved to be a crucial stabilizing factor on their return as indicated by Luis and Miguel:

LUIS: I returned home to my mother and sister after being locked up for eight years in Massachusetts. It was a terrible thing for my mother and the rest of my family . . . they didn't have the money to visit me and just had to wait here, hoping I would eventually come back. (August 2, 2003)

MIGUEL: I don't think that nobody is a saint, you know what I mean, but they're (deportees [added by the authors]) desperate, you know, 'cause they don't know nobody, nobody help them out, you know, nobody got

them good luck. I got my mother and my family here. At least I got that . . .
there is no way out in here if you don't. (January 25, 2003)

Similarly, Tony's mother was instrumental in laying a foundation for his resettlement, whereas Freddy described the feeling of being integrated after his family welcomed him back unconditionally:

D.B.: Did you get any support from your family when you came back?

TONY: Yes, they supported me, thank God. They bought me clothes, shoes, everything, you know, everything I needed, they sent it over. My mother came and brought me stuff.

D.B.: Did she come to stay with you for a while?

TONY: Yes, she came for about a month. She stood here with me, to find me a place where I could stay.

D.B.: Is that where you are now?

TONY: Yes, I'm there since 2001. And you know, they supported me, they still support me, right now, you know, because when I need a few dollars, you know, I gotta call them, and they also help me with the rent. (April 1, 2003)

FREDDY: In the barrio where I live it's to the contrary, the people say that I'm an asset to the community because I do a lot of favors for people. Everyone around there wants me in the neighborhood because it's like always asking me to do this and that. . . .

D.B.: You do all kinds of things for people?

FREDDY: Yes, and I ask for nothing in return.

D.B.: And no one says you're a deportee?

FREDDY: Nope, nothing like that, never. (February 11, 2003)

These are undoubtedly the more positive experiences of family reattachment and solidarity that also extended to some of the heroin users. For example, one of the main shooting galleries where deportee addicts gathered and resided part-time was owned by a deportee's mother in Brooklyn, while another addict was consistently being placed in Hogar Crea by his mother and brothers as they sought to contain his "habit."

Others, however, were not so fortunate. Eleven members of the sample experienced rejections from their family, including from their mothers, aunts, uncles and more distant relations. In each of these cases, deportees felt bitter and resentful because they felt disowned, abandoned, and denigrated. Most of the subjects did not like to speak much about their rejection because it was a painful and recent episode.

In the previous chapter, Alex was one of the more expressive respondents on this subject. Tony2 also spoke about his mother as we sat in his threadbare room, having just pawned his small television set for food. Tony2's response was typical of those deportees who for years had had little contact with anyone in their family. Although they can remember the names of relatives, their addresses, the ages, and the physical conditions were becoming increasingly obscure and meaningless

D.B.: What about your mother? She never contacted you?

TONY2: She lives in Puerto Rico, but I don't know about her, she moved to an apartment and I don't have the new number. In December she sent me something to eat, yeah, December 5, you see this is the day, my mother. . . . (Tony2 looks at the calendar hanging from the wall)

D.B.: Yeah, I see December.

TONY2: But I don't have her new phone. My mother is Ines Mojica, Alma is my father's name, Mojica is my mother's. I don't lie, they were my parents, but I don't know no more, I don't know the address, nothing. She still goes to church; I think she's sixty-five or something, retired. (April 1, 2003)

FRIENDS, POLITICS, AND SELF-HELP

In addition to the family, many deportees did their best to provide social and economic support to one another, although, as was noted earlier, some deportees preferred to beat their own path to survival, often fearing that continued relations with other deportees would mire them in their marginality through stigma and the effects of deportees' "negative habits." Manolo reflects on the contradictory position in which deportees find themselves and how they sometimes are the only ones to whom they can turn.

D.B.: There are different types of deportees, right? Now, the last ones you talked about, the Americanized deportees, do you see them like they stay together, help each other?

MANOLO: Yes, they help each other, they stay together and they're more reasonable people. They also think positive, regret coming back here, and wanna leave from here 'cos they get so rejected. (May 10, 2006)

We encountered numerous groups of deportees socializing with one another and helping each other through job references, financial handouts, and advice on questions of the law and different aspects of Dominican culture.

9.6 THIS IS THE FIRST AND ONLY PAMPHLET PUBLISHED BY THE FLEDGLING "CASA DEL REPATRIA-DO," FOUNDED AT THE CHURCH OF FATHER ROGELIO CRUZ IN THE BARRIO OF CRISTO REY IN 2003.

On at least two occasions, these relations developed into attempts at self-organization.

First, in 2002, a deportee lawyer founded a support group after the first ever conference in the Dominican Republic dedicated to the issues of deportations at the Autonomous University of Santo Domingo. The group was helped by the radical priest Rogelio Cruz, who provided space for the group to hold its weekly meetings and offered strategic and organization advice. However, not long after the group's birth, Father Cruz fell victim to the church's hierarchy and a witch-hunt conducted by the then President Mejia, which eventually forced Father "Rogelio" to leave the island for an extended stay in Mexico to avoid being sent permanently to Spain on orders of the Catholic Bishop. Over time the group weakened and eventually dissipated.

Three years later, however, in June 2005, a second group was started by another deportee, René (see interview excerpt below and the beginning of chapter 5) and three friends, called "Bienvenido Seas, Inc.," a year after René's repatriation. René is an articulate and garrulous man in his fifties and came of age when the crack and cocaine trade was dominating much of the informal economy of his neighborhood, Washington Heights in Manhattan. René

9.7 RENÉ, THE FOUNDER OF BIENVENIDO SEAS, A SELF-HELP GROUP FOR DEPORTEES (*PHOTO: LUIS BARRIOS*).

did "hard time" in some of New York's most infamous prisons and intimately knows the obstacles that deportees face and the sociocultural and economic backgrounds from which many of them come.

> RENÉ: Listen, I was no saint, I've got to tell you, but I paid for what I did in some of the worst prisons in America, and I grew up in the barrio. I didn't grow up here. I spent nearly all my life there and so I know what it's like to be thrown back here with nothing. There's sixty thousand of us now back here and we're treated like crap. So we've gotta do something for ourselves. We've gotta advocate for ourselves and we've gotta win respect for ourselves. That's why we formed this organization, which is growing every day. But I don't want it to stop there, no way, I'm gonna get into politics and force this issue out in the open. (September 22, 2006)

René is currently the president of this nonprofit organization and ensures that the group meets at least once a month; every Wednesday evening, representatives go to the airport to receive the weekly batches of deportees. The group functions as a social support and networking organization to help deportees obtain resources and find broader acceptance in Dominican society, and to educate the community on the many issues of deportation and the everyday lives of deportees.[10] In the May 2010 elections for the Dominican Congress, René made good on his promise to run for office and gained substantial media attention and community support while putting forward a program advocating for and uniting the most marginalized segments of Dominican society. However, despite an excellent chance of success, René fell afoul of the country's Procuraduria General Radhamés Jiménez Peña (roughly equivalent to the U.S. Attorney General), who ruled that René be disqualified due to his past criminal record, even though René has committed no crime in the Dominican Republic. This is yet another example of stigma and social exclusion that confirms the experience of so many other deportees.

INDIGENCE

> D.B.: So, you've been on the streets for. . . .
>
> NAVY VETERAN DEPORTEE: I've been in the streets since about three days after my birthday. Let me see, November 20, since November 20 I've been in the streets. I'm going to one of my aunt's house and I take a shower over there and eat once in a while. Then I got tired of going there because, you know, I don't wanna impose, and I really need help, seriously 'cause I just can't adjust to this. This is not my way to live. I've never been, like, so, so down in my life. (August 22, 2003)

Of the sixty-five participants in our street sample, three could be described as indigent. Of these three, Alex (as mentioned earlier), appeared to have died through what some believe was a drug overdose (may have been suicide.) A second, the Navy veteran quoted above, "disappeared" and has not been seen since 2003. A third died in 2004 from alcohol and drug-related causes after spending many years sleeping on the streets of the colonial zone and suffering from what many believe was a "mental illness." In the Dominican Republic, there are no homeless shelters or social services for the indigent. Their only resources are their families, compassionate members of the community, and sometimes outreach efforts from the Catholic Church. We have little data on the day-to-day lives of indigent subjects, although we know a good deal about their past lives. Although we had only three cases in our sample, there were many more cases of deportee indigents in Santo Domingo and Santiago. They were frequently seen scavenging for food in the trash cans outside restaurants and sleeping wherever they could without being rousted by the local police. Josefina, who considers herself "surviving" in Santo Domingo described how close to the precipice she is:

> JOSEFINA: Good, the life of Josefina. We've been working here, as you can see, selling "ropa vieja" (a typical Dominican dish), putting out a little juice and doing what we can to support ourselves because the truth here

is, just imagine, there is nothing. There is no chance if you don't have a political connection or you don't know how to work the system and your family can't help you find work. The situation is fucked. For a person to be able to eat, you have to juggle a lot because there are days when you simply can't eat. It's ten or twelve o'clock during the day and you still haven't got ten or twenty pesos to buy a pound of rice, and for whatever reason you can't sell anything . . . that's the life of Josefina right now. (October 23, 2002)

CONCLUSION

Deportees make up a heterogeneous and heavily stigmatized population. Most members of this population would welcome some form of reintegration into mainstream economic Dominican society, and some indeed found their way into this strata. Many, however, were forced to exist in the socio-economic margins as they confronted the highly limited opportunity structure and the lack of a social network and support system that might have provided them with more sustainable ways to survive. Hence, for many, there was not much to their experience other than struggling in the informal economy, licit or illicit; for a few, it meant subsisting at the lowest level of society, compounding their already precarious psychological and social condition. For those faced with such pervasive marginality, heroin and other drugs became a means by which to cope, and years of sobriety gave way to the everyday life of the dope fiend and the inevitable decline of their physical and mental health to the point of death.

We found that, above all, economic survival depended particularly on the deportees having some valued social capital with which to weave their way back into Dominican society. Of course, for those who had left for the United States much later in life, the forced return home was less traumatic because many of their family and friendship connections were still intact. For those primarily raised in the United States, the negatively labeled "Dominicany-orks," the links with family and extended kin were often strained, which hampered the assimilation and acculturation processes and further impeded their abilities to economically resettle.

10.1 AN INCARCERATED DEPORTEE IN RAFEY PRISON, SANTIAGO (*PHOTO:* LUIS BARRIOS).

CHAPTER TEN

BACK IN THE HOMELAND: PART THREE

PRISON, DOMINICAN STYLE

*If you come here from over there, all of a sudden they put a label on you.
Then they find something to pin on you, and then they want to get rid of
you. That's what they do with every deportee. That's probably why you're
doing a survey, 'cause you found out how, out of a hundred deportees, sixty
wind up getting killed. Why is that?*

(U.S. NAVY VETERAN, OCTOBER 23, 2002)

"Hey Father Barrios, what you doing here? Remember me? Victor from Washington Heights."

"Yes, I remember you," Luis retorts, smiling at the inmate who approaches him. The two warmly embrace, and then Luis explains our presence.

"We're here to interview deportees, but the administration says there aren't any."

"There's loads of us here," says Victor. "We just don't tell 'em we're deportees 'cos, you know, they could treat you differently and you don't wanna stand out here, you know what I mean? I'll go and get you a bunch." (Field notes, Rafey Prison, June 5, 2007)

As noted in the chapter 9, life is extremely precarious and marginal for many deportees as they find themselves excluded from the few opportunities that exist in the formal economy and are bereft of family and community networks that have been left behind in the United States. Those who spent less time in the United States may be able to rekindle many of their old social and familial networks, but the prospects of living the rest of their lives in a highly dependent economy shot through with the colonizing structures of the West is still daunting. In this chapter, we examine another aspect of social and institutional marginality that many deportees experience: the Dominican prison system.

In May 2007, we visited two prisons in the Dominican Republic and conducted fifteen life history interviews with deportees. The first prison, Rafey, with approximately 750 inmates (down from 1,200 a couple of years before), is located near Santiago and had recently undergone major reforms under pressure from various European governments and human rights groups.[1] The other prison, Najayo, officially housed 2,300 but was said to have more than 3,400 inmates and is near Santo Domingo. Najayo is a traditional Dominican prison with a maximum security wing: desperately overcrowded, secured from the outside by the military with few prison guards on the inside, and a deplorable record on human rights abuses (see Stern and Coyle 2003).[2]

We conducted all of our recorded interviews at Rafey Prison, in an office provided by the administration. This ensured the subjects some confidentiality. Generally, they felt at ease to tell their stories, for which they were paid the equivalent of twenty dollars. The subjects were recruited by other deportees as indicated in the excerpt from our field notes. The administration initially denied that any deportees were in the prison—at least, they claimed to have no record of them. Then, as we waited in the reception area, Victor broke the impasse. Through Victor and another inmate, fifteen deportees offered to meet with us; when their interviews are viewed together, they provided an articulate voice on behalf of these normally invisible and highly marginalized human beings. We toured the second prison as well, escorted by inmates, and we talked informally with several deportees. It was impossible to conduct more formal face-to-face interviews, however, due to insufficient time and a lack of personal security, and the prison administration did not offer to make a space available to us for such interviews. Nonetheless, viewing first-hand another kind of institution that held deportees allowed us to gain a better understanding of the range of prisons and prison conditions in contemporary Dominican Republic.

We first provide some general background on the Dominican prison system, and then we describe the conditions of the two institutions we visited. Thereafter, we share the characteristics of the subsample and move into a discussion of the major themes that emerged from our data. We conclude that, although the subjects' deportee status places them at a higher risk for entering the chaotic, archaic, and largely unaccountable Dominican criminal justice system, the notion that they have returned to a life of crime is not validated. In contrast, the subjects mirror the findings of larger law enforcement data (Venator-Santiago 2005a, 2005b), which show that deportees are no more likely to be involved in crime than most other sectors of Dominican society, although they continue to feel socially and economically excluded.

THE DOMINICAN PRISON SYSTEM

The Dominican inmate population, which is housed in thirty-five institutions, has declined from around 16,500 inmates in 2003 to approximately 13,000 inmates in 2006 (Díaz Rodríguez 2006). This decrease occurred in the wake of a scathing review of the penitentiary system by the International Center for Prison Studies at the University of London, funded by the European Commission for Human Rights and the British Consulate (Stern and Coyle 2003). Among their findings, the authors stated:

> Over recent years there has been a series of trenchant reports on the prison system of the Dominican Republic, coming from inside and outside the country. The reports show a remarkable consistency in their analysis of the problems and in their recommendations for solutions. They all identify gross overcrowding as a major problem. . . . This level of overcrowding affects not only living space. It also puts intolerable pressure on health care, on cooking, on sanitary and washing arrangements, on visiting facilities and on all activities for prisoners. The reports also refer consistently to "a shortage of general resources and lack of any proper budgetary arrangements."
>
> (STERN AND COYLE 2003:14)

In another recent report based on a census of the inmate population (Díaz Rodríguez 2006), the following fundamental problems with the Dominican penal system are cited, despite recent reforms:

- A lack of resources
- Disinterest by the state
- A priority placed on the repression of crime and not on its prevention
- Lack of knowledge about the causes of crime or, at least, how these causes affect crime
- Lack of prison specialists
- Lack of rehabilitation programs inside prisons
- Overcrowded prisons
- Physical infrastructure of prisons in bad condition
- High number of inmates in preventive custody
- Lack of programs to socially reintegrate ex-inmates back into society

- Absence of a political prison
- High imprisonment rate compared to other countries

Clearly, the Dominican system is not a model of "modern" penitentiary policy and practice, and it is generally on a par with the appalling state of prisons encountered in almost all Latin American countries. A report from the U.S. Department of State confirms this.

> While prison conditions generally ranged from poor to extremely harsh, the government made advances with newer "model prisons" known as Correctional and Rehabilitation Centers (CRCs) where prisoners experienced improved conditions in comparison to the other facilities. According to the Office of the Attorney General, there were 18,701 prisoners and detainees held in 36 prisons, with an intended capacity of approximately 10,000. The new CRCs held 2,864 prisoners, while 15,837 prisoners were held in conventional prisons. Virtually all prisons, other than the CRCs, experienced extreme overcrowding. La Victoria prison, the largest in the country, held more than 4,000 prisoners in a facility designed for 1,300. This severe overcrowding led to an informal market wherein prisoners paid as much as 40,000 pesos (approximately $1,200) to acquire a bed. The cell blocks consisted of makeshift bed cubicles, stacked three high, in a densely packed warren of cells. Air circulation was a problem, and the danger of a fire outbreak was high.

(U.S. DEPARTMENT OF STATE 2009B)

The daily conditions of inmates can be gauged by the following (Díaz Rodríguez 2006):

- Only 6,300 beds are available to the more than 13,000 inmates.[3]
- Some institutions are so overcrowded that inmates sleep in the toilet areas.
- 60 percent of all inmates said they had taken no educational or rehabilitative courses.
- 90 percent of all inmates have not completed either high school or technical school (i.e., the most basic education needed to obtain a reasonable job).
- Between 50 percent and 70 percent of inmates are still being held in preventive custody despite recent prison and criminal justice reforms.

THE DEPORTEES AT RAFEY PRISON

As stated earlier, the first prison we visited was one of the country's five reformed institutions. The following field notes set the scene and give a more naturalistic context to the views and experiences expressed by the interviewees.

As we approach the prison gate of the men's prison, about forty to fifty women and ten of their children are waiting outside under a small awning to protect them from the baking mid-day sun. The prison is a large, yellow, concrete affair with walls about fifteen feet high topped by the customary barbed wire. It is nothing like most U.S. prisons, which seem to be built like fortresses, somber and forbidding. The sign outside announces that this is a "Center for Corrections and Rehabilitation" and lists all the different trades that can be learned here. We park our car in a small lot with but one other present. Opposite this institution is the female prison; interestingly, there is no one waiting outside to visit the inmates. After about five minutes, the large metal gate swings open and a large SUV appears. A young, squat man in his late twenties jumps out and approaches one of our party, a local lawyer who is arranging the visit. He tells her that he knows why we are there and that everything will be "sorted out" in due course. He then tells us to enter the gate and check in at the reception. We thank him for his efforts, and a young guard stands by as we enter. Everything is mechanical, no electrically operated doors, no surveillance cameras, and when we are patted down there are no metal detectors or any of the usual high-tech gadgetry that one sees at airports and high school entrances, let alone prisons. Two of the guards are concerned about the cell phones, but these are looked at and then given back. The major contraband they seem to checking for are guns, and we are then patted down a second time in a very casual manner and asked to proceed across the well-kept gardens into the prison proper. As we walk about thirty yards to the prison doors, we see inmates strolling around in blue trousers and red shirts. Some are gardening, others are carrying baseball gear, and others seem to be just chatting with the guards. The atmosphere is relaxed at least for the moment. . . .
We enter another reception area, which is basically a desk behind which sits a young man and woman with a signing-in book. Once again, they ask us if we have any guns, and then we're told to deposit our bags behind the desk and take out whatever we need for the interviews. After I do this, I realize I've not even been asked for my ID, which seems strange; I sign the visiting book, although no one seems to be too bothered whether I do or I don't. On fulfilling all our check-in duties, we are told to take a seat and wait for the administrator handling our visit.

As we do so, the atmosphere changes, becoming more energized with groups of primarily Dominican men (and a few Haitians) coming in and out through a prison gate with heavy metal bars, behind which lies a dark corridor. The men approach the gate and talk animatedly to one or two guards, who then escort them one at a time to a side room called an "area de cacheo," where they are searched for weapons. Once this ritual is completed, the men continue to another destination and then shortly thereafter return. We wait for about an hour, watching the same interactions, with most inmates looking straight ahead not glancing to either side. Suddenly a tall, blond inmate emerges. He is the first Anglo I've seen during our visit, and on his return he catches my eye. He breaks his step and leans over, "What are you doing here?" he asks. "Are you coming to visit, to check up on things?" "Sort of," I reply, and I ask him about his background. "I'm Dutch," he says, "Got seven years for drug smuggling, it's very difficult." I answer him in Dutch, which surprises him. "I can't talk now but I'll be back." The inmate leaves, returning a few minutes later, whereupon I get his story (translated from the Dutch).

DUTCH INMATE: The situation here is "zwaar" (heavy), "erg zwaar" (very heavy). There's more than 160 Dutch inmates here in this country. There's five of us in this prison alone. You have no idea what it's like here. They have no conception of human rights. I was in La Victoria before here, I spent ten months there. It's like hell there! Guys with knives, machetes, guns, drugs, you name it. There were quite a few Dutch there, about fifty of us. Sickness everywhere, AIDS, tubeculosis, people dying, terrible food, and we have no one here, no family, nothing, and the Embassy does very little for us. If you complain they take it out on you, they're vicious. You can disappear, anything can happen to you. It's difficult to talk to the other inmates. Many of them are illiterate and I'm a gringo. They think I have money and I've got nothing. If you have money you don't end up here, you just buy everyone off. I got busted with three kilos but there was no real trial. I had a lawyer but he didn't know what was going on. It's all money, you just have to keep giving everyone more otherwise you don't stand a chance. There's no sense of justice, nothing that we're used to in Europe. It's completely corrupt, everything from start to finish. The slightest look, an argument with someone, and you've had it. They'll knife you for nothing, chop your arms off—seriously. It's hard to believe. You've seen films about these places, but you think it must be Hollywood or something—but no, it's the truth.

DAVID BROTHERTON (D.B.): Is it better here than the previous prison?

DUTCH INMATE: Yeah, it's better, but it's not what it looks like to you. It looks not bad, eh? They say they have programs and the guards talk to you. It's time I got a job here, I try to occupy myself as much as possible, but I'm always on edge. Look at me! I don't look at anyone. I just look straight ahead. Never make eye contact, never. Just keep myself to myself and try to survive. I'm used to a country that believes in rehabilitation, you know, you're supposed to learn something.

D.B.: Do you do any exercise?

DUTCH INMATE: Well, they play baseball here and walk around a bit. But again, if I do play it can easily land in a conflict, and before you know it you're getting cut. That's how it is.

D.B.: Can you write about this to anyone?

DUTCH INMATE: I can write up some of the complaints but I can't pass them on to anyone here. You can't do that here, you just don't. They don't have that mentality, you know, that you could have genuine complaints and something should be done about it. No, if you complain there's something wrong with you. They take it as an insult, like you've done something to them personally and they'll get you back. You see, you can't win, so I just keep my head down and do what I can to survive. I've got about four years to go. Many of the others are worse off than me—they are really suffering. If nothing happens I think you will see a number of suicides or people just getting killed. It's a desperate situation here, but no one seems to care. I don't understand. (Field notes, June 5, 2007)

The Dutch inmate clearly experienced difficult conditions at Rafey despite the reforms, part of which can be attributed to his identity as an "outsider" in such a closed and socially competitive institutional setting. In addition, his frame of reference for criminal corrections consists of the norms in his native Holland, a country renowned for its progressive treatment of inmates and its long history of prison reform, a far cry from the norms of a Third World country with a long history of dictatorship and human rights abuses. Nonetheless, he was also adamant that conditions at Rafey were superior to those at his previous institution, La Victoria, one of the worst prisons in the Dominican Republic and one that has much in common with those of Najayo, as we shall read a little later. In the accounts that follow, we share the experiences of other imprisoned Dominican deportees and try to answer the following questions: How did these subjects find themselves in the very institutions that most of them swore were in their past? Is there any truth to the claims often repeated by the media and politicians that many of these deportees are incorrigible career criminals?

DEMOGRAPHICS AND CHARACTERISTICS OF FIFTEEN IMPRISONED MALE DEPORTEES AT RAFEY PRISON

We will discuss the following primary characteristics of the sample as we try to understand the pathways of these deportees back to the prison system and their trajectories in their enforced homeland.

TABLE 10.1 CHARACTERISTICS OF IMPRISONED DOMINICAN DEPORTEES
(*N* = 15)

Prior criminal record	3 deportees
Formerly legal residents of the United States	12 deportees
Average number of children in the Dominican Republic	2.5 children
Age range	25–43 years
Working in formal economy prior to detention	11 deportees
Reporting problems with alcohol/drugs	2 deportees
Average number of years since being deported	5 years

Settlement, Family, and Work

Most of the participants in our prison sample were legal residents of the United States and had been raised there since early childhood. Only three were living illegally in the United States, but even they had each spent more than five years in the New York City area. With most of their families in the United States, the majority had been returned to the Dominican Republic with little social support and effectively had to start their families and their work careers all over again. Remarkably, most had managed to do that; only three were not living with a partner when they were arrested. Nearly all of them had Dominican children, an average of 2.5 each, with whom most had close relationships. Some of them did their best to hide their present whereabouts from their children to avoid distressing them:

> ANGEL: My daughter doesn't know that I'm in prison. I told her that I'm in a rehabilitation center. She always tells me when I call her—she's seven years old—she tells me, "Daddy, when are you coming? Are you coming to see me?" (June 5, 2007)

In addition, most subjects spoke of working in the formal economy, either full-time or part-time, prior to being arrested. Construction, telemarketing, security, tourism, taxi driver, computer sales, and small restaurant ownership were some of the fields mentioned. These characteristics of the subjects suggest that, in general, they were resettling and were not drawn from that stratum of the deportee population who were indigent and barely surviving. This, of course, is not to say that they did not experience social and psychological difficulties in adapting to the new ways of life.

VICTOR: When I got deported, they gave me a card, supposedly to go back to the National Palace of the Police where they got psychological therapy. But they didn't do none of that. You go there and you have to give them some money for whatever, and they're just like "'Yo, you got to blend in." There is no help, no re-socialization into this society. Like, I heard England does that, is that right? Do they re-insert you, like if you never been there? Not here, they don't! (June 5, 2007)

The deportees' time spent in prison was particularly burdensome for their families, a form of collateral damage much written about in the United States (Mauer and Chesney-Lind 2002; Travis 2005; Travis et al. 2005), because they were all the primary breadwinners and their incomes were desperately needed by their working-class and lower middle-class families. Some of them were also responsible for other family members who had also run into difficulties with the capricious practices of the Dominican legal system. Franklyn describes a particular set of trying circumstances that reflect how common the experience of deportation has become among certain families.

FRANKLYN: My brother is here with me right now, and he has the papers with him from the United States that say he's crazy. I don't know what to do about him, he needs his meds, he's walking around not knowing where he is. You know how they are here. They have to release me so I can take care of him. But not only that, I have to pay the monthly rent on my house, its twelve hundred pesos and I have three children. My children don't have Pampers, they don't have milk, and I'm here as a prisoner suffering and so are my children. (June 6, 2007)

Perhaps because of their "success" in finding work and a new family life, these subjects made contradictory statements about returning to the United States. They talked both of wanting to get back to the United States, either legally or illegally, and of being resigned to the fact that their futures lay in the Dominican Republic, despite the obvious difficulties. For those who still had their families "back there," the dream of one day seeing them again never left them.

FELIX: One day I want to get back to the United States again, even if it's just for one day to see my children, my son and daughter. I want the opportunity for a day or perhaps a week, and then they can drag me back here. I want to see my children, to hug them, to kiss them, to talk to them just a little bit, to have dinner with them, you know, see how they were. See that they weren't junkies and that they had studied and had been doing well in life. I would love to know this. It's the only thing I want to do in life before I die! (June 5, 2007)

Pathways Back to Prison

Although certain politicians, media pundits, and law enforcement representatives would have us believe that deportees are leading factors behind the rise in crime, our interviews did not bear out these claims. Only three of the fifteen had been before a judge and convicted, whereas the rest were there in preventive detention. Of course, interviewees may not always tell the truth about the reasons for their arrest; however, we have found most interviewees to be honest in their responses. Although some might not reveal certain aspects of their lives, we did not find any accounts of participants' pasts that were fabricated,[4] and we assume the same holds true for this subsample. We concluded that most found themselves pulled once again into the criminal justice web due to a momentary loss of self-control, victimization by the police, or pure happenstance. Most notably, their return to prison had little to do with crimes of opportunity or rational action, the favored paradigms of so much contemporary criminology. Both José's and Luis's accounts are typical of this sample:

D.B.: What happened?

JOSÉ: How do I explain it to you? The computer company where I work is close to my home in Villa Oga, I live at the Embrujo Primero. When I got my salary check, since I have my father and my mother here and she's a bit elderly, I give her some money. "Here, mother," I will say, "Have five hundred pesos. . . ." So I went to get my children, whom I always pick up from school. It was Friday the 12th and I said to my children, "Katherine, let's bring something to your grandma, and I'm also going to take you to have McDonald's." I drove my car and stopped in front of my mother's house, pushed the horn and got out, and what happened? I have one brother living with my mother and there are, like, four more tenants. As it turns out, the DDCD (antidrugs police) had gone there and found twenty-two grams, but there were no tenants there at the time, it was empty. They took the drugs, at least that's what they said but you don't know if it's true or not, because nobody saw anything. Then, five months later, I'm visiting my mother, and they are there again looking for someone who was supposedly living there. I was standing there with my mother and I take out my twelve thousand pesos and give five hundred to my mother. Right then the DDCD arrives, jump on me, and say, "This is the guy that we're looking for," referring to me. I said to them "No, you're mistaken, you're not taking me to prison, you didn't find anything. Show me the arrest order against me, against José Antonio Peralta Guilera." Do you understand?

D.B.: Yes.

JOSÉ: "Show me the order that allows you to break into my home." My home is Fifth Street, Number 5, but the house they were breaking into was 176th Street. I mean, they were after the other person. Then he says "Ok, I'm not going to arrest you and I am going to investigate why you were deported." (June 5, 2007)

LUIS: I'm a prisoner because I made a mistake. I was in a house working where they found drugs, but I was not selling those drugs, I had nothing to do with them. Unfortunately for me, that's the case. If God wills it, the judges will understand this and accept that I didn't know anything. They will understand that this was simply a house where I was working. It's as simple as that. . . . (June 6, 2007)

It is worth noting that five study participants were arrested in similar circumstances for having some relationship to a piece of real estate (housing or a shop) where drugs (usually cocaine) were thought to be stored. None of the subjects admitted to being involved in the drug trade, and none of them said they were regularly using drugs other than alcohol. Rather, they were swept up in raids carried out by the special drugs unit (usually trained by the United States) who always found an assortment of drugs at the site, which led to a roundup of the "usual suspects." Other subjects were arrested for a range of offenses such as nonpayment for food in a restaurant, fighting with a female partner, an argument over the sale of a computer, a robbery without any evidence being produced, possessing a gun that had been used in a crime some years before; the list goes on. According to the subjects familiar with U.S. law, most of these cases would not have gone this far in their former homeland, but the lack of (adequate) representation and the absence of habeas corpus meant that they had no option but to linger in prison until they could see a judge, who would most likely send them home.[5]

Three subjects, however, were not in this category. Two of these deportees were in prison for ten or more years having committed homicide(s), and both of them had records of violent crimes in the United States. One of the subjects, Mr. R., had achieved some notoriety in the New York area and had simply continued his criminal career in the Dominican Republic, taking advantage of new opportunities in the drug trade with politicians linked to the Colombian cartels. His story further illuminates the extraordinary corruption that is part and parcel of the country's political and criminal justice culture.

D.B.: So you came out and then went back to the streets, got busted again. And then?

MR. R.: I did an armored car robbery and I killed everyone.

D.B.: When did they bust you?

MR. R.: In 1990, I came out of prison too wild, I didn't last no time on the streets. I did time, I came out in June 1989, and then in December 1989 I committed that crime, and then got busted again going to prison in 1990.

D.B.: So what happened when you got back here?

MR. R.: I came back here, started dealing, started making money. I made it up again. But then I got caught for eight murders.

D.B.: What year was that?

MR. R.: In 1996, I got caught for eight murders. So I started talking to the politics people, they knew I could be useful to them. Always the politics people are more dirty than they look. So this big political person says, "I'm going to help you with that, don't worry." So they took me out; they discharged the cases and I came out.

D.B.: Wow.

MR. R.: So then this time I was doing the same thing again, taking people out, it was all linked to drugs, only with this other politics person. And then it all went down, but this time this politics person didn't have any words with anyone and he let me take the whole thing. and this time it was for something I didn't do, I didn't go to kill this one, I went to kill another one, my boy went to kill him. I was with him in the same moment that we were told to kill him, and so they gave me twenty years for being an accomplice.

D.B.: And this is because the guy you were working for didn't have. . . .

MR. R.: The balls to take it . . . to accomplish it, yeah. Right now I'm contesting it in the Supreme Court. My sentence is going to either get knocked up or they are going to reduce it to ten years. But basically the other politics person didn't help me, I got fucked over. . . . I don't feel like I should be ashamed of what I've done and what I've done right here. What I got to do now is fix what I did, try to make a better life from now on.

D.B.: Right.

MR. R.: But if you ask me how many people I killed, I killed more than eighty people, and I'm still young! I can tell, you're looking at me and thinking, "You don't look like a killer."

MR. R.: It's just part of life. (June 5, 2007)

The Daily Regime

In general, inmates were grateful that they were at Rafey Prison as opposed to any other prison. Victor's account of his daily routine does not sound very inviting to outsiders, but there is a semblance of order, a regime of control and predictability, and the presence of professional staff, all of which are exceptions to the rule. This appreciation is relative; no one wanted to be here, and there is little going on in terms of rehabilitation, but inmates at least remained confident that they would remain alive (the Dutch inmate was the only one who expressed fears for his life). In some ways, the inmates have been conditioned to tolerate this kind of life. If they were from poor and marginalized backgrounds, their lives might be much the same as prison life: hanging around, struggling for a living, becoming wedded to the informal economy (Venkatesh 2006), and searching for some form of meaning in the everyday. At Rafey we found a mixture of the rational penitentiary model, with strict controls on time and space, and the culture of a "developing" country, with its more opaque social and economic relationships and its rejection of industrialized efficiency and of meritocratic rationales in various occupational systems (although there is a generally strong regard for credentials, which provide a sense of status, even though in practice these credentials do not signify a high level of training).

D.B.: Tell me about an average day, what would you do on an average day?

VICTOR: Average day? Go to the yard, spin around, use the phone.

D.B.: So you get out at what time?

VICTOR: They do a count at seven.

D.B.: Seven o'clock.

VICTOR: Yeah. There is a TV in every block, before there wasn't none of that.

D.B.: Okay.

VICTOR: You have water, cold water, a little refrigerator with the bottle.

D.B.: Oh, good.

VICTOR: Before, there was none of that, nothing. They drank it from the thing with diseases. They used to get rashes because there wasn't a filter in there, now they do it.

D.B.: Okay. So you get up at seven, they do a count, you get washed. . . .

VICTOR: Wash up, go to the morning breakfast, come back, go to the yard. . . .

D.B.: Does everybody eat together?

VICTOR: Yeah, everybody. Everybody is Dominican here, so there is really no gang.

D.B.: And breakfast, what's after that?

VICTOR: Breakfast . . . then they lock everybody up until nine, then they open up the yard, washing clothes. (June 7, 2007)

Comparing the Prison Experience: United States versus the Dominican Republic

We have already noted some of the differences between the United States and the Dominican Republic vis à vis prison conditions, but it is worth recounting how these deportee inmates saw the contrast. Although Rafey was by far one of the best facilities in the country, many of the complaints mirror the findings of the external evaluations of the system. At the same time, these "insider" perspectives provide some valuable insights from those who have gone through both regimes of punishment and social control.

Lack of Due Process, Absence of Transparency, and No Legitimacy

How does a criminal suspect obtain legal representation in this country? Who knows the law? Without a legitimate state machine that dispenses rational order, maintains a set of clear punishments, displays a commitment to due process, and safeguards against impunity, the system breeds vigilantism and informal forms of justice. In addition, the lack of court oversight of the prison system and the inefficiency of the justice bureaucracy leaves inmates in jail for much longer periods than are necessary, often on the basis of charges that cannot be substantiated. In the United States, there are many cases of inmate abuse and wrongful arrest, many of which are influenced by race, but there still exists a jury system based on one's peers and the important constitutional right to have legal counsel, which in most states has led to different forms of free or low-cost legal aid.

ANGEL: I'm waiting a year in here because there is a law that says that you can't spend more than twelve months in here without seeing a judge, so I've got about three months to go.

D.B.: Do you have a lawyer?

ANGEL: I have a lawyer, but I never see him. I saw him the first day when I was in court, when he came up and says, "Do you need a lawyer?" "Yes," I said. He took my name and I never saw him again.

D.B.: So he represented you in court?

ANGEL: I've never been to court, but his name shows up on the papers that they send me.

D.B.: So you're waiting for a judge to set you some bail?

ANGEL: Yes, I've gotten nothing, and I don't have any help. I don't have anything, and I don't see anyone, I'm just a nothing, just a nothing right now. (June 6, 2007)

JOSÉ: It's a crazy system here . . . they keep you here forever and often nothing gets resolved. Maybe you killed someone and maybe you didn't. Maybe you did a robbery and maybe you didn't. Often there's no evidence or not sufficient evidence, and it just depends on what the judge thinks of you. That's why they keep a lot of people here and then let them go without any charges. But think about the people who have been the victims. Suppose they still think that you did it, what are they going to do? Many people don't believe this system means anything, and if they still think you killed their family member even though you are free, they could come and kill you, just because no one has any faith in the system. (June 5, 2007)

Lack of Communication

For those inmates who lived close to the prison, visits from family members were quite regular, and this was the least of their complaints. For those

10.2 DEPORTEE INMATE PEERING OUT THE WINDOW DURING AN INTERVIEW (*PHOTO:* LUIS BARRIOS).

who had to rely on telephone communications with relatives and friends, however, the situation was much more arduous. In the U.S. state and federal prison system, each inmate is given a fixed amount of time to call per month, and, although the calls are costly, they are usually paid by the recipient of the call. The reality of phone use, however, is usually more chaotic, and there are many accounts of physical conflicts over phone use. In our previous research with gang members, there was frequent mention that control over the phones was often a factor in prison gang fights and gang development. At Rafey, phone use was organized as described by Mr. A., which obviously led to a great deal of frustration on the part of inmates. In the unreformed prisons, telephone access is even more constrained and is usually regulated by the gangs that control the specific areas of each institution.

> MR. A.: This place is hard man, very difficult. If you got to make a phone call, you got to make a line in the hot sun. You have to get burned just to make a phone call. And then you only get five minutes, just five minutes. What can you say in five minutes? Then after five minutes you have to get, and if you want to go again you start all over at the back of the line in the hot sun. And like today, the communications are down, and so we don't talk to anyone, and this can last for . . . who knows when? (June 5, 2007)

But the biggest contrast with the United States may be the lack of mail at Dominican prisons. In the United States, inmates cherish their ability to write to friends and associates, and the arrival of mail from the outside is a crucial line of communication to the outside world. Through this medium, inmates fight their cases, conduct intimate relations, and stay in touch with their families. In the Dominican Republic, the postal system barely functions, and it can take weeks or even months for a letter to be delivered between different parts of the country, if it arrives at all. No one in our sample ever mentioned receiving mail at Rafey, and documents related to their cases had to be delivered by hand to the recipient.

Lack of Rights

> D.B.: What are the conditions right here?
> VICTOR: Well, right now this system is like . . . it's a First-World system in a Third-World society. Like, they try to implement everything that they have over there but without, like, the rights. It's, like, very dictatorial, they do what they want and that's it. It's like the Spanish government is supporting them, and we are not Spanish, we are Dominicans. So they

are implementing their rules of that country here to the prison system, and it's a lot of totalitarianism. (June 5, 2007)

Victor is somewhat confused about the influence of the Spanish on the recent prison reforms. He is correct, however, that these reforms have arrived without any thought given to the provision of rights for inmates. In the United States, the prisoners' rights movement mushroomed in the 1960s and 1970s, especially after the massacre at Attica and elsewhere, and the movement continues to this day. Prisoners everywhere in the United States have a sense of their basic human rights—incarcerated inmates are constantly filing complaints of maltreatment from prison staff, the prison medical system, and the prison administration. Outside reform groups regularly visits correctional institutions to help monitor prisons and hold the administrations accountable. This culture of rights, obligations, and responsibilities is completely missing in the civil society of the Dominican Republic, so it should come as no surprise that it is nonexistent in the society of captives.

Lack of Work and Educational Opportunities

At Rafey there was a strong attempt to link the inmate experience with some form of job training and minimum levels of education, particularly literacy. This was in stark contrast to the mainstream prisons, where inmates had little else to do other than attend religious services, play baseball in the prison yard, hang out with other inmates, or spend time alone. Two deportee inmates spoke positively about the efforts at Rafey, but the second also mentioned how lackadaisical these efforts were. In comparison, the inmates spoke about participating in a range of trainings during their stay in the U.S. prisons, although a number also mentioned that these opportunities had been curtailed in recent years. We have detailed elsewhere how little was provided for non-citizens in U.S. prisons, other than elementary English language lessons and the ability to spend time in the prison library. This latter point is important because, to our knowledge, prison libraries in the Dominican Republic simply do not exist. It is therefore extremely difficult for inmates to learn about the law and the intricacies of the system that incarcerates them.

JULIO: It's not bad here, it could be worse. You get some basic education, mainly for those who can't read and write and a chance to take a few courses like in agriculture, baking, computers, that kind of thing. And you get to play some sports, some baseball and basketball. (June 5, 2007)

D.B.: So there is no education?

VICTOR: Yeah, it's not like in the States where they make you go, like they got somebody from Albany there checking. You know, they'll say, "What do you know how to do? Plumbing? Then you go to plumbing school. Sheet metal? You go to sheet metal school. Or if you don't have a decent reading or math level, you're going to school. Here they don't care; they're just like 'hang out if you want.' (June 5, 2007)

Lack of Safety

As previously stated, the conditions of physical safety had improved greatly at Rafey.

JORGE: It's a lot better than before, because before you had to sleep with one eye open all the time. You had to, otherwise someone could easily kill you, stab you, shoot you, whatever. So, it's a bit better now. (June 5, 2007)

Nonetheless, as reported earlier in our field notes at the beginning of the chapter, conflicts between inmates are not uncommon, and it is not advisable to complain to the guards about mistreatment. Another interesting finding at Rafey was the absence of organized prison gangs that alternately prey on and protect inmates, whereas in other Dominican prisons these inmate organizations are common due to the complete lack of internal social controls provided by the state. In U.S. prisons by contrast, inmates generally spoke of feeling "safe" despite the widespread existence of prison gangs throughout the system. A few inmates had spent time in solitary confinement for fighting, and at least three of them had joined prison groups like the Triniterios (see chapter 5).

Lack of Health Care and Hygiene

D.B.: What happened to you?

JUAN: They bust in through the door and shot me in my leg here (he points to a festering wound in his calf). The bullet is still in there, and I've been here three weeks already.

D.B.: Have you seen a doctor?

JUAN: I'm supposed to see someone tomorrow, but I've no money to pay for anything. They'll only treat you if you can pay.

D.B.: But this could get seriously infected.

JUAN: It is already but they don't care. If you don't have the money then. . . .

D.B.: You have no right to see a doctor?

JUAN: You can complain, and I do because I'm in a lot of pain, but no, there's
no rights here, even though this is one of the best prisons in the country.
(June 5, 2007)

Although the level of hygiene at Rafey was generally quite high, with interviewees talking of access to fresh water (although it often had to be bought),
bathing facilities, and relatively sanitary toilets, there was little mention of
medical treatment. J. recounted how treatment is still linked to the ability
to pay. Although many U.S. institutions have subcontracted out their medical care programs, the state still has to ensure that prisoners receive a basic
level of treatment. Such medical and health programs help keep down the
rate of contagious diseases such as tuberculosis and AIDS. In addition, there
is widespread use of drug therapy to manage the increasing population of
inmates with mental health problems, and many critics of the system point to
the cynical use of "meds" to socially control the inmate population.

Rampant Corruption

D.B.: Was the prison inside here the same as in La Victoria?
MR. R.: Before?
D.B.: Yeah.
MR. R.: Sure, if they wanted you to kill somebody, the cops used to come to
the jail to talk to me, I used to talk to the colonel, and he would tell me,
"What day is it? Ok, you go to the streets till Monday." I used to go out
to the streets, you know, I used to do what I had to do and come back in.
They used to accuse me of the murder, and then the guys here would say,
"It couldn't have been him, he's been locked up; he couldn't have done it."
You understand, it's the same system . . . that is the system!" (June 5, 2007)

As shocking as Mr. R.'s account may be, such reports are commonplace in all
of the Dominican Republic's penitentiaries. The system is run primarily by
largely unaccountable military leaders, "colonels" or "generals" who use the
institutions as a kind of fiefdom from which they extract monetary gain to
supplement their already substantial incomes.[6] A lawyer who accompanied
us to the field site recalled another recent incident:

LUISA: A couple of years ago there was a report in the newspapers, all over
the front page, of the director of prisons here at Rafey sitting on the obe-
lisk in the middle of Santiago drinking a bottle of rum with a leader of a
drug cartel who had just been sentenced to twenty years. There he was

with this terrible drug lord in full view of everybody. They took a photo of him and everything, and of course we got the usual cries of surprise from the government and the guy was removed from his post. But he wasn't kicked out of the military. He wasn't charged with anything, and it was business as usual. That's our system in a nutshell. (June 6, 2007)

Consequently, inmates expressed remarkable confidence in the professionalism of the U.S. system, frequently saying that correctional officers were generally well behaved and responsible. They did not accept bribes, although very little mention was made of anyone at the senior level. Of course, one reason for the difference is that correctional workers in the U.S. system are paid much better than their counterparts in the Dominican Republic, and there is a veritable industry of professionals and service providers sustained by billions of tax dollars. Institutional corruption in the U.S. prison system, while not as overt as in the Dominican Republic, is alive and well, but it is discretely hidden from many of the inmates. In other words, the corruption exists in the laws passed by "get tough" politicians who are often tied to the correctional industry and in the array of subcontracts meted out to telephone companies, private security companies, and prisons run for profit. Thus, prisons in the United States are part of a large and expanding corporate security industry whose profits are mostly open and legal, rather than an essential part of the informal economy constituted by drug dealers, colonels, gang leaders, and crooked politicians.

Inadequate Space and Sleeping Arrangements

Alberto: I sleep in a room with fifty-seven others, they have cells like nine to each cell, and we have six of these on each side, and then a small one with three in it.

D.B.: Is it noisy?

ALBERTO: Yeah, a lot of people talking, different ideas. . . .

D.B.: And a lot of tension?

ALBERTO: Yeah, it's difficult. You are never alone. Sometimes we got days when people wake up angry, then there are times when people get angry because they have to wait in line for water, to buy it. . . . You have to buy everything, the most basic things. (June 5, 2007)

Again, a great deal has improved at Rafey, and the inmates welcomed these changes. The large cells that Alberto refers to are a world away from the teeming confinements that we found at Najayo and at La Victoria prison, about which we wrote some years ago (Brotherton and Barrios 1997). But inmates still have no personal space and are always living with the moods, strange noises at night, loud voices, shouts, screams, and laughter of others. In the United States, although some inmates sleep in large dormitories and others are in cells with as many as three other cellmates, prison authorities are mindful that each inmate should have a certain amount of space.

Conjugal Visits

There was one area, however, that the inmates felt was better in the Dominican Republic than in the United States: the ability of loved ones and friends to visit the inmates two or three times a week and to have physical contact with their visitors.

> D.B.: Do they set up conjugal visits here?
> RAFAEL: Yeah, you got your conjugal visits inside. . . .
> D.B.: Once a week?
> RAFAEL: Three times a week, Friday, Saturday, and Sunday. (June 5, 2007)

This opportunity for inmates to be with their partners, girlfriends, and children was an extremely important difference with the U.S. system, and in many ways was a much more humanistic part of the Dominican system. Most inmates recognized this contrast and looked forward to their visits, which made them feel more "normal," unlike the dehumanized inmate so carefully constructed in the U.S. media and ruthlessly patrolled by the interlocking U.S. systems of policing, welfare, criminal justice, and prisons (Wacquant 1997; Garland 1990).

What's Next?

Of course, all of the deportee inmates wanted to return home as soon as possible. The three who were adjudicated and still had several years to serve were the least anxious and were patiently "doing their time." Nonetheless, they all talked of their future plans, which involved improving their education, trying new business ventures, looking for training opportunities, taking better care of their families, and moving to a new location to get away from "bad" influences in their communities.

> MARIA (M.): From your experience as a deportee, how do you plan to face the future?
> PUNTIEL: Behave well, behave well and work hard.

M.: What else?

PUNTIEL: To be honorable. I already have a lot of experience and I'm not the same person as before. Yes, I want to work, so give me a chance. I'm a new man, and I'm not the guy I was when I was twenty. I'm now forty and I have another mentality. (June 5, 2007)

M.: And what plans do you have?

RODRIGUEZ: To work, as I told you, to finish my career. I was studying psychology, general psychology at the Autonomous University. I want to see if I can finish these studies and become a clinical psychologist. I think I can do it if God wills it. (June 5, 2007)

FRANKLYN: If my family can help me a little bit I want to start a little store, you know, selling beer, rice, beans . . . just a little store because there's not much money here to open a big place. Just enough to keep my wife and children. And, I'll also keep driving the cab because I don't want to die an old man with nothing in his pocket. You see these old men who nobody wants, old men who depend on everyone else because they have no money. It's terrible. (June 6, 2007)

ALEX: When I get out of here I'm going to my wife's neighborhood, and I'm going to have my daughter near me, and I'm going to get me a job. (June 5, 2007)

EDWIN: When I get out of here I'm gonna stand on my own two feet. I know I have a problem with alcohol and I have to confront it. But I can do things, I can work, I just have to set my mind to it, stay calm, conduct myself like an American but realize I have to make my life here. (June 5, 2007)

Getting "back in the mix" or "in the life" (i.e., returning to a life of crime and deviance) was not mentioned as a possibility. They sincerely believed that it would be possible for them to stay out of prison if allowed to live their lives as non-stigmatized members of society. Whether this was possible for them as deportees is debatable, but they seemed generally optimistic that, with the support of their new families in the Dominican Republic and with the help of their old families in the United States, it could happen. For them, time in prison was a setback and it would not happen again. In their eyes, they had let a situation get out of hand, or they had not been as circumspect as they should have about illegal activities in their community, or they simply did not realize they were vulnerable anymore because they had worked hard to socially reintegrate themselves and had achieved a certain level of success.

10.3 OUTSIDE RAFFEY PRISON (*PHOTO:* LUIS BARRIOS).

THE SITUATION AT NAJAYO PRISON

In this section we share the field notes from our visit to Najayo prison, some thirty miles outside of Santo Domingo. We have no official data on the numbers of deportees held here, but on the basis of estimates from the inmates themselves and on our visits to other similar institutions, it is likely that, of the total male inmate population of 2,000, fifty to one hundred inmates are deportees. As can be gleaned from the descriptions below, the conditions at this prison were inhumane, and all of the problems typical of the Dominican system were abundantly present: overcrowding, unsanitary conditions, lack of safety, lack of educational resources, administrative negligence, lack of due process, and so on. Nonetheless, through it all, most inmates survive the experience and adapt to the prevailing culture and subcultures. Unfortunately and disgracefully, one of the participants in this project did not. Freddie (see photo) died needlessly and willfully in the presence of guards, a phone call away from medical attention. In effect, he was condemned by his double stigma, a deportee and a junkie.

We drive about forty-five minutes from Santo Domingo to Najayo Prison, one of the largest penitentiaries closest to the capital, to visit several deportees who have been picked up in recent months for selling heroin. The visit has been arranged with Mr. L., a former male prostitute and long-time resident at the prison who consistently returns to do HIV/AIDS work with the inmates. One of them, "Freddie," we have just been informed, died a week ago while going through withdrawal from heroin and valium. There are currently 2,000

inmates in the male prison, 450 inmates in the female prison, and approximately 250 in the juvenile detention center.

We approach the gate, and our intermediary, Mr. L., gets out to talk to a guard.

"Is that an Americano?" asks the guard in Spanish.

"No, he's British," says Mr. L., "and this one is Puerto Rican (pointing to Luis)."

"OK, let them through. They have to check everything in. No cellulars, no "gaffas" (sun glasses), no earrings, and give me all your passports."

We enter the gates and are subjected to a cursory body search. I count thirteen security personnel who have two guns between them. Above there are two towers, also with guards armed with rifles. We carry on walking and meet the "Assistant to the Mayor of the Prison," a small man about forty years old and wearing a smart, silk shirt, sitting on a deck chair in the middle of a stretch of grass in front of the main prison gate, behind which are dozens of inmates. Standing beside the man are two muscular inmates with their shirts unbuttoned, displaying their pumped up chests. They both know Mr. L. and give me the impression that they are gay and somehow in the service of the Assistant. Mr. L. and the Assistant talk and joke. I'm struck by how relaxed the interaction is. Finally, with the Assistant's blessing, we walk over to the prison gates and a guard lets us in; there are four of us, myself, Mr. L., Luis, and M., who has been working as an informant throughout the study.

The prison is teeming with sweating bodies, crushed against one another, simply hundreds of faces wherever you look. I try to stay close to Mr. L. with both Luis and M. behind me as we thread our way through the crowd. I have no idea where we are headed when Mr. L. says we should aim for the "comedor" (the dining area). We enter a large eating area with long concrete tables and seating. At least 500 inmates are congregated, some sitting, some standing on the benches, and the atmosphere is noisy and tense.

"Hey Blondie, do you have five pesos."

"Hey, American, do you wanna chill?"

"Gringo, give me some money, I need help."

The requests and calls are relentless, and I look straight ahead trying not to make eye contact, just as the Dutch inmate had advised a couple of days before. M. is surrounded by inmates who badger him with questions in Spanish; he tells them we are there to do work, to interview deportees, and they should "back off." Then a woman who is visiting her husband catches the eye of Luis and shouts out that she was deported, as was her husband. Luis goes over and talks to her and arranges to meet her outside the day after. He seems to think he knows her from the Washington Heights community. She is one of the few women around at the moment in this sea of men, which is strange since we are here during visiting hours. Mr. L. says that we are too far away from the capital for many of the families to visit. Most of the inmates are extremely poor, and the twenty pesos it costs to get here is often too much for them.

We continue on, and the crowd following us gets bigger. Finally we reach a section that is separated from the dining area by tall gates, behind which lies the kitchen. This area consists of four large gas burners on which huge pots formerly used in sugar production are used to cook a stew. One inmate is using a garden spade to stir the concoction. This is all there is unless family members can supplement their diet.

We are joined by three deportees who have been contacted by M., and they act as a human shield against the other inmates. I recognize Omar from several years ago and give him a hug. He looks fitter than the last time I saw him, strung out and emaciated in a shooting gallery. He is with Derek, formerly from Brooklyn, who has been here for four months and expects to get out in another two months, and a third deportee whose name I don't get. We talk about the death of Freddie:

OMAR: He died about two weeks ago. He died in my cell. I was right there. They wouldn't do anything to save him. Nothing. That was hard to take.

D.B.: What do you mean they wouldn't do anything?

OMAR: They have no medical care here. Nothing. There's no doctor on call for the entire place.

DEREK: If you're ill in here, man, you've basically had it. There's nothing. The doctor comes twice a week, Tuesday and Thursday, that's it.

D.B.: Tell me about Freddie.

OMAR: Freddie was shaking real bad, vomiting on the floor. He was kicking (going through withdrawals from heroin [added by the authors]), but he was doing pills as well as heroin. It makes it worse. So I go to the front, to the guard, I shout to them an inmate is in bad shape, he needs help, it's very urgent. They just turned and said, "He's a drug addict. What do you expect?" Anyway, I went back and brought him down, and they brought him through the gates. This is about 2 a.m. I'm sitting with him. He's vomiting, shitting, basically he's dying, and the guards are there just filling out forms. They don't call the hospital, nothing. And he dies. They just waited until he died. "He's just another junkie."

DEREK: He's not the first to die, and he won't be the last. It happens here all the time. If there's trouble, a fight between inmates, someone goes down and shouts through the gate, and finally some guards will come in to break it up. It could take ten or fifteen minutes—by that time someone could be dead. That's how it is here. They don't give a fuck about us, and they never will.

Omar and Derek's accounts were chilling, and I visualize Freddie more and more during our interview, remembering how we talked about him growing up in Brooklyn, his history of drug use, and his deep desire to see his U.S. family again. But now the situation is getting more tense and we have to move on. Luis calls out, "Keep your hand on your wallet." But I'm so surrounded by inmates I can't even reach by back pocket as I get carried forward. Then I hear someone shout, "Are you missing your glasses?" I look down and see that someone has removed them from my shirt pocket. Miraculously, one of the deportees retrieves them from an inmate and hands them to me. "Keep them safe," he says.

Eventually, I am carried partly off my feet through the crowd and reach the second floor of the facility, where it is suddenly calm. There are ten cells, five on each side of a narrow corridor, with five or six inmates bunched up in each. I look down and see three kittens are playing on the floor, while inside another cell a small shop has been set up to sell sweets and cigarettes, with a young woman taking the money. This is the area where Mr. L. used to live for most of his stay, and many of the inmates are still here from the time he was released three years ago. I talk to Derek about his situation:

D.B.: Where are you sleeping?

DEREK: Downstairs, we have a little patio where we can cook. I prefer it to here. You have to pay three thousand pesos to be up here and two thousand for your mattress.

D.B.: Do you have a mattress?

DEREK: No, nothing. You'd think they'd supply them, but they give you nothing, no soap, nothing. You buy everything, and I don't have anything. So I'll just wait my time till they let me and him out. You know they planted all the stuff on us. Of course we were doing drugs and selling, but not when they busted us. We had nothing on us. They said we had six rocks and five grams of coke, but they put that on us. That's not right but that's what they do around here.

D.B.: How do they treat deportees here?

OMAR: It's hard here (he smiles). They are hard on Americans in here. (Field notes, June 7, 2007)

10.4 DAVID BROTHERTON INTERVIEWING FREDDY IN SANTO DOMINGO IN 2006. FREDDY DIED IN PRISON ONE YEAR LATER (*PHOTO:* LUIS BARRIOS).

CONCLUSION

We have described and analyzed the circumstances of some deportees who found themselves back in the prison system. For a few, their criminal involvement carried on as before in the United States. It was not surprising to them or to us that they were still doing serious prison time. However, the majority were there primarily due to their deportee stigma, often combined with the fact they lived in impoverished neighborhoods and the arbitrary, unaccountable nature of the Dominican criminal justice system. Even if they were innocent and could prove it, without the resources needed to hire a rep- utable lawyer or buy their freedom from the appropriate bureaucrat, they will surely be held for months or years in preventive detention. Not surprisingly, therefore, no one wanted to go back inside, and all looked forward to the time when they could resume their civilian lives, get back on track in terms of work, and stay away from "trouble" as far as their social circles were con- cerned. The extent to which all these intentions may be realized is another question. Some deportees did not want to wait to find out whether their fates would play out in the Caribbean land of their birth, as we shall discuss in chapter 11.

11.1 CHISMIN, RETURNED DEPORTEE, SELLING CLOTHES ON BROADWAY IN WASHINGTON HEIGHTS (*PHOTO*: LUIS BARRIOS).

CHAPTER ELEVEN

THE RETURN OF THE DEPORTEES

*Before being deported, a social worker with a lawyer visited me to discuss my
daughters. They gave me two options: You can take them with you or leave
them with your family. This was one of the hardest decisions I've had to make
in my life. I love my daughters and they are everything to me, but I'd never
bring them to the Dominican Republic to struggle. With pain in my heart,
I left them with my father and stepmother. My consolation was to tell myself
every day that I was a good mother and that I gave them a future. It was clear
to me that in Santo Domingo my daughters would not have a future, so
I sacrificed myself. In this city (New York [added by the authors]), if the poor
do not work they'll go to hell.*

(A RETURNED DEPORTEE, MAY 2009)

This book would be incomplete if we did not discuss those who managed to
return to the United States after being deported to the Dominican Republic.
For a variety of reasons, these individuals saw no hope for the future by
remaining in the Dominican Republic. They felt the pull of their families in
the United States so strongly that they had to return, whatever the risk. In
this way, deportees resisted their forced exile. Garnering whatever resources
they could to make it back across the extensive and massively patrolled U.S.
border, they often chose to risk their lives and join those eking out an existence as part of the indispensible undocumented work force in the shadows
of both the formal and informal economies in the United States.

On the basis of life history interviews of a subsample of eighteen returned
deportees living and working in the Washington Heights Community of New
York City, we highlight the survival stories of men and women engaged in

TABLE 11.1 DATA FROM THE 18 INTERVIEWED DEPORTEES WHO RETURNED
TO THE UNITED STATES

Average age	28 years
Charges and convictions	Drug-related
Average time before return to the United States	1.5 years
Number with family members in the United States	13
Male/female	14/4
Average time spent in U.S. prison	3 years

five kinds of economic activity: (1) drug selling, (2) street vending, (3) child care, (4) factory work, and (5) taxi driving. Together these narratives show the heterogeneity of the undocumented deportee community, the degree of integration of this population into the formal and informal economies and the social and economic challenges they face in resettling.

WHY GO BACK TO THE UNITED STATES?

Similar to other researchers of deportees (e.g., Berlin et al. 2008), we found that deportees returned to the United States because of "extreme poverty, violence, and discrimination." Many of these themes have been discussed in the previous chapters; deportees attempted to adapt to their new homeland, but they were often greeted with mistrust, fear, stigma, and outright rejection. The primary reason given by our deportees for returning to the United States, however, was to be with their families.

LUIS BARRIOS (L.B.): Tell me about going back to the Dominican Republic.
ESTRELLA (pausing, breathing deeply with her head lowered and tears in her eyes): I was having difficulty finding a job when I discovered that my name was on a list of criminals, and for this reason employers did not want to hire me. In this country, when you are a deportee it's like you have a public sign saying you are the worst of the worst. . . . On top of this I'm constantly thinking about my children and my wife. Asking myself, how are they really doing? But when we talked on the phone we spent more time crying and cursing than loving each other. After eight months I couldn't stand it anymore so I got back in a yola not knowing if I would arrive alive. . . . I thank God that I came back to my family.

I travelled with a photo of my wife and my three children thinking of that moment when we could reunite. Now here I am and I made it (he smiles). (August 19, 2009)

L.B.: How long were you in Santo Domingo before returning?

QUISQUEYA: The years I spent in the Dominican Republic without my daughters after being deported were a living hell. I did all sorts of things to survive. Things I never thought I would do, and now I feel ashamed. From 1999 to 2006 was an agony, I tried to kill myself more than five times, but thinking of my daughters gave me the strength to keep fighting. The rejection of people knowing that you were deported really hurt me. It was worse when this rejection came from your own family. It was like wearing a sign on your head. This makes you feel like shit. I think that we women carry the brunt of it all, especially when we have kids. To everybody in the Dominican Republic and New York, I was a bad mother because I had abandoned my daughters. I swear that I did not abandon them. I just wanted a better future for them, knowing that in Santo Domingo they would have no future. (September 1, 2009)

CHISMÍN: Every time I saw a girl in the street in Santo Domingo, I saw the face of my daughter, who was growing away from my love and my protection. I felt I had failed as a parent and had betrayed her. (August 22, 2009)

EL MAYIMBE: The mere thought of my wife and two children made me feel like I was dying alive. If torture exists, that's it. I could not sleep, eat, or live in peace. I felt that I was no longer a man and that I had betrayed them. There were many nights that I cried while looking at their pictures and dreaming of returning. I was so afraid that I would lose them. (August 16, 2009)

This feeling of loss, abandonment, and guilt ate away at many of the subjects, leading them to conclude that life was not worth living without making an attempt to return. The social and emotional pull was evident in each of their testimonies, as they recounted their feelings of despair and hopelessness at life in such a fractured state. Returning was a way to restore the family, redeem oneself, and show one's love and commitment to others. This conclusion is made more understandable when one considers the central role that family plays in the lives of most Dominicans, who often still care for their aging parents no matter the cost and who have large extended family networks that serve as important social and economic resources across the geographic divide. It is not surprising that interviewees saw their socioeconomic plight as secondary—though obviously important—in their decision-making process. They also insisted that, upon their return, they looked for a "legal" way to support their family.

For the men, an extremely important factor in their thinking was the psychological burden of being head of the family. Their identity was rooted in their roles as bread winner, father, and husband, and their failure to make good on their obligations led them to feel guilty, anxious, impotent, and incomplete, as both Verdugo and El Mayimbe related to us.

> VERDUGO: You do not understand. If you are a real man, you need to support your wife, your children, your mother, and your small siblings. I hate those fake men who enjoy taking advantages of their woman. These are not real men, they are a bunch of pussies. The real man goes out to the street and finds what he needs to bring home. You do whatever is necessary. If not, they are going to replace you. I always knew that I would have to return if I want to keep my family. I couldn't sleep, it was like living in hell, thinking about the possibility that she could find someone else. . . . You understand me? (October 1, 2009)

> EL MAYIMBE: I thought my wife would fall in love, get another husband, and give my children a new father. How much shit went through my head. However, the poor woman only had eyes for me and was always giving consoling me from New York by telephone. My family became a kind of engine to keep me fighting until I found a way to return. (August 16, 2009)

HOW DO DEPORTEES RETURN?

In chapter 3, we discussed how some of the undocumented emigrants first came to the United States, some as children with their relatives and others alone as adults. Many of their peers later became legal citizens by gaining amnesty during various government initiatives, particularly during the 1980s. None of our sample participated in those initiatives for the variety of reasons already discussed. The costs described by the participants who immigrated to the United States in the 1970s were much less than the payments demanded from more recent immigrants. Some paid as much as $20,000 to return to the United States, although most were able to make the journey for $5,000 to $8,000—still an enormous amount for someone from a poor family, unless they have been able to set aside proceeds from their past endeavors in the

TABLE 11.2 FREQUENCY OF DEPORTEES' METHODS OF RETURN TO THE UNITED STATES

Yola via Puerto Rico	11
Stowaway on tourist ship to Miami	3
Flew to Miami with false documents	4
Money paid to return to the United States	$5,000–$15,000

informal economy (primarily drugs). Nearly all of our participants had been deported for their direct or indirect relationship with this economy.

Therefore, most of the subjects incurred debt to make it back to the United States. At least some of the money they earned upon returning was being used to pay off loans that were usually secured through their extended family. Furthermore, a number of them had been cheated out of substantial sums by con artists in the community, who posed as immigrant smugglers to prey on the vulnerable. A third important difference in the return journey was that most travelled back through Puerto Rico and Miami; one participant returned via Mexico, and none returned through Canada, which we had heard in previous interviews was another pathway. One explanation for this might be that these borders have become extraordinarily militarized[1] (Ngai 2004; Massey 2003). Smuggling links between these ports of entry have become more sophisticated, and about half of the participants recounted the role played by a Dominican/Cuban/American "mafia" with connections to key workers in the transportation and border control systems. This purported organized crime group was able to maintain many of the routes through Miami, thereby exercising a great deal of control over the market, including the going rate of bribes.

BY YOLA TO PUERTO RICO

Interviewees made extraordinary efforts to return. The degree of guile, courage, and perseverance reflect their deep desire to be reunited with their loved ones and to escape the futureless lives that most were convinced would be their lot in the Dominican Republic.

L.B.: How did you come to the United States?

EL NEGRO: By yola. I paid $5,000 to transport me from Nagua to Puerto Rico. In total, there were seventeen of us, eleven men and six women. It was a nightmare. I thought we were not going to make it. The waves were, like, forty feet high. We were feeling sick, hungry, and thirsty. After twenty-eight hours, I was so relieved when I could see the lights in Puerto Rico. We managed to avoid the U.S. Coast Guard, and once in Mayaguez a friend was waiting to take me to San Juan. From San Juan I took a plane to New York, and now I'm talking to you. (September 25, 2009)

QUISQUEYA: To return was rather complicated. I talked to my father and my brothers, and they began looking for $8,000 to get me on a raft to Puerto Rico. The first time, I was screwed out of $8,000 because the bastards who organized the trip had us for fourteen hours out at sea, out of the town of Samaná . . . I am ashamed to talk about it. Those bastards took us to Santo Domingo from the northeast to the south. We were told to hide in the forest until sunrise, because that way it's better to travel. They just left with our money. When the sun rose, we realized that we were in Samaná Grande on Palenque Beach. The second time, after paying another $8,000, the Dominican Navy intercepted us at sea and arrested us. We then found out that those who were transporting us actually worked for these officers, and it was all a plan to steal our money. The third time was a charm, and I made it to Puerto Rico after paying about $6,000. My poor father did so many things to get the money to reunite me with my daughters. He always said that, if I killed myself, that he would carry that burden on his conscience forever. He was very concerned about how I felt without my daughters. (September 1, 2009)

BY SHIP TO MIAMI

L.B.: How did you come to the United States?

EL TIGRE: I paid $10,000 to an organization that brings you in a rice cargo ship from the Dominican Republic to the Port of Miami. They hide you, give you a meal, and allow you to go to the toilet. How many people knew that I was aboard I have no idea, but they treated me very well. Once I was in Miami, I had to wait two hours before getting out of the ship. Later they put me in a bus, La Cubanita,[2] that brought me to New York City in about twenty hours. (September 25, 2009)

TRINITARIO: I spent every day thinking about returning. In the Dominican Republic you always hear people talking about wanting to leave the country, how it's done and how it's paid. I met several people in this type of business, Dominicans tangled up with a mob of Cubans transporting people for $20,000 in cargo ships to Miami. I talked to my father and my older sister, with whom I don't have a very good relationship, but they were willing to help me get the money. A group of taxi drivers where I worked also made several collections. The trip was easier than I imagined. I got on the boat in Santo Domingo, a slow but safe journey, and two days later I was in Miami. I came the whole way so damn scared I couldn't sleep or eat, while looking at a picture of my baby the whole time. Once in Miami, I rode with other people on a bus to New York City on September 27, 2008, after two years of forced exile away from my family, my people, my work, and this country, which for me is my home because I grew up here. I was finally able to be reunited with my family again, especially with my daughter. Now I feel complete, now I want to continue living and fighting. I got back the reason to continue looking for a future. (October 5, 2009)

BY AIRPLANE TO MIAMI

L.B.: How did you come to the United States?

LOCO: I paid $15,000 to take a plane from Santo Domingo to Miami International Airport. The people that I paid have a solid organization. Everybody is part of this mafia, starting with officers working for the Dominican Immigration Office to those working for the Immigration and Naturalization Services at Miami. Once I got to the airport, Terminal E, they told me to stand next to my red luggage and wait. This is exactly what I did. I have to tell you that I was very scared. Later on, an officer came to me and told me to follow him. Shortly after, another officer verified my fake documents, which they all knew. Later on, this officer escorted me to the immigration area and I was free. Then I saw this guy with a sign with my fake name. I introduced myself to him, and he took me to the La Cubanita bus to New York City. (October 6, 2009)

EL MAYIMBE: Several friends told me about return trips where they pay about $15,000. I talked with my wife, and the whole family collected the money. It was a kind of family loan that I would repay gradually once I started working again. In August 2004, I was handed a Dominican passport with my photo, another name, and a tourist visa for two weeks. This of course was all false. I had to enter the United States through Miami, where they were waiting for me. This was very well prepared. I discovered when we were in Miami that about eight other people came on the same flight. Then we boarded a bus that brought us to New York. Once in New York, I was able to reunite with my family. They had a welcoming party with food, rum, and music. My return left me sort of hanging for at least two weeks. I didn't want the kids to go to school while my wife stayed at home with me in the apartment. I feared losing them again, and I had nightmares and stress that stopped me from sleeping. I don't know how many times I went to the children's bedroom to see them. My wife would tell me that they were fine, to let them sleep in peace, but I just kept wanting to hug and kiss them. I was the same with her. (August 16, 2009)

BY PLANE, TRUCK, HORSE, AND BOAT VIA MEXICO

L.B.: How did you come back?

CAMILLA: I wasn't thinking of coming back, but my mom said to me, "You're gonna have to go because you have your children there. I know you want to be with me, you but have to go." That's when I decided I had to come. We took a flight to Nicaragua . . . the international negotiations between the Dominican Republic and Nicaragua didn't require that much paperwork to travel. You only had to pay for a visa. You have your passport and a visa for thirty days. When we got to Nicaragua, the man kept talking to us, making us dream about it . . . and then he cheated us! After that we were on our own. Me and my brother, we got to Honduras. First we got a bus to take us to somewhere called "Las Garitas"—it's like a migration area, all sand at the border. But before we went by horse to the crossing . . . that was, like, an easy ten kilometers. After that, they took us into a room inside a house where we rested. At night, we left in one of those big trucks to San Felito, a port which opened the way to the border with Guatemala. Then we went to a place in Guatemala that they call "Ocos" (sic). It's controlled by the immigration smugglers and the police who just take their bribes. From there we got to the state of Chiapas . . . then we had to cross the Atlantic in a yola. We went from nine in the morning 'till twelve at night . . . to the city of Veracruz by sea and arrived at a tourist city called "Guatulco" (sic). That was the nicest thing about Mexico. From there we were put on a bus to Acapulco. From Acapulco we were taken in that part of the truck where the driver sleeps, they put fifteen of us in there where usually only one would fit! From there we got to the Federal District, where we were put in a hotel for two days, but the situation was not good. . . . I tell you, you have to be really motivated and have a lot of discipline to get where you're headed, as you go through a lot. After that we crossed to Monterrey. In Monterrey you're almost like at the United States, and from there I remember that we got to another city that shares a frontier with Mexico. Over there, we were taken across by two kids, two coyotes. We crossed the Rio Bravo, and when we arrived we were already on American soil. From there we were picked up and spent like an hour walking and hiding from migration officials. We got to a ranch, where we stayed hidden in the forest and were taken to a city called San Benito, Texas, where we stayed a week. After that, we got to Houston, Texas, and from Houston, Texas, we got here. I remember that it was November 30th when we arrived here in the United States. The journey was sort of a little long. . . .

L.B.: How much was all of this?
CAMILLA: We paid about $4,500 each, including the guy who cheated us. (July 3, 2009)

SURVIVING IN NEW YORK CITY

Once in New York, what then? How does one survive not only as an undocumented person but as a returned deportee facing at least three years in a federal prison? We begin this section with field notes that describes the informal street economy during the early part of our research in Manhattan.

Today I took the number 1 train to Washington Heights, alighting at the 145th Street station. It is 8:30 AM. I like this walk from 145th Street to 152nd Street. I can see and feel how people struggle in the streets, and I always find someone

11.2 152ND AND BROADWAY—THE CENTER OF THE WASHINGTON HEIGHTS COMMUNITY (*PHOTO:* LUIS BARRIOS).

I know. Today is no different. I found Doña Altagracia selling her customary *habichuelas con dulce*.[3] We talk for a while about her family in New York City and in the Dominican Republic. I continue walking until I get to 152nd Street, where I'm doing the interviews. I use the office of a friend who owns a travel agency on the corner. While waiting, I start observing some guys I had previously interviewed. This corner is *un punto de droga*[4] and there are thirteen young men hanging around, all of them dressed up. They know I'm here and allow me to observe.

Two of them are selling heroin and cocaine, and the rest are *matando el tiempo*.[5] They are young, with the eldest about thirty years old. They talk, eat, and socialize. Today someone has brought a table with four chairs, and they start playing dominoes, calling each other nicknames and ritually push each other around, making fun of one other. Those who are not playing are watching and telling the players the best way to win. It seems that people who watch always think they know better than those who are playing.

Every five minutes someone stops to buy drugs, everybody else checks to make sure the police are not around or that a buyer is not an undercover. They do this surveillance automatically, instinctively. When they are not sure, they ask the person directly: "Are you a police officer?" Legally the person needs to disclose his or her identity, otherwise, once they are in court, they can dismiss the case.

This is a corner where trust is essential. You can't be too paranoid if you want to hang out here. One of the dealers told me that they help out those without a job, giving them a little something to support their family. This is our welfare system in the Heights. Every two hours, the guys rotate, some take on the role watching for the police and screaming *fo*[6] or *ta'bien*.[7] According to my interviews, no one on this corner is making more than $100 a day, even though these are the same guys that the U.S. Drug Enforcement Agency or New York City Police Department describe as the major drug dealers and big shots in the community. Nothing could be further from the truth. (Field notes, February 21, 2003)

As indicated in the field notes, the streets of Washington Heights, historically home to the Dominican community, are awash in the practices and social actors of both legal and illegal economies. This community is one of the most impoverished in New York City, where, according to city estimates in 2008, the overall poverty rate for individuals was 22 percent (Roberts 2010).[8] It is also home to an increasingly large subpopulation of returning deportees who need to find ways to support themselves and the families that they returned to be with.[9]

11.3 A PUBLIC ELEMENTARY SCHOOL IN THE WASHINGTON HEIGHTS COMMUNITY NAMED AFTER ONE OF THE FOUNDERS OF THE DOMINICAN REPUBLIC (*PHOTO:* LUIS BARRIOS).

In the following, we provide accounts of the daily lives of five occupations favored by returning deportees: the drug seller, the chiripero, the babysitter, the taxi driver, and the factory worker.

THE DRUG SELLER

L.B.: Tell me about your day from the moment you wake up till you go to sleep.

EL NEGRO (smiling, getting comfortable in his seat, breaking his silence and finally saying): Well, my brother, the streets are tough. I don't feel very proud of what I am doing, I know it's wrong. But I have to live. If I don't sell these drugs, somebody else will. It's not that I wanted to sell drugs again, but things are not very good. I didn't find work, I never finished school, and I don't know what else to do because I never finished a career. There are times that I think that this is my destiny.

But you asked me how my day begins. When I wake up, I stay in bed for a moment wondering how I'm going to get money that day. I have three young boys and a woman that all need to be fed and maintained. On top of this, the apartment needs to be paid for, or else the landlord will kick you out in a second. Thinking about this at 7:00 AM gives me a headache, especially with the boys messing around and fighting before going to school. In the midst of all of this screaming, I try to plan for my

 appears along right margin: THE RETURN OF THE DEPORTEES

281

day. I need to bring home at least $100 daily, and that's not easy. So I tell myself to stop thinking shit and to prepare for the streets.

I jump up, take a shower, and put my clothes on. By then, the boys have already left, and I am alone with my woman. I eat my breakfast . . . I have always liked oatmeal with milk and bread with black coffee. Before I leave, I place myself in the hands of the Virgin of Altagracia. I go to the altar that I have built for her and leave her flowers, candles, and water. I also hold the amulets that my mother gave me for protection. These are beads that represent both Santa Barbara and Papa Candelo. I say my prayers and I ask my little Virgin to protect me and my family, and let me make today's money and keep the police away. I can't deny that I am always afraid that something might happen to me, and my family will be left to fend for itself. In this line of work, something always happens, whether it's the hospital because they hurt you, the cemetery because they kill you, or the jail because they arrest you and then deport you. But that's life. You have to take risks, especially when you're the head of a family. I tell people in my building that I'm going to my office. Well, I give my woman a kiss and say goodbye till the night time when I return, if God allows me.

After this I go to the streets. You already know that I help Rasputin sell drugs on the corner of 152nd Street and Broadway. I start the day standing on the corner around 9:30 AM, and I stay there till 9:00 PM, which is when we divide up everything and go home. Whether it's raining, cold, hot, or snowing, you've got to stand on that fucking corner. It's a dangerous job, but at least I don't have the drugs on me if the police come. I just take the orders and collect the money on the corner. Then I call someone to deliver and tell the person where to pick them up. Of course, I have to be aware when people start screaming that somebody suspicious is coming because the police are everywhere. It's a job that makes you very nervous, and it's full of risks. There are times when you feel very insecure but, my friend, I have to continue. It's in those moments that I start functioning on automatic pilot to stop me from dropping everything and going home. At those times I think about my family having something to eat, which helps me keep going.

Those twelve hours that I'm standing there are full of agony and pain, especially when the weather is not good. If it's not the police messing with you, it's a hustler trying to take your money or your drugs. These people need to be taken care of. We might hit them, shoot them, or just kill them. In this work it's either you or the other person. You can't think too much about it or feel pity. The rules of the street are real simple when you sell drugs: if you don't kill them, they will kill you.

On that corner I eat my lunch as well as my dinner. I also talk and socialize with the guys who stop by. Some of them stay there the whole fucking day, doing nothing. Probably they don't have any other place to go. There are a few businesses which we pay to let us use their bathrooms.

Around 9:00 PM we close the business. They pay us and everybody goes home because tomorrow is another working day. On the way, I call my woman to see if we need anything and to tell her that I am on my way, tired like a dog. God has been good to me. (September 25, 2009)

THE CHIRIPERO

L.B.: Tell me about your working day, from the moment you wake up till you go to sleep.

CHISMÍN: My day begins at 6:00 AM. I get out of bed and look out the window to see if nature will be good to me. If it's raining or snowing, my day is fucked. This is a serious problem for those who sell on the streets. If I cannot go out, my income for the week gets chaotic, therefore I have to try to do something else to compensate. If the day is good, I am definitely heading out to the streets. You already know that I have four children, my wife, and my mother-in-law, and they eat a lot. My wife is on welfare, but that shit doesn't give her enough, just misery. And let me tell you, when we put together what they give her and what I earn, we are still short, we always have to make miracles so that we have enough money. In this country, you can be an honest person and they are still going to fuck you.

Once I leave my house, I put myself in the hands of God. My God always protects me. Still, when I'm ready to leave the apartment, I always tell myself that this could be the day they are going to arrest me and have me deported again. It is very painful every morning, when I look at my wife and my children thinking that I may not be coming back. She always gives me that look as if we were saying goodbye, and I hate thinking about that possibility. This shit gives me chills and headaches because I don't want to be separated again from my family. But I can't stay at home because I am still the man of the family.

By 8:00 AM I am on my way to a friend's house, which is where the four of us store the merchandise. We give him something to use his apartment as a storage area. I sell children's and men's clothing and underwear for men and women. The first thing I do is sort out the merchandise that I want to carry with me in a suitcase with wheels and a book bag I carry on my back. I always carry some clothes in my hand for my customers to see. To carry and walk with all of this, up and down, is like carrying Jesus' cross. It weighs a lot, but at least I earn a living honestly.

Since I don't have a government permit to sell this merchandise, I can't stand on any corner to sell like others. I would love to have a permit, but since I was deported and I entered the country illegally, I have no choice. If I go to Police Plaza to get a permit, they can arrest me right there.

Once you are on the street, you have to move and approach people if you want to sell. I move in a rectangle from 135th and Broadway to 155th and Broadway. I then do the same on Amsterdam Avenue. I do this route about six times a day, going into each of the businesses, mainly bodegas, barbershops, and beauty salons. The guys on the corners also buy my clothes.

On a daily basis, probably in twelve hours I make about $300 dollars, but taking out expenses it's only $75. The rest goes to the investment I made buying the merchandise. I do this seven days a week because I need to make up for the days I can't sell. I eat lunch in the street every day, but I try not to spend too much.

It's a disgrace, but there's always a cop on the street who will stop you and ask for your permit and identification. I guess they do their work and I do mine. With these people, it's always a discussion about power. When you say that you don't have a permit, they take away your merchandise and confiscate it. And once in a while a corrupt cop comes along who takes your money as well, but where can you complain? Going to the precinct is out of the question. You are illegal, you are invisible, and you do not exist in this country. To avoid being arrested you have to present a photo ID or they will arrest you right there. I have a fake ID that works very well. Once you show them the ID, they give you a ticket to show up in court but I don't dare to pass by. Either way I have to accept many losses and setbacks, because when I lose the merchandise that's my living. These weaklings should be arresting the drug sellers, not decent people like us! When they take your merchandise I have to start from the beginning again, and the family goes into crisis mode; we have to be very careful how we spend our money.

This shit has happened to me three times in the last five months. I lost everything, money and merchandise. Two motherfuckers that call themselves police officers took away everything. When this happens you feel so weak that it's better to erase everything from your mind. Of course, they know that I'm not going to the precinct complaining about corrupt cops. But my biggest fear is to be arrested. I am afraid because I do not want to be deported again. Sometimes I dream about this. I see myself running with police officers running after me. I always wake up sweating, very anxious and agitated. Just thinking about the possibility that they can take away my merchandise creates some kind of daily panic, but I'm learning how to live with these feelings without getting ill.

Around 8:00 PM I return home to shower, eat, and hear the problems before heading to bed. If there is a lotto I always play it to see if I can get out of this devil's lair and head back to my country with all my family. Then I tell myself, "Ok, Chismín, you made it through this day, tomorrow is another day." Of course, it will be the same story, the story of the poor. (August 22, 2009)

THE BABYSITTER

L.B.: I understand that you already have a job as a nanny. Tell me what a workday is like for you.

QUISQUEYA: A friend of mine got me this job. They are very good people. They know I'm undocumented and that I have been deported to the Dominican Republic and returned to New York to be with my family. They are a lovely family, with a daughter and a son. It's been two years that I've worked with them, and when I started the girl was three years old and the boy one year old. I speak a little English, but they always told me to only speak Spanish to the children. You have to listen to them, I don't know how the hell they learned Spanish in such a short time, and I keep trying with this fucking English that I sometimes know and sometimes don't know what the hell I am saying!

I have to be at work at 7:00 AM before they leave. They live by 88th Street and Riverside Drive. I start by preparing breakfast for the children. I bathe them and put them in clean clothes. The lady of the house always prepares a list of places where she wants me to take them. There is a bookstore called Barnes & Noble that has activities for children every day, and she likes me to take them there. I don't understand much of what is happening but I like to see the children enjoy themselves. The girl is in preschool from 9:00 AM to 1:00 PM, so I take her there and pick her up from Monday through Friday. The boy stays with me, because he is still very young. I read to him in Spanish and take him to the places that the lady says.

Then they eat the lunch I make for them, sleep for a while, and at about 3:00 PM I take them to the playground. I love taking them to the park because I always find a group of friends who do the same work as me, raising children that are not ours. We support each other and listen to each other's stories. We also refer people to jobs either as nannies or cleaning apartments. When we're in the park together, we always laugh because people see all these black women with all these white kids and they look at you as if saying that they know they are not yours. I guess they know that we are nannies, but anyway I don't care because to me, although I did not give birth to them, I always think I'm their real mother. In the evening I cook for everyone. These people like Latino food. I don't know where the hell they learned to eat rice, beans, and meat every day.

I get up at 5:00 AM to deal with my own housework and be at work by no later than 7:00 to 7:30 AM in my nanny job. I leave that house at 6:00 PM and get home at about 8:00 PM to cook and deal with children, tired as a bitch to work for free for my other family.

L.B.: Where do you find the strength to keep going?

QUISQUEYA: Firstly from my family. They are my inspiration and my reason to continue going on. I also go to an evangelical church that knows my history of being deported and returning with false papers, but they accept me, love me, and help me. They pray with me a lot, and that gives me strength. God has become someone with more importance in my life after my return, and my brothers and sisters in my church are always available to help me in whatever I may need. I do not know where I would be without them. (September 1, 2009)

THE FACTORY WORKER

L.B.: What does a day's work look like for El Mayimbe?

EL MAYIMBE: I had to find work again and start making money to support the children. I went with a friend to a women's clothing factory in Long Island. These people specialize in recruiting undocumented immigrants, paying them a misery of a wage while never paying social security or medical benefits. But fuck that, I needed a job and with another fool I went, and they gave me a job.

I get up at 4:00 in the morning to be at work by 6:00 AM. We are a group of friends who all go in one car. We all share the cost of gas and tolls. We leave work at 5:00 PM and we get home around 7:00 PM, tired, hungry, and with little inclination to listen to problems or to deal with matters at home. We do this six days a week. At least Sunday is free and for my family.

At first this was frustrating, earning less money than those who were documented, working more hours, and with working conditions that were not optimal. The mere thought that I was now an undocumented immigrant hurt and bothered me. I felt inferior to my coworkers, and this gave me great shame. What comforted me was that I could keep food on the table for my kids and I became a man again. I think I was born to work in factories.

L.B.: Where does your energy come from?

EL MAYIMBE: Well I'm not the only deportee that returned or the only undocumented person in this city, and that comforts me. But of course, I don't want people to know that I am a returnee or that I'm undocumented. That is a shame, and I am not in the mood to put up with stupid people. However there is a club of Sanjuaneros in exile in the Bronx where I go every week to play dominoes and play pool, and I find a lot of support there. It's a place where people like me will talk about their problems, even if just drinking a beer. No one judges you; they accept you, respect you, and make you feel like a person. (August 16, 2009)

THE TAXI DRIVER

TRINITARIO: My dad managed to get me some work as a taxi driver with one of his cars, but now it's different. I'm an illegal, a fugitive undocumented immigrant, driving a taxi and listening to people's problems.

L.B.: What is a working day like for you?

TRINITARIO: I start and finish at the time that I want. I am my own boss. But, starting early and finishing late is a necessary routine because in this work there is a lot of competition. Usually I go out and leave my daughter at school at 7:30 in the morning and continue driving. I go back and pick her up at 3:30 in the afternoon and leave her with a baby-sitter while I look for clients. I'd say I'm out for about twelve hours a day in order to have a reasonable income to help me cover expenses and save at least a little to get out of this country and die in peace in Santo Domingo.

L.B.: Where does your energy come from?

TRINITARIO: Beyond the unconditional support that my family has given me, I have to thank the group of drivers who have functioned as another family. This is a group of men and women, many of them immigrants who respect, protect, and help in whatever. What one needs one says into the microphone of the base, and someone always comes with the answer. It may be furniture, food, clothing, work, going to a dentist because you have no health insurance. Open your mouth and let them know, and you'll realize you're not alone in this country. Again, we taxi drivers hear the people's problems. (October 5, 2009)

THE ROLE OF THE UNDERGROUND ECONOMY

As Venkatesh (2008) demonstrated, the role of the underground economy is pivotal in many poor communities that have long suffered social disinvestment and a scarcity of work opportunities that pay a living wage with opportunities for social mobility. In this sense, the Washington Heights community is no different from other marginalized neighborhoods, except that it is a transnational community, with the majority of its residents having strong links to both countries. The economy of this community reflects this transnational location; thus, the work that is available to returning deportees reflects these community characteristics.

El Negro chose the drug trade as his best way to earn a sufficient income for his wife and children. This opportunity exists via the connections between the Dominican Republic and the drug cartels of Colombia. It has long been established that many consumers of illicit drugs come from New Jersey to Washington Heights to satisfy their needs. Drug spots in the area serve both the local market of Manhattan as well as further afield. El Negro simply played a low-tier role in this well established economic practice of the neighborhood, no doubt continuing a role he played before he was imprisoned and deported several years prior. He had to decide whether to earn his living "honestly," such as Chismín as a chiripero or Trinitario as a taxi driver, while choosing which would realistically provide him with sufficient resources on a regular basis.

For many outside of this community who choose to ignore the context of the socioeconomic situation, drug selling might be seen as a moral or even a criminological issue (i.e., continuing a criminal career), but El Negro was already a criminal by dint of being an illegal returnee. If caught, he would face imprisonment regardless of the nature of his employment.

Moreover, all five work narratives show the extensive relationship between the formal and informal economies of the city. El Negro serviced many working and middle-class clients of New York City with his product, for which there is an enormous and continuing demand in the United States despite billions of dollars being spent over the last two decades on the war on drugs (see Brotherton and Martín 2009). Quisqueya's work as a babysitter allowed her middle-class Upper West Side family to maintain a lifestyle to which they are accustomed. In many respects, she and so many like her, with or without official documents, make the lifestyles of the middle class possible (Ehrenreich and Hoschild 2004; Young 2009), and many would argue that the immigrant situation drives the vast political economy of the United States by providing limitless cheap colonized labor in food production, restaurant services, construction, child care, health services, and manufacturing (Bacon 2008). Trinitario worked hard to provide transport in an area that is poorly served by the city's yellow cabs; Chismín engaged in the illegal practice of selling legal products on the street, a custom that is common in Latin America; and El Mayimbe provided cheap, undocumented labor in a factory that produces for the formal market.

The links and networks between the formal and informal economies are therefore intricate, massive, and fluid, and they have become even more interconnected during the past several decades as both social and economic policies have been dominated by neoliberal ideology, which views capitalistic markets as the panacea for all social problems. Such thinking has led to a sharp curtailment in business regulations and government oversight, effectively promoting the underground economy by increasing the precariousness of legitimate work opportunities and encouraging "shady" entrepreneurship (Venkatesh 2008). This allows the proceeds of an illicit enterprise, such as the drug trade, to become an important portion of the money being circulated in the banking system.[10]

VARIEGATED SOCIAL SUPPORT SYSTEMS

How do people in such trying situations keep going? The economic situation is hardly life sustaining, but engaging in the relentless daily grind with little end in sight is probably better than remaining unemployed in Santo Domingo. Nonetheless, the frustration with not being able to move ahead, the precariousness of employment itself, and the constant threat of law enforcement all take its psychological toll on returnees (see later in this

TABLE 11.3 PROCESSES OF ADAPTATION

Social dimension	Type of involvement	Effects on well-being
Families as social support	Psychological involvement and social support	Positive social relationships; produce happiness and settlement
Friends as social support	Peer social acceptance	Social support and inclusion; helps them cope
Community as social support	Social bonding	Perception of control; a sense of relatedness to other people

chapter). Participants stated that it was their range of social supports that enabled them to face the day, address their multiple problems head on, and sustain their lives. Survival was achieved through a network of friends, family, generalized members of the community, and work associates who did not judge them as criminal outsiders but as essential and valued members of the community (Nelson and Prilleltensky 2005:351).

In one way or another, subjects placed a strong emphasis on being included socially in their microcommunity, which gave them a renewed identity as a father, husband, wife, or worker and not just as a despised and helpless deportee as they experienced in the Dominican Republic. Furthermore, their reunification with their family brought them joy and happiness and was in complete contrast to the anguish, alienation, and despair that they felt during their exile. This interconnectedness that they now enjoyed produced a semblance of self-control, personal security, and a deeper sense of belonging, all of which convinced them that returning was the right and only decision they could have made. Their need now, in order to cope, is to look forward, to not let the fear of being discovered paralyze them, and to be grateful for this special time that may not last long.

TRAUMA AND COLLATERAL DAMAGE

The last theme that has been in evidence at all times throughout this project relates to the psychosocial wounds experienced by the subjects and the collateral damage to which they refer. What must it be like to always be aware that this may be the last time your false papers will pass inspection? Or that the innocent transaction with a cop may lead to further questions and the discovery of your true identity? Or that your employer is coming under increasing pressure from authorities to no longer employ the "undocumented," let alone the "deported?" This state of permanent anxiety is, of course, not healthy, and it wears both on the individual and on their relationships with others despite the brave face they put on for family and friends. For example, Jaramillo revealed the psychological effects of this condition and the frustration that it produces:

JARAMILLO: This is a racist country. Before I was deported, they always found a way to remind me that I was trash. In prison they treated me like trash, and when they deported me they treated me the same way. Now that I've returned, nothing has changed, it's still the same—they continue treating me like garbage. I need to face this painful reality every day. What is wrong with these people? (March 1, 2003)

CONCLUSION

There is no doubt that deportees are returning to the United States and that this phenomenon needs to be studied from a perspective other than one that claims deportees are returning to commit further crimes (Rumbaut 2008; Bernstein 2007). Our data demonstrate that this phenomenon is about much more than an immigrant's criminal or legal status; rather, it is about the current processes of global and transnational resettlement, social control, social reproduction, strategies of resistance, the nexus of the formal and informal economies, and the narratives and sufferings of both personal and collective trauma.

In many ways, the participants in our study are similar to other, more "legitimate" refugees or exiles in that much of their life is a consequence of human rights violations; as deportees, however, such violations cannot be considered. They are essentially non-persons, people who have to live in the deepest crevices of the subterranean world of the "undocumented" with families and loved ones who are often from the legitimate world of the mainstream. In this massive contradiction, they are caught between openness and concealment, resettlement and threatened expulsion, opportunity and risk. Many of the interviews revealed that, although returned deportees express their intense relief at having "made it," they are always aware that the dream could once again become a nightmare.

CHAPTER TWELVE

CONCLUSION

Whereas recognition of the inherent dignity and of the equal and inalienable rights of all members of the human family is the foundation of freedom, justice and peace in the world,

Whereas disregard and contempt for human rights have resulted in barbarous acts which have outraged the conscience of mankind, and the advent of a world in which human beings shall enjoy freedom of speech and belief and freedom from fear and want has been proclaimed as the highest aspiration of the common people,

Whereas it is essential, if man is not to be compelled to have recourse, as a last resort, to rebellion against tyranny and oppression, that human rights should be protected by the rule of law,

Whereas it is essential to promote the development of friendly relations between nations,

Whereas the peoples of the United Nations have in the Charter reaffirmed their faith in fundamental human rights, in the dignity and worth of the human person and in the equal rights of men and women and have determined to promote social progress and better standards of life in larger freedom,

Whereas Member States have pledged themselves to achieve, in co-operation with the United Nations, the promotion of universal respect for and observance of human rights and fundamental freedoms,

Whereas a common understanding of these rights and freedoms is of the greatest importance for the full realization of this pledge....

(THE UNIVERSAL DECLARATION OF HUMAN RIGHTS, ADOPTED ON DECEMBER 10, 1948 AT THE UNITED NATIONS IN NEW YORK)

This has been a long journey. We spent almost seven years interviewing, observing, investigating, testifying, interpreting, and analyzing the life-worlds of deportees at multiple locations in two countries, working until we were able to draw conclusions. When we started the project in 2002, we thought that the entire process would take two to three years, but with little to no funding (we wrote several grant proposals to both public and private agencies, but no financial support was ever forthcoming despite encouraging reviews) and the enduring complexity of the issues, we felt that we could not end our data collection until we interviewed the returning deportees in Manhattan.

We sincerely hope that the life-course narratives along with our various ethnographic reports from the field, as framed in a critical sociological and criminological analysis, have been sufficient to raise awareness of the destructive and inhumane criminal justice and immigration processes being conducted in the names of the citizens and taxpayers of the United States and beyond. It has been sixty-one years since that momentous occasion in New York City when the Declaration of Human Rights was signed by every member state in the wake of the horrendous casualties and crimes against humanity perpetrated before and during World War Two.

Still we are treated to daily reminders of the abuse of those rights supposedly enshrined in our respective constitutions and nation state laws. The photographic scenes of perverse indignity perpetrated at Abu Ghraib by a government and its agents in the name of defeating tyranny and the plethora of images broadcast around the world in the wake of Hurricane Katrina demonstrate how unequal, unjust, and punishing life has become for many in the United States—not as the exception but as the rule. We issue our report in an epoch when torture and extreme mistreatment have become sanctioned by laws. We witness a studied indifference in the total contravention of the spirit and substance of the Declaration of Human Rights countenanced by war exceptionalism in the pursuit of terrorists or by the everyday structured rituals of racism, classism, and sexism that make our discriminatory practices so banal. We locate our study therefore within this more generalized knowledge of the flagrant and celebrated abuses of the human condition and suggest that the voices heard in the previous pages be placed in that context. We write reflexively at a time when we have tended repeatedly to forget who we are as democratic citizens, as members of a world family completely interdependent on one another, and as purveyors of hope and enterprise often stirred ironically by those immortal words at the foot of the Statue of Liberty[1]:

Give me your tired, your poor,
  Your huddled masses yearning to breathe free,
  The wretched refuse of your teeming shore.
  Send these, the homeless, tempest-tost to me,
  I lift my lamp beside the golden door!

BETWEEN HOPE AND REJECTION

At the beginning of the book we asked the following questions: What happened to the immigrant's dream such that it became a nightmare? What happened to the hope and ambition of these subjects? How was it channeled into such "deviant" pathways that they received the heavy societal sanctions that not only tore them away from their families within the United States but also from the United States itself, condemning them to exile in their homeland? Certainly there are numerous sociological and criminological theories that purport to explain these processes of deviance through reference to opportunity structures, drift, innovative subcultures, and even criminal seduction. All of these theories have been applied in various degrees in our analyses.

In addition, there are immigration theories, particularly those pertaining to the concept of segmented assimilation, that speak of the mix of social and cultural capital as the immigrant enters a downward cycle of social mobility, acculturating him or herself to the subterranean worlds of the street and the resistant identities of the "underclass." In this reading of the wayward immigrant, the imaginary landscape is replete with gangs, drugs, and the usual assemblages of subcultures, informal economic webs, and social practices that typify the proletariats and subproletariats of the globalized inner city. There are many such narratives in our data that testify to the explanatory power of such theories, but these are all only part of the picture. Our data demonstrate and demand a fuller, more culturally contextual and fluid analysis that points to the savage mix of history and politics in the era of capitalist late modernity and in particular to the peculiarly punitive turn society has taken in its chosen modes of government and population control.[2]

BULIMIA AND A CONTRADICTORY THEORY OF EXCLUSION

Thus we settled on the theoretical notion of social bulimia as developed over the last decade in the work of criminologist Jock Young. In the form of the deportee we see the massive contradictions of dependency and colonialism, of a seductive capitalism and the needs and imaginations of emigrants and immigrants, and the interests of elite-dominated security states whose leading parties continue to fashion crime and immigration controls on the backs of the poorest and most vulnerable sections of society. It is out of this torrid confluence of social forces and public policies that the deportee emerges, pushed and pulled through low-tier schools and immigrant neighborhoods, put to work in low-status occupations or finding niches in legal and illegal "off the books" occupations, and finally consumed by criminal justice institutions now umbilically tied to border controls that virtually seal their fate in an era of anti-rehabilitation.

The deportee therefore becomes much as Bauman (2004) had foreseen: the epitome of the "wasted life" in the contemporary post-Fordist United States and increasingly in other developed capitalist democratic societies in Europe (see later in this chapter). On the one hand driven out and marginalized by the unequal trading relations and histories of colonial and imperial plunder, and on the other lured by the old wants of the industrialized economy and the new wants of the post-industrial middle classes, many were brought to the United States by parents fleeing from dictatorship and/or attracted to the endless promises of the American Dream that are so profoundly a part of the Latin American and Caribbean consciousness. What they encountered was different than what they had imagined. Those who came early as children were often pleasantly surprised; after adjusting to the language and customs of their new homeland, they did their best to settle, to learn the customs and norms of their new transnational habitus, and to live up to the aspirations of their parents. As they remembered their trips to Macy's, the sparkling lights of Christmas, the plentiful pantries, and the free milk in elementary school, our participants recounted those times when New York City did indeed seem to be a land of opportunity welcoming those tired and huddled families from the barrios of Santo Domingo. Those who came to the United States later in life were not so lucky—their families were unable to guide them and give them the ethnic capital and grounding that immigration scholars currently emphasize for purposes of integration. For these latter immigrants, the story was destined to be rather more disappointing. They went straight into the business of surviving in a postindustrial world where the influence of the illicit drug trade was becoming increasingly integrated into the general political economy of the nation. The drug culture had always been part of the fabric of New York City's social life, whether in the days of prohibition and the speakeasies of Harlem and the Lower East Side in the 1920s, to the heroin that flooded the city during the Vietnam war, to the cocaine that became a normal part of nightclub life in the 1970s and early 1980s, to the crack epidemic that seemed to leave such a visible trail of physical devastation during the late 1980s and 1990s.

The trajectory of these first-generation participants, these rather typical contemporary immigrants, took a turn for the worse, not simply because of what they did or did not do, but because the laws in the United States changed, turning the racialized communities from which they came—their spaces, networks, survival mechanisms, and statuses—into increasingly criminalizable units of control and expulsion. In this we see the bulimic paradox, the inclusion/exclusion dialectic, as immigrants were recast as incontrovertible villains with no salvageable histories, no sufficient offerings of penance and remorse, no acceptable commitments to self-reform, and no possibilities of family or community restoration. As we wrote in an earlier field note, with the stroke of a judge's pen, the immigrant becomes an ex-resident of the United States, forever banished from what was for many—though not all—their presumed homeland. In this social fact, the intensity of the bulimic act—as the agent of the state backed by the full force of the United States Congress—determines not only the subject's fate but also that of his or her family and loved ones for decades to come. The vindictiveness of this practice, this ritual of extreme judicial control, cannot be underestimated; no other sociocultural act more graphically displays the contempt with which the United States holds the 1948 Declaration of Human Rights.[3]

THE HOMECOMING

Of course, it could have ended differently. Immigrants could have been deported to a country that may have welcomed them, like the sons and daughters of the nation that they are, albeit somewhat blemished ones. Instead they become the Other of the Other, carrying the stigma of the past with the meanings and identities of the present. They represent both the bitter reminder of the flipside of the American Dream and the threat of the criminal, that peculiarly remorseless "American" stereotype that the U.S. corporate media and its political enablers have been infamously projecting for the past three decades. Who wants to live with the former and who wants to hear of the latter? Who needs reminders of the inescapable nature of their Dominican misery? Who wants yet another confirmation that those transnational spaces are not what they once were and that the balance of class forces in the wake of neoliberal political, economic, and criminal justice doctrines and in the midst of the world's crisis-ridden financialization have ensured that their capacity to labor has become obsolete?

If we dig a little deeper, we find that the deportees represent further reminders of a world that might have been, of a lost opportunity to make good on one

12.1 MANOLO IN 2003 IN SANTO DOMINGO (*PHOTO:* WILLIAM COSSOLIAS).

of the most progressive constitutions during the second half of the twentieth century under the tutelage of the intellectual political leader Juan Bosch. Every day that the government of the Dominican Republic refuses to put the issue of deportees on the agenda of bilateral relations with the United States and demand that Washington at least help pay for the reintegration of those they so efficiently reject is further proof of the spinelessness that defines the kleptocracy that has ruled this half of the island for much of the last one hundred years.

Finally, the participants in our study are examples of the generalized nature of the phenomenon: included/excluded subjects who have their counterparts all over the developing world, throughout the Caribbean, Central America, much of South America (particularly in Colombia, Ecuador, and Brazil), and South-East Asia, and they are present in increasing numbers in the prisons of Spain, Italy, Britain, France, Portugal, Greece, Germany, and Holland (Welch and Schuster 2008; Calavita 2003; De Giorgi 2010). In both Spain and Italy, immigrants make up more than 30 percent of the inmate population. Calavita calls them a "reserve army of delinquents," and others have likened them to a global migrant underclass whose otherness has provoked successive moral panics that rationalize extreme measures of criminalization or "hyper-incarceration" (De Giorgi 2010) while fueling political campaigns of the extreme right. We must not overlook the irony that this punishing language toward the immigrant is prevalent in countries that for decades relied on immigrants for low-cost labor for the industries of Northern Europe and the United States, countries whose citizens were themselves the victims of exclusionary laws and discrimination.

WHAT OF RESISTANCE?

None of the factors which sociologists believe to be the determinants of human behaviour—education, religious belief, political attachment—correlated with the incidents of heroic resistance against evil. Somehow, the ability to resist is not fully dependent on social conditioning.

(BAUMAN, INTERVIEWED BY MADELEINE BUNTING 2003)

The topic of resistance is an important part of our conclusion because the criminological literature pays little attention to that which cannot be explained by the kinds of social conditioning variables that Bauman refers to above. The result is that the bulk of criminological narratives is based largely on economistic and mathematical principles, with nary a human being in sight (Young 2007). Although the literature regarding the sociology of immigration is more varied, it still favors the use of large secondary data sets to measure the demographic flows of immigrants and the great waves of ethnic cohorts as they pass through the social, educational, and occupational sieves of U.S. society. When the concept of resistance is applied, however, it is usually used to explain the downward mobility of immigrants in theories of segmented assimilation, where it is viewed mainly as an oppositional disposition[4] to mainstream socialization, particularly the rejection of middle-class "white" norms in public school settings.[5]

We found this form of resistance in our participants as they joined street gangs, did not have particularly successful educational or work careers, entered the criminal justice system, and struggled with the norms of the Dominican Republic (which might be seen more as a case of culture conflict); however, this is only one side of the dialectic. The resistance we are wont to emphasize is that[6] which privileges the agency of individuals as they seek meaning in everyday life and contest power relations in highly colonized contexts, an approach that is rare among immigration treatments that offer relatively few long-term, in situ, ethnographic investigations (see Smith [2005] and Gregory [2007] as two of the exceptions) that might provoke such analyses.

We observed resistance in our participants at multiple levels, and this resistance has an existential air about it as deportees search for ways to sustain themselves socially, physically, mentally, and economically in a society that is profoundly absurd, irrational, hypocritical, liquid, and anxious. How else can one describe laws that introduce new penalties (i.e., deportation) for a person who has already served a criminal sentence more than twenty years ago? How does the act of fragmenting hundreds of thousands of "American"

families through enforced exile serve the purposes of increasing domestic social order? How does one find the social and psychological resources to live
below the radar in the United States while greasing the wheels of both formal and informal economies and ensuring the lifestyles of the middle classes?
How does it feel to be blamed for crimes in a country where the elite seem to
have no moral or legal boundaries (see Brotherton et al. forthcoming)?

Therefore, we found resistance in the form that Gregory (2007) witnessed
in the occupation of public spaces and in the many instances and processes
of sociocultural and economic innovation. The examples are numerous and
varied. It is there as Luis1 set up his chess school in the middle of a shopping
street in Santo Domingo as a way to encourage the productive use of time, to
stimulate the intellect, and to provide a site for social interaction between deportees and non-deportees. It is in the struggle of Luis2, who finally finished
his law degree at the Autonomous University after starting it more than fifteen
years before while he was incarcerated in the United States for seven years
while visiting on holiday. On a daily basis Luis2 now provides legal counsel
to the residents of his blighted neighborhood, representing those who find
themselves in the nation's prison hellholes under the auspices of preventive
detention, and he works to build bridges among deportees to counter their
cultural isolation and social stigma. It is in the work of René and his advocacy group, which aims to provide a political voice for not only the deportees
but for all those who suffer from social exclusion in a society that openly
discriminates against the fifth of its population with Haitian blood. It is present in Guido as he continues alone with his farm despite the departure of his
family, who are unable to tolerate the privations of Dominican rural life and
the absence of opportunity. It exists in the returnees to New York City who
navigate their way back across U.S. borders to reunite with their families, to
reinsert themselves into the U.S. political economy at the lowest ends of the
occupational hierarchy, and who risk a minimum of three years imprisonment just for being there.

These are just some instances of the resistance that runs through narrative after narrative of liminal deportees and returnees who have spent their
entire lives struggling against, living with, and accommodating dependency
in its manifold forms. Each trip in a "yola" across the Mona Passage to Puerto
Rico, or on planes with fake passports through Miami, or on buses, boats,
and freight trucks from Santo Domingo through Central America and into
Manhattan, is a form of resistance against the fatalism and the certainty of
subsistence living that is the lot of so many Dominicans, especially those who
do not have access to remesas. It is a resistance of not giving up, of refusing to lose the dream, of doing one's utmost to maintain and retain personal

appearance and dignity despite it all, of fulfilling one's family obligations, such as keeping the kids clothed, encouraging them to study, and helping them to "make it" in an unforgiving world, without lacing one's messages with the stuff of conspiracy while living in the shadows.[7] This resistance emanates from the other side of the assimilation imaginary, the side that is overwhelmed by the American inclusionary rhetoric that always works in tandem with the needs of the political economy (Calavita 1992); it is an historical process artfully summed up by Ngai (2004:5): "The telos of immigrant settlement, assimilation, and citizenship has been an enduring narrative of American history, but it has not always been the reality of migrants' desires or their experiences and interactions with American society and state. The myth of 'immigrant America' derives its power in large part from the labor that it performs for American exceptionalism."

Resistance, then, cannot be easily measured, as is the predilection of most social science. It does not fit into a convenient equation that can be mathematically manipulated to reveal almost anything the author wants, however absurd and inconsequential the formulation. This is why so few social scientific studies fail to predict social disturbances, uprisings, economic crises, and even revolutionary movements, and why most middle-class academics only come into action post facto to give the sequence of events a patina of social scientific predictability. If there is one thing our study has shown, it is that the "truths" of our participants' lives are complex and often contradictory as they at times blame each other for their plight, wax nostalgic about their treatment in the United States, or hope against hope that, if only "the American people knew what we are going through," they would find their moral compass once again and end this injustice that "surely must be unconstitutional."

NEW PRACTICES AND POLICIES OF INCLUSION?

So what should be done? Perhaps it is more fitting to ask what could be done, given the balance of forces in both societies at the moment. When one looks at the United States and the confused state of immigration controls and policies, it is hard to be optimistic. There is tremendous fear and apprehension on the part of the dominant white population as they see their economic futures in jeopardy, and few political voices with any clarity and power are able to explain and take positions against those institutions and polices that have largely created this crisis. In this climate of high anxiety and ontological insecurity (Young 2007), in which the middle classes in particular exhibit a heightened "fear of falling" (Enhrenreich 1990), it is the immigrant, particularly of the undocumented variety, who are identified as the scapegoat. The racist and xenophobic policies emanating from Arizona are just another example of a long history of "blaming the victim" and tagging the immigrant with every social and economic ill that has befallen the United States throughout much of the country's history (Ngai 2004; Zinn 2005).[8] This fear and anxiety are particularly acute in states such as Arizona, with its militarized borders, history of highly racialized politics, and vast new subdivided housing estates (or what Garreau [1992] calls "edge cities")[9] that have been severely affected by the collapse in housing values due to the recent capitalist financial crisis.

In this era, then, it is difficult to conceive the degree to which there will be a sufficient political constituency to tip the balance back toward a more "rational" and humane center, to return the United States to at least a criminal justice/immigration system that gives judges the power to grant administrative relief and allows families to stay intact, or to put into perspective the so-called "threats to society" by those charged with the ever increasing category of "aggravated felony" (the recent establishment of a deportation panel review by New York Governor Patterson is a notable exception).[10] This is especially so when the federal government and various states are desperate to cut their incarceration costs by expelling the non-citizen as quickly as possible and Republican shock jocks in the monopolized media are desperately seeking a constant stream of alien symbols to keep the imagination of that not-so-silent majority exercised. In addition, in this age of the Kafkaesque security state, with its massive law enforcement bureaucracies and integrated enforcement agencies such as the Department of Homeland Security, it is hard to see where the political will exists to dismantle the current constructs in the furtherance of democracy without a massive shift of public opinion and social protest.[11]

In effect, the social control logics—the specialized knowledge, practices, rituals, and disciplines of the security state that are part and parcel of the globalized political economy of punishment—are there for all to see and have become entirely normative in both popular and social scientific discourse. Each day that due process is trampled with regard to deportable felons, that lawyers are not provided, that immigrants are kept uninformed of their rights (what is left of them) with many failing to understand the consequences of their pleas and the consequent removal procedure, brings us closer to authoritarian rule. The constant incursion of Immigration and Customs Enforcement in prisons across the United States—in particular in the nation's largest human warehouse on the East River in New York City, Rikers Island—is a civil rights issue. Calling for reform and drastic changes to the immigration and deportation laws is not about "them"; rather, it is about "us." To this end we should support those groups that are at the cutting edge of the advocacy and protest movement in the area of human and immigration rights (listed in Appendix D).

With respect to the government of the Dominican Republic (and other receiving nations), there is much that can be done to mitigate the situation. The issue of deportation must not be passively accepted as a fait accompli by those nations. It could be part of a joint effort to force it onto the agenda of international relations between the United States and the variously affected countries. More specifically, the Dominican government can take a much more proactive approach and advocate for their returning citizens in the United States, ensuring that they are treated properly. They should work with local organizations to visit U.S. prisons on a regular basis to check on conditions and provide more professional services and meaningful long-term assistance on their arrival in the Dominican Republic. Instead of viewing deportees as a burden and allowing—or even fueling—the stigma that surrounds their identities and pasts to go unchecked, the government could engage in a public educational campaign to explain to the Dominican public the history of the U.S. immigration laws and the impossible web of legal and social controls that are ensnaring more and more of their compatriots. Finally, the Dominican government could remove all formal legal and social barriers to the integration of deportees by stopping the practice of informing employers of their deported status, allowing deportees to run for political office, and recognizing that deportees have talents and skills that could be used for the more general development of Dominican human capital in a world of increasing economic competition.

MORE RESEARCH

There is so much more that we would like to see accomplished on this subject. We wish we could have heard more from the families and associates of the deportees, both in the United States and in the Dominican Republic. It would have been valuable to look at the experience of deportees in different areas of the Dominican Republic and to have carried out more grounded ethnographic research in these comparative regions. In future research, there is a great need to hear more extensively about the experience of female deportees and how their treatment might differ from their male counterparts in the Dominican Republic. Finally we would very much like to engage in a multisite study to compare the experiences of Dominican deportees to those of other recipient nations. To conduct these kinds of long-term, collaborative, and highly intensive research projects, investigators need the interest and support of funding agencies. Funding of this nature has been difficult for us to acquire; nonetheless, with or without such aid we will continue to work with such parties in the respective recipient countries and in the United States, be they social scientists, lawyers, or advocacy groups, to collect what data we can and to provide relevant critical sociological and criminological analyses. Without exaggeration, we feel this area of global (in)justice goes to the heart of a question that is increasingly being asked by young and old alike in developed and developing countries: Whither has democracy gone in the new millennium? We hope that our small study on behalf of the voiceless will make a contribution to this debate and prompt more concern from those who have the ability to make the difference.

APPENDIX A: DOMINICAN CENTRAL BANK OCCUPATIONAL DATA

BANCO CENTRAL DE LA REPUBLICA DOMINICANA DEPARTAMENTO DE CUENTAS NACIONALES Y ESTADISTICAS ECONOMICAS DIVISION DE ENCUESTAS

TABLE 1 POBLACIÓN DE 10 AÑOS Y MÁS POR CONDICIÓN DE ACTIVIDAD SEGÚN GÉNERO Y RAMA DE ACTIVIDAD ECONÓMICA, TOTAL PAÍS 2005

ECONOMIC SECTOR	POPULATION OF WORKING AGE	ECONOMICALLY ACTIVE POP	EMPLOYED	UNEMPLOYED TOTAL	LONG TERM	NEW	INACTIVE
Total	**7,144,757**	**3,992,210**	**3,276,373**	**715,837**	**415,113**	**300,725**	**3,152,547**
Agriculture and farming	489,381	489,381	477,820	11,561	11,561	0	0
Mines	6,982	6,982	5,895	1,087	1,087	0	0
Manufacturing industry	578,517	578,517	486,728	91,789	91,789	0	0
Electricity, water, and gas suppliers	30,830	30,830	26,194	4,637	4,637	0	0
Construction	239,367	239,367	213,378	25,989	25,989	0	0
Commerce	775,649	775,649	707,458	68,191	68,191	0	0

ECONOMIC SECTOR	POPULATION OF WORKING AGE	ECONOMICALLY ACTIVE POP	EMPLOYED	UNEMPLOYED TOTAL	LONG TERM	NEW	INACTIVE
Hotels, bars, and restaurants	229,860	229,860	191,607	38,253	38,253	0	0
Transport and communications	251,284	251,284	238,491	12,793	12,793	0	0
Financial advisors and insurance companies	72,533	72,533	62,307	10,227	10,227	0	0
Defense and public administration	168,081	168,081	147,545	20,537	20,537	0	0
Other services	849,004	849,004	718,952	130,053	130,053	0	0
Pop without occupational sector	3,453,271	300,725	0	300,725	0	300,725	3,152,547
Men	**3,552,500**	**2,442,920**	**2,173,352**	**269,568**	**162,208**	**107,360**	**1,109,580**
Agriculture and farming	457,182	457,182	446,919	10,263	10,263	0	0
Mines	6,881	6,881	5,794	1,087	1,087	0	0
Manufacturing industry	374,283	374,283	335,523	38,760	38,760	0	0
Electricity, water, and gas suppliers	20,006	20,006	17,191	2,815	2,815	0	0

Construction	230,949	230,949	206,940	24,010	24,010	0	0
Commerce	492,451	492,451	459,992	32,459	32,459	0	0
Hotels, bars, and restaurants	98,428	98,428	88,439	9,989	9,989	0	0
Transport and communications	224,425	224,425	215,524	8,901	8,901	0	0
Financial advisors and insurance companies	38,603	38,603	34,521	4,082	4,082	0	0
Defense and public administration	115,193	115,193	103,644	11,549	11,549	0	0
Other services	277,162	277,162	258,868	18,294	18,294	0	0
Pop without occupational sector	1,216,940	107,360	0	107,360	0	107,360	1,109,580
Women	**3,592,257**	**1,549,291**	**1,103,021**	**446,270**	**252,905**	**193,365**	**2,042,967**
Agriculture and farming	32,199	32,199	30,902	1,298	1,298	0	0
Mines	101	101	101	0	0	0	0
Manufacturing industry	204,234	204,234	151,206	53,029	53,029	0	0
Electricity, water, and gas suppliers	10,824	10,824	9,003	1,822	1,822	0	0

ECONOMIC SECTOR	POPULATION OF WORKING AGE	ECONOMICALLY ACTIVE POP	EMPLOYED	UNEMPLOYED			INACTIVE
				TOTAL	LONG TERM	NEW	
Construction	8,418	8,418	6,439	1,980	1,980	0	0
Commerce	283,198	283,198	247,466	35,732	35,732	0	0
Hotels, bars, and restaurants	131,432	131,432	103,169	28,264	28,264	0	0
Transport and communications	26,859	26,859	22,967	3,892	3,892	0	0
Financial advisors and insurance companies	33,931	33,931	27,786	6,145	6,145	0	0
Defense and public administration	52,889	52,889	43,901	8,988	8,988	0	0
Other services	571,843	571,843	460,084	111,759	111,759	0	0
Pop without occupational sector	2,236,331	193,365	0	193,365	0	193,365	2,042,967

Sources: Retrieved from: http://www.bancentral.gov.do/english/index-e.as.

TABLE 2 EMPLOYED POPULATION IN THE FORMAL SECTORS AND HOURLY SALARIES PER SALARY DECILES ACCORDING TO ACTIVITY, ENTIRE COUNTRY 2005

ACTIVITY SECTOR	RECEIVED SALARY	DECILES									
		1	2	3	4	5	6	7	8	9	10
Employed population (total)	**1,437,260**	143,726	143,726	143,726	143,726	143,726	143,726	143,726	143,726	143,726	143,731
Agriculture and farming	59,056	18,243	10,036	4,880	4,625	5,154	4,449	2,811	1,861	3,153	3,845
Mines	5,241	0	142	410	180	807	358	489	1,109	967	782
Manufacturing industry	356,009	27,066	42,692	67,199	49,375	41,295	32,581	30,995	24,456	18,730	21,622
Electricity, water, and gas suppliers	26,194	1,478	2,282	2,950	2,761	1,772	2,662	3,525	2,126	2,285	4,355
Construction	31,601	620	1,381	2,134	1,830	2,749	2,760	2,878	4,174	5,211	7,866
Commerce	211,993	24,568	22,278	15,347	25,769	27,573	23,659	18,858	21,226	15,567	17,149
Hotels, bars, and restaurants	86,665	12,887	11,005	9,890	11,413	12,523	8,927	8,495	6,404	3,263	1,860

ACTIVITY SECTOR	RECEIVED SALARY	DECILES									
		1	2	3	4	5	6	7	8	9	10
Transport and communications	64,357	2,936	4,515	3,813	4,067	6,579	8,000	8,692	8,922	9,759	7,076
Financial advisors and insurance companies	46,758	606	1,698	1,897	2,052	3,552	7,904	7,232	5,248	7,331	9,241
Defense and public administration	147,545	16,123	15,422	9,669	14,967	13,105	15,621	14,229	16,001	18,692	13,719
Other services	401,845	39,201	32,278	25,539	26,688	28,619	36,808	45,523	52,203	58,769	56,218
Hourly salaries (average, rd$)	**57.09**	**12.61**	**18.77**	**22.61**	**26.69**	**31.35**	**37.20**	**46.36**	**61.09**	**88.86**	**225.35**
Agriculture and farming	41.28	11.58	18.77	22.48	26.45	30.97	36.97	46.27	59.13	91.62	238.51
Mines	63.50	0.00	19.38	22.32	26.43	30.59	35.20	47.98	62.92	86.35	133.65
Manufacturing industry	42.71	12.44	19.00	22.40	26.64	31.38	37.22	46.16	61.81	88.13	191.69
Electricity, water, gas suppliers and	62.38	12.89	18.67	22.60	26.83	31.25	37.24	45.46	59.26	91.92	178.09

ACTIVITY SECTOR	RECEIVED SALARY	DECILES									
		1	2	3	4	5	6	7	8	9	10
Construction	84.70	12.80	18.81	22.57	26.51	31.55	36.94	45.02	60.18	90.17	191.80
Commerce	50.58	12.14	18.64	22.87	26.60	31.47	37.22	46.09	62.41	88.25	213.39
Hotels, bars, and restaurants	36.76	12.90	19.07	22.90	26.76	31.10	36.36	46.81	60.32	91.04	290.76
Transport and communications	76.56	11.74	18.94	23.17	26.71	31.09	37.46	46.06	59.60	90.62	316.34
Financial advisors and insurance companies	76.53	14.73	19.14	22.48	26.90	31.62	37.63	46.59	61.38	90.21	188.28
Defense and public administration	53.71	13.64	18.63	22.83	26.68	31.32	36.96	46.74	60.38	88.35	184.34
Other services	73.16	13.08	18.50	22.78	26.87	31.39	37.35	46.52	61.03	88.48	253.29

Source: Retrieved from: http://www.bancentral.gov.do/english/index-e.as.

APPENDIX B

INTERNET RESOURCES

GUIDE FOR IMMIGRANT ADVOCATES

Deportation Resource Manual: A Practical Guide for Immigrant Advocates
http://alabamaappleseed.org/publications/Immigration/Deportation%20Guide%20
    Final.pdf
Know Your Rights Information Packet About Detention, Deportation, and Defenses
    Under U.S. Immigration Law—National Immigrant Justice Center
http://www.ansarilawfirm.com/docs/Know-Your-Rights-NIJC.pdf
Immigration Detention—What Are My Rights?—National Immigration Project
http://www.ansarilawfirm.com/docs/Immigration-Detention-What-are-my-rights.pdf

POSTDEPORTATION: RESOURCES FOR ATTORNEYS

Practice Advisory on Filing Post-Departure Motions to Reopen or Reconsider
Center for Human Rights and International Justice at Boston College
http://www.bc.edu/centers/humanrights/projects/deportation/resourcesat.html
Practice Advisory on Non-Immigrant Waivers
Returning to the United Sates Following Removal: A Guide to Non-Immigrant Visas
Center for Human Rights and International Justice at Boston College
Retrieve from: http://www.bc.edu/centers/humanrights/projects/deportation/
    resourcesat.html

APPENDIX C

IMMIGRANT RIGHTS

IMMIGRANT RIGHTS

http://www.immigrantsolidarity.org/resource.htm#rights
Guide for state groups dealing with anti-immigrant worker legislation (PDF reports)
  by the National Employment Law Project:

- State Anti-Immigration Legislation Guide
- Anti-Immigrant Workers Compensation Bills 2006
- State Employer Sanctions Bills 2006

TALKING POINTS

Myths about Undocumented Immigrants English and Spanish (National Council of
  La Raza)
Toolkit for State/Local Police Enforcing Immigration Laws (National Council of
  La Raza)
The toolkit addresses the various proposals to deputize state and local police to enforce
  federal immigration laws, including the CLEAR Act. The toolkit contains sample
  materials that you can adapt and use to fight these proposals, including sample
  letters, press releases, talking points, and intake forms. It also includes many useful
  tips for lobbying, working with the media, and coordinating with coalitions
  (PDF report).

USEFUL LEGAL INFORMATION AND RESOURCES

More information is available from the National Lawyers Guild (NLG) "Know Your Rights" pamphlet, available in English, Spanish, Farsi, Arabic, Punjabi, and Portuguese; and the American Immigration Lawyers Association (AILA) (question and answer sheet).

KNOW YOUR RIGHTS

Know your rights when you are questioned by the police, FBI, INS, or any other law enforcement agents.

Trainings and wallet-sized palm-cards (Spanish, Arabic, English, and Urdu) are available from the Know Your Rights Committee of Commonwealth Human Rights Initiative (CHRI). The back of each card lists places to call for legal assistance, help in finding a lawyer, and other resources.

You have these rights in the United States (regardless of your immigration status!):

- Say you want to see a lawyer.
- You do not have to sign any paper without a lawyer with you.
- You do not have to let the police, FBI, INS, or anyone else come into your house without a "warrant" (special paper from a judge). Tell your roommates not to let them in without a warrant.
- You do not have to answer any questions about your immigration.

PRO-IMMIGRANT ORGANIZATIONS FIGHTING DEPORTATION

NEW YORK

FAMILIES FOR FREEDOM

Founded in September 2002, Families for Freedom is a New York-based, multi-ethnic, defense network by and for immigrants facing and fighting deportation. We are immigrant prisoners (detainees), former immigrant prisoners, their loved ones, or individuals at risk of deportation. We come from dozens of countries, across continents. Families for Freedom seeks to repeal the laws that are tearing apart our homes and neighborhoods, to build the power of immigrant communities as communities of color, and to provide a guiding voice in the growing movement for immigrant rights as human rights.

Contact Information
3 West 29th Street
New York, New York 10001
Phone: (646) 290-5551
Fax: (800) 895-4454
Website: http://www.familiesforfreedom.org

NEW YORK UNIVERSITY IMMIGRANT RIGHTS CLINIC

Director: Prof. Nancy Morawetz

The New York University Immigrant Rights Clinic is a leading institution in both local and national struggles for immigrant rights. Our students engage in direct legal representation of immigrants and community organizations in litigation at the agency, federal court, and, where necessary, Supreme Court levels, and in immigrant rights campaigns at the local, state, and national levels. Each student, along with a student partner, will typically have the opportunity to represent either an individual or set of individuals in litigation (such as a removal proceeding or appeal, detention litigation, or a civil suit) as well as engage with a community organization in a campaign (such as an organizing project or legislative campaign). We choose our docket in consultation with our community partners and engage in work that is responsive to community needs. Students have direct responsibility for these cases and the opportunity to build their understanding of legal practice and the field of immigrant rights law and organizing.

Contact Information
Website: http://www.law.nyu.edu/academics/clinics/year/immigrantrights/index.htm

POST-DEPORTATION HUMAN RIGHTS PROJECT

The Post-Deportation Human Rights Project, based at the Center for Human Rights and International Justice at Boston College, offers a novel and multitiered approach to the problem of harsh and unlawful deportations from the United States. It is the first and only legal advocacy project in the country to systematically undertake the representation of individuals who have been deported from the United States.

Contact Information
Jessica Chicco
Supervising Attorney
Post-Deportation Human Rights Project
E-mail: pdhrp@bc.edu
Phone: (617) 552-9261

Prof. Daniel Kanstroom
Boston College Law School
E-mail: kanstroo@bc.edu
Website: http://www.bc.edu/centers/humanrights/projects/deportation/aboutpdhrp.html

NORTHERN MANHATTAN COALITION FOR IMMIGRANT RIGHTS

Northern Manhattan Coalition for Immigrant Rights works with more than 6,000 families each year on issues such as immigration, citizenship, deportation, and voter participation with a focus on keeping families together, facilitating integration, and building community power.

Contact Information
Northern Manhattan Coalition for Immigrant Rights
665 West 182nd Street, 1st Floor

New York, NY 10033
Phone: (212) 781-0355, ext. 300
E-mail: info@nmcir.org
Website: http://www.NMCIR.org

FAMILY UNIFICATION & RESETTLEMENT INITIATIVE

The objective of the Family Unification & Resettlement Initiative is to offer alternatives that foster faith, hope, and confidence that life can be worthwhile. The organization aims to assist in the reintegration of deported persons by collaborating with other service agencies.

Contact Information
144 West 127th Street
New York, New York 10027
Phone: (646) 698-2172/2174
Fax: (646) 698-2184
E-mail: familyunif@hotmail.com
Website: http://www.familyunification.net

THE NEW SANCTUARY MOVEMENT

The New Sanctuary Movement is a nonprofit, public interest legal foundation dedicated to furthering and protecting the civil, constitutional, and human rights of immigrants, refugees, children, and the poor. The Center is generously supported by the California Legal Services Trust Fund, the Liberty Hill Foundation, and its many members. Students, lawyers, and other volunteers are encouraged to join the Center's efforts to protect and promote domestic and international civil and human rights.

Contact Information
Website: http://www.newsanctuarymovement.org

THE NEW SANCTUARY COALITION OF NEW YORK CITY

The New Sanctuary Coalition of New York City is an interfaith network of immigrant families, faith communities, and organizations, standing together to publicly resist unjust deportations, to create a humane instead of a hostile public discourse about immigration, and ultimately to bring about reform of the United States' flawed immigration system.

Contact Information
239 Thompson Street

New York, NY 10012
Phone: (646) 395-2925
Website: http://www.newsanctuarynyc.org

DETENTION WATCH NETWORK

Detention Watch Network is a coalition that addresses the immigration detention crisis head on. Together we work to reform the U.S. detention and deportation system so that all who come to our shores receive fair and humane treatment.

Contact Information
1325 Massachusetts Ave. NW
Washington, DC 20005
Website: http://www.detentionwatchnetwork.org

NEW YORK STATE DEFENDERS ASSOCIATION: IMMIGRANT DEFENSE PROJECT

The Immigrant Defense Project, formerly an initiative of the New York State Defenders Association, defends the legal, constitutional, and human rights of immigrants facing criminal or deportation charges. We are the nation's first project founded to respond to the devastating 1996 immigration laws that placed hundreds of thousands of immigrants at risk of mandatory detention and deportation for virtually any interaction with the criminal justice system.

Contact Information
Website: http://www.immigrantdefenseproject.org

THE NEW YORK IMMIGRATION COALITION

The New York Immigration Coalition (NYIC) is an umbrella policy and advocacy organization for more than two hundred groups in New York State that work with immigrants and refugees. As the coordinating body for organizations that serve one of the largest and most diverse newcomer populations in the United States, the NYIC has become a leading advocate for immigrant communities on the local, state, and national levels. The NYIC's membership includes grassroots community organizations, not-for-profit health and human services organizations, religious and academic institutions, labor unions, and legal, social, and economic justice organizations. With its multiethnic, multiracial, and multisector base, the NYIC provides both a forum for immigrant groups to share their concerns and a vehicle for collective action to address these concerns.

Contact Information
Website: http://thenyic.org

THE LEGAL AID SOCIETY

The Legal Aid Society's Criminal Practice is the largest public defender program in the country and serves as the primary provider of indigent defense services in New York City. The Criminal Practice includes criminal defense trial offices in the Bronx, Brooklyn, Manhattan, and Queens; a Criminal Appeals Bureau; a Parole Revocation Defense Unit; and a Special Litigation Unit. Representation is provided in 225,000 cases each year. There are also special units to address the needs of specific client populations, including mentally ill and chemically addicted clients; adolescents who are prosecuted in criminal proceedings; and incarcerated clients. Society social workers in the Defender Services Program provide comprehensive services in conjunction with our defense representation. The Rikers Island Paralegal Program deploys paralegal staff directly in the City jails to assist in our client representation.

Areas of practice: Noncitizen New Yorkers detained by the Immigration and Customs Enforcement (ICE) at the Bergen, Monmouth, Hudson, and Sussex County Jails in New Jersey and/or their family members, may call for advice and possible legal representation in their cases. Immigrants detained at other immigration detention facilities and in upstate New York prisons and/or their family members can call the hotline for advice only.

When to call: The hotline operates on Wednesdays and Fridays from 1:00 p.m. to 5:00 p.m. Collect calls from detention facilities and prisons are accepted. Noncitizens with pending Immigration court cases at 26 Federal Plaza or 201 Varick Street (non-detained) should go to the Immigration Representation Project (IRP) on the 12th floor at 26 Federal Plaza, room 1207. Screening is held one week a month, Tuesday through Friday, from 9:00 a.m. to 11:00 a.m. Call (212) 577-3300 to obtain the schedule for IRP screening days. Appointments for all noncourt cases are made through the Immigration Law Unit's Legal Assistance outreach program (212) 577-3300.

Contact Information
Immigration Law Unit Hotline: (212) 577-3456
Website: http://www.legal-aid.org

UNITED STATES

AMERICAN CIVIL LIBERTIES UNION—IMMIGRANTS' RIGHTS FREEDOM NETWORK

The American Civil Liberties Union (ACLU) is our nation's guardian of liberty, working daily in courts, legislatures, and communities to defend and preserve the individual rights and liberties that the Constitution and laws of the United States guarantee everyone in this country.

Contact Information
Website: http://www.aclu.org

AMERICAN GATEWAY

Founded in 1987 as the Political Asylum Project of Austin (PAPA), American Gateways began as a response to the legal needs of the large number of Central American refugees arriving at the Texas border in the 1980s. Like the thousands of others American Gateways has helped through the years, these refugees were fleeing violence and war in their home countries in search of a safe haven. American Gateways offers safety and hope for a new life to hundreds of men, women, and children every year, from approximately seventy-five countries around the world.

Contact Information
Website: http://www.americangateways.org

HEARTLAND ALLIANCE'S NATIONAL IMMIGRANT JUSTICE CENTER

Heartland Alliance's National Immigrant Justice Center (NIJC) is dedicated to ensuring human rights protections and access to justice for all immigrants, refugees, and asylum seekers. NIJC provides direct legal services to and advocates for these populations through policy reform, impact litigation, and public education. Since its founding three decades ago, NIJC has been unique in blending individual client advocacy with broad-based systemic change.

Contact Information
Website: http://www.immigrantjustice.org

HUMAN RIGHTS WATCH

Human Rights Watch is one of the world's leading independent organizations dedicated to defending and protecting human rights. By focusing international attention where human rights are violated, we give voice to the oppressed and hold oppressors accountable for their crimes. Our rigorous, objective investigations and strategic, targeted advocacy build intense pressure for action and raise the cost of human rights abuse. For thirty years, Human Rights Watch has worked tenaciously to lay the legal and moral groundwork for deep-rooted change and has fought to bring greater justice and security to people around the world.

Contact Information
Website: http://www.hrw.org

IMMIGRATION EQUALITY

Immigration Equality is a national organization fighting for equality under U.S. immigration law for lesbian, gay, bisexual, transgender, and HIV-positive individuals. Founded in 1994 as the Lesbian and Gay Immigration Rights Task Force, we have grown to a membership of 10,000 people in cities all over the country. We are run by a Board of Directors and have full-time staff in our National Headquarters in New York. Immigration Equality is funded by donations from our members as well as by generous support from private foundations.

Contact Information
Website: http://www.lgirtf.org

NATIONAL COUNCIL OF LA RAZA

The National Council of La Raza (NCLR) is the largest national Hispanic civil rights and advocacy organization in the United States and works to improve opportunities for Hispanic Americans. Through its network of nearly 300 affiliated community-based organizations, NCLR reaches millions of Hispanics each year in forty-one states, Puerto Rico, and the District of Columbia. To achieve its mission, NCLR conducts applied research, policy analysis, and advocacy, providing a Latino perspective in five key areas: assets/investments, civil rights/immigration, education, employment and economic status, and health. In addition, NCLR provides capacity-building assistance to its Affiliates who work at the state and local levels to advance opportunities for individuals and families. Founded in 1968, NCLR is a private, nonprofit, nonpartisan, tax-exempt organization headquartered in Washington, DC. NCLR serves all Hispanic subgroups in all regions of the country and has regional offices in Chicago, Los Angeles, New York, Phoenix, and San Antonio.

Contact Information
Website: http://www.nclr.org

NATIONAL IMMIGRATION PROJECT

National Immigration Project is a national nonprofit organization that provides legal assistance and technical support to immigrant communities, legal practitioners, and all advocates seeking to advance the rights of noncitizens. For nearly forty years, the National Immigration Project has been promoting justice and equality of treatment in all areas of immigration law, the criminal justice system, and social policies related to immigration. We are especially committed to working on behalf of disenfranchised and vulnerable populations, including battered women, people with HIV/AIDS, children, and noncitizen criminal offenders. Members of the National Immigration

Project include lawyers, law students, legal workers, judges, jailhouse lawyers, and all those seeking to defend and expand the rights of immigrants in the United States.

Contact Information
Website: http://www.nationalimmigrationproject.org

THE CENTRAL AMERICAN RESOURCE CENTER

The Central American Resource Center (CARECEN) is a community-based organization that seeks to foster the comprehensive development of the Latino community in the Washington metropolitan region. CARECEN was founded in 1981 to protect the rights of refugees arriving from conflict in Central America and to help ease their transition by providing legal services. Today our programs provide direct services in immigration, housing, and citizenship while also promoting empowerment, civil rights advocacy, and civic training for Latinos.

Contact Information
Website: http://www.carecendc.org

THE CENTER FOR GENDER & REFUGEE STUDIES

The core mission of the Center for Gender & Refugee Studies (CGRS) is to protect the basic human rights of refugee women and girls by advancing gender-sensitive asylum laws, helping advocates successfully represent women in need of protection, and preventing these refugees from being forcibly returned to the countries from which they have fled. In addition to engaging in scholarly research, policy work, and impact litigation, CGRS carries out original research and advocacy initiatives around human rights violations in specific countries or regions of the world. CGRS also seeks to address root causes for migration flows, including injustices and human rights violations against women in refugee-producing countries.

Contact Information
Website: http://cgrs.uchastings.edu

THE NATIONAL IMMIGRATION FORUM

Established in 1982, the National Immigration Forum is the leading immigrant advocacy organization in the country with a mission to advocate for the value of immigrants and immigration to the nation. The Forum uses its communications, advocacy, and policy expertise to create a vision, consensus, and strategy that leads to a better, more welcoming America—one that treats all newcomers fairly. Ultimately, our vision is to create U.S. immigration policy that honors our nation's ideals, protects human dignity, reflects our country's economic demands, celebrates family unity, and provides opportunities for progress. For over two decades, the Forum has occupied a unique role, knitting together alliances across diverse faith, labor, immigrant, nonimmigrant, and business constituencies in communities across the country. These alliances come together under the Forum's leadership to develop, execute, and evaluate legislative and administrative advocacy strategies.

Contact Information
Website: http://www.immigrationforum.org/about

HOMIES UNIDOS

Homies Unidos believes in the inherent right of youth, families, and their communities to pursue their dreams and achieve their full potential in a just, safe, and healthy society. For ten years, Homies Unidos has been a catalyst for change, working to end violence and promote peace in our communities through gang prevention, the promotion of human rights in immigrant communities, and the empowerment of youth through positive alternatives to gang involvement and destructive behavior. In fact, we are living proof that prevention works and that peace is possible.

Contact Information
Website: http://homiesunidos.org/about

CALIFORNIA IMMIGRANT INTEGRATION INITIATIVE OF GRANTMAKERS CONCERNED WITH IMMIGRANTS AND REFUGEES (GCIR)

California Immigrant Integration Initiative (CIII) seeks to develop a comprehensive immigrant integration agenda and to strengthen the immigrant integration infrastructure in local communities across California. The initiative was organized in 2007 and currently involves twenty-seven statewide and local funders. Through a partnership with the Institute for Local Governments, CIII also engages municipal and county governments in its efforts. In a time of significantly reduced public and philanthropic resources, CIII provides funders a forum to identify strategic partnership and funding opportunities and work together to leverage the influence and impact of their leadership and grant dollars.

Contact Information
Website: http://www.gcir.org/about/ciii

IMMIGRATION CLINIC–UCLA LAW

The Immigration Clinic at University of California Los Angeles (UCLA) is a joint venture between the UCLA law school and the Public Counsel's Immigrants Rights Project (IRP). This five-unit course will be graded P/U/NC. Students will spend four hours each week in the classroom and an additional eight hours per week on casework at IRP offices. The classroom portion of the course will include both substantive immigration law topics that are related to the student's clinical work and skills training such as interviewing, research and writing declarations, fact development, and some trial advocacy. Students are likely to engage in tasks such as client intake; preparation of asylum petitions, applications for relief under the Violence Against Women Act (VAWA) and the Victim of Trafficking and Violent Crime Prevention Act (VTVPA); and possibly appearances before the asylum office and the immigration court. The precise work conducted in any semester will depend on the clients who need representation and the posture of their cases.

CASA CORNELIA LAW CENTER

Casa Cornelia Law Center is a public interest law firm providing quality legal services to victims of human and civil rights violations at no charge. The Center has a primary commitment to the indigent within the immigrant community in Southern California. Casa Cornelia strives to educate others regarding the impact of immigration law and policy on society and the public good.

Contact Information
E-mail: lawcenter@casacornelia.org

LEGAL AID SOCIETY OF SAN DIEGO

Legal Aid is available to low income individuals and disadvantaged communities for a variety of legal problems, including consumer, family disputes, welfare and health benefits, immigration and poverty law issues such as landlord/tenant disputes, disability support, and family benefits payments. Federal Poverty Income Guidelines determine eligibility for free legal services.

Contact Information
Website: http://www.lassd.org

DOMINICAN REPUBLIC

CENTRO BONÓ

Programa-proyecto: Servicio Jesuita a Refugiados/Migrantes
Ciudad: Santo Domingo, Republica Dominicana

SERVICIO DE VOLUNTARIADO IGNACIANO DE REPÚBLICA DOMINICANA (SERVIR-D)

- Se presenta a la sociedad dominicana, el 1 de diciembre de 2004.
- Como un ESPACIO PARA UNIR a quienes buscan la manera de cambiar nuestra realidad, a quienes sueñan con una tierra de hermandad y amor.

Donde cada persona sea tratada como tal y alcance sus derechos de vivir en plenitud su dignidad: en educación, salud, alimentación, vivienda, arte y creatividad, trabajo, deporte, descanso, participación civil, fe.

- Como una RED DINAMIZADORA de todos los esfuerzos que ya se están haciendo en muchas partes para llevar a cabo este sueño.
- Como un APOYO Y PUENTE para quienes buscan modos de poner su vida, sus estudios, su profesión, su trabajo, sus capacidades, su tiempo, su corazón al servicio de los demás.
- Como una MÍSTICA Y PEDAGOGÍA de acercamiento entre personas que se descubren hermanas en este ayudarse y servirse mutuamente, en este vivir y ser fraternidad.
- Como un DESEO DE DESCUBRIR JUNTOS los tesoros y dones de esta tierra y de toda la tierra, en cada una de las personas a quienes se sirve.
- Como una NUEVA MANERA DE VIVIR Y DE CREER, buscando en todo amar y servir.

SERVIR-D coordina y anima el trabajo de voluntarias y voluntarios que quieran disponer de su tiempo y persona para colaborar gratuitamente en un servicio de bien social a través de alguna de las instituciones que dirige la Compañía de Jesús de República Dominicana y de otras instituciones hermanas. Por medio de su red de apoyo empresarial busca además los recursos económicos necesarios para realizar esta misión.

Contact Information
Website: http://www.servird.org/servird.php?p=documentos

FUNDACIÓN BIENVENIDO SEAS

Una fundación que ayuda a los repatriados que llegan a la Republica Dominicana. This foundation helps deportees who arrive in the Dominican Republic.

Contact Information
Website: http://bienvenidoseasrd.blogspot.com

NOTE:

Retrieve all immigration forms from:
English: http://www.uscis.gov/portal/site/uscis
Spanish: http://www.uscis.gov/portal/site/uscis-es

NOTES

1. THE STUDY

1. The official U.S. figure of Dominicans deported during this time frame is 30,000; however, in a report in the Santo Domingo newspaper *el Listin Diario* (Corcino, 2006, p. 6), the National Police stated that they have 19,000 registered as deported, whereas the National Council for the Control of Drugs said that they have a further 27,000 listed as deported. Another recent report from the Northern Manhattan Coalition for Immigrant Rights estimated unofficially that 50,000 Dominicans were deported between 1996 and 2008 in contrast to the "official" U.S. Immigration and Customs Enforcement figures (Northern Manhattan Coalition for Immigrant Rights, 2009).

2. An important coedited work recently published by De Genova and Preutz (2010) that contains deportation, illegal immigration, and asylum-seeking case studies from around the world should also be noted.

3. There has also been a report published by an advocacy group in cooperation with the immigration law clinic of New York University on the social and legal trauma of deportation (Northern Manhattan Coalition on Immigration 2009). Another unpublished analysis of secondary data based on the case files of 475 deportees was performed by Venator-Santiago, 2005a.

4. In this recent report from the immigration law clinics of UC Berkeley and UC Davis, legal researchers estimate that, between 1997 and 2007, more than 80,000 legal permanent residents have been deported, leaving behind more than 100,000 children, 44,000 under the age of five. The report states that directives from the U.S. Department of Homeland Security issued in 2009 will result in an increase in deported "green card" holders and therefore an increase in the collateral consequences for young U.S. citizens and their families.

5. For example, Janowitz (1978) suggests that social control rests on a societal value commitment that has at least three goals: the reduction of coercion, the elimination

of human misery, and the elevation of the role of rationality in social organization and interactions. Park and Thomas saw immigration within a constellation of broader influences. For example, "The immigration problem is unique in the sense that the immigrant brings divergent definitions of the situation and this renders his participation in our activities difficult. At the same time this problem is of the same general type as the one exemplified by 'syndicalism,' 'bolshevism,' 'socialism,' etc., where the definition of the situation does not agree with the traditional one. The modern 'social unrest,' like the immigrant problem is a sign of the lack of participation and this is true to the degree that certain elements feel that violence is the only available means of participating" (Park and Thomas 1927:52).

6. It could be argued that Lewis drew attention to the effects of race, class, and gender structuring in the U.S. inner city with respect to the immigrant, much as Dubois had drawn our attention to the color line in his revisionist masterpiece of Reconstruction (see Dubois 2006/1935).

7. In a recently acclaimed study of second-generation "incorporation" into the U.S. mosaic (see Kasinitz et al. 2008), the authors summarize data that included interviews by phone with more than 3,400 subjects, with another 333 in-depth interviews and 172 follow-up interviews, and ethnographies "where second generation and native groups were intersecting" (p. 13). Much of this data collection took place in the city's poorest neighborhoods from 1998–2003. Subjects were asked to recall their experiences of immigration during a period in which New York State prisons boasted almost 70,000 inmates, approximately 90 percent of whom were nonwhites coming from many of the same neighborhoods as the interview subjects. Remarkably, in this narrative of successful immigrant integration there is but one mention of prison, one mention of the criminal justice system, and no mention of deportation.

8. Small wooden boats.

2. SETTING AND SAMPLE

1. The creation of the moral conscience is the final goal of social evolution. To strive to be a human being is a good thing. The beautiful thing, the useful thing, the just thing and the real thing all aimed at the establishment of a society in which the social conscience is so educated and evolved that kindness becomes a natural principle exercised by all men and women. (Translated by the authors).

2. The Taino were a nonslave-holding subgroup of the Caribbean Arawaks, many of whom were murdered or worked to death within three decades of Columbus's arrival or died from European diseases against which they had no resistance.

3. Approximately 48,442 square kilometers, or approximately 18,000 square miles.

4. Three key military figures are remembered in this feat alongside the people: Colonel Rafael Tomás Fernández Domínguez, Colonel Francisco Alberto Caamaño and Colonel Manuel Ramón Montes Arache.

5. Famed Dominican-American author Junot Diaz describes Balaguer as: "a Negrophobe, an apologist to genocide, an election thief, and a killer of people who wrote better than himself" (Diaz 2007:90).

6. Social Christian Reformist Party (PRSC).

7. Dominican Revolutionary Party (PRD).

8. Dominican Liberation Party (PLD).

9. In 2007, 602,093 Dominicans were living in New York City, which was 25.8% of the New York City Latina/o population: distribution by boroughs: Bronx, 32.8%; Manhattan, 41.9%; Queens, 15.5%; Brooklyn, 18.5%; and Staten Island, 3.7%. These numbers do not include the hundreds of thousands of undocumented Dominican citizens (Limonic 2007).

10. "Blacks and mulattoes make up nearly 90% of the contemporary Dominican population; yet no other country in the hemisphere exhibits greater indeterminacy regarding the population's sense of racial identity" (Torres-Saillant 2000:1086–1111).

11. The criticism of the Central American Free Trade Agreement (CAFTA) is virtually the same as that of the 1994 North American Free Trade Agreement (NAFTA), between the United States, Canada, and Mexico. In the name of opening markets among these countries, NAFTA ensures that the benefits of the abolition of tariffs on a range of imports and exports realized largely by the heavily subsidized agribusinesses of the United States at the expense of local farmers. The same is true of most other large firms that exercise their comparative advantage on a very unequal economic playing field.

12. Between 1983 and 1985, the state sugar industry produced the highest tonnage in its history, roughly 800,000 tons per year, which amounted to 60% of the country's needs. In 1986, the directorship of the industry was handed to Carlos Morales Troncoso who was also in the pay of the Central Romana Corporation, a private sugar-producing company. In terms of dependency, the Dominican Republic's alignment with CAFTA ensured that economic development will be tied to U.S. interests to a greater extent than before. To emphasize this policy, President Fernandez abolished the tax on high-fructose corn syrup, which was designed by the Dominican Congress to protect the country's vulnerable sugar industry. This decision was made at the behest of the U.S. soft drink industry, which claimed that such "protectionism" would preclude the Dominican Republic from joining CAFTA. Nothing was said of the massive subsidies given to U.S. corn producers or the extraordinary political and economic power wielded by soft drink companies such as Coca-Cola (information courtesy of historian Frank Maya-Pons).

13. This far outweighs the value of the republic's mineral and agricultural products such as nickel, coffee, cacao, tobacco, and sugar, although the free trade zones are not growing to the extent they once did. In 2003, some 170,000 workers were employed in free trade zones, with more than 250 U.S. companies taking advantage of the cheap labor and corporate tax–free provisions.

14. Hence, nearly all free trade zones are usually union-free, with employers using the armed might of the state to discourage would-be labor organizers.

15. During this period, however, and especially during the first administration of Leonel Fernandez (1994–1997), the economy was "liberalized" by dismantling many of the paternalistic supports of the Balaguer years and replacing them with

so-called free market mechanisms of wealth creation and distribution. The result has been growth of the middle- and upper-middle classes, which can be seen in the mushrooming condominiums in new urban and suburban zones, U.S.- and Spanish-financed shopping malls, and several new private schools and universities. The indigenous class reconfigurations also include the many Dominicans who have made their money in the United States or in Spain and who now invest in the private property market, either to speculate or to claim their holiday home in the sun, a sure sign of status for the successful, socially ascending emigrant.

16. This is high compared to Cuba, which has 7 infant deaths per 1,000 births, but about average when compared to Jamaica or Trinidad.

17. These statistics come from a combination of the New Internationalist Basic Indicators for 195 countries (*One World Almanac* 2009), the International Monetary Fund, and the CIA World Factbook (Central Intelligence Agency, 2010), with the exception of the per capita income detail. According to the government's office of national statistics, the average wage for 3.4 million of the working population in 2007 was around $3,600 per year, i.e., approximately $300 per month.

18. The Dominican Republic currently ranks as the country with the third worst social investment record in Latin America (Valdez Albizu 2009).

19. It is estimated that two in five Dominican families receive help from abroad, similar to what Cesar Chavez, the renowned Chicano labor activist, said of Mexico, that the country's policy of exporting its labor was its most important social safety valve.

20. The increase in firearms possession is staggering. Brea de Cabral and Cabral Ramírez (2009a) estimate that the carrying of firearms increased over 840% between 1999 and 2005 (aside from the police and the military) and that 30% of the residents in Santo Domingo own a firearm of some sort.

21. A number of political commentators have started to refer to the country as a "narco state" given the level of drug trafficking and the complicity of so many layers of the government and the dominant classes. The United States lists the Dominican Republic as one of the 20 leading drug transit countries meeting the demand in the U.S. drug market and as one of the leading centers of money laundering in the world (United Nations Office of Drugs and Crime 2007).

22. This is accomplished with police-inspired "cordon sanitaires" around high-crime neighborhoods and with regular sweeps of drug hot spots and the round-up of the "usual suspects."

23. Like most developing nations, the Dominican Republic supplies very sketchy data on employment and unemployment figures because so many of the country are working in part-time or in self-employment occupations and because of the extensive presence of the informal economy.

3. LEAVING FOR AMERICA

1. Our orientation to this concept comes from the work of Cullen (2003). Cullen argues that the concept of the American Dream has a long history and has at least

four connotations. First, it is a dream that filled the imaginations of many early religious dissenters who sought a space to practice their own particular worship of God. Second, it is found in the notion of upward mobility and is a crucial part of America's dominant culture and ideology as found in the early work of Adams (1931) called the "Epic Dream." Adams describes the dream as that "of a land in which life should be better, richer and fuller for every man." Third, Cullen argues that the dream is contained in the notion of home ownership, as embodied by the Homestead Act of 1862 and more recently by the suburbanization of America; one might point to the recent subprime mortgage crisis as an indication of the yearning for this dream to become a reality. Fourth, Cullen states that the dream conveys the notion of personal fulfillment; although this idea is contained in the statements of Lincoln and of the Puritans, it is particularly virulent in the culture of Hollywood and the consumer ideology that pervades much of our lives.

2. Sometimes subjects did not really understand or want to respond to questions on poverty, and there were a number of reasons for this reticence. One is that their current state was still characterized by extreme deprivation, and so to think back to another period in the poverty cycle appeared redundant. It might have been different if they had moved on economically, but instead they had emigrated and done their best to attain a dignified living situation, and now they were back, not far from where they had started. Second, the terminology we were using was too condemning, too stigmatizing. For people who had experienced the United States and its culture of "blaming the victim," to openly discuss one's experience of poverty is to situate oneself as The Other, which was too painful coming on top of their already stigmatizing label as a deportee. The third reason was that many left the Dominican Republic in early childhood and could not recount much of that earlier period easily. Certainly they were told something about their prior circumstances by their parents and other family members, but even these memories were not easy to recall, which might also reflect the tendency of immigrants to look toward the future and not to the past.

3. We are aware that European democracies such as Portugal and Spain also have never had a full accounting of their authoritarian and fascist pasts.

4. According to a local priest, "Of course the local military take a cut from all those trying to leave. Rarely is anyone stopped from going, as long as you pay your way. I see them all the time in my congregation, saving up to make it across. How else can they go? They can't get visas so they take their chances on the sea."

4. SETTLEMENT

1. In their book on second-generation New Yorkers, these researchers point out that Dominicans were the least likely to see upward social mobility. It is worth quoting their findings in more detail: "The Dominicans probably present the clearest case for concern. With a comparatively high level of African ancestry, Dominicans face high levels of discrimination, both in the public space and in the housing market. Unlike the parents of West Indians, few of their parents spoke English on arrival.

They arrived in the United States with very low levels of education and continue to have low incomes. Their nearest "proximal host" population, Puerto Ricans, are also quite poor, and the neighborhoods they share have some of New York's worst schools. . . . It is not clear whether Dominicans, caught between remaining in one of the poorest immigrant communities and assimilating into the poorest of the native communities, enjoy much second generation advantage." (2008:363–364).

2. It might be easier to come up with such categories to explain sociocultural "acceptance" or "rejection," or, as Zhou puts it, how immigrants become "absorbed by different segments of American society, ranging from affluent middle-class suburbs to impoverished inner-city ghettos, and that becoming American may not always be an advantage for the immigrants themselves or for their children" (1999:210).

3. "Making it in America is a complex process, dependent only partially on the motivation and abilities that immigrants bring with them. How they use these personal resources often depends on international political factors—over which individuals have no control—and on the history of earlier arrivals and the types of communities they have created—about which newcomers also have little say. These complex and involuntary forces confront the foreign born as an objective reality that channels them in different directions." (Portes and Rumbaut 1994:93)

4. This is not to overlook the fact that many participants talked of their family sending money back to their grandparents and other family members in the Dominican Republic or of buying small properties in their homeland for visits during vacation.

5. In New York City, the school names attended by the subjects are familiar. Most of them are large schools with several thousand students and are often synonymous with low graduation rates, low test scores, high rates of violent incidents, and high teacher turnover. It is only in the last few years that New York City has been held accountable for the fact that it has short-changed the city's public schools by billions of dollars while overseeing a clearly inequitable schools budget formula. The previously elected New York State governor, Elliot Spitzer, pledged to end this injustice (see Spitzer's budget speech, January 30, 2007).

6. When this interview was carried out, Chino was just another heroin junky in Santo Domingo; at the moment he is in rehabilitation for the fourth time in the last six years.

7. Sassen (2001) describes the structuring of New York's labor market from the 1970s to the 1990s and shows how it has become increasingly stratified, offering fewer and fewer avenues for low-end workers as manufacturing has declined rapidly and has been replaced by low-paying service jobs and occupations geared to the educated middle and upper classes. Pessar (1986) also noted the increasing bifurcation of the labor market in the 1980s and its effect on Dominican male and female workers. Portes and Zhou (1992) meanwhile emphasized the importance of social capital for Dominican settlement, based on what they call bounded solidarity and enforceable trust, which has played an important part in the economic heterogeneity of the Dominican community, belying its stereotype of being locked into low-end occupations and the drug trade.

5. PATHWAYS TO CRIME

1. Of course, in other locales the spatial distance between the classes may be much greater.
2. D.B. (author) tried to ask Manny on various occasions about his child without success.
3. In discussing conservative positivism and liberal structuralism, Young says, "Both have very simple rational/instrumental narratives. In the first, crime occurs because of choice—depicted as an availability of opportunity and low levels of social control, particularly where individuals are impulsive and short-term oriented. Curiously (or perhaps not), every intellectual attempt is made to distance crime from structural inequalities and social injustice. Rather, we have pallid, calculative individuals committing crime where it is possible, coupled with putative victims who as likely targets are in turn attempting to calculate their optimum security strategies" (Young and Brotherton 2006).
4. When I (D.B.) last interviewed Alex in Santo Domingo, he was indigent and begged me to find him some work; he was a trained printer and knew carpentry. But his depression, the demons of his past, and the lack of any meaningful future were perhaps too much for him. According to other deportees, Alex overdosed on heroin at the end of 2003, not long after this interview, and his body was never found.

6. PRISON

1. The subject here is talking specifically about an immigration attorney; generally such representation is either deficient or completely absent. Another report on Dominican deportees (Northern Manhattan Coalition for Immigrant Rights 2009) confirmed this finding. In an analysis of removal proceedings against Dominicans between 2004–2007, more than half of the defendants had no representation at the proceedings. It should also be noted that one of the busiest immigration lawyers in the Washington Heights area was a man named Victor Espinal, whom we interviewed early in our study. *The New York Times* reporter Nina Bernstein recently revealed that Mr. Espinal was a fraud and possessed no legitimate legal credentials to practice in the United States. He has since been arrested and awaits trial on multiple charges of professional misrepresentation, fraud, and grand larceny (Bernstein 2009).
2. The worst representation seemed to be reserved for the immigration appeals court, where the court is not obliged to provide a lawyer because the subject is not a U.S. citizen and therefore is not entitled to the same constitutional rights of due process (see next chapter). Only 35 of the original 65 subjects reported having a lawyer defend them in these hearings.
3. Between 1980 and 1992, the average maximum sentence for a violent offense declined from 125 months to 88 months; however, the reverse was true for drug offenses, which increased from 47 months to 82 months (Beck and Brien 1995).

Moreover, the number of people going to prison for drug offenses also increased exponentially. According to the U.S. Department of Justice, between 1980 and 1992 court commitments to state prisons based on drug charges increased by 1000 percent; during the same period, convictions for violent offenses only increased by 51 percent (Maguire and Pastore 1996).

4. In 1998 a grassroots organization called Critical Resistance was formed "to build an international movement to end the Prison-Industrial Complex." Its first major conference was held at the University of California, Berkeley in the same year.

5. Examples include the ban on the use of public housing, being barred from a wide array of occupations, prohibitive restrictions on associations for return inmates, and the constant drug testing and surveillance that is required by probation officers.

6. These high rates of prison spending in many states, in light of the fiscal crisis, have become untenable. We now see radical measures to reduce prison spending and the prison population in states like New York, California, and Arizona (e.g., Archibold 2010).

7. Perhaps this was due to the deep feelings of resentment toward the U.S. criminal justice system; perhaps this was due to the vast majority of interactions between inmates and guards at that institutional, dehumanized level as maintained by Zimbardo (2008).

8. This is no longer the case regarding the Trinitarios, as there are reports of the group throughout the United States as well as in Europe and the Dominican Republic.

9. The Asociación Ñeta is a self-described prisoners' rights organization founded in 1979 by Carlos "La Sombra" (the shadow) Torres-Irriarte (although his birth name is Melendez) while he was serving time in Oso Blanco, the correctional facility located at Rio Piedras in Puerto Rico. Torres-Irriarte started the group to heighten the solidarity of inmates, to stop the rampant abuse by prison guards, and to provide mutual protection against a predatory prison gang called "G27" or the "Insects." On March 30, 1981, "La Sombra" was murdered on orders by the leader of the Insects, El Manota, who himself was murdered in revenge on September 30, 1981. There are five basic goals or "norms" that the group struggles to achieve within the prison culture: share, peace, education, harmony, and respect. A sixth principle of the group often mentioned in their texts is the commitment to the struggle. The group remained in Puerto Rico primarily as a prisoners' organization throughout the 1980s, eventually becoming the biggest inmate organization in the system. Because inmates in Puerto Rico can vote in elections, this gave the group power and leverage with both prison authorities and politicians.

10. It is difficult to say exactly when the Latin Kings started. Some say that it was in the Illinois prison system during the late 1940s, originating as a prisoner self-help group for Latino inmates; community leaders in Chicago recall that it began as a street group called the Latin Angels during the 1950s, later becoming the Latin Kings during the 1960s. Another explanation for the group's origin is that the group was formed in 1966 after youth workers organized a "shout out" to gang members from the Spanish Kings, Junior Sinners, and the Jokers (Knox 2000). In time, the Chicago Latin Kings developed an auxiliary wing called the Latin Queens, a group

that had a similar manifesto and owed allegiance to the organization's Supreme Crown, Gustavo Colón (aka Lord Gino), also known as the "Sun King." During the early to mid-1980s, the Latin Kings spread beyond Chicago to other cities of the Midwest, such as Milwaukee (Hagerdorn 1998), where a combination of deindustrialization and the anti–working class, anti-minority policies of the Reagan administration locked many inner city youth into the so-called "underclass."

11. Alex liked to fight. He grew up in that subculture; to him it was almost second nature. Alex also liked the drama, the excitement, the sport, and the honor that goes with it. Fighting, as Katz shows (1988), is extremely seductive and allows for moments of transcendence. In the prison setting, the unrelenting boredom, the intense struggle over minimal resources, the hypermasculine culture that saturates prison life, and the conspiracies and intrigue that are part of inmate–inmate and inmate–administration relations contribute to the fighting culture. It is in this context that Alex's account should be understood.

7. DEPORTED

1. We publish this field note in its entirety for two reasons. First, because it places the reader in greater proximity to the context of subjects who are experiencing what is likely to be the most traumatic event in their lives; second, this information can help the reader understand and perhaps empathize with this process.

2. There are approximately 40 immigration detention camps in the United States, formerly run by the Immigration and Naturalization Service and now under the direction of the Department of Immigration and Customs Enforcement (ICE), which, in turn, is under the purview of the Department of Homeland Security. According to ICE's government web site (http://www.ice.gov/index.htm), there are almost 20,000 inmates in these detention facilities. Since 2004, sixty-four detainees have died in custody (Bernstein 2007), prompting a Senate amendment that calls for an office of detention oversight within the Department of Homeland Security.

8. BACK IN THE HOMELAND: PART ONE

1. See chapter 9 for a discussion of the different kinds of "positive" coping strategies used by the deportees to avoid the criminal justice system and find their different paths toward social and cultural integration.

2. Journalist Luis Garcia, who was at the time the director of communications at the Education Department, openly complained to the administration of the National Police because he was mistakenly labeled as a drug-related deportee in police records (Reyes 2007). As a result of this error, it was revealed for the first time that two agencies retained files of deportees: the National Police, which has approximately 27,000 records up until the end of 2006, and the *Dirección Nacional de Control de Drogas* (the National Council for Drug Control), which had 17,000 records as of 2006.

3. The term "1.5-generation" refers to people who immigrate to a new country before or during their early teens.

4. We have not dealt with the role played by private security in maintaining social order vis a vis the deportees, but these forces are important and play a role similar to what Huggins (1999) calls the "rent a cop." Below is a field note of a beating given to Bory, a deportee associated with the heroin users in our sample. It is not so far removed from the methods used at Abu Ghraib. The field researcher, Yolanda Martín, interviewed Bory shortly after the incident while he was being held in a cell at the local police station:

> "Bory entered La Nacional, one of the largest supermarkets in town, and decided to sit on some boxes by the exit. One of the security guards identified him as a "deportado that always steals from the store." Bory did not have anything on him, no drugs and no store merchandise. Six of the private security guards took him to the storage room. Bory was tied to a high bar with a rope and blindfolded with a plastic bag placed on his head. He was then splashed with a bucket of water. One of the guards grabbed a stick and started to beat him on the back, head, chest, and legs. Others followed with punches. Bory was let down to the floor, still blindfolded. Guards then threw kicks at his stomach and legs; then they seated their victim, and the supervising guard started to interrogate him. They all think that Bory was working in tandem with an employee to steal hard liquor. They told Bory the hitting would continue until he gave the name of the employee. Bory had not collaborated with anyone and could not provide any names. Bory was beaten harder, again with the stick. Bory begged them to stop: "Please, please don´t. You´re gonna end up killing me." At that moment, the police arrived. Another employee working at the supermarket had called the police to intervene. Bory tells me that, had it not been for the police, he'd be dead by now" (Martín 2010).

5. In 2003, one of the country's most renowned lawyers, Angel Julian Serulle, proposed to the government of President Hipólito Mejia a solution for this human pollution problem, smacking of the segregationist thinking that used to be common in dealing with little understood diseases such as tuberculosis and leprosy: "In conjunction with the North Americans, it (the Dominican government [added by the authors]) should begin construction of a rehabilitation center on a Dominican island in order to confine and reeducate Dominicans deported from the United Status for serious crimes." Serulle stated that it would allow these citizens to transform themselves into productive members of society instead of being a threat. He added that, after being reeducated, these convicts should be "thrust into the productive market" (Perez 2003).

9. BACK IN THE HOMELAND: PART TWO

1. For example, in an innovative view of the informal sector, Gregory describes a range of occupations and levels of entrepreneurship that are as much an expression of resistance, i.e., "weapons of the weak" (Scott 1985) in a colonized political economy, as they are forms of economic subjugation and accommodation.

2. Willis (2000) refers to the purpose of work in advanced capitalist countries as a means of cultural enfranchisement, helping to frame class, race–ethnic, and gendered identities. "It brings a sense of self and maturity which is achieved through insight and experience rather than through the mere acquisition of years" (Willis 2000:89). Nonetheless, for many young people in these "advanced" societies, the world of work eludes them, "making conditional what should have been a birthright, working-class kids now have to aspire to their own necessary status!" (Willis 2000:88). In the Dominican Republic where unemployment and underemployment are the norm and not the exception, we need to rethink work's pivotal role in the cultural production of both youth and adult societies.

3. In recent years, the Fernandez government has proposed a new set of plans to address this tourist neglect of the capital. In league with a consortium of Spanish and Italian investors, Fernandez seeks to build an island just off shore, with imported sand for the beaches and a string of upscale hotels to cater to the international leisure class. The government has presented this project to the public as the Dominican version of the "Dubai model," in which the oil-rich sultanate, whose profits are based on the sweated labor of thousands of heavily exploited Pakistanis and Indians, has built a series of lavish resorts for the global super-rich. Of course, if such a project were to come to fruition in Santo Domingo, it will only further stratify the local work force.

4. Eddie died in July 2009. He was 56 years old and was the sole source of income for his 16-year-old son and his paraplegic brother.

5. We should also mention that, once a year, Manolo looks forward to the arrival of a Floridian named Frank who comes with a group of teenage baseball players for a summer camp in Santo Domingo. During the four weeks that the youngsters hone their baseball skills in a country obsessed with the sport, Manolo is paid a living wage to help in the camp's daily organization. Manolo also recruits two or three other deportees to participate; with their bilingual skills and knowledge of the local area, they are able to leave their state of subsistence, at least momentarily.

6. (Santo Domingo Field Notes [Brotherton, May 1, 2005]): George is propped up in his hospital bed; the left side of his face is drooping, and he cannot speak. He talks with his eyes. He is wearing an adult size diaper because he is completely incontinent. His wife is sitting on a chair at the bottom of his bed and greets us with a hug and a kiss. Next to George's bed is a mattress where his wife sleeps at night. His wife is his nurse and will take care of him, filling the void in care where only those who can pay are serviced. George is hooked up to some kind of "drip." Manolo goes over to him and hugs him and tells him he's brought his friends to see him. "Remember Davy, George? Remember the interview he did with you all those years ago?" George tries to look at me, and I go over and hug George and in his ear I say softly, "It's me, George, it's me, Davy. It's so good to see you George, so good to see you." As I retreat from the bed, George's eyes follow me intensely; he tries to move his lips, and saliva drips down his chin as he strains to mutter something. I feel tears well up in my eyes. It's heartbreaking to see this man, who was so animated when I last saw him, now so close to death. I turn to his wife again and she begins to tell me about the costs of the medical

care. She needs two thousand pesos just to keep feeding him the medicine; otherwise he will die straight away. She then says he needs a brain scan to see the extent of the damage, but that will cost about two hundred dollars and it has to be done in another hospital. I give her fifty dollars and Luis gives her another fifty dollars, and she says she should be able to get the rest from her sister. If she can get the money by tomorrow, she can take George across town in a taxi and get the scan done, and then return to have a hospital doctor analyze the results. There is no ambulance service to take George, and the wife will have to manage the task of moving a deathly sick man alone with her family members. To the right of him are three other patients in their beds, surrounded by their respective families. We stay for about fifteen minutes more, and I hold George's hand and wipe his sweaty brow. Manolo says that we have to go, at which Luis approaches George and begins to recite a prayer. He turns to all the patients and says the prayer loudly so that all may feel blessed. I cannot help feeling that these are George's last rites.

7. Two weeks after this interview I (David Brotherton) saw Alex again, and this time he was more agitated. His arm was in plaster and he was obviously in pain. He asked me for some money to get his prescription pills, which would alleviate his suffering. He explained that he had gotten into a fight with some gang rivals three days previously and that the Dominican hospital did not provide any pain medication free of charge; he had spent all his money getting his arm x-rayed and set (he had broken two bones in his wrist). I gave Alex fifteen dollars and arranged to see him again when he would introduce me to more deportees from New York who had joined his organization. He said he had a chapter of thirty members, almost of them deportees. After three days I tried to find Alex, but he failed to materialize. Finally, someone who knew of him told me that he was in the infamous La Victoria prison. I never saw Alex again, even though I have persistently asked about his whereabouts. Perhaps, like George, the deportee-cum-teacher did not survive the ordeal.

8. I (D.B.) was introduced to Guido and his American-born family by his uncle, who was related to a work friend of my wife's in Manhattan, and I came to know him well during the first phase of the research in 2002 and 2003. I visited his farm several times in 2002, but it was not until four months after we were introduced that he finally revealed to me that he was a deportee. "I don't let anyone know about it," he said. "They hear about it, and right away they gonna treat you differently— that's just the way it is here." Recently we talked about his beginnings on the farm, and in other parts of this study Guidorevealed much more about his deportation experience.

9. On a recent visit to Santo Domingo, I (D.B.) accompanied Luis2 on one of his business missions for the city. We drove to a patch of wasteland sandwiched between two major roads, one of which led to the airport. As I alighted from Luis2's relatively new SUV, he put his pistol in his back pocket. "Do you expect trouble, Luis?" I asked. "No, not really," he answered. "But you never know. There are squatters here, and we'll have to move them if we sell this land." Thus Luis2, a highly stigmatized deportee, was now working to remove other stigmatized residents of the city. I mentioned this irony to him as we drove back. "Yes," he said.

"It's a fucked up situation all round, but we live in the Dominican Republic, how much more fucked up can it be?"

10. Recently, the group started a television program and a bimonthly magazine, and in 2009 they opened three more chapters in Santo Domingo with more deportees: Guachupita, 27 de febrero, and Borojol.

10. BACK IN THE HOMELAND: PART THREE

1. Ironically, Rafey Prison was severely damaged in a recent hurricane; during repairs, it was found that the facility had been built upon unsafe foundations.
2. Staying at this prison in a so-called maximum security wing but in effect living in extreme luxury was the infamous drug dealer Roland Florián Felix. Florián was killed on My 16, 2009 by the prison's captain. Florián was supposed to be the most feared "capo" in the Dominican Republic and had served 15 of his 20-year sentence for smuggling 950 kilos of cocaine from the Dominican Republic to Puerto Rico.
3. This finding is misleading because most, if not all, inmates have to buy their mattresses from someone inside the prison. Of the three prisons we have visited over the last eight years, including the largest prison (La Victoria) in the Dominican Republic, we found no institutional provision of any beds!
4. Triangulation is one way to check on these accounts, e.g., ask family members about certain events and then check these accounts against those of the interviewees, or interview participants multiple times over a number of years so as to reveal discrepancies if an account is fabricated.
5. Under new judicial guidelines, six months is the maximum time a person may be held in preventive custody, but the degree to which this is being enforced is questionable, especially for those with few resources for legal advice and representation.
6. In a fairly recent reorganization of the prison system, the Procuradariá General is supposed to oversee this branch of the government and ensure some kind of transparency and accountability, but widespread reports of escapes, abuse, drug use, and violence still abound throughout the system.

11. THE RETURN OF THE DEPORTEES

1. On average, $2 billion of U.S. taxpayers' money is spent on border enforcement in the southwest United States.
2. Transport company from Miami to New York.
3. The literal translation is "beans with sugar," a Dominican dish that is famous in the south of the country.
4. The site or the corner where they sell drugs.
5. This is a figure of speech that is roughly equivalent to "killing time."
6. In Spanish, this word means that something does not smell good.

7. This Spanish expression is an abbreviation for "Everything is OK."
8. This figure differs from that of the U.S. Census Bureau, which found poverty rates of 18.6 percent for individuals and 15 percent for families. This is because New York City has raised the annual income threshold of poverty to $30,000 for a family of four because of high housing costs, whereas the federal government uses the standard measure of $22,000.
9. In a recent New York City second-generation study (Kasinitz et al. 2009), Dominicans were found to have the lowest median household income and the highest rate of unemployment; they were more economically disadvantaged than either native Puerto Ricans or African Americans.
10. This could be seen recently during the global financial crisis; a United Nations Report indicated that a large percentage of money in the banking system came from money laundering (Groendahl 2009 and Madrak 2009): "Antonio Maria Costa, head of the UN Office on Drugs and Crime, said he has seen evidence that the proceeds of organized crime were 'the only liquid investment capital' available to some banks on the brink of collapse last year. He said that a majority of the $352bn (£216bn) of drugs profits was absorbed into the economic system as a result."

12. CONCLUSION

1. Socialist poet Emma Lazarus wrote "The New Colossus" in 1883. It was engraved at the bottom of the Statue of Liberty in 1903:

Not like the brazen giant of Greek fame,
With conquering limbs astride from land to land;
Here at our sea-washed, sunset gates shall stand
A mighty woman with a torch, whose flame
Is the imprisoned lightning, and her name
Mother of Exiles. From her beacon-hand
Glows world-wide welcome; her mild eyes command
The air-bridged harbor that twin cities frame.
"Keep ancient lands, your storied pomp!" cries she
With silent lips. "Give me your tired, your poor,
Your huddled masses yearning to breathe free,
The wretched refuse of your teeming shore.
Send these, the homeless, tempest-tost to me, I lift my lamp beside the golden door!"

2. The Arizona state legislature and Republican governor Jan Brewer recently signed into law the most punitive sanctions against "illegal immigrants" in the United States. Punishments for residing illegally (i.e., not having legal documents when apprehended by state agents) in a state that depends heavily on Mexican and Central American labor include six months imprisonment and fines of $2,500. The Catholic Cardinal of Los Angeles, Roger Mahoney, has likened provisions of the bill to "Nazism," whereas the government of Mexico has said it will review all of its current agreements of cooperation with the state of Arizona (Archibold 2010).

3. Two important reports that attest to the vindictive and potentially unconstitutional actions of state agents as they pursue deportable populations have been published recently in New York City. In the first report from the Immigration Justice Clinic of Cardozo Law School (Chiu et al. 2009), the authors found that Immigration and Customs Enforcement (ICE) agents illegally entered and searched residences while seizing non-targeted individuals "based solely on racial or ethnic appearance or on limited English proficiency" during numerous home raids on undocumented immigrants in New York and New Jersey (p.1). In a second report from the non-profit organization Justice Strategies (Shahani 2010), the author alleged that the administration at New York's largest jail, Rikers Island, was working hand in hand with ICE, issuing "immigration detainers" that place an administrative hold on incarcerated suspected non-citizens for the flimsiest of reasons. The author states, "While Homeland Security purports to target the most dangerous offenders, there appears to be no correlation between offense level and identification for deportation" (p.1). The first author (David Brotherton) issued a report on home raids conducted by ICE in immigrant communities in Long Island during 2007 in which a basic policy of guilt by association was used to sweep more than one hundred non-citizens—supposedly connected to "gangs"—into the deportation system (Brotherton 2010).
4. To be fair, the theory of segmented assimilation has many variants. The model that explains downward mobility through what is sometimes called "dissonant acculturation" (i.e., overly rapid acculturation to the U.S. norms and values) resonates with criminology theories regarding the experience of second-generation immigrants. The descriptions of the cultural interplay are usually very thin, however, and engagement with any critical criminological literature is almost nonexistent.
5. Much of the notion of oppositional behavior comes originally from an assortment of works such as Cohen (1955), Ogbu (1978), and Willis (1977). These earlier sociological and anthropological contributions, however, are more complex than the renditions of later criminological and immigration researchers who often favor notions of social reproduction (Brotherton 2007) over processes of colonization or critiques of capitalist processes as a mode of production, a system of exchange relations, an incubator of class relations, or a driving force of contemporary global culture. In addition, there is little consideration of subcultural practices that have transformational possibilities rather than adaptational certainties (Barrios et al. 2006; Barrios 2003).
6. Gregory (2007) pursues this version of resistance in his ethnography of tourism in the resorts closest to Santo Domingo; Conquergood (1997, 1992) does the same in his long-term work with the Latin Kings of Chicago, as do Scott (1985) in his work with Malaysian peasants and Ferrell (1996, 2005) in his study of graffiti artists and dumpster divers.
7. In the recent study of second-generation New Yorkers by Kasinitz et al. (2008), the authors were "cautiously optimistic" that their immigrant subjects were making it in New York City because, in part, of the benefits of the civil rights movement, and the various legislative efforts to combat structural racism. They found, interestingly, that such immigrants are generally more successful than their native

counterparts due to the positive attitudes of their parents, who still believed in the possibilities of the American Dream; the pro-immigrant political climate of New York; and the range of "second chance" opportunities that New Yorkers are still able to enjoy.

8. However, with the Republican Party doing everything it can to suppress potential Democratic voters (e.g., as we have seen in its campaigns to maintain laws against voting for ex-felons in Florida and throughout much of the South), does the timing of this legislation have anything to do with the growth of the Latino population and its roughly two-to-one voting record in favor of Democratic candidates several months before the mid-term elections? (Palast 2010).

9. Garreau describes "edge cities" as the new suburban sites that are constructed at freeway intersections and often near major airports. They attract postindustrial corporations, such as those involved in information technology, which employ primarily middle-class workers. Such cities are planned hierarchically with housing and parkways intertwined with corporate campuses, quite distinct from the traditional modernist city's street grids. Originally, they were designed to be free of urban ills such as crime and racial strife, but critics have pointed to the growth of class segregation within these new growth zones, and many have suffered from a massive devaluation of housing prices caused by the subprime mortgage crisis.

10. On May 3, 2010, Governor Patterson of New York became the first governor to call for a review panel to try to stop the rising tide of deportations from New York. In his press release he stated the following: "Some of our immigration laws, particularly with respect to deportation, are extremely inflexible. However, federal law allows governors to pardon individuals in certain cases in order to remove the deportation consequence of a State criminal conviction. In some small way, we hope this initiative will help set an example for how to soften the blow in those cases of deserving individuals caught in the web of our national immigration laws. We hope it will prove that justice can always find a way" (see http://www.state.ny.us/governor/press/050310Deportation.html).

11. On May Day 2010, we may have seen the first major sign of this movement. According to various media reports, up to a million Latino/as and their supporters took to the streets of Los Angeles, California, and other cities to protest the unjust laws against immigrants and, in particular, the proposed anti-immigrant, racial profiling laws in Arizona.

REFERENCES

Abu-Jamal, Mumia. 2009. *Jailhouse Lawyers: Prisoners Defending Prisoners v. the USA*. San Francisco, CA: City Lights Publishers.

Adams, James Truslow. 1931. *The Epic of America*. Safety Harbor, FL: Simon Publications, 2001.

Alba, Richard and Victor Nee. 1999. Rethinking Assimilation Theory for a New Era of Immigration. In *The Handbook of International Migration: The American Experience*, eds. Charles Hirschman, Philip Kasinitiz, and Josh DeWind. New York: Russell Sage Foundation.

Alexander, Jeffrey, Ron Everman, Bernhard Gisen, Neil J. Smelser, and Piotr Sztompka. 2004. *Cultural Trauma and Collective Identity*. Berkeley, CA: University of California Press.

Amnesty International Report. 2009. *Dominican Republic*. May 28. http://www.unhcr. org/refworld/docid/4a1fadf164.html (accessed September 19, 2009).

Archibold, Randal C. 2010. Arizona enacts stringent law on immigration. *The New York Times*, April 23, A1.

Bacon, David. 2008. *Illegal People: How Globalization Creates Migration and Criminalizes Immigrants*. Boston: Beacon Press.

Bandura, Albert. 1977. *Social Learning Theory*. New York: General Learning Press.

Barrios, Luis. 2010. Reflections and Lived Experiences of Afrolatina/o Religiosity. In *Afrolatino/as in the U.S.A.: A Reader*, eds. Miriam Jimenez and Juan Flores, 252–261. Durham, NC: Duke University Press.

Barrios, Luis. 2008. Los hijos e hijas de Mamá Tingó: Culturas juveniles y violencia, en un proyecto llamado Palenque. In *Otras Naciones: Jóvenes, transnacionalismo y exclusión*, eds. Mauro Cerbino and Luis Barrios. Quito, Ecuador: Facultad Latinoamericana de Ciencias Sociales-FLACSO.

Barrios, Luis. 2007a. *Coquiando: Meditaciones subversivas para un mundo mejor*. Santo Domingo, República Dominicana: Editorial Búho.

Barrios, Luis. 2007b. Gangs and Spirituality. In *Gangs in the Global City: Alternatives to Traditional Criminology,* ed. John M. Hagedorn, 225–247. Chicago: University of Illinois Press.

Barrios, Luis. 2004. *Pitirreando: De la desesperanza a la esperanza.* San Juan, Puerto Rico: Editorial Edil, Inc.

Barrios, Luis. 2003. The Almighty Latin King and Queen Nation and the Spirituality of Resistance: Agency, Social Cohesion, and Liberating Rituals in the Making of a Street Organization. In *Gangs and Society: Alternative Perspectives,* eds. Louis Kontos, David Brotherton, and Luis Barrios, 119–135. New York: Columbia University Press.

Barrios, Luis. 2000. *Josconiando: Dimensiones sociales y políticas de la espiritualidad.* Dominican Republic: Editora Aguiar.

Barrios, Luis and David C. Brotherton. 2004. Dominican Republic: From poster child to basketcase. *NACLA, Report on the Americas.* 38;3(November/December):11–13.

Barrios, Luis, David C. Brotherton, and Marcia Esparza. 2006. Barcelona desde Nueva York. Amor de Rey de Corazón: Transnazionalizando la resistencia. In *Jóvenes Latinos en Barcelona: Espacio público y cultura urbana,* eds. Carlos Feixa, Laura Porzio, and Carolina Recio, 281–294. Barcelona: Anthropos-Ajuntament de Barcelona.

Basch, Linda, Nina Glick Schiller, and Cristina Stanton Blanc. 1994. *Nations Unbound: Transnational Projects, Postcolonial Predicaments, and Deterritorialized Nation-States.* Amsterdam: Gordon and Breach Science Publishers.

Baum, Jonathon, Rosha Jones, and Catherine Barry. 2010. *In the Child's Best Interest?: The Consequences of Losing a Lawful Immigrant Parent to Deportation.* International Human Rights Law Clinic, University of California, School of Law.

Bauman, Zygmunt. 2004. *Wasted Lives: Modernity and Its Outcasts.* Cambridge, UK: Polity.

Beck, A. J. and P. M. Brien. 1995. Trends in the U.S. Correctional Populations: Recent Findings from the Bureau of Justice Statistics. In *The Dilemmas of Corrections,* eds. V. C. Hass and G. P. Alpert. Long Grove, IL: Waveland Press.

Beck, Ulrich. 1992. *Risk Society: Towards a New Modernity.* Thousand Oaks, CA: Sage.

Behar, Ruth. 1993. *Translated Woman: Crossing the Border with Esperanza's Story.* Boston: Beacon Press.

Berlin, Daniel, Erin Brizius, Micah Bump, Daren Garshelis, Niloufar Khonsari, Erika Pinheiro, Kate Rhudy, Rebecca Shaeffer, Sarah Sherman-Stokes, and Thomas Smith. 2008. *Between the Border and the Street: A Comparative Look at Gang Reduction Policies and Migration in the United States and Guatemala.* Washington, DC: Georgetown Law School.

Bernstein, Nina. 2009. An immigration attorney is accused of being a fraud, and his clients scramble for help. *The New York Times.* February 25, http://www.nytimes.com/2009/02/25/nyregion/25immigration.html?_r=1&ref=nina_bernstein (accessed December 19, 2009).

Bernstein, Nina. 2007. New scrutiny as immigrants die in custody. *The New York Times,* June 2, A1.

Betances, Emelio. 1995. *State and Society in the Dominican Republic.* Boulder, CO: Westview Press.

Biernacki, Pat and Dan Waldorf. 1981. Snowball sampling: Problems and techniques of chain referral sampling. *Sociological Methods and Research* 10;2:141–163.

Black, William. 2005. *The Best Way to Rob a Bank Is to Own One: How Corporate Executives and Politicians Looted the S&L Industry.* Austin, Texas: University of Texas Press.

Blumstein, Alfred. 1995. Youth violence, guns and the illicit-drug industry. *Journal of Criminal Law and Criminology* 86;1:10–36.

Bolívar-Diaz, Juan. 2009. El peor año de Leonel. *Hoy Digital,* August 15, http://www.hoy.com.do/tema-de-hoy/2009/8/15/289643/El-peor-ano-de-Leonel (accessed January 22, 2010).

Boris, Eileen. 1995. The racialized gendered state: Constructions of citizenship in the United States. *Social Politics* 2;2:160–181.

Bosch, Juan. 2009. Frases y pensamientos de Juan Bosch en el centenario de su natalicio. *El Jaya,* http://www.eljaya.com/200908-1/n-frases.php (accessed March 14, 2009).

Bosch, Juan. 2003. *De Cristóbal Colón a Fidel Castro: El caribe, frontera imperial.* La Habana: Editorial de Ciencias Sociales.

Bosch, Juan. 1970. *Composición social Dominicana: Historia e interpretación.* República Dominicana: Publicaciones Ahora.

Bourdieu, Pierre. 1977. *Outline of a Theory of Practice.* Cambridge: Cambridge University Press.

Bourgois, Philippe. 2001. Culture of Poverty. In *International Encyclopedia of Social and Behavioral Sciences,* 11904–11907. Amsterdam: Elsevier Science Ltd.

Bourgois, Philippe. 2002. *In Search of Respect: Selling Crack in El Barrio,* 2nd ed. New York: Cambridge University Press.

Bray, David. 1984. Economic development: The middle class and international migration in the Dominican Republic. *International Migration Review* 18;2:217–236.

Brea de Cabral, Mayra and Edylberto Cabral Ramírez. 2009a. Homicidios y armas de fuego en República Dominicana. *Revista Electrónica Psicología Científica,* May, http://psicologiacientifica.com (accessed September 2009).

Brea de Cabral, Mayra and Edylberto Cabral Ramírez. 2009b. Violencia y proliferación de armas de fuego. Estudio de conocimientos, creencias, actitudes y vivencias en estudiantes universitarios del sector público en República Dominicana. *Revista Electrónica Psicología Científica.* http://www.psicologiacientifica.com/bv/psicologia-260-6-violencia-y-proliferacion-de-armas-de-fuego-estudio-de-conocimientos-creencias-actitudes-y-vivencias-en-estudiantes-universitarios-del-sector-p (accessed September 2009).

Brennan, Denise. 2004. *What's Love Got to Do with It?: Transnational Desires and Sex Tourism in the Dominican Republic.* Durham, NC: Duke University Press.

Brotherton, David C. 2010. Expert report. Adriana Aguilar v. Immigration and Customs Enforcement Division of Homeland Security, New York, United States District Court, Southern District.

Brotherton, David C. 2008. Exiling New Yorkers. In *Keeping Out the Other: Critical Analysis of Immigration Control Today,* eds. David C. Brotherton and Phillip Kretsedemas, 159–178. New York: Columbia University Press.

Brotherton, David C. 2007. Beyond social reproduction: Bringing resistance back into the theory of gangs. *Theoretical Criminology* 12;1:55–77.

Brotherton, David C. 2003a. The deportees of Santo Domingo. Paper presented at the Deportations and Society Conference, March 11, Santo Domingo, Dominican Republic.

Brotherton, David C. 2003b. Dominican deportees suffer in America's failing war on drugs, *London Guardian*, June 14, 19.

Brotherton, David C. 2003c. The life and conditions of Dominican deportees. *NACLA Report on the Americas*. September:3–7.

Brotherton, David C. and Luis Barrios. 2009. Displacement and stigma: The social-psychological crisis of the Dominican deportee. *Crime, Media, Culture: An International Journal* 5;1:29–55.

Brotherton, David C. and Luis Barrios. 2004. *The Almighty Latin King and Queen Nation: Street Politics and the Transformation of a New York City Gang.* New York: Columbia University Press.

Brotherton, David C. and Luis Barrios. 1997. November: Notes on prisons in the Dominican Republic. *Humanity & Society* 214:425–434.

Brotherton, David C. and Phillip Kretsedemas, eds. 2008. *Keeping Out the Other: Critical Analysis of Immigration Control Today.* New York: Columbia University Press.

Brotherton, David C., S. Will and S. Handelman, eds., forthcoming. *How Did they Get Away With It? Lessons from the Financial Meltdown.* New York: Columbia University Press.

Brotherton, David C. and Yolanda Martín. 2009. War on drugs and the case of Dominican deportees. *Journal of Crime and Justice* 32;2:21–48.

Bunting, Madeleine. 2003. Interview with Zygmund Bauman. *London Guardian*, April 5, http://www.guardian.co.uk/books/2003/apr/05/society (accessed January 22, 2010).

Burgess, Ernest. 1921. *Introduction to the Science of Sociology.* Chicago: University of Chicago Press.

Calavita, Kitty. 2003. A "reserve army of delinquents": The criminalization and economic punishment of immigrants in Spain. *Punishment and Society* 54:399–413.

Calavita, Kitty. 1992. *Inside the State: The Bracero Program, Immigration, and the INS.* New York: Routledge.

Caldeira, Teresa. 2000. *City of Walls: Crime, Segregation, and Citizenship in Sao Paulo.* Berkeley, CA: University of California Press.

Carlson, Eve B. and Constance J. Dalenberg. 2000. A conceptual framework for the impact of traumatic experiences. *Trauma Violence Abuse* 1;1:4–28.

Cashdan, Elizabeth. 2001. Ethnocentrism and xenophobia: A cross-cultural study. *Current Anthropology* 42:760–765.

Central Intelligence Agency. 2010. *The World Factbook: Dominican Republic.* http.www.cia.gov/library/publications/the-world-factbook/geos/dr (accessed April 20, 2011).

Chang, Jeff. 2005. *Can't Stop Won't Stop: A History of the Hip-Hop Generation.* New York: St. Martin's Press.

Chavez, Leo R. 1997. *Shadowed Lives: Undocumented Immigrants in American Society.* Ft. Worth: Harcourt-Brace Jovanovich College Publishers.

Chiu, Bess, Lynly Egyes, Peter Markowitz, and Vasandani Jaya. 2009. *Constitution on Ice: A Report on Immigration Home Raid Operations.* New York: Cardozo Law School.

Chomsky, Noam. 2006. *Failed States: The Abuse of Power and the Assault on Democracy.* New York: Metropolitan Books.

Christie, Nils. 2000. *Crime Control as Industry*, 3rd ed. Florence, Kentucky: Routledge.

Christie, Nils. 1993. Crime control as industry. *Probation Journal* 40:102–104.

Cloward, Richard A. and Lloyd Ohlin. 1960. *Delinquency and Opportunity*. New York: Free Press.

Cohen, Albert. 1955. *Delinquent Boys*. New York: Free Press.

Cohen, Ronald. 1978. Ethnicity: Problem and focus in anthropology. *Annual Review of Anthropology* 7:385–410.

Cole, David. 2000. *No Equal Justice: Race and Class in the American Criminal Justice System*. New York: New Press.

Coleman, James S. 1961. *The Adolescent Society*. Glencoe, IL: Free Press.

Conquergood, Dwight. 1997. Street Literacy. In *Handbook of Research on Teaching Literacy Through Communicative and Visual Arts*, eds. James Flood, Shirley Brice Heath, and Diane Lapp, 354–375. New York: Simon and Schuster Macmillan.

Conquergood, Dwight. 1992. Life in Big Red: Struggle and Accommodations in a Chicago Polyethnic Tenement. In *Structuring Diversity: Ethnographic Perspectives on the New Immigration*, ed. Louise Lamphere, 95–144. Chicago, IL: University of Chicago Press.

Corcino, Panky. 2006. Mas de 23,000 deportados desde E.E.U.U. *El Listin Diario*, March 26, p. 6.

Cordero-Guzmán, Héctor, Robert C. Smith, and Ramón Grosfoguel, eds. 2001. *Migration, Transnationalization and Race in a Changing New York*. Philadelphia: Temple University Press.

Coutin, Susan B. 2007. *Nations of Emigrants: Shifting Boundaries of Citizenship in El Salvador and the United States*. Ithaca, New York: Cornell University Press.

Courtwright, David T. 2005. Mr. ATOD's wild ride: What do alcohol, tobacco, and other drugs have in common? *The Social History of Alcohol and Drugs* 20;1:105–140.

Cressey, Donald and Edwin Sutherland. 1978. *Principles of Criminology*. Philadelphia: J. B. Lippincott.

Crick, Malcolm. 1989. Representation of international tourism in the social sciences: Sun, sex, sights, savings, and servility. *Annual Review of Anthropology* 18:307–344.

Cross, Frank. 2007. *Decision Making in the U.S. Courts of Appeals*. Palo Alto, CA: Stanford University Press.

Cullen, Jim. 2003. *The American Dream: A Short History of an Idea that Shaped the Nation*. New York: Oxford University Press.

Curtis, Richard. 2003. Crack, cocaine and heroin: Drug eras in Williamsburg, Brooklyn. *Addiction Research and Theory* 11;1:47–63.

Curtis, Richard and Travis Wendel. 2007. You're always training the dog: Strategic interventions to reconfigure drug markets. *Journal of Drug Issues* 37;4:867–892.

Danticat, Edwidge. 1999. *The Farming of Bones*. New York: Penguin.

De Genova, Nicholas. 2005. *Working the Boundaries: Race, Space and Illegality in Mexican Chicago*. Chicago: University of Chicago Press.

De Genova, Nicholas and Natalie Peutz. 2010. *The Deportation Regime: Sovereignty, Space and the Freedom of Movement*. Durham, NC: Duke University Press.

De Giorgi, Alessandro. 2010. Immigration control, post-Fordism, and less eligibility: A materialist critique of the criminalization of immigration across Europe. *Punishment & Society* 12;2:147–167.

DeCesare, D. 1998. Deported "Home" to Haiti. *NACLA, Report on the Americas.* November/December:6–10.

Devine, John. 1996. *Maximum Security: The Culture of Violence in Inner-City Schools.* Chicago: University of Chicago Press.

Diario Libre. 2007. Pepe Goico fue al tribunal con un bizcocho morado. *DiarioLibre. com*, January 16, http://www.diariolibre.com/noticias_det.php?id=122986&l=1 (accessed September 30, 2010).

Diaz, Junot. 2007. *The Brief Wondrous Life of Oscar Wao.* New York: Riverhead.

Díaz, Rocío. 2009. *República Dominicana: Sigue la crisis energética*, November 1, http://es. globalvoicesonline.org/2009/11/15/republica-dominicana-sigue-la-crisis-energetica (accessed December 2, 2009).

Díaz Rodríguez, Luz. 2006. La solución carcelaria: La Fundación Institucionalidad y Justicia, Inc. *FINJUS*, November, http://www.finjus.org.do/Articulo.aspx?ListId= 57&Entid=69 (accessed December 4, 2009).

Douglas, Mary. 1966. *Purity and Danger: An Analysis of Concepts of Pollution and Taboo.* London: Routledge Classics.

Dow, Mark. 2004. *American Gulag: Inside U.S. Immigration Prisons.* Berkeley, CA: University of California Press.

Du Bois, William and Edward Burghardt. 2006. *Black Reconstruction: An Essay toward a History of the Part which Black Folk Played in the Attempt to Reconstruct Democracy in America, 1860–1880.* Notre Dame, IN: University of Notre Dame Press, 1935.

Du Bois, William and Edward Burghardt. 1999. *The Souls of Black Folk,* new ed. New York: W. W. Norton & Company, 1903.

Ehrenreich, Barbara. 1990. *Fear of Falling: The Inner Life of the Middle Class.* New York: Perennial.

Ehrenreich, Barbara and Arlie Hochschild, eds. 2004. *Global Woman.* Boston: Holt McDougal.

Elsner, Alan. 2006. *Gates of Injustice: The Crisis in America's Prisons*, 2nd ed. Upper Saddle River, NJ: FT Press.

Ewick, Patricia and Susan S. Silbey. 1995. Subversive stories and hegemonic tales: Toward a sociology of narrative. *Law & Society Review* 29;2:197–226.

Fagan, Jeffrey. 1990. Intoxication and Aggression. In *Drugs and Crime: Crime and Justice, a Review of Research*, vol. 13, eds. Michael Tonry and James Q. Wilson, 241–320. Chicago: University of Chicago Press.

Fanon, Frantz. 1963. *The Wretched of the Earth: A Negro Psychoanalysts Study of the Problems of Racism and Colonialism in the World Today.* New York: Grove Press.

Feeley, Malcolm and Jonathan Simon. 1992. The new penology: Notes on the emerging strategy of corrections and its implications. *Criminology* 30;4:449–474.

Ferrell, Jeff. 2005. *Empire of Scrounge: Inside the Urban Underground of Dumpster Diving, Trash Picking, and Street Scavenging.* New York: New York University Press.

Ferrell, Jeff. 2001. *Tearing Down the Streets: Adventures in Urban Anarchy.* New York: Palgrave St Martin's.

Ferrell, Jeff. 1996. *Crimes of Style: Urban Graffiti and the Politics of Criminality.* Boston: Northeastern University Press.

Ferrell, Jeff, Keith Hayward, and Jock Young. 2008. *Cultural Criminology: An Invitation*. London: Sage.

Ferrell, Jeff and Mark S. Hamm, eds. 1998. *Ethnography at the Edge. Crime, Deviance, and Field Research*. Boston: Northeastern University Press.

Fiallo, Billini and José Antione. 2003. *Trascendencia histórica de la Constitución de 1963*, November 5, http://www.perspectivaciudadana.com/contenido.php?itemid=4445 (accessed August 23, 2009).

Firestone, Shulamith. 1959. *The Dialectic of Sex: The Case for Feminist Revolution*. Repr. New York: William Morrow, 1979.

Foner, Nancy and George M. Fredrickson, eds. 2004. *Not Just Black and White: Historical and Contemporary Perspectives on Immigration, Race, and Ethnicity in the United States*. New York: Russell Sage Foundation Publications.

Fordham, Signithia. 1996. *Blacked Out: Dilemmas of Race, Identity, and Success at Capital High*. Chicago: University of Chicago Press.

Fuller, Regina. 2009. *From Slavery to Exclusion: Perceptions of African Identity in the Dominican Republic and Brazil*. http://www.wofford.edu/uploadedfiles/community-scholars/new_cos_page/fuller_spread.pdf (accessed January 12, 2010).

Galeano, Eduardo. 1973. *Open Veins of Latin America: Five Centuries of Pillage of a Continent*. New York: Monthly Review Press.

Gans, Herbert. 1992. Second generation decline: Scenarios for the ethnic and economic futures of post-1965 American immigrants. *Ethnic and Racial Studies* 15;2:173–192.

Garcia, Francisco. 2009. Trabajo infantil en la República Dominicana. *Diario Libre*, September 7, http://fgarcia.diariolibre.com/?p=100 (accessed February 23, 2010).

Garland, David. 2002. *The Culture of Control: Crime and Social Order in Contemporary Society*. Chicago: The University of Chicago Press.

Garland, David W. 1990. *Punishment and Modern Society: A Study in Social Theory*. Chicago, IL: University of Chicago Press.

Garreau, Joel. 1992. *Edge City: Life on the New Frontier*. New York: Anchor.

Gerson, Daniela. 2004. Alarm growing in Dominican Republic over influx of deportees from America. *The New York Sun*, October 21, 1.

Giddens, Anthony. 1991. *Modernity and Self-Identity: Self and Society in the Late Modern Age*. Cambridge, MA: Polity.

Glick-Schiller, Nina, Cristina Blanc-Szanton and Linda Basch, eds. 1998. *Towards a Transnational Perspective on Migration: Race, Class, Ethnicity, and Nationalism Reconsidered*. New York: New York Academy of Sciences.

Goffman, Erving. 1960. *Stigma: Notes on the Management of Spoiled Identity*. Repr. Upper Saddle River, New Jersey: Prentice-Hall, 1963.

González-Acosta, Edward D. 2008. Discrimination, oppression, and identity in Dominican society. *Dominican Today*, January 2, http://www.dominicantoday.com/dr/opinion/2008/1/2/26566/Discrimination-Oppression-and-Identity-in-Dominican-Society (accessed December 19, 2009).

Grandin, Gregory. 2006. *Empire Workshop: Latin America, The United States, and the Rise of the New Imperialism*. New York: Metropolitan Books.

Grasmuck, Sherri and Patricia R. Pessar. 1991. *Between Two Islands: Dominican International Migration*. Berkeley, CA: University of California Press.

Gregory, Stephen. 2007. *The Devil Behind the Mirror: Globalization and Politics in the Dominican Republic.* Berkeley, CA: University of California Press.

Griffin, Clifford E. 2002. Criminal deportation: The unintended impact of U.S. anti-crime and anti-terrorism policy along its third border. *Caribbean Studies.* 30;2:39–76.

Groendahl, Boris. 2009. UN crime chief says drug money flowed into banks. *Reuters. com*, January 25, http://www.reuters.com/article/idUSLP65079620090125 (accessed January 2, 2010).

Guarnizo, Luís E. 1997. The emergence of a transnational social formation and the mirage of return migration among Dominican transmigrants. *Identities* 4:281–322.

Guarnizo, Luis E. 1994. Los Dominicanyorks: The making of a binational society. *The Annals of the American Academy of Social and Political Science* 533;5:70–86.

Habermas, Jürgen. 2001. *On the Pragmatics of Social Interaction: Preliminary Studies in the Theories of Communicative Action.* Cambridge, MA: MIT Press.

Hagedorn, John M. 1998. *People and Folks: Gangs, Crime and the Underclass in a Rustbelt City,* 2nd ed. Chicago, IL: Lake View Press.

Hall, Stuart, Chas Critcher, Tony Jefferson, John N. Clarke, and Brian Roberts. 1978. *Policing the Crisis: Mugging, the State and Law and Order.* London: Macmillan.

Hamm, Mark S. 2007. High crimes and misdemeanors: George W. Bush and the sins of Abu Ghraib. *Crime, Media and Culture* 3;3:259–284.

Handlin, Oscar. 1951. *The Uprooted: The Epic Story of the Great Migrations That Made the American People.* Boston: Little Brown.

Harcourt, Bernard E. 2001. *Illusion of Order: The False Promise of Broken Windows Policing.* Cambridge: Harvard University Press.

Harvey, David. 2007. *A Brief History of Neoliberation.* New York: Oxford University Press.

Headley, Bernard. 2008. Criminal deportees: What we know and don't know. *Jamaica Gleaner,* July 14, http://www.jamaica-gleaner.com/gleaner/20080714/cleisure/cleisure3.html (accessed December 19, 2009).

Hersch, Joni. 2008. Profiling the new immigrant worker: The effects of skin color and height. Journal of Labor Economics 26;2:345–386.

Hirschman, Charles, Philip Kasinitiz, and Josh DeWind. 1999. *Handbook of International Migration: The American Experience.* New York: Russell Sage Foundation.

Hoy Digital. 2009. El Papa denuncia la pobreza y el narcotráfico en República Dominicana. *Hoy Digital,* April 3, http://www.hoy.com.do/el-mundo/2009/4/3/272604/El-Papa-denuncia-la-pobreza-y-el-narcotrafico-en-Republica-Dominicana (accessed January 4, 2010).

Huggins, Martha K. 1999. *Political Policing: The United States and Latin America.* Durham, NC: Duke University Press.

Human Development Office. 2008. *Human Development Report—Dominican Republic—2008: Human Development a Matter of Power.* Santo Domingo, Dominican Republic: United Nations Development Programme.

Hunt, Geoffrey, Stephanie Riegel, Tomas Morales, and Dan Waldorf. 1993. Changes in prison culture: Prison gangs and the case of the Pepsi Generation. *Social Problems* 40;3:398–409.

International Monetary Fund. 2009. *IMF Executive Board Concludes 2009 Article IV Consultation with the Dominican Republic,* November 16, http://www.imf.org/external/np/sec/pn/2009/pn09128.htm (accessed December 19, 2009).

Janowitz, Morris. 1978. *The Last Half Century: Societal Change and Politics in America.* Chicago: University of Chicago Press.

Johnson, Kevin R. 2009. The intersection of race and class in U.S. immigration law and enforcement. *Law and Contemporary Problems* 72;4:1–36.

Kanstroom, Daniel. 2007. *Deportation Nation: Outsiders in American History.* Cambridge, MA: Harvard University Press.

Karmen, Andrew. 2001. *Crime Victims: An Introduction to Victimology,* 4th ed. New York: Wadsworth Publishing.

Kasinitz, Philip, John Mollenkopf, Mary Waters, and Jennifer Holdaway. 2008. *Inheriting the City: The Children of Immigrants Come of Age.* New York: Russell Sage Publication.

Katz, Jack. 2003. Analytical Induction. In *International Encyclopedia of the Social and Behavioral Sciences,* vol. 25, eds. Neil J. Smelser and Oaul B. Baltes, 480–484. New York: Elseiver Science Ltd.

Katz, Jack. 1988. Seductions of Crime: Moral and Sensual Attractions. In *Doing Evil.* New York: Basic Books.

Katznelson, Ira. 1982. *City Trenches: Urban Politics and the Patterning of Class in the United States.* Chicago: University of Chicago Press.

Kempadoo, Kamala. 1999. *Sun, Sex, and Gold.* Lanham, MD: Rowman & Littlefield Publishers, Inc.

Knox, George. 2000. *Introduction to Gangs,* 5th ed. Peotone, Illinois: New Chicago School Press.

Kurzman, Ira. 2008. Democracy and Immigration. In *Keeping Out the Other: Critical Analysis of Immigration Today,* eds. David C. Brotherton and Philip Kretsedemas, 63–80. New York: Columbia University Press.

Levitt, Peggy. 2001. *The Transnational Villagers.* Berkeley, CA: University of California Press.

Levitt, Steven D. and Sudhir Alladi Venkatesh. 2000. An economic analysis of a drug-selling gang's finances. *Quarterly Journal of Economics* 115;3:755–789.

Lewis Oscar. 1965. *La Vida: A Puerto Rican Family in the Culture of Poverty.* New York: Random House Lichter.

Limonic, Laura. 2007. *The Latino Population of New York City, 2007.* Center for Latin American, Caribbean & Latino Studies. New York: Graduate Center, City University of New York.

Lonegan, Bryan. 2008. American Diaspora: The deportation of lawful residents from the United States and the destruction of their families. *New York University Review of Law & Social Change* 35:55–81.

Lyng, Stephen. 2004. *Edgework: The Sociology of Risk-Taking.* New York: Routledge.

Madrak, Susie. 2009. UN advisor: Drug money propped up banks during crisis. *Crooksandliars.com,* December 13, http://crooksandliars.com/susie-madrak/un-advisor-drug-money-propped-banks-d (accessed December 23, 2009).

Maguire, Kathleen and Ann L. Pastore, eds. 1996. *Sourcebook of Criminal Justice Statistics 1995.* U.S. Department of Justice, Bureau of Justice Statistics. Washington, D.C.: U.S. Government Printing Office.

Martín, Yolanda C. 2010. Wasting away: Substance abuse and health risk outcomes among Dominican deportees. PhD diss., Graduate Center, City University of New York.

Martínez, Jr., Ramiro and Abel Valenzuela, Jr., eds. 2006. *Immigration and Crime: Race, Ethnicity, and Violence.* New York: New York University Press.

Maslow, Abraham. 1954. *Motivation and Personality,* 1st ed. New York: Harper & Row.

Matza, David. 1964. *Delinquency and Drift.* New York: John Wiley and Sons.

Massey, Douglas. 2003. *Beyond Smoke and Mirrors: Mexican Immigration in an Era of Economic Integration.* New York: Russell Sage Foundation.

Matthei, Linda Miller and David A. Smith. 1998. Belizian Boys 'n the Hood? Garifuna Labor Migration and Transnational Identity. In *Transnationalism from Below,* eds. Michael Peter Smith and Luiz Eduardo Guarnizo, 270–290. New Brunswick, NJ: Transaction Publishers.

Mauer, Marc. 1999. *Race to Incarcerate.* New York: New Press.

Mauer, Marc and Meda Chesney-Lind, eds. 2002. *Invisible Punishment: The Collateral Consequences of Mass Imprisonment.* New York: New Press.

Mayer, Robert. 2001. Strategies of justification in authoritarian ideology. *Journal of Political Ideologies* 6;2:147–168.

Melossi, Dario. 2004. Theories of Social Control and the State between American and European Shores. In *The Blackwell Companion to Crimin*ology, ed. Colin Sumner. Oxford: Blackwell.

Merton, Robert K. 1938. Social structure and anomie. *American Sociological Review* 3;October:672–682.

Mestrovic, Stjepan Gabriel. 2005. *The Trials of Abu Ghraib: An Expert Witness Account of Shame and Honor.* Boulder, CO: Paradigm Publishers.

Miller, Teresa. 2005. Immigration law and human rights: Legal line drawing post-September 11: Symposium article: Blurring the boundaries between immigration and crime control after September 11th. *Boston College Third World Law Journal* 81:1–43.

Moore, Joan. 1978. *Homeboys: Gangs, Drugs, and Prison in the Barrios of Los Angeles,* 1st ed. Philadelphia: Temple University Press.

Morawetz, Nancy. 2000. Understanding the impact of the 1996 deportation laws and the limited scope of proposed reforms. *Harvard Law Review* 113;8:1936–1962.

Morgan, Patricia. 1996. Unknown, unexplored, and unseen populations: An introduction into the truly hidden worlds of drugs and alcohol research. *Journal of Drug Issues* 26;1:1–4.

Moya Pons, Frank. 2008. *La otra historia Dominicana.* Santo Domingo: Librería La Trinitaria.

Moya Pons, Frank. 1998. *The Dominican Republic: A National History,* 2nd ed. Princeton, NJ: Markus Wiener Publishers.

Nadelman, Ethan A. 1998. Commonsense drug policy. *Foreign Affairs* 77;1:111–126.

Nelson, Geoffrey and Isaac Prilleltensky. 2005. *Community Psychology: In Pursuit of Liberation and Well-Being.* New York: Palgrave, McMillan.

Ngai, Mae M. 2004. *Impossible Subjects: Illegal Aliens and the Making of Modern America.* Princeton, NJ: Princeton University.

Noguera, Pedro. 1999. Exporting the undesirable: An analysis of the factors influencing the deportation of immigrants from the United States and an examination of their impact on Caribbean and Central American societies. *Wadabagei: A Journal of the Caribbean and Its Diaspora* 2;1:1–28.

Northern Manhattan Coalition Report 2009. *Dominicano, Deportado, y Humano: The Realities of Dominican Deportations and Related Policy Recommendations.* New York: Northern Manhattan Coalition.

Oakes, Jennie. 2005. *Keeping Track: How Schools Structure Inequality,* 2nd ed. New Haven: Yale University Press.

Ogbu, John. 1978. *Minority Education and Caste: The American System in Cross-Cultural Perspective.* San Diego, CA: Academic Press.

Ojito, Mirta. 1998. Change in laws sets off big wave of deportations. *The New York Times,* December 15, A5.

One World Almanac. 2009. London: New Internationalist.

Owen, Barbara. 1998. *In the Mix: Struggle and Survival in a Women's Prison.* Albany, NY: State University of New York Press.

Pager, Devah. 2003. The mark of a criminal record. *American Journal of Sociology* 108;5:937–975.

Palast, Greg. 2010. Behind Arizona immigration law: GOP game to swipe the November election. *Truth Out,* April 27, http://www.truthout.org/behind-the-arizona-immigration-law-gop-game-to-swipe-the-november-election58877 (accessed May 12, 2010).

Parenti, Christian. 2009. *Lockdown America: Police and Prisons in the Age of Crisis,* New ed. New York: Verso.

Perez, Máximo Manuel. 2003. No planea EEUU que se flexibilicen las deportaciones. *Listin Diario,* September 24, 3.

Park, Robert E. 1961. Cultural Conflict and the Marginal Man. In *The Marginal Man.* Bay of Islands, New Zealand: Russell & Russell Pub, 1937.

Park, Robert E. and William I. Thomas. 1927. Participation and Social Assimilation. In *Source Book for Social Psychology,* ed., Kimball Young, 47–53. New York: A.A. Knopf.

Payan, Tony. 2006. *The Three U.S.-Mexico Border Wars: Drugs, Immigration, and Homeland Security.* Santa Barbara, CA: Praeger.

Perkins, John. 2004. *Confessions of an Economic Hit Man,* 3rd ed. San Francisco, CA: Berrett-Koehler Publishers.

Perelló, Julio. 2010. Hipólito Mejía debe alejar a "Pepe Goico" de su entorno. *Último Minuto/Serie26,* http://ultimominutolibre.blogspot.com/2010/09/opinionhipolito-mejia-debe-alejar-pepe.html (accessed, September 30, 2010).

Petersilia, Joan. 2003. *When Prisoners Come Home.* New York: Oxford University Press.

Pessar, Patricia R. 1986. The Role of Gender in Dominican Settlement in the United States. In *Women and Change in Latin America,* eds. June Nash and Helen Safa, 273–294. South Hadley, MA: Bergin and Garvey.

Pope, Alexandra. 2007. International tourism growing for fourth year in a row, UN organization says. *Dominican Today,* November 9, http://www.dominicantoday.

com/dr/tourism/2007/11/9/26028/International-tourism-growing-for-fourth-year-in-a-row-UN-organization (accessed December 7, 2009).

Portes, Alejandro and Rubén G. Rumbaut. 2001. *Legacies: The Story of the Immigrant Second Generation*. Berkeley, CA: University of California Press.

Portes, Alejandro and Rubén G. Rumbaut. 1994. *Immigrant America*. Berkeley, CA: University of California Press.

Portes, Alejandro and Min Zhou. 1994. Should immigrants assimilate? *Public Interest* 116;Summer:18–33.

Portes, Alejandro and Min Zhou. 1993. The new second generation: Segmented assimilation and its variants. *Annals of the American Academy of Political and Social Science* 22;2:217–238.

Portes, Alejandro and Min Zhou. 1992. Gaining the upper hand: Economic mobility among immigrant and domestic minorities. *Ethnic and Racial Studies* 15;4:491–522.

Precil, Privat. 1999. Criminal deportees and returned teens: A Migration Phenomenon, a social problem. *The Panos Institute of the Caribbean* May.

Ramírez, Juan M. 2008. Informe del PNUD pone de relieve. May 28, http://67.199.16.148/el-pais/2008/5/28/91565/Informe-del-PNUD-pone-de-relieve (accessed October 22, 2009).

Reiman, Jeffrey. 2006. *The Rich Get Richer and the Poor Get Prison*, 8th ed. Upper Saddle River, New Jersey: Allyn & Bacon.

Reyes, Juan. 2007. Deportados y errores en lista policial. *Listin Diario*, May 6, 5.

Ribando, Clare M. 2005. *Dominican Republic: Political and Economic Conditions and Relations with the United States*. CRS Report for Congress. March 8, http://www.dtic.mil/cgi-bin/GetTRDoc?Location=U2&doc=GetTRDoc.pdf&AD=ADA461397 (accessed November 23, 2009).

Riessman, Katherine, ed. 1993. *Narrative Analysis: Qualitative Research Methods*. Thousand Oaks, CA: Sage Publications, Inc.

Roberts, Sam. 2010. Calculating poverty in New York: More by city standard, and less by federal one. *The New York Times*, March 2, 1A.

Rohter, Larry. 1997. In U.S. deportation policy, a Pandora's box. *The New York Times*, August 10.

Rose, Mike. 1999. *Lives on the Boundary: The Struggles and Achievements of America's Underprepared*. Austin, TX: Touchstone Publishing House.

Rumbaut, Rubén G. 2006. On the past and future of American immigration and ethnic history: A sociologist's reflections on a silver jubilee. *Journal of American Ethnic History* 25;4:160–167.

Salmi, Jamil. 1993. *Violence and Democratic Society: New Approaches to Human Rights*. London: Zed Books.

Sánchez-Fung, José R. 2008. Money demand in a dollarizing economy: The case of the Dominican Republic. *The Journal of Developing Areas* 42;1:39–52.

Sánchez-Jankowski, Martin 2003. Gangs and social change. *Theoretical Criminology* 7;2:191–216.

Sánchez-Jankowski, Martin. 1991. *Islands in the Street: Gangs and American Urban Society*. Berkeley, CA: University of California Press.

Santacruz Giralt, María L. and José Miguel Cruz Alas. 2001. La maras en El Salvador. *MPC* 2001:15–107.

Santos, Emmanuel. 2008. *Debt crisis in the Dominican Republic.* October 14, http://socialistworker.org/2008/10/14/dominican-republic-debt (accessed November 13, 2009).

Sassen, Saskia. 2001. *The Global City: New York, London, Tokyo.* Princeton, NJ: Princeton University Press.

Sayad, Abdelmalek. 2004. *The Suffering of the Immigrant.* Cambridge, MA: Polity.

Schwartz, Richard D. and Jerome H. Skolnick. 1962. Two studies of legal stigma. *Social Problems* 10;2:133–142.

Scott, James. 1985. *Weapons of the Weak: Everyday Forms of Peasant Resistance.* New Haven: Yale University Press.

Shahani, Aarti. 2010. *New York Enforcement of Immigration Detainers.* New York: Justice Strategies.

Shaw, Clifford and Henry D. Mackay. 1942. *Juvenile Delinquency in Urban Areas.* Chicago: University of Chicago Press.

Sibley, David. 1995. *Geographies of Exclusion: Society and Difference in the West.* New York: Routledge.

Simon, Jonathan. 2007. *Governing Through Crime: How the War on Crime Transformed American Democracy and Created a Culture of Fear.* New York: Oxford University Press.

Smith, Michael Peter. 2000. *Transnational Urbanism: Locating Globalization.* New York: Blackwell.

Smith, Robert. 2005. *Mexican New York: Transnational Worlds of New Immigrants.* Berkeley, CA: University of California Press.

Solís, Ubaldo. 2008. Desigual distribución de la riqueza y falta de servicios impiden desarrollo. *La comunidad*, May 30, http://lacomunidad.elpais.com/usolis4587/2008/5/30/desigual-distribucion-la-riqueza-y-falta-servicio-impiden (accessed September 10, 2009).

Spradlin, Lynn Kell and Rick D. Parsons. 2008. *Diversity Matters: Understanding Diversity in Schools.* Belmont: Thomson Wadsworth.

Stern, Vivien and Andrew Coyle. 2003. *Prison Reform in the Dominican Republic.* London: International Center for Prison Studies.

Suarez-Orozco, Carola and Marcelo Suarez-Orozco. 2001. *Children of Immigration.* Cambridge, MA: Harvard University Press.

Sykes, Gresham M. 1958. *The Society of Captives: A Study of a Maximum Security Prison.* Princeton, NJ: Princeton University Press.

Tejada, Diógenes. 2010. Llegan 81 dominicano repatriados de los Estados Unidos. *Hoy Digital*, September 22, http://www.hoy.com.do/el-pais/2010/9/22/342991/Llegan-81-dominicano-repatriados-de-los-Estados-Unidos (accessed September 22, 2010).

Thomas, William Isaac and Florian Znaniecki. 1927. *The Polish Peasant in Europe and America.* New York: Alfred A. Knopf.

Thrasher, Frederic. 1927. *Gang: A Study of 1,313 Gangs in Chicago.* Chicago: New Chicago School Press.

Tonelson, Alan. 2002. *The Race to the Bottom: Why a Worldwide Worker Surplus and Uncontrolled Free Trade are Sinking American Living Standards.* New York: Basic Books.

Torres-Saillant, Silvio. 2000. The tribulations of blackness: Stages in Dominican racial identity. *Callaloo* 23;3:1086–1111.

Torres-Saillant, Silvio and Ramona Hernández. 1998. *The Dominican Americans (The New Americans)*. Santa Barbara, CA: Greenwood Press.

Travis, Jeremy 2005. *But They All Come Back: Facing the Challenges of Prisoner's Reentry*. New York: Urban Institute Press.

Travis, Jeremy. 2002. Invisible Punishment: An Instrument of Social Exclusion. In *Invisible Punishment*, eds. Meda Chesney-Lind and Marc Mauer, 15–16. New York: New Press.

Travis, Jeremy, Elizabeth Cincotta McBride, and Amy L. Solomon. 2005. *Families Left Behind: The Hidden Costs of Incarceration and Reentry*. New York: Urban Institute Press.

Travis, Jeremy, Amy L. Solomon, and Michelle Waul. 2001. *From Prison to Home: The Dimensions and Consequences of Prisoner Reentry*. Washington, DC: The Urban Institute.

Uggen, Christopher and Jeff Manza. 2002. Democratic contraction? Political consequences of felon disenfranchisement in the United States. *American Sociological Review* 67;December:777–803.

United Nations Office of Drugs and Crime-NODOC 2007. *World Drug Report*. http://www.unodc.org/unodc/en/data-and-analysis/WDR-2007.html (accessed October 22, 2009).

United Sates Department of State. 2009a. *Background Note: Dominican Republic*. Bureau of Western Hemisphere Affairs, June, http://www.state.gov/r/pa/ei/bgn/35639.htm (accessed December 2, 2009).

United States Department of State. 2009b. *Human Rights Report: Dominican Republic*. Bureau of Democracy, Human Rights, and Labor, March 11, http://www.state.gov/g/drl/rls/hrrpt/2009/wha/136110.htm (accessed September 10, 2009).

United States Drug Enforcement Administration. 2002. *Drugs, Money and Terror*. http://www.justice.gov/dea/pubs/cngrtest/ct042402.html (accessed July 17, 2009).

University of California–Berkeley School of Law and University of California–Davis School of Law. 2010. *In the child's best interest? The consequences of losing a lawful immigrant parent to deportation*. http://www.law.berkeley.edu/files/IHRLC/In_the_Childs_Best_Interest.pdf (accessed April 1, 2010).

Valdez, Solangel. 2009. De España a RD: El impacto de las remesas en la economía. *Antena*. http://www.antenaenlinea.com/index.php/reportajes/49-reportajesportada/591-de-espana-a-rd-el-impacto-de-las-remesas-en-la-economia (accessed September 11, 2009).

Valdez Albizu, Héctor. 2009. *Discurso del Gobernador del Banco Central en la conmemoración del sexagésimo segundo aniversario del Banco Central de la República Dominicana*. October 23, http://www.bancentral.gov.do/notas_del_bc.asp?a=bc2009-10-23 (accessed September 12, 2009).

Vargas, Robert. 2001. *Mueren 200 dominicanos en el éxodo de ilegales*. http://www.puertorico.com/forums/politics/3402-domicanos-comen-carne-humana-en-su-intento-de-llegar-puerto-rico-de-los-eu.html (accessed May 3, 2009).

Venator-Santiago, Charles. 2005a. *The Impact of United States Deportation Policies on Dominicans*. New York: Dominican Studies Institute, CUNY, Research Monograph Series.

Venator-Santiago, Charles. 2005b. *Lost in Paradise: Some Reflections on the Deportation of Dominicans to the Dominican Republic*. New York: Dominican Studies Institute, CUNY, Research Monograph Series.

Venkatesh, Sudhir. 2006. *Off the Books*. Cambridge, MA: Harvard University Press.

Venkatesh, Sudhir. 1997. The social organization of street gang activity in an urban ghetto. *American Journal of Sociology* 1031:82–111.

Vigil, Diego. 1988. *Street Life and Identity in Southern California*. Austin, TX: University of Texas Press.

Wacquant, Loic. 2008. *Urban Outcasts: A Comparative Sociology of Advanced Marginality*. Cambridge: Polity Press.

Wacquant, Loic. 2002. Deadly symbiosis. *Boston Review,* May 1, 1–25.

Wacquant, Loic. 1997. *From Welfare State to Prison State: Imprisoning the American Poor*. http://mondediplo.com/1998/07/14prison (accessed November 29, 2009).

Wallace-Wells, Ben. 2007. How America lost the war on drugs. *Rolling Stone*, December 13.

Warner, W. Lloyd and Leo Strole. 1945. *Yankee City Series 3*. New Haven: Yale University Press.

Welch, Michael. 2003. Ironies of social control and the criminalization of immigrants. *Crime, Law and Social Change* 39;4:319–337.

Welch, Michael. 2002. *Detained: Immigration Laws and the Expanding I.N.S. Jail Complex*. Philadelphia: Temple University Press.

Welch, Michael and Liza Schuster. 2008. American and British construction of asylum seekers: Moral panic, detention and human rights. In *Keeping Out the Other: A Critical Introduction to Immigration Control*, eds. David Brotherton and Phillip Kretsedemas, 138–158. New York: Columbia University Press.

Western, Bruce, Becky Pettit, and Josh Guetzkow. 2002. Black Economic Progress in the Era of Mass Imprisonment. In *Invisible Punishment: The Collateral Consequences of Mass Imprisonment*, eds. Marc Mauer and Meda Chesney-Lind, 165–180. New York: Free Press.

Willis, Paul. 2000. *The Ethnographic Imagination*. Cambridge, MA: Polity.

Willis, Paul. 1977. *Learning to Labor: How Working-Class Kids Get Working-Class Jobs*. Westmean, UK: Saxon House.

Wirth, Louis. 1928. *The Ghetto*. Chicago: University of Chicago Press.

Wucker, Michelle. 2000. *Why the Cocks Fight: Dominicans, Haitians, and the Struggle for Hispaniola*. New York: Hill and Wang.

Wynn, Jennifer. 2002. *Inside Rikers: Stories from the World's Largest Penal Colony*. New York: St. Martin's Griffin.

Young, Jock. 2009. Moral panic: Its origins in resistance, ressentiment and the translation of fantasy into reality. *British Journal of Criminology* 49;1:4–16.

Young, Jock. 2007. *Vertigo in Late Modernity*. London: Sage Publications.

Young, Jock. 1999. *The Exclusive Society: Social Exclusion, Crime and Difference in Late Modernity*. London: Sage Publications.

Young, Jock. 1971. *The Drugtakers: The Social Meaning of Drug Use*. London: Paladin.

Young, Jock and David C. Brotherton. 2006. Cultural criminology and its practices: A dialogue between the theorist and the street researcher. Paper presented at the annual meeting of the American Sociological Association, Montreal Convention Center, August 10, Montreal, Quebec, Canada.

Zilberg, Elana. 2006. Gangster in guerilla face: A transnational mirror of production between the USA and El Salvador. *Anthropological Theory* 7;1:37–57.

Zilberg, Elana. 2004. Fools banished from the kingdom: Remapping geographies of gang violence between the Americas (Los Angeles and San Salvador). *American Quarterly* 56;3:759–779.

Zilberg, Elana. 2002. From riots to rampart: A spatial cultural politics of Salvadoran migration to and from Los Angeles. Ph.D. diss., Department of Anthropology, University of Texas at Austin.

Zimbardo, Phillip G. 2008. *The Lucifer Effect: Understanding How Good People Turn Evil*. New York: Random House.

Zinn, Howard. 2005. *A People's History of the United States: 1492–Present*. New York: Harper.

Zolberg, Aristide R. 2008. *A Nation by Design: Immigration Policy in the Fashioning of America*. Cambridge, MA: Harvard University Press.

INDEX

Asociación Ñeta, 141–152, 336n9
assimilation, 18–19. *See also* segmented
    assimilation
"at-risk" environments, 111
attendants, tourism, deportees as, 216–217
attorneys. *See* lawyers
authoritarian policing culture, in Dominican
    Republic, 203–205
autonomy, and American Dream, 58
AVV (alternative visions to violence) pro-
    grams, 143

babysitters, returned deportees as, 285–286
Baez, Ramón, 40
Balaguer, Joaquin, 35, 330n5
Banco Central de la Republica Dominicana,
    305–308
banking industry, in Dominican Republic, 40
"Barrio Seguro" (safe neighborhood) initiative,
    Dominican Republic, 45
Barrios, Luis, 8, 10, 27
Belize, Garifuna ethnic community of, 14
Bernard, Peter, 184
betrayal, feelings of upon being deported, 193–197
Bienvenido Seas, Inc., 238–240
border crossings, into United States, 73–74,
    275–279
Bory (deportee), 338n4
Bosch, Juan, 33
Brea de Cabral, Mayra, 42, 45, 332n20
Brooklyn, New York, environment of in 1970s,
    81–82
Brotherton, David C., 8, 14, 27
bulimia, social, 22–23, 164, 202, 295–297.
    See also stigmatization of deportees
business aspect of imprisonment, 140–142

Cabral Ramírez, Edylberto, 42, 45, 332n20
California Immigrant Integration Initiative
    (CIII), 325
call centers, in Dominican Republic, 217–218
Camilla (deportee), 278–279
capitalism: limbic, 122; in neoliberal ideology, 289
Cardozo Law School Immigration Justice
    Clinic, 343n3
Caribbean miracle, Dominican Republic as, 40–41
Carlos (deportee), 72–73, 152–153
Casa Cornelia Law Center, 325–326
Celia (deportee), 233
Celio (deportee): American Dream, 56–57,
    58–59; drugs trade in Dominican Republic,
    227; family life, and crime, 129; getting to
    America, 73–74; prison gangs, 151–152
Center for Gender & Refugee Studies (CGRS),
    324

Central American Resource Center
    (CARECEN), 324
Centro Bonó, 326
Cesar (deportee), 231
Chicago School of Sociology and Pragmatism,
    17–18, 87
childbirth in prison, 157
Chino (deportee): college in United States,
    104–105; drugs environment in neighbor-
    hood, 113–114; lifestyle dilemmas and
    crime, 121–122; school life in United States,
    100; violence in environment while settling
    in United States, 87–88
chiriperos, returned deportees as, 283–285
Chismín (deportee), 194, 270, 273, 283–285
Chiu, Bess, 343n3
CIII (California Immigrant Integration
    Initiative), 325
civil war, in Dominican Republic, 34–35
classes, in Dominican Republic, 331–332n15
club gangs, 84–87, 89
Cohen, Ronald, 197
collaborative methodology, 25
collateral damage: of deportation, 163–164, 177;
    of returning to United States, 290
college: attendance by deportees while in
    United States, 104–106; while in prison, 144
colonial political economy, 213–214
commerce, jobs in, 213
communication, in Dominican versus U.S.
    prison systems, 257–258
compliance, with deportation orders, 178–179,
    180–182
confusion, feelings of upon being deported,
    193–197
conjugal visits, in Dominican versus U.S.
    prison systems, 263
conservative positivism, 335n3
constitutive criminology, 17
consumer capitalism, and identity, 122
contemporary sociogeography, Dominican
    Republic, 36–37
correctional officers, in U.S. prisons, 145–147,
    158–159, 262
correctional system. *See* prison experiences of
    deportees
corruption: in Dominican Republic, 254; in
    Dominican versus U.S. prison systems,
    261–262; in U.S. law enforcement, 130–132
Cossolias, William, 8
counseling, in prison, 143–144
court-appointed lawyers, 136–137
Courtwright, David T., 122
Coutin, Susan B., 13
Coyle, Andrew, 245

123; overview, 117–118; straight life versus street life, 121–122; wrong place at wrong time, 123–125

Pessar, Patricia R., 334n7

phone use, in prisons, 258

"Plan for Democratic Security" initiative, Dominican Republic, 45

police: attitude towards drugs in United States in 1980s, 123, 131–132; corruption of in Dominican Republic, 199; stigmatization of deportees, 203–205; violence by in Dominican Republic, 44–45

Polish immigration, 18

political economy, Dominican Republic, 37–40

politics, of deportees, 237–240

population by age, of Dominican Republic, 37

Portes, Alejandro, 20, 93, 334n3, 334n7

Post-Deportation Human Rights Project, 318

postdeportation resources, 313

poverty: in Dominican Republic, 211; indirect violence of, 67–69; in New York, 342n8, 342n9; as reason for emigration, 59–63; reticence of subjects regarding, 333n2; and violence, 42

Precil, Privat, 13

prejudice towards deportees. See stigmatization of deportees

presidents, of Dominican Republic, 34–36

preventive detention, 62–63, 341n5a

print media, and stigmatization of deportees, 203

prison experiences of deportees: overview, 46–47

—in Dominican Republic: daily regime, 255–256; inmates' plans for future, 263–264; Najayo Prison, 265–269; overview, 26, 243–246; pathways back to prison, 252–255; Rafey prison overview, 246–252; versus United States prison system, 256–263

—in United States: conditions in, 138–140; female prisons, 156–159; gang life, 148–156; legal representation, 136–137; mandatory sentences, 138; overview, 135; prison-industrial complex, 140–142; relationship with correctional officers, 145–147; surviving alone, 142–145

prison-industrial complex, U.S., 140–142

prison-only gangs: Rat Hunters, 148–149; Trinitarios, 149–151

private security, in Dominican Republic, 338n4

privatization of energy industry, Dominican Republic, 39

processing of deportees, in Dominican Republic, 190–192

professionalism of U.S. prison system, 147, 262

pro-immigrant organizations: Dominican Republic, 326–327; New York, 317–321; United States, 321–326

prosperity, promise of as reason for emigration, 55–59

psychological crisis of deportees. See social-psychological crisis of deportees

psychological survival: in prison, 142–145; on return to United States, 290

public defense lawyers, 136–137, 179, 321

public schools, New York City, 334n5

public sector employment, deportees in, 221–223

Puerto Rican immigrants, 19

Puerto Rico, deportees returning via, 275–276

Puntiel (deportee), 263–264

Quisqueya (deportee), 273, 276, 285–286

race: neighborhoods, 83–87; school life and, 102–103

racial composition, of Dominican Republic, 37

racism: and neighborhood culture while settling in United States, 84; in prison, 145–147

Rafael (deportee), 83, 138, 263

Rafey prison: characteristics of imprisoned deportees in, 250; daily regime, 255–256; inmates' plans for future, 263–264; overview, 244, 246–249; pathways back to prison, 252–255; settlement, family, and work, 250–252; versus United States prison system, 256–263

Ramon (deportee), 231

Raoul (deportee), 136

Raphael (deportee), 101

Rat Hunters gang, 148–149

rational action, crimes of, 252

rational choice theory, 125–126

reattachment, family, 235–236

recidivism of deportees, 47, 190

rejection of deportees, by family, 236–237. See also social-psychological crisis of deportees

remesas, for deportees, 233–234

René (deportee), 110, 238–240

representation, legal. See legal representation

resettlement of deportees in Dominican Republic: getting processed, 190–192; homecoming, 297–298; overview, 189–190. See also work experiences in Dominican Republic

—return to prison: daily regime, 255–256; inmates' plans for future, 263–264; Najayo Prison, 265–269; overview, 243–246;

Ulster correctional facility, 164–176
unconstitutional aspects of deportation, 343n3
underground economy, returned deportees
in, 288–289. *See also* informal economy,
deportee work experiences in
undocumented returnees. *See* return of
deportees to United States
United Nations Office of Drugs and Crime, 44
United States: military invasions, of
Dominican Republic, 34–35; new practices
and policies of inclusion, need for, 301–303;
prison system, versus Dominican prison
system, 256–263; pro-immigrant organizations fighting deportation, 321–326
—deportation from: flight back, 185–186; legal
process of, 177–184; notes from deportation
hearing, 164–176; overview, 163–164
—immigration to: emotional impact of, 70–72;
modes of entry in United States, 72–76;
overview, 53–55; reasons for, 55–69. *See also*
settlement in United States
—imprisonment in: conditions in, 138–140;
female prisons, 156–159; legal representation, 136–137; mandatory sentences, 138;
overview, 135; prison-industrial complex,
140–142; relationship with correctional
officers, 145–147; surviving alone, 142–145
—pathways to crime in: corruption, 130–132;
drugs, 113–117; family life, 126–130; overview, 111–113; peer pressure, 117–125; rational choice theory, 125–126
—return of deportees to: life after return, 279–
287; overview, 271–272; reasons for returning, 272–274; ways of returning, 275–279
Universal Declaration of Human Rights,
293–294
University of California Los Angeles (UCLA)
Immigration Clinic, 325–326
upper-middle class, in Dominican Republic,
331–332n15
The Uprooted, 19
upstate New York prisons, 150
urban community, in transnationalism, 21
urban spatial segregation, and stigmatization
of deportees, 206
U.S. Department of State, 45, 246
U.S. Navy veteran deportee, 211, 240, 243

Venator-Santiago, Charles, 46–47, 49
Verdugo (deportee), 274
victimization, prison gang membership to
avoid, 150
Victor (deportee): daily regime in prison in
Dominican Republic, 255–256; education

in Dominican prisons, 260; inability to
adapt as deportee, 234–235, 251; lack of
rights in Dominican prisons, 258–259
vindictiveness: in deportation process, 343n3;
in incarceration system, 140
violence: by correctional officers in prison,
145–147; direct and indirect, 67–69; in
Dominican Republic, 42–45, 71–72; neighborhood, 87–89; by private security in
Dominican Republic, 338n4; related to drug
gangs in New York City, 89–90; against
women, in Dominican Republic, 43–44.
See also domestic abuse/violence; gangs

wages, in Dominican Republic, 309–311, 332n17
Washington Heights, 111, 279–280, 288–289
Waters, Mary, 343–344n7
Welch, Michael, 141
Willis, Paul, 339n2
Wirth, Louis, 18
women deportees: female prisons, 156–159;
gang life, 154–156; overview, 46; pathways
into crime for, 129–130. *See also specific
deportees by name*
women, violence against in Dominican
Republic, 43–44
work experiences in Dominican Republic:
overview, 211–213
—in formal economy: educators, 218–220;
farmers, 220–221; public sector, 221–223;
tourist industry, 213–217; Zona Franca
Workers, 217–218
—in informal economy: drugs trade, 227–232;
indigence, 240–241; remesas, 233–234; self-
employment, 232–233; sex trade, 224–227;
social supports, 234–240; street sellers,
223–224
working-class occupations, of deportee's parents, 94–96
work opportunities, in Dominican versus U.S.
prison systems, 259–260
work, role of, 339n2
wrong place at wrong time, 123–125

yolas to Puerto Rico, deportees returning by,
26, 275–276
Young, Jock, 22–23, 121, 202, 335n3
youth violence, in Dominican Republic, 71–72

Zhou, Min, 20, 334n7
Zilberg, Elana, 13
Znaniecki, Florian, 18
Zona Franca, Dominican Republic, 40,
217–218, 331n13